Communication and Information Technology in (Intercultural) Language Teaching

Communication and Information Technology in (Intercultural) Language Teaching

By

Mariusz Marczak

CAMBRIDGE SCHOLARS PUBLISHING

Communication and Information Technology in (Intercultural) Language Teaching,
by Mariusz Marczak

This book first published 2013

Cambridge Scholars Publishing

12 Back Chapman Street, Newcastle upon Tyne, NE6 2XX, UK

British Library Cataloguing in Publication Data
A catalogue record for this book is available from the British Library

ISBN (10): 1-4438-5143-4, ISBN (13): 978-1-4438-5143-5

To Eliza, Melania and Mateusz

TABLE OF CONTENTS

LIST OF FIGURES

LIST OF TABLES

ACKNOWLEDGEMENTS

It would not have been possible for me to write this book without the help and support of the people whom I would like to give particular mention at this point.

As the present book is a revised version of my PhD dissertation, first and foremost, I wish to thank my PhD supervisor, professor Hanna Komorowska, Warsaw University. It was a great honour for me to have an opportunity to work under her academic guidance, which I found extremely stimulating and instrumental in completing this publication. I would particularly like to thank her for the understanding and constructive criticism that I received from her throughout the writing process.

In addition, I am truly grateful to professor Romuald Gozdawa-Gołębiowski, Warsaw University, and professor Krystyna Drozdział-Szelest, Adam Mickiewicz University, Poznań, for invaluably constructive criticism.

I am obliged to many of my colleagues who in various ways supported me as I worked on this publication. In particular, I would like to thank Marek Bielecki, NKJO, Łowicz, and Jan Dutka, NKJO Sieradz, for their readiness to help as well as for acting as professional role models for me to follow.

I also wish to express gratitude to Michael Houten and Aiden Thorne, British Council, for introducing me to the world of in-service teacher training and modern technologies in language education as well as dr Anna Tomczak, Białystok University, for words of encouragement and sharing vital resources with me.

Last but not least, I am truly indebted and thankful to all my family, who showed unrelenting support, understanding, patience and resourcefulness that enabled me to work in comfort.

INTRODUCTION

The twenty-first century so far has been a period of increased internationalisation and globalisation, which has been stimulated by educational, economic and professional mobility as well as the steadily growing use of information and communication technology. In the wake of the process, not only the already-heterogeneous societies of today are becoming even more multilingual and multicultural. In relatively monolithic contexts, the ICT-enhanced flow of information in what is referred to as *knowledge society* has translated into the diversification of people's viewpoints and lifestyles, and intercultural encounters are being experienced even by those who do not travel abroad. As a consequence, the ability to cope with otherness, communicate successfully with strangers, be it from one's immediate or more remote social circles, and use ICT is now an indispensable key with which to unlock the cultural riddles of reality.

The responsibility for the provision of this key to members of society lies, to a large extent, with the education system, particularly with foreign language teachers, who by default are supposed to prepare learners for contact with strangers and effective international/intercultural communication. Therefore, it is desirable that modern day EFL teaching embraces not only the development of language skills per se, but also intercultural training and the implementation of computer technology.

The idea of promoting intercultural awareness and developing learners' ICT skills has been endorsed by international organisations, e.g. the Council of Europe, the United Nations and UNESCO, as well as international and national educational documents, including *The Common European Framework of Reference for Languages* (CEFR 2001), *UNESCO Guidelines on Intercultural Education* (UNESCO 2006) and *Podstawa programowa* (MEN 2008) for public schools in Poland.

This book constitutes an attempt to demonstrate how the aforementioned international language teaching agenda translates into actual classroom practices at national level, as illustrated by the situation in Poland. To be more precise, the aim of this book is to research the manner in which teachers of English in Poland utilise information and communication technology in the EFL classroom for the purpose of teaching language and culture as well as fostering the development of learners' intercultural competence. Moreover, the research conducted is supposed to demonstrate whether selected Computer Assisted Language Learning (CALL) software, available in Poland, permits the development of the learner's intercultural competence, and which of its components are featured within the programs.

In Chapter One the notion of culture is elucidated, as well as the interrelation between culture, language and communication, including an analysis of earlier publications in this area, e.g. Whorf (1956), the literature of the 1970s and 1980s, e.g. Geertz (1973), Lakoff & Johnson (1980), and the most recent publications, e.g. Moran (2001) or Riley (2007). The chapter additionally outlines the role of the cultural component in foreign language teaching on the basis of the glottodidactic literature of the last twenty-six years, e.g. Richards & Rogers (1986), Aleksandrowicz-Pędich (2005), and Komorowska (2009). The author analyses the validity of teaching culture within language education and discusses the changing status of a native-speaker teacher of English in today's world, where English functions as a *lingua franca*, i.e. a language for international communication (Kachru 1985; Medgyes 2001; Graddol 2006; Ronowicz & Yallop 2007).

Chapter Two is devoted to the very concept of intercultural teaching and its role in language education. The need to develop foreign language learners' intercultural competence is discussed here as well as the presence of an intercultural component in international educational documents. This chapter also presents intercultural teaching through a comparison with the so-called British Studies/Landeskunde approach. Particular attention is drawn to the model of *intercultural competence* as proposed by Byram (1997) and numerous other authors, e.g. Ruben (1976), Komorowska (1999), Jandt (2001) and Kohonen (2001). Chapter Two ends with a presentation of Risager's (2007) extended model of intercultural competence.

Chapter Three accounts various implementations of the intercultural approach to foreign language teaching, with regard to the EFL context, as advocated by Byram (1998), Zarate et al. (2004) and Bandura (2007). It opens with a discussion of learner and teacher roles in intercultural language teaching. Subsequently, alternative approaches to intercultural teaching are presented, along with an array of techniques in intercultural language teaching (Damen 1987; Corbett 2003).

Chapter Four concerns computer assisted language education. It features an description of the developmental stages of CALL, presents types of CALL software and computer-based work modes in the foreign language (e.g. Warschauer 1996; Gajek 2002; Belisle 2007; Krajka 2007).

Chapter Five outlines the utilisation of ICT for the purpose of intercultural language teaching. It demonstrates the rationale of the use of ICT, including the internet, in intercultural teaching, along with the potential advantages and disadvantages of ICT-enhanced instruction (e.g. Fitzpatrick 2007; Gajek 2007; Risager 2007). Computer-enhanced techniques in intercultural language teaching are also discussed here (e. g. Liaw 2006; Żylińska 2007; Levy 2007; Gajek 2009). In addition, a range of criteria for the evaluation of computer assisted language (and culture) learning materials are reviewed (e.g. Byram 1991; Cunningsworth 1995; Skopinskaja 2003; Hanušova 2006; Davies 2009). Finally, a checklist of criteria for the evaluation of the intercultural component of CALL software is proposed.

Chapter Six delineates the aims, research questions, methods and techniques which were used in order to examine to what degree and in what manner Polish EFL teachers utilise ICT while teaching English as a foreign language and developing learners' intercultural competence. The research was administered on a sample of 105 EFL teachers from Poland's primary and junior/senior high schools as well as teacher educators employed at the country's teacher training colleges. It aimed at diagnosing the following: the technological and organisational setting in which Polish ELF teachers function; their attitudes to ICT, ICT skills and qualifications; the manner in which Polish teachers utilise ICT while teaching English as a foreign language and developing learners' intercultural competence as well as ICT-related problems which they face. Subsequently, the results of the study are presented, together with conclusions drawn from the findings.

Chapter Seven is a report of a research study in which 6 CALL multimedia programs, addressed to junior/senior high school EFL learners, were evaluated. The evaluation focused on the presence of intercultural content and activities in the programs examined. The evaluation was based on an original evaluation checklist proposed by the author of the study, and it was motivated by the following research questions:

- Does CALL software targeting lower/upper secondary school level audiences available in Poland permit learners to work on the major components of intercultural competence such as: attitudes, knowledge, skills of interpreting and relating, skills of discovery and interaction, critical cultural awareness?;
- Does CALL software targeting lower/upper secondary school level audiences available in Poland feature technological functionalities which facilitate intercultural learning such as: advanced search options, task

authoring tools, cultural explanation, insightful audio-visuals, annotation tools, supplementary cultural materials, and online communication tools?

The chapter also contains a discussion of the findings and is rounded up by a set of conclusions drawn from the results obtained within both research modules, comments on the validity of the results and implications for further research. The present author believes that the research will permit improvement in language teaching and teacher education with regard to intercultural training and the implementation of ICT. At the same time, it will allow a revision of the content of internationally available CALL software in terms of the features which foster intercultural training. Finally, the studies conducted may potentially motivate further research pertaining to the teaching of language and culture with the use of information and communication technology in the foreign language classroom.

CHAPTER ONE

VIEWS OF CULTURE AND THE PLACE OF CULTURE IN EFL TEACHING

"Tolerance, inter-cultural dialogue and respect for diversity are more essential than ever in a world where peoples are becoming more and more closely interconnected."
—Kofi Annan, Former Secretary-General of the United Nations

1. Culture

1.1 The Concept of Culture

As culture is extremely broad in scope, it has been defined in a multitude of manners, and from numerous perspectives. It was nearly 60 years ago that Kluckhohn and Kroeber (1952) had arrived at over 160 definitions of the term, while two decades later, in the 1970s, Kaplan and Manners (1972) deemed culture too complex for analysis. Sztompka (2002) reports that today the number of definitions has increased to over 200, and Gozdawa-Gołębiowski (2006) tentatively suggests that an interdisciplinary definition of culture is impossible.

As Riley observes, the notion is "highly polysemic, not to say frustratingly ambiguous, and yet it is (...) essential to any understanding of the modern social sciences" (Riley 2007: 21). Consequently, one cannot discuss the process of teaching culture, or – more pertinently to the purpose of this book – language and culture, without venturing to understand the concept. Aleksandrowicz-Pędich (2005) observes that *culture* embraces the fine arts as well as good manners, but also behavioural styles, values, perceptions and thought patterns. Paradoxically, this multi-faceted nature of the notion may be an advantage, as a variety of definitions helps one look at culture extensively, i.e. inclusively rather than exclusively, which in Aleksandrowicz-Pędich's (2005) view, is an indispensable component of the intercultural approach to foreign language teaching.

Fenner (2000) briefly outlines the evolution of the term *culture* throughout history. According to her, up to the Early Renaissance culture was viewed as "the classical cultural heritage" (Fenner 2000: 143). In Romanticism the term was expanded to embrace "national culture and identity" (Fenner 2000: 143) and people's way of life. In the 20th century culture ceased to be perceived as national and set; instead, people's power to construct their own culture through a selection of multiple identities was recognised, which added a personal dimension to the concept. Particular cultures began to be perceived as "creative responses to the human condition" (Bredella 1988: 3).

Culture has been examined by various sciences, which, in turn, have developed different perspectives on it. In the 1940s, anthropologists Kluckhohn and Kelly proposed that culture was "all those historically created designs for living explicit and implicit, rational, irrational, and non-rational, which exist at any given time as potential guides for the behaviour of men" (Kluckhohn & Kelly 1945: 54).

Culture as communication derives from Hall, who in his seminal work *The Silent Language* (Hall 1959) demonstrated how particular culture groups use a repertoire of means through which their members communicate, e.g. language in both its verbal and non-verbal forms, such as kinesics, oculesics or olfactics, to name a few.

In the 1970s Chałasiński (1973) emphasised that culture was a projection of people, and their group/individual values. In addition, he referred to culture as "the shape of human life" (My translation) (Chałasiński 1973: 9), which linked culture to human personality and its development over time. Another social view of culture came from Crommager, who defined culture as ”a bundle of patterns of behaviour, habits of conduct, customs, laws, beliefs, and indistinctive responses that are displayed by a society" (Crommager 1970: 161).

At roughly the same time, Geertz (1973) presented culture as dynamic, and defined it as values, beliefs or attitudes that people develop in specific social contexts. What this definition implies is that values, beliefs and attitudes do not last unchanged over time. Instead, they constantly fluctuate depending on the social situation in which a given group of people or its individual members find themselves. Geertz claimed that culture was "a historically transmitted pattern of meanings embodied in symbols, a system of inherited conceptions, expressed in symbolic form by means of which men communicate, perpetuate and develop their knowledge about and attitudes towards life" (Geertz 1973: 89). Especially the end of the quotation is significant, as it puts emphasis on people's attitudes and implies that those attitudes are subject to constant change. A similar view was more recently expressed by Suchodolski (1987), who suggested that culture only appears to be permanent, while it actually evolves perpetually. Other congruent views of culture derive from Leach (1982) as well as Montgomery (2003), who also highlighted culture as dynamic, i.e. unstable over time and subject to permanent change.

In the 1980s, a socio-historical perspective on culture was adopted by Valette (1986), who depicted culture as two components: (i) sociological, which covered attitudes, customs, daily activities, including language, values and ways of thinking (thought patterns); and (ii) heritage, i.e. the history of civilisation, which features geography, history as well as scientific and artistic achievements.

Goodenough (1964) viewed culture as ways of perceiving, relating and interpreting the world, a universal knowledge possessed by all people. This definition is congruent with Kramsch's (1998b) and Alptekin's (1993), both of which present culture as a filter, or frame, of perception through which people conceive of reality. On societal level, Goodenough (1964) believed that culture is a combination of knowledge and beliefs that people need in order to be accepted by a particular social group. As Hofstede remarked, culture is a kind of "collective programming of the mind which distinguishes the members of one group or category from people of another" (Hofstede 1994: 5).

A noticeable trend in the discussion of culture throughout the 1980s was an attempt to draw attention to the explicit and tacit elements of it, as illustrated by the metaphor of culture proposed by Weaver (1986). He conceptualised culture as an iceberg, whereby he indicated that every cultural system consists of three layers: (i) behaviour, which is its most salient aspect, thus placed above the water surface; (ii) beliefs, which are half-tacit and half-observable, e.g. in part they may be explicitly expressed or clearly implied by the members of a cultural community; and (iii) values and thought patterns, which remain invisible unless carefully examined. A similar iceberg metaphor was offered by Levine and Adelman (1993), who placed language and artefacts above the water level, and put beliefs, attitudes and values underneath it.

Irrespective of the details of either model, the iceberg metaphor indicates that what outsiders to a given culture notice at first is behaviour, however, what they are normally blind to is the motives behind the behaviour observed.

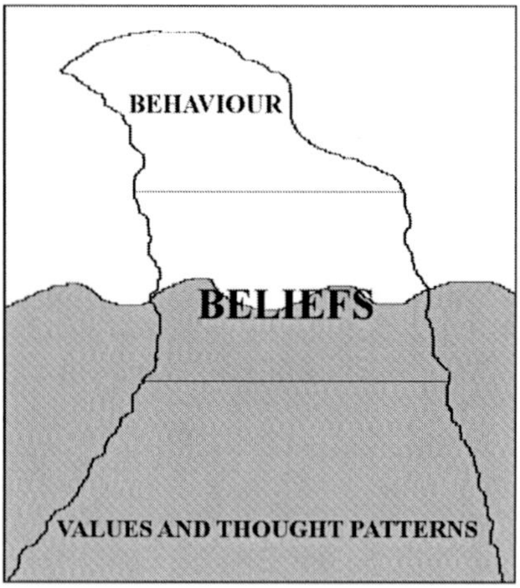

Fig. 1-1

Williams (1965) distinguished between three categories of anthropological categories of culture" (i) ideal, i.e. viewed as a process or state of human development with regard to universal values; (ii) documentary, within which culture is a body of work that constitutes a record of human thought and experience; and (iii) social, where culture is treated as a broadly-perceived way of life which embeds meanings and values, and which, as Leach (1982) states, may be used differently by various sub-groups within a given society.

At the turn of the 1980s and 1990s social sciences examined culture as the attitudes, beliefs and thought patterns shared by particular social groups (Nostrand 1989), or – in Brislin's (1990) words – they targeted the ideals, values and assumptions that members of communities commonly chose to adhere to.

In the 1990s language educators ventured to define culture for the purpose of foreign language teaching as a reality of products, exemplified by literature, music and artefacts; beliefs, values and institutions; as well as behaviour, manifesting itself in the customs, work and leisure of cultural groups (Tomalin & Stempleski 1993). If Tomalin and Stempleski's model is delineated along the lines of the iceberg metaphor of culture, it may be seen as an extension of the explicit layer of culture, i.e. behaviour, as it adds cultural products and institutions to it. This idea seems to be supported by Byram (1989), who observes that societal institutions can be described through observable behaviour. However, he notes that their cultural significance surfaces only when it is analysed in terms of meanings and beliefs that underpin them.

In addition, Tomalin and Stempleski perceived culture as civilisation and distinguished two of its types: "achievement culture" (Tomalin & Stempleski 1993: 6), also labelled as 'Big C' culture (Halverson 1985; Tomalin & Stempleski 1993), which embraces history, geography, art, music, and architecture; and 'little c' culture (Tomalin & Stempleski 1993), or 'small c' culture (Halverson 1985), which comprises customs, traditions, and practices. In Tomalin and Stempleski's (1993) view, 'little c' culture includes: behaviours (customs, habits, dress, foods and leisure), products (popular literature, folklore, popular music, popular art and artefacts), and ideas (beliefs, values and institutions). A similar distinction was made more recently by Khanevitch (2005), who talked about 'big C' culture as *high culture* or *elite culture*, and used the term *popular culture* for 'little c' culture, with the caveat that most of the popular culture of today is mass culture at the same time as it is distributed and promoted through the mass-media.

In humanistic sciences culture will normally denote the manner in which social groups represent themselves to the outside world through e.g. literature, art or artefacts as well as the processes that they engage in order to preserve such representations throughout the course of history (Kramsch 1999).

Culture as a general concept is normally defined from the perspective of culture-general behavioural patterns, attitudes and values (Moran 2001), the knowledge of which, in Kohls and Knight's (1994) view, underlies intercultural awareness. This kind of awareness enables one to examine potential aspects of culture which can lead to intercultural conflicts (Moran 2001).

Culture approached from the angle of intercultural communication is mostly studied in terms of factors that relate to "(...) the capacity and ability to enter other cultures and communicate effectively and appropriately, establish and maintain relationships, and carry out tasks with people of these cultures" (Moran 2001: 5). What is taken into account here is therefore the processes that accompany intercultural communicative situations which can help people mediate the differences that they experience in such contexts. Byram's (1997; 2008) intercultural communicative competence, set to be the goal of intercultural foreign language teaching, embraces this view of culture.

Culture may also be perceived as a platform for various communities within larger social groups, e.g. "the haves and the have-nots, the privileged and the underprivileged, or the oppressors and the oppressed"

(Moran 2001: 5), to struggle in order to secure the social, economic or political position that they would like to occupy. The same view has been aptly expressed by Fiske, who sees culture as: "(…) not a relatively harmonious and stable pool of significations, but a confrontation between groups occupying different, sometimes opposing positions in the map of social relations (…)" (Fiske 1989: 58). He continues to add that "(…) the process of making meanings (which is, after all, the process of culture) is a social struggle, as different groups struggle to establish meanings that serve their interests" (Fiske 1989: 58).

All in all, Moran (2001: 4-5) has attempted to systematise the views of culture that have emerged so far by assigning them to seven distinct categories: (i) culture as civilisation, (ii) culture as communication, (iii) culture as a general concept, (iv) culture in terms of intercultural communication, and (v) culture as a platform for group community interaction, (vi) culture as dynamic construction between and among people, and (vii) culture from the perspective of evolutionary psychology.

Currently, culture is viewed as a filter which shapes people's perceptions of the world. It is also an entity that individuals do not only passively enter through socialisation, but are capable of shaping themselves. Therefore, within intercultural communication – in congruence with the views of anthropologists such as Leach (1982), Suchodolski (1987) and Montgomery (2003) – culture is recognised as dialectic in nature and dynamic (Fenner 2000).

In evolutionary psychology it is recognised as a set of universals, such as music, language or facial expressions, which human beings use to communicate. Yet, this view of culture – although reminiscent of what Hall (1959) proposed in the 1950s – does not so much focus on difference, but rather perceives culture in terms of common biological features that stem from the nature of the human brain (Moran 2001). Similarly to Bonvillain (1997), Camilleri Grima also credits culture with the power to provide the "rules of the [communication] game" (Camilleri Grima 2002: 9). However, what must be observed is that although these concepts all relate to appropriate ways of communicating in a given language and culture, they mostly signify verbal expression, thus ignoring what Hall (1959) put to the fore.

In Moran's opinion, arriving at a synthetic anthropological definition of culture is an impossible task due to the various approaches and perspectives adopted by particular scholars, but also because of the complexity of culture per se. Thus, what he postulates as a solution to the conundrum is that "We have to accept and embrace the complexity of culture. The challenge is finding a simple approach to its complexities" (Moran 2001: 23).

More insight into culture in the context of language teaching can be gained if one examines how culture relates to language and, or even more broadly, to communication.

1.2 Language and culture

According to Zawadzka (2004), the relationship between language and culture has been under examination since the eighteenth century. The sciences involved in the study of the issue include: linguistics, ethnography, social psychology and cognitive psychology, but the problem has been most closely investigated within: (linguistic) anthropology, sociolinguistics and ethnolinguistics.

Anthropological perspective. It was in anthropology that the link between language and culture was fully recognised. As respected anthropologist Malinowski (1922) proposed in the 1920s, cultures should be studied through direct participation, and with attention to all the possibly observable practices of social groups, including language. In Malinowski's (ibid.) view, language was not a mere expression of culture but also a means of encoding culture, thus he believed that language was interwoven into the fabric of culture.

In the 1950s American Structural Linguistics raised the question of whether it was the world that people lived in that shaped the language that they used. The Sapir-Whorf Hypothesis (Whorf 1956) provided a negative answer by maintaining that the opposite was true, i.e. the language people spoke determined the way they perceived the world. "Language is not simply a reporting device for experience but a defining framework for it" (Whorf 1956: 252).

Relatively recently, Douglas Brown (1986) subscribed to this point of view by claiming that words shape people's lives, as the verbal labels people use to understand what they observe have an impact on information recall, sentence structure, and thought patterns, while organised discourse, e.g. an emotional speech, may have the power to persuade.

On the other hand, scholars such as Wardhough (Douglas Brown 1986), or more recently Pinker (2002), formulated anti-theses provided evidence to devalue the Sapir-Whorf Hypothesis.

The two schools of thought were in a sense conciliated by linguistic anthropologist Boas (1986), who observed while European languages enable their speakers to discuss abstract ideas, as European civilisation is based on philosophy, Indian languages are much more specialised in that they allow their speakers to express mostly daily activities. However, he concluded that Indian languages are not restrictive; they simply reflect the world and needs of the communities that they serve.

Douglas Brown (1986) stated that as world views differ, the language used to express them is likely to be relative and specific, but at the same time, he postulated that the debate on the Sapir-Whorf Hypothesis in the light of research findings is totally irrelevant to language educators. He expressed the view that irrespective of whether it is language that shapes human perception and culture or whether it is the environment – or culture – that moulds linguistic expression, the same conclusion can be drawn from the dispute: language and culture interact.

In modern times, Gozdawa-Gołębiowski (2006) is also of the opinion that language and culture are inseparably interconnected, however, the debate on the Sapir-Whorf hypothesis continues. Pawelec (2006) analyses three possible interpretations of the hypothesis: *linguistic determinism*, *linguistic relativism*, and the *thinking for speaking* perspective, and concludes that the latest one, i.e. *thinking for speaking*, seems to best reflect reality, where language offers its speakers a possible frame of mind, a perspective on the world that they may adopt; the final choice, however, lies with the speaker. Corbett is more cautious and prefers to view languages as "maps of *cultural priorities*, not *cognitive possibilities*" (2003: 8).

One must be cognisant of the fact that despite the research and findings of American Structuralism, linguistics was almost simultaneously – for a long time – dominated by the view of language proposed by Chomsky (1965), who practically removed culture from any considerations of the nature of language as he discussed language from the perspective of linguistic competence, i.e. purely linguistic rules which would enable language users to receive and produce language accurately.

At the same time, Hockett (1960) expressed his belief that language is a culturally transmitted phenomenon which is passed on from one generation to another. Interestingly enough, as psycholinguists Krauss and Chiu (1998) recently noticed, this cultural transmission occurs through language per se. Cognitive psychologist Vygotsky (1962) also viewed language as determined by cultural processes – an expression of contextual world.

Sociolinguistic perspective. It was within sociolinguistics, especially ethnography of communication, that Chomsky's limited view of language was elaborated through the introduction of Hymes' (1972) concept of communicative competence, which apart from linguistic competence highlighted the necessity of sociolinguistic competence, viewed as a tool which would enable language users to act not only accurately but also appropriately, depending on a given context of language use.

Larson and Smalley related language to culture by defining the former as a form of human behaviour – linguistic behaviour. Consequently, they believed that language depends on culture, which, as they claimed, "guides the behaviour of people in a community" (Larson & Smalley 1972: 39).

A number of scholars and researchers examined the bond between language and culture through the 1980s/1990s, e.g. Lakoff and Johnson (1980) proposed that metaphors represent people's experience; Blum-Kulka et al. (1989) examined speech acts and discourse as means of cultural expression; Halliday (1990) underlined the strong interconnection between language and culture, and claimed that the grammar, vocabulary and metaphors that people use are culture, while Keller (Kramsch 1993) traced stereotypes and self/other-perceptions as cultural components of language.

In the 1990s Kuper (1999) presented an inclusive definition of culture which covered: knowledge, including traditions, a social group's history, common sense, beliefs, attitudes, values and language.

In the same decade Duranti defined a relatively young scientific discipline aimed at studying "language as a cultural resource and speaking as a cultural practice" (Duranti 1997: 3), which most recently, Riley (2007) labelled as linguistic anthropology, anthropological linguistics or ethnolinguistics. As a matter of fact, it may be stated that its very emergence confirms that language and culture relate to each other.

As Riley illustrates, ethnolinguists relate language to thought by maintaining that "language is at one and the same time the tool, the contents and the form of human thought" (Riley 2007: 9), and thought and thinking patterns, in turn, are elements of culture. "Human beings can think because they are blessed with the gift of language, but their thoughts are necessarily expressed in and on the terms of the specific language they use, 'their mother tongue'. Germans think like Germans because they think in German" (Riley 2007: 25).

Zawadzka (2004) rounds up the findings of ethnolinguistics, sociolinguistics and linguistic anthropology with regard to the bond between language and culture and maintains that the above-cited sciences collectively view language as an element of culture, its product, carrier, and a tool for constructing the latter. Additionally, it is a record of culture-bound perception modes, but also a tool with which to receive and interpret reality. An illustration is provided by Sharwood-Smith's (2007) discussion of cultural shibboleths, in the course of which the author states that language can serve as a gate-keeping practice through which social/cultural strangers can be detected.

Pedagogical perspective. Valdes (1986) maintained that language, thought and culture are inextricably interwoven, and illustrated this by examining what cultural information can be detected within language. Language carries cultural values, such as efficiency, which is reflected through the brevity and directness of American English. Words in a language system often illustrate the environment in which a particular social group uses it. For example, Boas (1986) reported that in Eskimo languages there are many more words for snow than in any other language.

Even the structure of language has cultural significance, as the degree of formality that speakers use is culturally-motivated. In addition, language exerts influence on people, e.g. when the language of advertising enters daily vocabulary, in much the same manner as people influence language; after all, the language of advertising is created by people themselves (Valdes 1986).

Sell (1995) demonstrates that language is a component of culture by stating that without knowing the culture beyond a given language system, one cannot understand what signified objects are denoted by particular linguistic signifiers. As Sell explains, language cannot be interpreted literally, as what meets the eye is not what the text purports to express. This hidden layer of text is only decipherable to someone who is familiar with the culture within which it was originally encoded. Sell even suggests that seemingly nonsensical statements in a language may be ascribed a logical meaning to by a person who has an extensive knowledge of the culture behind it. In a similar vein, Jones (1990) sheds light on the relationship between language and culture by discussing how a text is received by a reader. The degree to which the reader finds a text understandable depends on the degree to which the culture of production, i.e. the culture from which the text originates, is in congruence with the culture of reception, i.e. the culture of the reader.

As Bakhtin (1992) remarks, language is saturated with other people's intentions, which reflect the thought patterns, ideals and values that others live by. McCarthy and Carter (1994: 155) refer to the latter collectively as people's "cultural frames of reference". Montgomery and Reid-Thomas (1994) maintain that culture and language are interrelated and culture is actually expressed through the medium of language.

Byram and Fleming (1998) view language as a carrier of culture in that the former helps speakers maintain a sense of belonging to social groups through the connotations and associations that it conveys. However,

Kramsch (1993) comments that if language is defined exclusively in such terms – which it very often is – and if it is reduced to the role of a cultural transmitter, it is not a part of culture. She suggests that language be perceived as a social practice, in which case, culture becomes its core element. In Taylor's words, language expresses meanings, which are a part and reflection of social practices – modes of social relation (Byram 1989). Stubbs (1995) seems to subscribe to this point to view when he notices that phraseological analysis of the collocations of a given language system depicts the perspectives of its users, e.g. sexism in the world perceptions of the native speakers of English.

Pulverness states that "To attempt to divorce language from its cultural context is to ignore the social circumstances which give it resonance and meaning" (Pulverness 1999: 101). Kramsch (1999) also sees culture as constructed through language, and adds that attitudes and ideas do not exist outside language.

Fenner (2000) sees culture as text, which in form and content is both an expression of culture and its carrier. She actually equates language with culture and does not doubt that language is indeed culture. Simultaneously, it must be underlined that her view of language as text exceeds the verbal dimension, and covers e.g. works of visual art, such as paintings, which converges with Corbett's (2003) extended view of text.

The realisation of intricate bonds between language and culture has led various scholars to developing a number of words that capture both notions under a single umbrella term, e.g. Kramsch's (1989) and Agar's *languaculture* (1994), or Fantini's (2002) *linguaculture*. In culture pedagogy Byram, Morgan et al. (1994) have coined *language-and-culture*, Crozet and Liddicoat (1997) have come up with *culture-in-language* and Galisson uses *language-culture* (Risager 2007). Moran (2001) chooses to apply the term *language-and-culture*, which seems to represent a moderate view of the link between language and culture, within which both components can be perceived separately, as well as in combination. He believes that language is a product of culture, it is used by cultural groups to execute their practices and name the perspectives that they follow when analysing the world. Simultaneously, language is also used to participate in and identify with a culture. All in all, to him language and culture are mutual reflections of each other – they can be seen in and through each other.

Montgomery claims that "(...) culture is implicated in every instance of language in use" (2003: ix), and language is used against a cultural background of social practice, value, belief and symbol.

Aleksandrowicz-Pędich (2005) states that language is an integral component of culture in many ways: it is a carrier of culture, its direct manifestation, as well as a benchmark for tracing cultural alterations. Her view resounds the words of Kramsch (1989), who maintained that language does not only express but also embodies and symbolises cultural reality.

Bogusławski (2006) argues that culture cannot exist without language, as e.g. moral norms, religious behaviours, customs, inventions, technology, sports and artistic activities, i.e. components of culture, are impossible without language. At the same time, language suffices for all of them to come into being.

Finally, Ash (2007) confirms that language and culture interact, as he observes that differences in language dialects in the United States of America appear to be determined by the cultural groups that use them. Evidence which supports this statement is the fact that the boundaries of language dialects across the United States coincide with the lines of cultural regions.

1.3 Culture and communication

The need to separate a discussion of the bonds between language and culture from that of the links between culture and communication stems from the fact that not all communication involves language. Hall (1959) testified to this point of view by observing that Americans speak only 5-11 minutes during the day. Most of their daily communication is, therefore, realised through non-linguistic means. As Birdwhistell (1960) revealed, 65% of meanings expressed in one-on-one communicative exchanges are conveyed nonverbally.

Morain (1986) classifies the nonverbal modes of communication as: body language, e.g. gestures, facial expressions and touch; object language, manifested through the use of clothes, realia, designs or patterns; and environmental language, which he sees as certain aspects of space, architecture or colour which define man's nature. Tomczak (2005) demonstrates a more comprehensive classification of non-verbal components of communication which includes: kinesics (the use of body language), proxemics (the use of distance and space), chronemics (the use of time), haptics (the use of touch), olfactics (the use of smell), oculesics (the use of eye contact), sartorial codes (the use of appearance), the use of objectual systems (realia) and paralanguage (polite noises).

Language has already been demonstrated as a cultural phenomenon, but body language has also been discovered to be culture-bound by scholars such as Hall (1959), Banks (1975), or Wylie and Stafford (1977) – similarly to the other non-verbal aspects of communication, e.g. haptics, proxemics (Hall 1966) and oculesics (Lustig & Koester 1999; Jandt 2001). Recently, Kurtchenia reported that non-verbal aspects of communication are actually "the most culturally-influenced part of human behaviour" (Kurtchenia 2005: 102). Consequently, it may be assumed that communication per se is also strictly related to culture, as illustrated below.

In the 1960s Hymes (1967) highlighted the socio-cultural nature of communication by maintaining that while communicating speakers make choices, e.g. of when, where and to whom to speak and what to discuss, which are determined by the social context of a communicative situation, i.e. the participants, the setting, and the objectives one wishes to achieve.

As early as in the 1970s, Samovar and Porter (1972) observed the culture-bound character of intercultural communication when they proposed five features of culture that have a significance for intercultural communicators. They maintained that culture is (i) ethnocentric, i.e. people have a tendency to place their own culture before any other that they come into contact with, which affects their perception of the new or the different. Samovar and Porter (ibid.) emphasised that (ii) culture is not innate, thus it needs to be learned in the course of one's life. What is worth stressing is the fact that such cultural learning is both conscious and subconscious, as on the one hand cultural knowledge may be transmitted to children from their parents through explicit instruction, while on the other hand such knowledge may be simply acquired through observation. One way or the other, culture is (iii) transmissible. Samovar and Porter highlighted that language can be used as a conveyor of culture, but the transmission might also be realised through culturally significant symbols or nonverbal actions. Culture is also (iv) selective in that out of a vast repertoire of human behaviours, every cultural group selects a set of patterns that it desires to follow in the light of its leading values and assumptions. Finally, culture is (v) dynamic, i.e. it is subject to constant change through diffusion, borrowings or innovations. Those alterations, however, mostly concern the surface rather than the deep structure of culture, with the latter being much more resistant to change.

The cultural character of communication has been elucidated ever since the 1970s up to the present moment. For instance, similarly to language, communication has been at times perceived as not only a manifestation of culture, as presented above, but also as a means through which culture may be created. Breen and Candlin expressed this view in the 1980s by stating that communication is a"(...) convention-creating as well as convention-following activity" (Breen and Candlin 1980: 91).

In the same decade, Samovar et al. stated that culture is "(...) the foundation of communication" (1981: 24), and explained that culture informs language performance in terms of speaker roles, turn-taking practices, content, meaning of messages and message interpretation principles.

Tajfel (1981) underlined the fact that people's social identities, such as ethnic, national, gender-, class- and age-related, are strongly involved in communicative interactions. Le Page and Tabouret-Keller (1985) supported him, as they envisaged communication to go far beyond an exchange of information. They saw it rather as a form of interaction which involves the social identities of its participants. Byram and Fleming (1998) also give communication a cultural angle by adding that a person's identity constitutes a bond between him/her and the social groups and cultural practices that he/she identifies with. Communication is therefore a constant interplay between those identities, which take a more or less dominant position, depending on the language involved or the relationship between the interlocutors.

In the 1990s Garton (1992) ascribed one more role to communication by stating that communication is essentially social interaction in the course of which not only information but also cultural and historical values are transmitted. As Porto (2000) illustrated, the range of decisions that speakers take on how to communicate with others is reflective of their social values, which are not universal but culture-bound.

Penz built on Garton's (1992) and Porto's (2000) view of communication as social interaction involving socio-cultural values and proposed that this interaction is additionally used as a means of the acquisition of "cultural values and interactive rules of communication" (Penz 2001: 105).

Ronowicz (2007) has also displayed a view of communication similar to that of Garton, and stated that what effective communication involves is not only an awareness of historical symbols but also of "the complicated reality of everyday life and social consciousness of (...) [a given] language community" (Ronowicz 2007: 6). With regard to language communication, he has underlined the vitality of second-level meanings acquired by language through cultural associations, which are constantly in flux.

Riley has gone even further as in actual fact he has equated culture with communication by claiming that as culture is transmitted between generations through communication, "the communicative practices through which culture is transmitted are themselves part of culture" (Riley 2007: 40). According to him, the bond between communication and culture is best illustrated by the fact that research in language acquisition to date, including error analysis, contrastive analysis or studies of interlanguage, has failed to explicate interference solely in linguistic terms. It was Hymes who drew attention to the sociolinguistic side of communication, and inspired studies of sociolinguistic transfer (Riley 2007).

Consequently, the twenty-first century to date has seen scholars, such as e.g. Meinardi (2007), perceive communication from an intercultural angle. In Meinardi's view, communication is an act in which the speakers' deictic circles clash. Those deictic circles comprise the speakers' communication codes: language, context and culture. Therefore, communication cannot be perceived only in terms of its linguistic aspects as it inescapably entails an exchange of contextual and cultural clues. It is particularly relevant to intercultural communication, where although the linguistic codes of the speakers involved may happen to at least partially dovetail, the same is not normally true about their contextual and cultural perspectives (Meinardi 2007).

2. Teaching language and culture

2.1 Culture in foreign language teaching: a historical overview

Before the nineteenth century language learning did not follow any specific principles which would be codified by a particular teaching method. Learning was, therefore, natural in that it occurred through face-to-face contact with native speakers in the multilingual societies of that time or through private tuition, which was reserved for the elite. As an alternative, young aristocrats would conventionally set out on a journey across Europe with the intention to expand horizons and learn foreign languages (Aleksandrowicz-Pędich 2005). During such journeys, culture was experienced directly rather than studied in any systematised way.

The nineteenth century and the first half of the twentieth century in foreign language teaching was dominated by the Grammar-Translation Method – also referred to as the Classical Method (Richards & Rogers 1986) – which reflected the needs of the then society and set as its major purpose the development of the ability to read classical target language literature. It must be explained here that the languages taught through the method were Latin and Greek, viewed as a tool with which the upper social classes would augment their familiarity with the intellectual achievement of mankind (Aleksandrowicz-Pędich 2005). Since Latin and Greek did not serve the purpose of daily communication, the method was intended to help learners increase their intellect, and learning through it was frequently conceived of as mental exercise (Larsen-Freeman 1986).

On the one hand it can be stated that the role of culture in the foreign language classroom within this method was elevated, on the other hand, paradoxically, the method reduced the very concept of culture to the fine arts only – literature, in particular, which in Lessard-Clouston's (1997) view, was the major cultural medium of that time. Consequently, the Grammar-Translation Method focused mostly on high culture, the civilisation of the target language, while ignoring elements of low culture (Komorowska 2006b), which learners need to be familiarised with if they are to communicate successfully with representatives of other cultures.

In a modernised version of the Grammar-Translation Method, the cultural content was expanded to cover facts and figures about the target language country as well as its life and institutions. The picture of the target culture drawn by textbooks was perceived as educationally appropriate for learners, therefore, it was taught as such. What is worth stressing, however, is the fact that although the method permitted learners to use their mother tongue in a lesson, it did not induce any reference to their native culture (Neuner 2003).

Towards the end of the nineteenth century the Direct Method came into being, which was very much a response to the critique of the Grammar-Translation Method by linguists such as Vietör, Gouin, Jespersen and Sweet (Richards & Rogers 1986); it thus primarily emphasised language work in the form of oral communication, and was supposed to incite classroom conversation. The kind of culture that was dealt with within the method embraced rather formal aspects of life in the target language country, e.g. geography (Larsen-Freeman 1986). Occasionally, elements of material culture and lifestyle were introduced (Komorowska 2006b). However – yet again – only the target culture was tackled.

Throughout the 1950s, 1960s and 1970s, a number of publications by Hall (1959), Nostrand (1967a), and Seelye (1974) suggested that foreign language and culture teaching ought to better reflect the personal needs of language learners. At the same time, culture was supposed to be presented in a more digestible, straight-forward manner. Despite that, the foreign language teaching methodology of the period was so strongly influenced by two strands of psychology, Behaviourism and Cognitivism, that little notice of those ideas was taken within the two resultant methods that followed.

After World War II, in the Audio-Lingual Method, which grew on the back of the rising popularity of behavioural psychology, the stress was put on the learning of language patterns through mechanical repetition of language chunks. This grammar-based view of language practice, in which language learning boiled down to students imitating a model by *overlearning* fragments of dialogues, practically ousted any discussion of culture out of the classroom. It was so due to the belief that the verbal behaviour of humans was a universal set of habits which could be developed through rote learning (Richards & Rogers 1986).

As Neuner (2003) and Komorowska (2006b) indicate, culture in the form of daily routine was incidentally incorporated into the language drilled, but the teacher neither made any reference to it, nor issued any cultural comments. Aleksandrowicz-Pędich (2005) admits that cultural instruction was part of the method, but it was delayed until learners achieved a relatively high level of proficiency in the target language.

In the 1960s' Cognitive Method, learners' attention was drawn to conscious language learning. The teacher here assisted learners not only in analysing formal aspects of language, including grammatical rules, but also developing language learning strategies which would aid their linguistic development (Komorowska 2006b). In practice, the method completely ignored culture, as it essentially focused on procedural matters and metacognitive awareness (Richards & Rogers 1986).

Since the Second World War, English language teaching methods have, almost by default, been devoid of teaching/learning materials based on literary texts (Brooks 1968; Richards & Rogers 1986; Larsen-Freeman 1986; Komorowska 2009). In the 1960s Brooks (1968) once again de-emphasised the role of literature in foreign language learning as a manifestation of culture. Simultaneously, he underlined that the forms of culture to be taught ought to comprise aspects of everyday life, such as behaviour or lifestyle, as well as the beliefs and attitudes that underpin them. Roughly that time witnessed the emergence of Communicative Language Teaching, which, by definition, was to prepare foreign language learners for oral communication in the target language. Although potentially the method lent itself perfectly to cultural, or even intercultural, teaching, in actual practice it did not make use of the potential at all. It placed at its centre the development of the four major language skills: listening, speaking, reading and writing (Aleksandrowicz-Pędich 2005). As Komorowska (2006b) states, reading and listening texts which were utilised in the method for the purpose of skills development indeed featured elements of knowledge about the target culture, but there was no proper follow-up. Although professional literature emphasised the development of communicative competence, communicative skills and the importance of sociolinguistic context (Hymes 1972; Savignon 1972; Canale & Swain 1980), it found little reflection in the actual teaching practice in the communicative classroom. To do justice to communicative teaching, it may be added that it did demonstrate to students a body of sociolinguistic patterns related to specific speech acts – mostly through authentic texts – that learners were supposed to indiscriminately follow in particular communicative settings (Neuner 2003). However, the rules were viewed as representative of all native-speaker communication, without any recognition of the heterogeneity of the target language society, and with disregard to the cultural circumstances of intercultural communicative situations.

The late 1970s saw the appearance of the so-called designer, humanistic methods of teaching, such as the Silent Way, Suggestopaedia or Community Language Learning. As they mostly concentrated on de-suggesting students' negative feelings or reducing their learning inhibitions by establishing a friendly and supportive atmosphere in the classroom (Larsen-Freeman 1986; Komorowska 2006b), culture once again was cast aside. Even if it incidentally surfaced, either through the themes tackled or the activities practised, it was not explicitly taught or discussed.

Due to a dramatic increase in migration and direct intercultural contacts, both for personal and professional purposes, that began to characterise social interaction in the 1980s, real attention was directed towards the educational and communicative needs of language learners (Komorowska 2006b). The noticeable mobility of societies coincided with a rapid development of international trade contacts, which spawned the proliferation of courses in business English. As a result, the need was finally highlighted to equip language learners not only with purely linguistic skills but also essential aspects of cultural knowledge which would help corporate institutions successfully establish and maintain international trade links (Aleksandrowicz-Pędich 2006; Komorowska 2006b). Komorowska (2006b) stresses the fact that such intercultural business contacts did not necessarily require their participants to follow the socio-cultural rules of the target language community, but rather necessitated a knowledge of rules governing international/intercultural interaction.

As the relevance of cultural instruction to foreign language teaching was being increasingly realised, so was the nature of culture per se. Societies and their socio-cultural practices were closely examined by scholars, e.g. Preston (1981), and information was collected on differences in four categories of conventions which characterised human behaviour within particular societies: (i) punctuality, politeness or intimacy; (2) frames: turn-taking and presentation patterns; (iii) non-verbal communication: e.g. oculesics, kinesics, the use of silence or politeness; and (iv) the nature of language (Morgan 1998). Language was in consequence discovered afresh, as it began to be viewed through the prism of its functions in communication, e.g. persuading or deceiving (Thanasoulas 2001).

Towards the beginning of the 1990s it was finally realised that communication was a "a highly cognitive, as well as affective and value-laden activity" (Thanasoulas 2001: 4), while learning culture in a foreign language course offered learners an opportunity to not only delve into the target language community's perspectives but also to decentre and look anew at their own behaviour and viewpoints as culture-determined (Byram 1989; Kramsch 1998a). It was realised that in order to fully grasp the nature of the target culture learners would have to experience it from the insiders' perspective, while, at the same time, they would need to defamiliarise themselves with their own culture. It was recognised that this kind of learning would additionally require willingness to understand other points of view and readiness to empathise (Byram 1997). Yet another realisation was the need to demonstrate to learners the dynamic nature and heterogeneity of culture, especially in the modern-day world.

As Thanasoulas (2001) indicates, three stances on the position of a cultural component in foreign language teaching have emerged so far: (i) culture as a language learning aside, a kind of fifth skill which is supposed to be developed alongside the other major language skills; (ii) culture as an inherent element of communicative competence and intercultural communicative competence, which contains intercultural awareness; and (iii) culture as a knowledge to be developed as a general educational objective, a body of 'an all-encompassing knowledge which, to a certain extent, has determined – facilitated or precluded – all other types of "knowledge"' (Thanasoulas 2001: 5).

Although the rapid development of social sciences in the current post-communicative era has resulted in much more recognition of the need to include culture in foreign language teaching than before (Aleksandrowicz-Pędich 2005; Komorowska 2006b; Bandura 2007), it finds limited reflection in the daily practice of foreign language teachers (Lubecka 1994; Bandura 2007).

As Aleksandrowicz-Pędich (2005) summarises, the difference between the view of culture in foreign language teaching today and the past lies in a departure from the relaying of fact-based, declarative knowledge, which was the convention of the *Landeskunde* approach, and a shift towards more focus on attitudes to otherness, empathy, intercultural knowledge and skills, as well as elements of intracultural education, where the learner attempts to increase self-awareness by exploring their own culture.

In contemporary pedagogy, culture is additionally perceived as a multi-faceted entity, which contrasts with its monolithic, and largely national, image, transmitted by the British Studies approach. A comprehensive presentation of the explicit and implicit components of culture to be taught in the intercultural language classroom comes from Moran (2001). The explicit components embrace: cultural products and practices as well as communities and their individual members. At the same time, the explicit elements are underpinned by concealed perspectives, which must be explored if intercultural understanding is to be brought about.

Moran (2001) perceives culture as a number of *cultural knowings* to be developed in learners through the suggested content and activities. Only then can the desirable outcomes be attained:

	Content	**Activities**	**Outcomes**
Knowing about	cultural information	gathering information	cultural **knowledge**
Knowing how	cultural practices	developing skills	cultural **behaviours**
Knowing why	cultural perspectives	discovering explanations	cultural **understanding**
Knowing oneself	self	reflection	self-**awareness**

Table 1-1

In order to develop the expected outcomes of intercultural teaching, which are: cultural knowledge, behaviours, understanding, and increased self-awareness, the following content is supposed to be dealt with: (a) cultural information, (b) practices (c) perspectives, and (d) the learner's self. The activities which can be utilised while tackling the content are to involve: (i) gathering the kind of cultural information which may function as the foundation of the learner's cultural exploration; (ii) developing skills which will enable the learner to observe and follow culture-bound behaviours; (iii) discovering explanations with a view to investigating perspectives and attaining intercultural understanding; and (iv) reflecting on one's self, which seems to be the prerequisite for the understanding of others.

To sum up, in the intercultural classroom culture is recognised as dynamic (Fenner & Newby 2000), inclusive (including a myriad of components), heterogeneous (delineated by occupation or age), multiple (involving individual people's numerous identities), contemporary (manifested in the present and future rather than the past), and a process (resulting in the development of behaviours and products) (Bolt 2001).

2.2 For and against teaching culture in the EFL classroom

Scholarly arguments have been voiced in favour of both incorporating as well as abandoning culture in the English-as-a-Foreign-Language (EFL) classroom.

Opposition to teaching culture. An example of the critique of cultural education in EFL settings comes from Valdes (1986), who has issued a warning to language teachers that studying language and culture may create a mental block, a kind of barrier to learning, in learners. According to that view, exposure to a foreign culture may lead to all kinds of negative responses from learners in the EFL classroom, which in extreme cases may develop into anger, fright or even repulsion. Occasionally, those negative reactions may even be aggravated by the nature of the target language itself.

However, it ought to be mentioned here that what Valdes warns against is only one of the possible scenarios in teaching culture, and one which is most likely to materialise in situations where culture is taught in a superficial and insensitive fashion on the part of the teacher. What is more, in the light of the theory of acculturation proposed e.g. by Douglas Brown (1986), it can be stated that acute anxiety caused by language/culture learning experiences is only a temporary stage in learners' linguistic/cultural development, which with time is likely to be followed by full recovery, i.e. either cultural adaptation or assimilation. If students' feelings are taken into account, and culture is carefully explored and analysed, negative emotions will be alleviated and counteracted. In sum, Valdes' (1986) point of view may rather be viewed as a call for an informed and well-organised approach to culture teaching, which would allow for commentary on the culture taught.

Calls for the removal of cultural education from language courses have been particularly strongly expressed in English-as-a-Lingua-Franca (ELF) contexts, where English is supposed to be taught as a language for international communication. Even the very choice of English as the target language in ELF settings has caused deep concerns, as due to the belief that cultural elements will surface in the classroom in one form or another, the language taught and its culture have been perceived as tools for linguistic and cultural indoctrination. For instance, in the 1990s Holly

(1990) labelled teaching ELF as ideological and cultural colonisation, while roughly a decade later Alexander (1999) and Gnutzmann (2000) warned against language imperialism in the ELF classroom. Alexander (ibid.) additionally feared that the international dominance of English might lead to a reduction in importance or even obliteration of other, local languages.

Komorowska (2006c) observes that the afore-mentioned reasoning, referred to as a *trap scenario* (Komorowska 2006c: 114), may have been fuelled by the ever-persisting concerns of language educators about the domination, or cultural imperialism, of English in language teaching worldwide, which are reminiscent of the voices directed towards English as a foreign language in the 1980s.

By and large, English language teaching, be it in ELF and EFL contexts, has been suspected of smuggling socio-cultural norms of the target language community into the foreign language classroom in an attempt to impose them on unsuspecting language learners, who might with time replace their own ideologies and cultures with the target ones, be it consciously or incidentally.

To counteract the fear of the trap scenario amongst educators, the concept of teaching English as an international language, or a lingua franca, has been altered. Its new conception now bases on the premise that a universal language system for international communication, which a lingua franca purports to be, should serve the purpose of pragmatism and cultural neutrality, which would make it fit for use by any user across the world. The language system should at the same time potentially capacitate its users to convey any cultural content through it (Gozdawa-Gołębiowski 2006). Gozdawa-Gołębiowski (ibid.) sees international English simply as a decline in the original national status of the language – a by-product of the international use of English today. He perceives this de-nationalisation of English as a natural phenomenon which stems from the fact that in intercultural contexts, especially where the culture-referential systems of co-communicators diverge, culture-bound elements of ELF, such as cultural artefacts, idiomacy and facto-graphical references, become naturally eliminated.

What this implies for the ELF classroom is that when English is taught as an international language, it ought to be culturally-neutral (Gozdawa-Gołębiowski 2006), which might be interpreted as an attempt to cast culture out of the ELF classroom.

However – similarly to other scholars before, e.g. Loveday (1981), Kramsch (1993) or Tomalin and Stempleski (1993) – Gozdawa-Gołębiowski (2006) himself immediately admits that complete eradication of culture from language education may not be possible. It was already in the 1980s that Loveday (1981) adamantly stated that the culling of culture from English as a lingua franca was an illusion, as in communicative situations the culture of its users would inescapably emerge, even if the simplest, routine language was involved.

Kramsch (1993) expressed the belief that if "language is seen as social practice, culture becomes the core of language teaching" (Kramsch 1993: 8), while Tomalin and Stempleski (1993) saw culture as inescapable in the foreign language classroom, as they proposed that it be "systematically treated as a regular feature of the language lesson" (Tomalin & Stempleski 1993: 7), with special emphasis on the development of cultural awareness through a focus on 'little c' culture, i.e. culturally-determined behaviour.

With such arguments in mind, Gozdawa-Gołębiowski (2006) today only postulates that on cultural level English be taught without the dominance of the cultural reality of one specific country or cultural-linguistic region, without attempting to curb culture per se. He implies that a compromise solution might be an intercultural approach to language teaching when in conclusion to an article in which he ponders the role of culture in the ELF classroom, he himself answers the title question: "An Intercultural or Anticultural Approach?" (2006: 112) by tentatively pointing towards the former alternative.

Multiple other scholars have confirmed that the lingua franca context does require some form of (inter)cultural training, e.g. Byram (1997; 1989; 1998; 2008), Tsvirko (2005), Komorowska (2006b) and Aleksandrowicz-Pędich (2006). In addition, Gałkowski (2006) suggests three possible positions of a cultural component in lingua franca courses for educators to choose from: (i) retaining the teaching of anglo-centric culture as a platform for international communication; (ii) turning lingua franca instruction into a culturally-neutral discipline; and (iii) replacing culture teaching with elements of contemporary ethnography, as originally advocated by Byram and Fleming (1998).

Arguments for teaching culture. In general, the proposition that has dominated the language teaching scene is that the cultural component does occupy its place in foreign language teaching, which has been supported by numerous arguments, as demonstrated below.

In the light of the findings of Gardner and Lambert (1972), who researched the influence of motivation on success in foreign language learning and concluded that integrative motivation increased learning efficacy, it may be concluded that teaching culture may have a motivational value. Although Gardner and Lambert's (1972) research results cannot be viewed as conclusive – Brown's (1986) research debunked their original suggestion – it might be putatively assumed that by teaching learners about the target culture the teacher may happen to develop integrative motivation in at least some of their learners, or simply increase their learner's positive attitudes towards the target language culture, overall.

As Midgley (1980) and Lustig (1988) have demonstrated, counteracting learners' ethnocentricity, which in intercultural contacts makes them assume that their cultural practices are universal or more natural than those of others, is crucial in language teaching. Such a goal might be achieved when culture is taught in a comparative fashion, where learners compare their own culture with others and realise that a large portion of human behaviour is not natural, as it is normally assumed, but culture-dependent (Ochs and Schieffelin 1984). As Byram confirms, "If FLT contributes to re-interpretation of pupils' own behaviour by introducing them to those in other cultures, it can surely claim to have a significant role in young people's education" (Byram 1989: 50).

Byram (1984) has also proposed that if culture is taught with proper attention to contrasts between the learner's native culture and its target counterpart, the learner's awareness shifts from monocultural to intercultural. Douglas Brown (1998) seems to be more complacent and maintains that even if culture is taught superficially, it adds up to the learner's knowledge of other cultures at large. To him, familiarity with many different cultures renders a person ready to accept otherness; that is, it increases the learner's tolerance. In general, both Byram (1984) and Douglas Brown (1998) agree that teaching culture may help the learner progress on a continuum between monocultural to bi- or multi-cultural awareness.

Valdes (1986) believes that teaching culture is a precondition of elucidating appropriate language meaning to learners, without which sociolinguistic accuracy in both reception and production will become virtually impossible.

On a pragmatic note, Byram (1989) explains that if the target language is taught with disregard to its culture, it does not only undermine the nature of language itself, but also jeopardizes learners' success in a foreign language by perpetrating cultural transfer, i.e. the semantic interference that makes learners attribute L1 meanings to target language words. It is a natural consequence of the lack of familiarity with the target language culture, which the learner compensates by resorting to their L1 cultural knowledge, readily available to them. Negative transfer (interference) – which was originally associated with language per se (Selinker 1972) – also seems relevant to cultural aspects of language use, and as such, once more demonstrates the bond between language and culture. In order to avoid intercultural transfer Byram (1989) – and more recently also Riley (2007) – advise foreign language teachers to focus on both linguistics, i.e. phonology and syntax, as well as sociolinguistics and pragmatics, i.e. functions of language.

Byram (1989) also proposes that introducing a cultural component into foreign language teaching gives learners an opportunity to experience foreign cultures through the target language, and that can serve the purpose of reducing prejudice and encouraging tolerance towards others. At the same time, cognisant of Goodson and McGivney's (1985) suggestion that cultural learning will naturally emerge out of language teaching – as teachers falsely assume, he postulates that culture teaching be meticulously planned. Proper planning must cover not only the teaching procedures, but also the materials to be used, as cultural information that learners obtain is most often incidental, distorted and culturally biased. "The distortion is then increased by exaggeration of the typical, by concentration on the differences between the foreign language and home culture" (Byram 1989: 16). Coursebooks offer a stereotypical – somewhat superficial and touristy – picture of the target language culture, they distort reality, and in effect, are naturally rejected by learners as too idyllic. Such materials will not turn learners into effective language users, no matter how hard the teacher tries.

Instead, teachers should attempt to draw a true picture of the target culture, with special attention to cultural experience and emphasis on empathy. One of the aims of teaching culture in the foreign language classroom would be to attempt to develop in learners an understanding of human language and culture, and the interplay between them, as one might add. This kind of pedagogical aim would: enrich learners' knowledge, raise awareness, and help teachers inspect what learners intuitively assume to know about language and culture (Byram 1989).

Byram (1989) proposes that teaching culture serve two curricular aims: (i) behavioural and (ii) symbol-and-meaning oriented. When culture is taught with a behavioural intent alone, it focuses on making learners imitate cultural practices, without any study of underlying values. In consequence, this kind of teaching only engineers learners' behaviour without encouraging any deep-level learning which would involve reflection.

Culture may also be taught along the lines of the symbols-and-meanings view, where it serves the purpose of making learners discover social symbols and phenomena, learn how to interpret them, develop new competencies, and reflect on their own culture. Byram (1989) endorses this kind of aim-setting in teaching culture, as it does not treat learners instrumentally, and its aim is not to develop any arbitrarily predetermined forms of behaviour. Instead, the learners are expected to be able to determine their own actions on the basis of the their interpretations of particular social contexts.

In a similar vein, Crozet and Liddicoat (1997) suggest that by teaching culture in a cross-cultural fashion teachers add up to their learners' effectiveness in communication, whereas Byram and Fleming (1998) claim that language learning must involve not only developing linguistic skills but also cultural awareness, which helps learners understand those who speak the target language more fully. Otherwise, even relatively simple linguistic units, such as words or phrases, will not be completely grasped by learners.

Porto (2000) deems culture important in foreign language teaching on two planes: (i) pedagogical and (ii) educational. Pedagogically, culture enables students to use the target language appropriately, i.e. in agreement with the social rules that underpin it. Educationally, it helps the foreign language teacher develop learners not only linguistically, but also socially and cognitively. If that is the case, in addition to what learners unravel about the target language culture, they are given an opportunity to develop a number of skills through which they can interpret, explore and explain the world – universal, transferable skills which might be useful to learners outside the foreign language classroom.

The reasons for which culture ought to be incorporated into foreign language teaching courses also transpire from Tomalin and Stempleski's "seven goals of cultural instruction" (Tomalin & Stempleski 1993: 7), which they adapt from Seelye (1988):

> "1. To help students to develop an understanding of the fact that all people exhibit culturally-conditioned behaviors.
> 2. To help students to develop an understanding that social variables such as age, sex, social class, and place of residence influence the ways in which people speak and behave.
> 3. To help students to become more aware of conventional behavior in common situations in the target culture.
> 4. To help students to increase their awareness of the cultural connotations of words and phrases in the target language.
> 5. To help students to develop the ability to evaluate and refine generalizations about the target culture, in terms of supporting evidence.
> 6. To help students to develop the necessary skills to locate and organize information about the target culture.
> 7. To stimulate students' intellectual curiosity about the target culture, and to encourage empathy towards its people" (Tomalin & Stempleski 1993: 7).

Tomalin and Stempleski's (1993) intercultural agenda for the EFL classroom is endorsed by Cortazi (1998), who stresses that today language teaching is supposed to prepare learners to cope with intercultural encounters and develop their sociopragmatic accuracy. Linguistic proficiency in Chomskyean terms does not involve cultural proficiency, which nevertheless needs to be developed due to the cultural nature of language and communication (cf. sections 1.2 and 1.3 of Chapter One). If a learner is only familiarised with generative aspects of the target language, they run the risk of becoming a *fluent fool* (Bennett 1997), or as Gozdawa-Gołębiowski (2006) has recently put it, a *culture monster*, who is sociopragmatically awkward, and may appear funny or even offensive.

The role of the cultural component of language courses in developing intercultural competence also reverberates – more or less directly – through the writings of other authors. For instance, Collie (1998) writes that as learners attempt to explore and understand various aspects of the target language culture, they engage in a study of values or relationships, which may provoke a range of reactions: from aggressive to positive. The teacher can, therefore, build on that in two ways: increase learners' motivation, as well as their cultural and social awareness, which can be achieved by steering learners through the cultural phenomena that they experience, so that they can reflect on them.

According to Kramsch (1999), the goals of teaching culture within the English teaching curriculum worldwide are three-fold: political, educational and ideological. From the political perspective, culture teaching is to aid international understanding and promote world peace, which broadly speaking are the goals of intercultural teaching. From the educational point of view, it is to increase learners' contact with cultural content, i.e. content which would further learners' *intellectual* and *humanistic* development. Finally, when cultural instruction serves an ideological purpose, it is used in immigration contexts, where its aim is to help newcomers to a given country assimilate or acculturate into its society.

Moran (2001) lists the possible outcomes of culture learning, which could also be interpreted as the possible roles which culture teaching might fulfil, should it be guaranteed a place in the foreign language classroom. The outcomes relate to the possibility of developing learners' "cultural understanding, cultural awareness, cultural adaptation, assimilation, integration, social change, communicative competence, identity transformation, and language proficiency" (Moran 2001: 6). To build on that, Penz (2001) believes that cultural awareness may foster the development of intercultural communicative competence or multiculturalism.

The intercultural purpose of culture teaching in the EFL classroom is succinctly expressed by Bolt (2001), who proposes that teaching culture today is "about how to bring culture into the class **from 'the world'** in such a way as to develop understanding and expression of it, as well as **bringing culture out of the learners** (...), and teach them how to express it for later use out in 'the world'" (Bolt 2001: 104, emphasis original).

Zawadzka (2004) demonstrates that linguistic competence without the addition of sociopragmatic and socio-cultural norms that govern communication will not suffice to adequately prepare learners for intercultural communicative situations, as Ronowicz and Yallop (2007) illustrate by citing examples of communicative failure experienced by foreign academics participating in university exchange programmes in Midwestern USA.

Finally, Budzko (2005) underlines that culture is an indispensible component of foreign language teaching as language is "the most representative element in any culture" (Budzko 2005: 21). According to her, the pedagogical value of culture teaching is the development of empathy, cultural understanding, open-mindedness, civic responsibility, sensitivity towards global issues, but also a better understanding of one's native culture. The value of increasing students' awareness of their own culture as an element of foreign language teaching is also stressed by Tsvirko (2005), who believes that it ultimately results in the development of students' self-awareness and intellect at large. In addition, she deems teaching culture so vital that she equates the status of language teaching and culture teaching, similarly to Crozet and Liddicoat (1997).

2.3 The changing status of the native speaker in language education

In 1985 Kachru graphically demonstrated that the international community of the users of English fall into three circles: (a) the inner circle, (b) the outer circle and (c) the expanding circle. The inner circle, also referred to as a norm-producing circle, amounted to roughly 380mln members and comprised speakers of English as a native tongue from countries such as UK, USA or Australia. The outer circle, labelled a norm-developing circle, with a membership of an estimated 300mln people, consisted of speakers of English as a second language, i.e. those who acquire the language in an indigenously different language and cultural context, e.g. in Singapore or India. The expanding circle, and the largest of the three, with a 1000mln-strong representation, included speakers of English as a foreign language, e.g. those who learn the language in non-

English speaking countries such as Spain, France, Poland, Russia or China. Kachru posited that while members of the inner circle provide language norms, those from the outer circle develop them, and EFL speakers only abide by the norms established externally (Kachru 1985; Kachru & Smith 2008).

However, the ever-increasing spread of English worldwide has been increasingly rendering Kachru's original model invalid. It is particularly observable in countries, such as Holland or Finland in Europe, where language learners develop their skills in English in circumstances which resemble a second language context, and where the level of linguistic attainment is very high. Moreover, increasing globalisation and permanent migration, be it for professional, business, political, military, touristic or study purposes, have strongly undermined the very concept of a native-speaker, as has been indicated by a number of researchers.

Kramsch (1998a) emphasises the fact that the status of native speakers has been overestimated and – at least in part – glorified. Despite prior claims by Krashen (1982) and Paikeday (1985) that native speakers have a feel for their native tongue, she remarks that it does not necessarily translate into linguistic accuracy.

Besides, as she demonstrates, it may be difficult to ascertain whether or not a person qualifies as a native. The native speaker status depends on the following three criteria: (i) birth(place); (ii) education; and (iii) social recognition, but each of them may be questioned on certain grounds. For instance, those who owe their native speaker status to birth may not actually fully qualify as natives, e.g. if they move out of their own country and lose touch with its reality – a very common situation in today's world (Kramsch 1998a).

As regards education, although McDavid in an interview by Paikeday (1985) stated that a person can become a native exclusively through language acquisition, Davies (1991) maintains that one might educate oneself to the point at which one could pass off as a native speaker. Kramsch (1998a) questions Davies' stance, given what such an education would entail, and prefers to call a well educated speaker simply a proficient language user.

With reference to social recognition, Davies (1991) himself refers to the concept of a native speaker as a myth only, as he observes that the native speaker status is determined in half by a person's knowledge, and in half by their identity, as it is perceived by a given social community. In other words, he admits that a person becomes a native speaker if others see them as one. Yet, Kramsch (1989) again voices reservations here, as she asks whether it is at all possible to become a native speaker if the status depends on the social conventions of language use.

Medgyes (1992; 2001) questions the feasibility of attempting to qualify people as native/non-native speakers, as the dichotomy seems to escape definition on both linguistic and sociolinguistic grounds. He observes that from the linguistic perspective, speakers of English in e.g. India qualify as neither native speakers nor non-natives, while bilingual children may have either more than one native language or no clearly definable native language at all. Sociolinguistically, it appears impossible – or very difficult – to establish what the native speaker status involves, as "Efforts to define native competence or native-like proficiency have yielded inconclusive results at best" (Medgyes 1992: 341).

In recognition of arguments such as the afore-mentioned as well as changing reality, Kachru has verified his original view of the circles by admitting that speakers of English ought to be perceived from the perspective of the level of target language proficiency that they represent rather than birthplace or residence. As Kachru (2004) observes – in a manner reminiscent of Medgyes' (1992) reasoning – in many places, e.g. in Singapore, the border between native and non-native users of English has been blurred so much that the old classification scheme does not apply to the current situation. Consequently, the inner circle "(…) is now better conceived of as the group of highly proficient users of English" (Graddol 2006: 110), irrespective of how they have developed their knowledge of the language or in what circumstances they use it. All in all, it seems much more useful to tell apart proficient users of the language, i.e. *functional natives*, from those with a low level of proficiency (Kachru 2004).

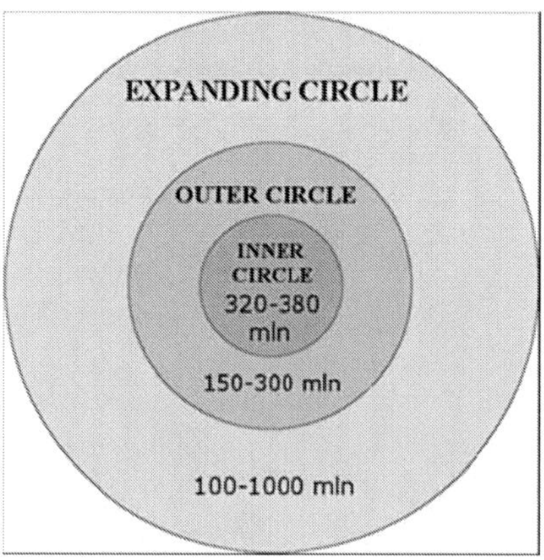

Fig. 1-2

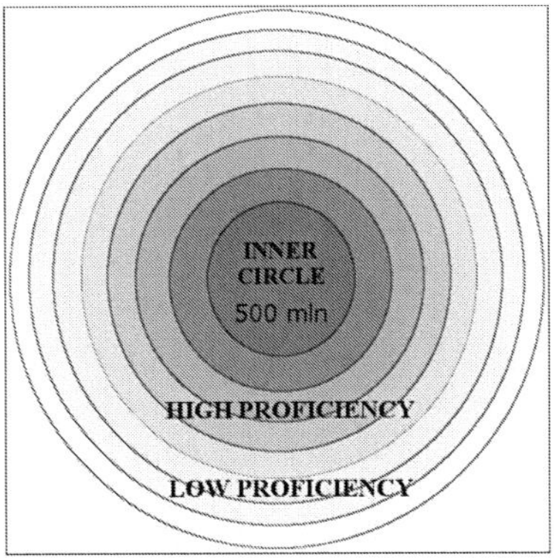

Fig. 1-3

Yet another significant implication of Kachru's model is that non-native speakers of English by far outnumber the native speakers themselves. If that is the case, nowadays English functions mostly as a lingua franca, i.e. a tool for international communication, which does not necessarily involve native speakers (Komorowska 2006c). English in the modern-day world is the leading language of science and technology, internet communication, book publishing, banking and economy (Komorowska 2006c). At the same time, English is also the dominant foreign language taught within European schooling systems, with a systematic increase in the percentage of all primary and secondary school learners of it. According to the *Key Data on Teaching Languages in Europe. 2008 Edition* (Eurydice 2008), over 50% of all primary school children in Europe learn English, and "in the great majority of countries, at least 90% of pupils learn English in general lower or upper secondary education (...), or both" (Eurydice 2008: 69). Thus, English has indeed become the dominant language of international communication.

Consequently, if "the way English is taught and assessed should reflect the needs and aspirations of the ever-growing number of non-native speakers who use English to communicate with other non-natives" (Graddol 2006: 87), EFL instruction is supposed to convert into education in English as an International Language (EIL) (Gozdawa-Gołębiowski 2006), or English as a Lingua Franca (ELF) (Graddol 2006), also occasionally referred to as ELF-ish (Sobkowiak 2008).

Research into the nature of language use in lingua franca contexts has already yielded certain implications for the ELF classroom. As Grosjean (1982) reports, people who constantly enter multiple cultures and experience socio-cultural heterogeneity in the course of their lives are very unlikely to happily mimic in the foreign language classroom the sociopragmatic competence of a native speaker, including the values of the target language culture; a very similar opinion has also been recently expressed by Paradowski (2008). Moreover, Paikeday (1985) rejects the idea of one speaker, one language and one culture throughout an individual's life as a fallacy which is at odds with reality. Therefore, Kramsch (1998a) proposes that speakers of English need to develop a form of adaptability which would enable them to select correct language forms and follow appropriate socio-cultural rules in intercultural, *lingua franca* contexts. That is relevant even for situations in which a non-native speaker of English comes into contact with a native-speaker outside the target language country. As Gnutzmann (2000) argues, in such situations conversation need not be modelled after a native speaker either, as in this case interaction takes place in an improvised, temporary social and cultural context where rules are mutually negotiated by both interlocutors.

Paradoxically, most teachers of English in the English teaching classrooms across the world who have been attempting to teach a native-norm-based English to their learners are non-native speakers themselves (Danova 1998). What is more, their language learners might never come into contact with native speakers in the foreseeable future, even when they complete school education. Therefore, as Poelzl (2003) suggests, in lingua franca contexts, where the model of language use is that of a non-native bilingual speaker, or a user of English, native-like accuracy ought to be replaced with intelligibility, including pronunciation standards. Most importantly, however, the goal of ELF is not to turn learners into imitations of native speakers, who would denounce their national identity, but successful intercultural communicators, who would be able to mediate between different cultures (Graddol 2006; Paradowski 2008; 2010).

As Ronowicz and Yallop (2007) warn, if in intercultural settings learners follow a native speaker model of English sociopragmatic competence and despite the limitations of their knowledge attempt to imitate target language behaviour, they will not be able to count on the usual sympathy that they could otherwise experience from natives in case of sociopragmatic failure.

Consequently, language communication in lingua franca situations on the one hand calls for a non-native language model, while on the other hand it brings forward (inter)cultural awareness as a vital language skill (Gajek 2002a). Teachers are no longer expected to instruct about the target language culture, but rather ensure that their students will successfully handle intercultural communicative situations through the medium of

English (Byram 2003); and perform in English as world citizens (Paradowski 2010).

In the light of the above, the native speaker in the language classroom has lost the privilege of the target language model, while a non-native speaker model appears to be more relevant to students' needs (Kramsch 1993; 1998a; Morgan 1998; Graddol 2006; Paradowski 2008; 2010).

At the same time, through globalisation/internalisation cultures mingle/clash to such a degree nowadays that cultural hybridity is beginning to become accepted as a natural component of the modern day world (Cooper 1998). Graddol (2006) illustrates this by his discussion of the emergence of people's multicultural, hyphenated identities, e.g. Polish-English or Pakistani-English, produced by social mobility and intermarriage. By and large, cultural diversity has been brought to the fore so much now that culture in the foreign language classroom must be more clearly than ever recognised as heterogeneous, and much less associated with the national than before (Byram 2008).

To sum up, although research findings reveal that certain native speaker teachers may be unable to handle intercultural mediation (Graddol 2006), it should be stressed that with a dose of intercultural training, which their non-native counterparts would also need to undergo, they could make very efficient intercultural language teachers – a point of view expressed e.g. by Bandura (2007). It needs reiterating at this point that within ELF teaching, it is not the native speaker who is denounced, but rather a native speaker model of language and language use, as less relevant to lingua franca communicative contexts. Medgyes (1992; 2001) explicitly states that both native English speaker teachers (NESTs) and non-native English speaker teachers (non-NESTs) can be equally successful, provided that they are adequately prepared. He suggests that NESTs be familiar with their learners' native tongue, whereas non-NESTs increase their target language proficiency. Paradowski (2010) reaffirms that stance while also adding the teacher's familiarity with the target language and learners' cultural systems as a prerequisite of successful language teaching.

2.4 Summary

This chapter has demonstrated that culture constitutes a complex entity which escapes definition in simple terms. The fact that over 200 different definitions of it exist (Sztompka 2002) illustrates that due to its complexity, culture has to be viewed from a number of perspectives.

Gozdawa-Gołębiowski's (2006) claim that offering a universal, interdisciplinary definition of the concept is unattainable implies that educators seeking to incorporate cultural education/training into their practice must tackle its diverse forms, e.g. the fine arts, classical and national heritage, individual and group identities, human behaviour, or etiquette. They must also be cognisant of which aspects and representations of culture best address their teaching objectives as well as learners' needs. Most importantly, they must not fall prey to the impression that culture can be comprehensively explored, as it is dynamic, negotiable, and is being constructed/reconstructed in real time (Geertz 1973; Suchodolski 1987; Fenner 2000).

What also stems from the present chapter is the fact that culture is undeniably at the core of language education, as whether the bond between language and culture is perceived from the Whorfian perspective (Whorf 1956) or the reverse (Wardhaugh 1976), language and culture are in constant interaction, and in language lessons this interaction must not be overlooked.

However, as language education embraces the teaching of communication, educators must be aware that communication reaches beyond language per se, and includes non-verbal components, e.g. the use of gestures, facial expressions, touch, object language, clothes, realia, as well as space (Hall 1959). Thus, it must be born in mind that effective communication involves an awareness of its non-verbal forms on the part of participants. Otherwise, it will be ridden with socio-cultural errors, or gaffes. The close link between culture and communication is particularly tangible in intercultural contexts, both in and outside the foreign language classroom, in which it must be taken into account.

Despite the intensity of studies devoted to the nature and roles of culture in the lives of individuals and societies, the findings have only minimally been percolating into the field of foreign language education throughout history, as a result of which, the cultural component of language courses has been either extremely limited, e.g. as in the Grammar-Translation Method or the Direct Method, or completely absent, e.g. as in the Audio-lingual Method or the Silent Way, from the tenets of teaching methods (Richards & Rogers 1986; Komorowska 2006b).

Only the turn of 1970s/1980s saw increased interest of language educators in teaching culture – inspired by Hymes (1972) – which translated into the teaching of socio-linguistic rules within the Communicative Approach. Yet, even then, the culture taught was limited in scope and application, as it related exclusively to the target language community, viewed as a cultural monolith.

The situation changed with the increased human mobility and globalisation processes of the end of the twentieth century, whereby the need to equip language learners with intercultural knowledge and skills was realised (Komorowska 2006b). That has had a profound impact on the perception of the native-speaker vs. non-native speaker dichotomy, as well as the native speaker's role in the language classroom while also inciting a debate on the justifiability of the presence of a cultural component in *English as a foreign language* vis-à-vis *English as a lingua franca* contexts. The arguments cited in the course of the debate indicate that both native and non-native speaker teachers as well as their learners require adequate intercultural training, be it in EFL and ELF classrooms (Byram 1997; Byram 2008; Gozdawa-Gołębiowski 2006; Aleksandrowicz-Pędich 2006).

As an aside, if non-native speakers genuinely claim possession of the English language, which Kachru (1985;2004) has argued, Canagarajah (1999) and Graddol (2006) predict that they are very likely to also dominate English language teaching methodology and materials and have them tailored to their needs – if only through the market force of demand.

Given Paradowski's (2010) view of the potential of non-NESTs for intercultural teaching, new materials created by them are likely to fulfil the following aims: develop learners as members of their own culture while fostering their interest in and respect for otherness; better correspond to learners' cross-cultural learning experience; assist students in contrasting and comparing cultures; as well as incorporate translation as a potential awareness-raising tool.

CHAPTER TWO

THE RATIONALE OF INTERCULTURAL TEACHING

1. Intercultural teaching as part of educational policy

1.1 The need to develop intercultural competence

Due to globalisation and increased human mobility, the contemporary world is saturated with multicultural communities where different cultures interact on a systematic basis. The phenomenon has become so common now that multiculturalism is no longer a feature of countries conventionally perceived as multi-ethnic, such as the United States of America or Australia. It has also become a permanent characteristic of countries such as Poland, i.e. those which have been traditionally viewed as relatively monocultural and monolingual. As Aleksandrowicz-Pędich (2005) claims, in Poland alone there are currently about twenty different ethnic groups. She also states that in the European Union, which is multicultural per se, the member states have culturally diversified to such a degree that they are collectively inhabited by representatives of roughly three hundred minorities. In addition, sociology has provided scientific evidence which demonstrates that each social group itself is a hub of sub-cultures which can be delineated along the lines of gender, age, generation, profession or interest. This presents a picture of a world where "Globalization, modernization, and the new technologies of communication have combined to produce many situations where the rules for identifying members and Strangers have become blurred. Urbanization and immigration in particular have produced societies where members are strangers to one another" (Riley 2007: 172-173). It is a world where effective communication is possible only if people can negotiate all the socio-cultural differences that they are bound to come in contact with on a daily basis, even if they do not travel. In other words, the international/intercultural nature of communication today requires intercultural (communicative) competence, as advocated by e.g. Lázár (2007) or Byram (1997; 2008).

Therefore, there is a need for intercultural education which would help people function in this culturally complex world and avoid communication breakdowns (Shandar 2005). Aleksandrowicz-Pędich (2005) also sees the purpose of such intercultural training as creating opportunities to sensitise people towards otherness, develop empathy as well as teach them how to objectively explore and value other cultures.

On the one hand she perceives intercultural language teaching as the realisation of the most basic goals of education at large, i.e. tolerance and openness. On the other hand she draws attention to the fact that language teaching must follow the intercultural approach, otherwise, through cultural oversimplifications and overgeneralisations, it will lead to the development of stereotyped views of other cultures or xenophobia in the learners.

Aleksandrowicz-Pędich additionally cites other possible consequences of the lack of intercultural training in modern education. They are: "intercultural misunderstandings"; "depression caused by dissatisfaction with contacts with foreigners in one's own country"; "persistent shock, which may interfere with effective learning or work"; "apathy"; "excessive aggression"; "the feeling of isolation or rejection; self-depreciation"; "job loss"; and the resultant: "financial difficulties", "addictions" and "health problems" (2005: 33, My translation). As it is evident from the above, intercultural understanding seems to condition success not only in people's private lives, but also business activity (Hampden-Turner & Trompenaars 2000; Aleksandrowicz-Pędich 2006). Hence, the suggestion that intercultural training be part of courses in ESP courses, including business English (Aleksandrowicz-Pędich 2006).

Another benefit one gains from intercultural training is a better understanding of self (Byram 2000a; Jandt 2001; Parmenter 2003; Aleksandrowicz-Pędich 2005; 2006) and one's own identity, which might be treated as an *added educational value* of the approach.

Language educators also believe that in the European context, intercultural teaching might help increase integration within the European Union (Aleksandrowicz-Pędich et al. 2003), as well as prepare learners for the role of European citizens – or "'better' member[s] of society" (Parmenter 2003: 121).

In the United States of America, which an indigenously multicultural, one might take intercultural education as redundant. However, as Malysheva (2005) explicates, despite the multi-dimensional heterogeneity of American society, its peoples tend to remain isolated, especially through the years of early school education, which frequently results in mutual prejudice, inter-racial and inter-ethnic tensions and conflicts. Thus, she suggests that it is essential even for American citizens to learn to shift perspectives and notice the viewpoints of others. She also gives one more vital reason for which the USA needs intercultural education. It relates to the role of the United States as a country involved internationally on economic, political as well as military levels. Its people need to develop an understanding of international/intercultural communities if this involvement is to be effective.

On a global scale, teachers believe that learning about other cultures would also contribute to the promotion of world peace. As intercultural teaching promotes democracy (Byram 2003; 2008), it is possible to view it as a way in which to counteract ethnic genocide or other forms of extremism, as Coste (Byram & Tost Planet 2000) remarks. "Acceptance of other people in their otherness and international solidarity are, therefore, the objective of the process of education in foreign languages" (Byram 2003: 58). Risager goes further and expresses the belief that in the long run intercultural teaching will help the international community establish transnational organisations and institutions that will better recognise and resolve global problems – a perspective she reiterates in one of her most recent publications *Language and Culture Pedagogy*, according to which, intercultural teaching is potentially conducive to the transformation of language learners into world citizens (Risager 2007).

Intercultural language teaching also encourages learners to assume responsibility for their own learning in that it teaches them to take independent decisions, draw conclusions, and reflect on experience. It engages learners more into the process of learning through the autonomy that fosters, e.g. with regard to topic choice, as well as the stress that it places on performance rather than declarative knowledge, exclusively (Bandura 2000).

Byram and Tost Planet (2000) indicate that intercultural teaching enables teachers to combine the traditional humanistic goals of foreign language education, i.e. acquainting learners with other people's lifestyles and cultural heritage, such as literature or art, with the more pragmatic goal of teaching students how to communicate. They claim that it is possible because communication within intercultural teaching is perceived as a complex network of interactions between people's perspectives, beliefs, values, and practices, not mere information exchange.

1.2 Intercultural teaching in international educational documents

European context. The need to develop students' intercultural competence is prescribed today by the official documents which shape national educational policies in Europe, North America or Asia. Notably, depending on a given country's geopolitical and cultural context, the problem of intercultural teaching is approached differently, however, the very notion of intercultural training has been universally recognised.

In *Recommendation No R (84) 18 on the training of teachers in education for intercultural understanding*, the Committee of Ministers of the Council of Europe recognised the multicultural character of European countries and their societies, increased migration, and the ensuing need for "a fuller understanding of the cultures and ways of life of other peoples" (Council of Europe, Rec. R(84): 1), and stressed the essential role of teachers in promoting mutual understanding across Europe. They also highlighted the need to prepare foreign language teachers to use an intercultural approach in order to increase "intercultural understanding and of the value and originality of each culture" (Council of Europe, Rec. R(84): 2).

Therefore, the ministers recommended that the governments of the member states include intercultural issues and the problem of understanding between different communities in both pre- and in-service teacher training schemes. The goals of the recommendations embraced: increasing teachers' awareness of various forms of cultural expression; persuading them to override ethnocentrism and stereotypes as potentially damaging to intercultural relations, and preparing them for increasing their learners' consideration of other cultures. The document also aimed at inciting 'the development and use of appropriate materials to support the intercultural approach in the training of teachers and in school in order to give a "truer" image of the different cultures of their pupils' (Council of Europe, Rec. No. R(84): 2). Finally, it called for the organisation of "national and international seminars and courses on the intercultural approach to education for teachers, teacher trainers, administrators and other persons involved in teacher-training" (Council of Europe, Rec. No. R(84): 2).

Recommendation No. R (98) 6 concerning Modern Languages of the Committee of Ministers of the Council of Europe aimed to promote education which would: teach learners respect for other ways of life; prepare them for functioning in an intercultural world; further bilingual and multilingual education; pay particular attention to redressing the balance between the languages and cultures taught; as well as offer children within the national school systems not only a chance to learn and appreciate the languages of others, but also their cultures.

The recommendation recognised the need to: offer learners preparation for international mobility, promote intercultural understanding and tolerance, teach students respect for other identities, and increase the effectiveness of international communication.

The specific measures recommended by the Ministers of the Council of Europe for incorporation into European education entailed: the general measures and principles of open-mindedness, respect for otherness, plurilingualism, and lifelong language learning, which implicitly relates to intercultural learning, given the indefinite nature of the latter process.

For early language education the document recommended the development of children's awareness of diversity in Europe. At secondary level, it postulated that learners' intercultural understanding be enriched and their changing cultural needs be met. For adult education, it set the task of facilitating intercultural understanding, and preparing learners for international cooperation. Finally, it called on teacher training to develop clearly set out competences, which, amongst others, were to include an intercultural skills.

Recommendation 1383 (1998) on Linguistic diversification, issued by the Parliamentary Assembly of the Council of Europe, saw language learning as instrumental in establishing international/intercultural understanding and tolerance as well as peace. It urged the Committee of Ministers to accelerate work on the introduction of the then-being-prepared *Common European Framework of Reference* and *the European Language Portfolio* (Council of Europe 2001). Finally, it encouraged the member states to increase emphasis on culture and society within their educational systems.

Recommendation 1539 (2001) on the European Year of Languages of the Parliamentary Assembly of the Council of Europe, emphasised the importance of linguistic and cultural diversity in Europe and by establishing the year 2001 as the European Year of Languages, intended to foster "the development of language policies encouraging, above all, cultural and linguistic diversity and promoting the integration of minorities and immigrants, social cohesion in general and human rights" (Council of Europe, Rec. 1539).

It emphasised that despite what its name might suggest, the European Year of Languages was intended to ameliorate linguistic and cultural openness to Europe and the world. It also saw language learning as a vehicle for intercultural and international dialogue, tolerance, and understanding to the advantage of the parties involved.

It called on the Committee of Ministers to introduce language policies which would promote not only linguistic but also cultural diversity social/ethnic integration, and recommended that the Ministers ought to persuade the Joint Council, the Advisory Council, the European Steering Committee for Youth and the Programming Committee of the Directorate of Youth and Sport to reintroduce courses in languages and intercultural learning for youth leaders.

The most important document in which the intercultural awareness of European citizens has been emphasised is the *Common European Framework of Reference for Languages: learning, teaching, assessment* (Council of Europe 2001), compiled by the Council of Europe. This seminal European educational document constitutes a blueprint of educational guidelines which are supposed to inform syllabus and curriculum design, examination setting and materials preparation across Europe. By laying out the basis of uniform objectives, content, methods of language/culture education as well as assessment criteria, it is also intended to permit transferability of language qualifications in Europe, and facilitate international cooperation of professionals involved in modern language teaching e.g. course designers, teacher trainers or teachers themselves.

The document is founded on the three central goals of the Council of Europe's policy on modern language teaching, originally presented in *Recommendation R (82) 18* of the Committee of Ministers of the Council of Europe: (i) European linguistic and cultural diversity is to be preserved and used as a ground for greater understanding; (ii) modern European language learning is to ensure pan-European communication, increase people's mobility and counteract prejudice and discrimination; and (iii) coordination of modern language teaching policies amongst individual European countries is supposed to increase the level of pan-European convergence.

Cognisant of the afore-mentioned language teaching prerogatives, the authors of the *Common European Framework* (Council of Europe 2001) highlight the co-existence of multiple cultures on the continent on the one hand, and the need to explore the complex relations between particular cultures, on the other. As the document adopts an action-oriented approach to language education, it lists out the key competences that are supposed to be developed in language learners. These fall into two categories: *general competences*, which comprise: knowledge, skills, existential competence, ability to learn; and *communicative language competence*, including linguistic, sociolinguistic and pragmatic competences. The elements of communicative language competence can be viewed as the essence of foreign language teaching. However, the addition of the so-called general competences unravels an intercultural bias in European language teaching policies; the more that the constituent elements of general competences are described with reference to Byram's (1997) model of intercultural communicative competence.

The *knowledge* component (*savoirs*) refers to declarative knowledge of language and culture, academic and empirical scientific or technical knowledge, which may be helpful in understanding foreign language texts. It also covers the knowledge of the socio-cultural realia which enhance functioning in a foreign language, and the knowledge of the value system of language communities.

The *skills and know-how* (*savoir-faire*) refers to procedural knowledge one needs in order to explore the target language and culture, as well as function successfully in the target language society. The CEFR (2001) exemplifies such skills as the ability to: use computer technology in language learning, use a dictionary or find one's way in a specific location.

Existential competence (*savoir-étre*) comprises a number of factors which influence success in language and culture learning, e.g. personality traits, attitudes towards others or willingness to interact. These are likely to evolve in the course of language learning, as they are subject to alteration in the light of experience. Such factors may determine e.g. the degree to which the learner is sensitive towards the possibility of intercultural misunderstanding.

Ability to learn (*savoir apprendre*) involves the procedures or learning strategies one utilises in order to explore linguistic and cultural knowledge. These are dependent on either the context in which the learner is supposed to learn or the learner's previous experience. If learners consciously reflect on their learning to date, they are likely to build a repertoire of their learning skills over time. As the CEFR (2001) suggests, the ability to learn is likely to relate to the above-mentioned competences.

A tool with which to develop learners' intercultural competence along the lines of the CEFR (2001) is t*he European Language Portfolio*, which was prepared and piloted by the Language Policy Division of the Council of Europe in the years 1998-2000, and published in 2001. Based on the educational guidelines of the CEFR (2001), it can be used in order to keep a record of one's language and intercultural experiences. It permits one to document their entire language and intercultural development throughout school education and afterwards, when one sets out to seek employment. Thus, it also embraces out-of-school experience. So far, 130 accredited versions of the Portfolio have been issued by both national governments as well as social and educational organisations, including the five Polish versions: for 3-6 year-olds, for 6-10 year olds, for 10-15-year-olds, for upper secondary and students, and for adults.

Since it aims at promoting plurilingualism and pluriculturalism in European education, its three parts are to foster intercultural language learning, as demonstrated in *European Language Portfolio. Principles and Guidelines* (Council of Europe 2004). Thus, the Language Passport enables one to keep a record of one's language proficiency and intercultural experiences; the Language Bibliography permits one to plan, reflect upon and assess one's learning; while the Dossier helps one document one's intercultural language learning attainments (Council of Europe 2004).

In 2008 the Council of Europe Ministers of Foreign Affairs launched the *White Paper on Intercultural Dialogue* (Council of Europe 2008), another document which has had an impact on the European educational policies. The document laid out a set of recommendations to the Council of Europe and its member states whose goal was to promote intercultural understanding, dialogue and respect. The publishing of the document coincided with the celebration of the *European Year of Intercultural Dialogue*, announced by the Council of Europe.

The paper underlined the role of intercultural dialogue in preventing animosities, and facilitating European development through the universal values of democracy, human rights and law-abidance. It also called for teaching intercultural competences, as well as creating opportunities for intercultural dialogue on international level. At the same time, it drew attention to the diversity of the world and intercultural understanding as a future necessity. It also expressed the intention of the Council of Europe to remain "(…) strongly committed to the transmission of intercultural competences through education" (Council of Europe 2008: 46).

The *White Paper on Intercultural Dialogue* spawned the creation and publication of *the Autobiography of Intercultural Encounters* (Council of Europe 2009), a document which in its character resembles the function of the European Language Portfolio. Its most important parts constitute: *the Autobiography of Intercultural Encounters* and *the Autobiography of Intercultural Encounters for Younger Learners*. As the title indicates, the autobiography serves as a tool for handling intercultural encounters, which it does by providing users with a series of questions that they are supposed to ask themselves in order to properly analyse an intercultural incident, reflect on it and learn, i.e. draw conclusions on action that might potentially be taken in the future. The autobiography incorporates the general competences recommended by the *Common European Framework of Reference*, as it parses intercultural encounters through questions that refer to: knowledge and skills, behaviour, attitudes and feelings, and action. The document can be used in different settings: individually, with the support of a facilitator or in a whole-class mode.

All in all, due to pivotal contribution of the Council of Europe, most European countries have incorporated socio-cultural and intercultural competence into their educational documents (Komorowska 2006a).

Intercultural teaching has also been endorsed by the European Centre for Modern Languages (ECML) in Graz. For example, in the years 2004-2007 the ECML released a multitude of publications on intercultural teaching, including classroom materials, within the research and development programme *Languages for social cohesion: Language education in a multilingual and multicultural Europe* (ECML 2004-2007). Two strands of the programme, *Coping with linguistic and social diversity – provisions, profiles, materials* and *Communication in a multicultural society: the development of intercultural communicative competence*, had a particular focus on multilingual and intercultural issues, e.g. linguistic diversity in Europe, intercultural exchanges, plurilingual and pluricultural awareness, intercultural communication in teacher training or language education. The ECML has also co-published *Teacher Training Modules* (Guenova et al. 2000), which is a collection of modules for intercultural teacher education.

Most recently, within the 2008-2011 programme, the ECML has financed research and materials production within three projects relating to intercultural language education: *CLIL-CD*, *ConBAT* and *FREPA/CARAP*.

The *CLIL-CD* (*Content and Language Integrated Learning – Curriculum Design*) project focused on the development of models of CLIL curricula to be used in teacher training as well as the foreign language classroom. It is worth observing that the *Professional Development Modules*, developed within the project, embraced *Interweaving psychological and pedagogical aspects in the CLIL classroom*, and tackled intercultural dynamics and multicultural and multilingual issues as well as affective factors and attitude awareness in CLIL education.

The *ConBAT* (*Content Based Teaching + Plurilingual/Cultural Awareness*) project incorporated intercultural training in the most explicit manner and targeted primary and secondary school teachers, teacher trainers, educational inspectors and decision-makers working in multi-linguistic and multi-cultural contexts. Its purpose was to assist educational institutions in accommodating learners from varied linguistic/cultural backgrounds in the classroom. The teacher training kit developed here was meant to support the management of diversity in the classroom through content-based and plurilingual activities relating to selected subjects across the curriculum.

Finally, the *FREPA/CARAP* (*A Framework of Reference for Pluralistic Approaches*) project aimed at promoting didactic approaches which involve the implementation of teaching/learning activities featuring more than one language and culture. The four pluralistic approaches promoted within the project included: (i) awakening to languages; (ii) intercomprehension of related languages; (iii) intercultural approach; and (iv) integrated didactic approach to different languages studied. The pluralistic approaches constitute a response to plurilingual and pluricultural/intercultural competences which are part of the *Common European Framework of Reference*.

It is worth noticing that in the light of the *FREPA/CARAP* project, the intercultural approach to language teaching has continued to establish itself as relevant to learners' needs and the goals of contemporary education, and it is now recognised as one of the four most essential teaching/learning approaches in modern-day Europe.

Moreover, the pluralistic approaches, promoted within the *FREPA/CARAP* project, target the three most essential elements of Byram's (1997) model of intercultural language education: knowledge (savoirs), skills (savoir-faire) and attitudes (savoir-être).

Polish context. In the Polish education system the document that informs curriculum design and materials writing for the purpose of teaching modern foreign languages at all levels of schooling is *Podstawa programowa wychowania przedszkolnego oraz kształcenia ogólnego w poszczególnych typach szkół*, which covers primary, lower, and upper secondary education. The latest version of the document introduced by the Polish Ministry of Education in 2009 (Rozporządzenie MEN z dnia 23 grudnia 2008 r.) emphasises the importance of the role of foreign language education in: fostering social growth by increasing learners' respect for own traditions and culture as well as those of others; preventing discrimination; and developing an attitude of curiosity, tolerance and openness towards other cultures.

At lower secondary level, the document suggests that knowledge of the target culture and one's own, including intercultural contexts, ought to be developed. It also stipulates that learners are supposed to be capable of self-assessing their own learning, e.g. with the use of the *European Language Portfolio*, which – inter alia – helps learners reflect on how they can use cultural texts.

At upper secondary level, *Podstawa programowa* expands language and cultural learning objectives through the inclusion of the problem of

European integration, and explicit attention to issues relating to intercultural encounters. For learners involved in bilingual education at secondary level, it sets the goal of becoming able to recognize civilisational and cultural context of language use as well as the significance of cultural symbols.

At the same time, it assigns to foreign language teachers the task of inciting learners' interest in cultural and civilisational heritage of the target language society in relation to their own national heritage; and fostering attitudes of curiosity and tolerance towards other cultures. In addition, it stresses the role of the teacher in organizing direct intercultural encounters for students through international exchange projects and collaboration programmes (Rozporządzenie MEN z dnia 23 grudnia 2008 r.).

Another crucial educational document that determines foreign language teaching in Poland is *Informator o egzaminie maturalnym od roku 2008. Język angielski* (CKE 2008), which is a detailed account of examination requirements and assessment criteria that are followed within the *Matura Exam* – an upper secondary school leaving examination. This examination is taken at two levels: basic and extended, which are differentiated in terms of both requirements and assessment, and is composed of two parts: written and oral. The written part is assessed externally by an independent examination board set up by the regional examination board (Okręgowa Komisja Egzaminacyjna), whereas the oral part is administered by the school examination board (Szkolna Komisja Egzaminacyjna). At the basic level, the written exam consists of three tasks: a listening task, a reading task and a written task, which involves writing a short piece, e.g. a note, postcard or invitation, and a longer one e.g. a formal/informal letter. At the extended level, the written exam comprises two parts: Part I, which contains a short lexical-grammatical test and an essay; and Part II, which takes the form of a listening comprehension task, a reading comprehension task, and a task which involves recognition of lexical and grammatical structures (CKE 2008).

As it has been demonstrated above, the written component of the *Matura Exam* at both levels focuses mostly on language skills, such as listening comprehension, reading comprehension and writing. In the writing tasks content, format, and language accuracy constitute the main assessment criteria. The only element of cultural knowledge which may be optionally assessed within the written task at the extended level – at the examiner's discretion – is the knowledge of the cultural realities of the target language country.

The oral exam at the basic level consists of two parts: (i) three guided talks, which involve obtaining/giving information, relating events, and negotiating; and (ii) a description of an image guided by two questions. At the extended level, the oral exam also has two parts: (i) a conversation prompted by a sheet of verbal and nonverbal cues, e.g. newspaper headlines or images; and a topic presentation, followed by discussion.

The assessment criteria for the oral exam at both levels include the knowledge of the socio-cultural realities of the target language area and Poland. They also make reference to issues of European integration and intercultural context. The extended level sets an additional criterion as the knowledge of socio-cultural norms which may facilitate one's functioning on the job market (CKE 2008).

Overall, it may be stated that although the *Matura Exam* tasks produce numerous opportunities for a display of the learner's intercultural competence and skills, no advantage is actually taken of that, and the intercultural component of language education is usually marginalized. It may well be that it is one of the most serious reasons for which few Polish teachers incorporate intercultural teaching into their classroom routine on a regular basis (Aleksandrowicz-Pędich 2005; Bandura 2007).

Simultaneously, it appears that the rationale for intercultural teaching has indeed reached Poland and received a degree of institutional recognition, which is reflected in the fact that the two documents which largely promote it in Europe, i.e. *the Common European Framework* and *the European Language Portfolio*, have been made available to the general public in Poland through their translated versions. *Europejski system opisu kształcenia językowego: uczenie się, nauczanie, ocenianie* (CODN 2004) was published in 2004. Additionally, five Polish versions of the *European Language Portfolio* have been produced for different age groups: *Europejskie Portfolio Językowe dla dorosłych* (CODN 2000); *Europejskie Portfolio Językowe dla uczniów od 10-15 lat* (CODN 2004); *Europejskie Portfolio Językowe dla uczniów od 6-10 lat* (CODN 2006); and *Europejskie Portfolio Językowe dla uczniów od 3-6 lat* (CODN 2007), complete with relevant companions, e.g. *Czego Janek się nauczy.... Przewodnik metodyczny dla nauczycieli do Europejskiego Portfolio Językowego dla uczniów od 10-15 lat* (Głowacka 2005). Therefore, all that needs to be done now is to ensure that the theory is instilled in teachers' minds and properly implemented.

Broader international context. In the United States of America, the US Department of Education and the National Endowment for the Humanities endorsed the preparation of a document which laid out a model of content- and skill-based standards in American foreign language education. The outcome of the cross-organisation project was a document published in 1996 under the title *Standards for Foreign Language*

Learning: Preparing for the 21st Century. Its three editions, published so far, define the role of foreign language education in American education and are meant to be used by teachers, administrators, and curriculum developers. In the course of the development of the programme – led by the American Council on the Teaching of Foreign Languages – the following statement of its underlying philosophy emerged:

> "Language and communication are at the heart of the human experience. The United States must educate students who are linguistically and culturally equipped to communicate successfully in a pluralistic American society and abroad. This imperative envisions a future in which ALL students will develop and maintain proficiency in English and at least one other language, modern or classical. Children who come to school from non-English backgrounds should also have opportunities to develop further proficiencies in their first language" (ACTFL 1999: 2).

As the philosophy statement indicates, cultural education is viewed here as a complement to language development which is necessary to enable people to reach proficiency in a foreign language. Attention to cultural teaching within the document becomes even more evident on closer inspection, as the text advocates learners' development within five areas, the so-called five C's.: (i) Communication, (ii) Cultures, (iii) Connections, (iv) Comparisons and (v) Communities.

(i) *Communication* is perceived within the standards as oral, writing, and literature-mediated. At the same time, it is stressed that language study furthers the acquisition of cultural knowledge and results in (ii) *cultural understanding*, which is a prerequisite of genuine mastery in a foreign language. In particular, the knowledge of socio-cultural contexts of communication is underlined. Language learning is also presented as an opportunity to broaden one's horizons through (iii) *connections* with other areas of knowledge which it may involve. (iv) *Comparisons and contrasts* described in the document are especially pertinent to the idea of intercultural education as they refer to insight into the nature of language and culture per se that foreign language learners gain, as well as the development of an intercultural perspective as a by-product of language learning. (v) *Communities* denote the environment in which foreign language learners are expected to be able to use the language(s) that they learn; this component calls for a recognition of what is culturally appropriate behaviour in multilingual and multicultural communities (ACTFL 1999).

In sum, the *Standards for Foreign Language Learning* verbalise the competences which ACTFL aims to develop as the ability to:

- "Communicate in Languages Other Than English" (*Communication*);
- "Gain Knowledge and Understanding of Other Cultures" (*Cultures*);
- "Connect with Other Disciplines and Foreign Acquire Information" (*Connections*);
- "Develop Insight into the Nature of Language and Culture" (*Comparisons*);
- and "Participate in Multilingual Communities at Home & Around the World (*Communities*)" (ACTFL 1999: 4).

In 2006 another vital educational document providing for intercultural education in the USA was released. *The National Security Language Initiative*, as the document was named, was designed by President Bush administration, and its main goal was to increase the learning and teaching of foreign languages strategically important to the USA in the light of the current political situation e.g. Chinese, Russian or Hindi. The document stipulates that foreign languages are an essential means with which to promote international/intercultural understanding and respect. The programme involves organisational and administrative measures to ensure continuity of foreign language education from kindergarten to tertiary level, including nationwide teacher training schemes, scholarship programmes, school partnerships, and youth exchanges. What is significant is that the programme does not only aim to increase the understanding of other cultures, but also familiarise strangers with America and its people (NSLI 2006).

International organisations which have incorporated intercultural education into their documents include the United Nations and UNESCO (Bandura 2007). For instance, in 2001 the United Nations General Assembly announced *the Global Agenda for Dialogue among Civilizations* (United Nations 2001), whose goal was to incite "Dialogue among civilizations (...) [as] a process between and within civilizations, founded on inclusion, and a collective desire to learn, uncover and examine assumptions, unfold shared meaning and core values and integrate multiple perspectives through dialogue" (United Nations 2001: 3).

The objectives of the agenda were to be realised by state governments, the United Nations, independent organisations and members of society through the following course of action: encouraging interaction and exchange among all individuals, creating opportunities for discovering commonalities among various civilizations and cultures; increasing acquaintance with other cultures; enhancing intercultural understanding, tolerance and dialogue; and promoting rejection of intolerance, violence and racism, especially among young people.

Asian countries have also responded to globalisation by internationalising their curricula, as is the case in Japan (Parmenter 2003). However, a distinct difference in their approach to the role of intercultural education can be discerned in that e.g. the Japanese internationalised curriculum is intended to highlight the cultural diversity of the world to the country's learners only in order to enhance the learners' representation of their own national culture (Parmenter 2003). It might thus be posited that the international lens through which Japanese learners acquaint themselves with other cultures is to sharpen their perceptions of the national.

A similar agenda has been set in the Near Eastern countries, e.g. Turkey, where elements of intercultural education are to help modernise Turkish society and develop a new national culture modelled after foreign examples. One of the linguistic and cultural changes promoted as part of the process is the introduction of the Latin alphabet in order to replace the old Arabic script (Raw 1998). The Japanese and Asian examples illustrate clearly that the ideology behind intercultural teaching is not universal and it does not have the same international appeal; it per se constitutes an intercultural issue, as it may be perceived in culture-bound ways across the world. As Parmenter (2003) explicates, Asia is undeniably a region of social, economic, political and cultural contrasts, which renders the idea of equality – promoted by the Euro-American vision of intercultural communicative competence – irrelevant to the local context. Hence, the difference in its interpretation and application.

2. Major assumptions beyond intercultural teaching

2.1 Intercultural teaching vs. British Studies

In Aleksandrowicz-Pędich's (2007) view, intercultural language teaching is supposed to serve the following purposes: to prepare learners for intercultural contacts in at school, at work and on a tourist visit; to enable learners to function within international societies which experience change due to migration; to empower learners to negotiate social interactions in the target language without experiencing discomfort; and to increase learners' awareness of their identity and native culture.

From the pedagogical perspective, the realisation of these goals requires that intercultural teaching be postmodernist in nature, which means that it elevates the position of the learning process, and not so much the very demonstrable outcomes that it may produce. In effect, learners' strategies, skills as well as meta-cultural awareness become more important than declarative knowledge, which had been emphasised within educational modernism, up to the 1980s. At the same time, in intercultural teaching the knowledge component must not be neglected (Risager 2007). As Byram (1997; 2008) postulated, knowledge is one of the essential components of intercultural competence, and it is supposed to be developed alongside attitudes and skills. It is neither an addition nor an inferior companion of the other intercultural competences. Similarly, Risager sees intercultural teaching not as a rejection of modernist educational tradition but rather "revitalisation of modernism within postmodernism" (Risager 2007: 164).

The differences between the modernist and postmodernist schools of thought are brought to the fore when one compares the qualities of the British Studies Approach, which was focused on content, with the Intercultural Approach, which primarily promotes the development of awareness and skills. Both approaches were compared by Bolt (2001: 101), as summarised below:

British Studies	Intercultural Teaching
Knowledge-based	Experiential (awareness and skills)
Focus: Target culture	Focus: Target and learner's native culture
Outcome: target culture, and native speaker	Outcome: variety of cultural outcomes
Teacher-centred	Learner-centred (autonomy)
Culture-dependent (target culture focus)	Generic (transferable)
Monolithic, national picture of culture	Heterogeneous picture of culture
Textbook-based	Centred on original resources
Goal: knowledge	Goal: skills, attitudes, knowledge

Table 2-1

In brief, Bolt (2001) depicts that in the modernist British Studies Approach declarative knowledge is the major concern of the teacher. Therefore, teaching mostly involves transmitting a pre-defined image of the target language culture to learners, who are only supposed to internalise it and retain for later recall. At the same time, only the target culture is taught, without any reference to learners' native culture and society.

Consequently, the end product of teaching is a model of the target culture and the native speaker which is imposed on the students by the materials used, and the teacher, who authoritatively controls the students' work and its effects, thus leaving no room for the development of learner autonomy.

Another characteristic aspect of the British Studies Approach is the nature of the cultural knowledge and information that it conveys, which has serious limitations in a two-fold manner. On the one hand the target culture is stencilled and passed on to students as a one-dimensional entity, perceived from a national perspective and without any allowance for sub-national diversity and individual difference. On the other hand, because of the monocultural approach, the knowledge is limited in application, as it covers a specific culture and its society – both seen as monolithic. Symbolic of those limitations is the fact that teaching is based mostly on textbooks, with little use of supplementary materials, such as realia (Bolt 2001).

The Intercultural Approach is illustrative of a shift in the teaching of culture towards (inter)cultural experience. The learners here do not passively receive knowledge, but immerse into the target culture and interpret it for themselves – thus learning becomes experiential, which leads to the development of cultural skills and an increase in cultural awareness. The knowledge that each learner arrives at is individual, and perceptions are not imposed. Simultaneously, both cultures are dealt with: the target culture and the learners' native culture, which makes learning relational as it involves comparison as well as reflection. As a result, learning outcomes are numerous: cognitive (knowledge), attitudinal (perspectives, emotions) and pragmatic (e.g. skills of comparison and relation).

Another benefit for learners is the development of autonomy in learning, which is necessary for intercultural exploration and interpretation. The resultant image of culture drawn in students' minds is thus much more diverse; it includes cultural sub-groups, and variation among individuals, which is facilitated by the use of original teaching/learning resources, such as real objects, commercials, official documents, tourist brochures, records of private conversations, notes, radio phone-ins, web forums, private video footage, clips featuring nonverbal communication. Due to the diversification of resources and techniques, but also thanks to the multi-dimensional character of the activities involved, the Intercultural Approach leads to the development of generic, transferable skills, which may be applied to the discovery, exploration, and interpretation of other cultures in contexts for which learners are not directly prepared (Bolt 2001).

Another person who adds to the discussion of differences between the two approaches mentioned above is Delanoy (1995), who succinctly demonstrates the dissimilarity between the British Studies/*Landeskunde* Approach of the modernist era and the Intercultural Studies, which he refers to as *New Cultural Studies*. A summary of his comparison is presented in a tabular form below:

Landeskunde	**New Cultural Studies**
Transmission of fact-based knowledge	Experiential (awareness and skills)
Static view of culture	Culture as dynamic; formation of culture
Objective image of culture	Subjective image of culture
Separable from language teaching	Language-in-culture
Culture in essence	Culture as signifying practice
Target outcome: native speaker	Learner outcome: intercultural mediator

Table 2-2

Delanoy (1995) sees *Landeskunde* – a name that derives from the German tradition of culture teaching pedagogy (Montgomery 1995; Risager 2007) – as monotonous and fact-based, but also mostly tied to class work. By contrast, he emphasises that in the *New Cultural Studies* – inspired by methods of anthropology and culture analysis (Montgomery 1995) – work modes may additionally involve school trips, role-plays and project assignments.

Another vital observation which Delanoy makes relates to the view of culture as dynamic, which is absent from Bolt's (2001) model. The novelty of intercultural teaching consists in the exploration – not presentation – of the dynamic intercultural relations between the varied sub-cultures within a given national society. Delanoy (ibid.) illustrates that by referring to the United States of America, where diverse cultures constantly interact while attempting to negotiate their position within the mainstream culture. Delanoy claims that such phenomena are observable to learners only in intercultural teaching, whereas the *Landeskunde* Approach blurs, the image of the target culture that it conveys.

Delanoy (ibid.) also underlines that intercultural teaching involves the learners' minds in that it does not only concentrate on inter- or intra-cultural differences, but helps learners realise that such differences clash within themselves. What this results in is the realisation on the part of the learners that their perceptions of culture are not objective, and they should be subject to scrutiny if cultures are to be genuinely discovered. Such a view of cultural development makes intercultural learning interpersonal at the same time.

Delanoy (ibid.) notices that intercultural teaching instigates the practical study of the close bond between language and culture in the foreign language classroom. That translates into students learning how to explore cultures with the use of the limited linguistic resources that they have at their disposal. In effect, learners develop an awareness of possible communication breakdowns which may be caused by their linguistic shortcomings, and also learn how to counteract the danger. In this respect, language study becomes inseparable from culture learning, while in *Landeskunde* the culture component was viewed as an addition to learners' linguistic development (Delanoy 1995).

Within intercultural teaching language and culture are also related to each other in yet another sense. Through the realisation that culture is not a *baggage* that is passed on from one generation to another but it is rather "(...) created, maintained and modified (...) through communication" (Bernaus et al. 2007: 46), learners find out that language is a means of cultural creation, expression, mediation and exploration.

In Delanoy's (ibid.) view, intercultural teaching has one more characteristic advantage. In contrast to *Landeskunde*, it does not attempt to present to students an essentialist image of the target, or their own, culture. Therefore, it avoids the trap of stereotyping, including both autostereotypes and heterostereotypes. In addition, *New Cultural Studies* help learners notice that the actions of individual representatives of a culture, including communication practices, are significant, as they are explicit manifestations of otherwise implicit cultural meanings. Culture is, therefore, "a signifying practice" (Delanoy 1995: 40).

Last but not least, intercultural teaching differs from traditional *Landeskunde* in that it ultimately aims to develop a different kind of language user. In modernist tradition learners were taught the target language in order to follow what could be collectively labelled as the native speaker's ways, both linguistically and culturally. In other words, the teacher had an ambition to turn their learners into imitations of native speakers. Unrealistic as the effort was, it yielded very little effect, given the circumstances (cf. section 2, Chapter One) and the techniques applied. Delanoy (1995) demonstrates that in *New Cultural Studies* the model of a native speaker is cast aside as irrelevant to the needs of an intercultural language speaker and replaced with that of an intercultural mediator, i.e. a person who is able to successfully engage in intercultural dialogue.

According to Delanoy, an intercultural speaker does not need to follow the example of a native speaker, who "can be ethnocentric, and (...) may lack those language skills in their own language which can facilitate communication with overseas people" (Delanoy 1995: 41). This reflects the language-in-culture perspective that intercultural teaching takes on in the foreign language classroom, as a result of which, culture cannot be taught is separation from language. Instead, it must be taught along with language if an intercultural mediator is expected to be able to explore other cultures and negotiate intercultural understanding.

2.2 Intercultural encounters

Foreign language and culture teaching as well as communication in the target language inevitably involve coping with intercultural encounters, i.e. situations in which one comes into contact with otherness. Such encounters with difference may either be direct, when one interacts with a native speaker in person, or in indirect, when otherness is experienced through text or video footage (Morgan 1998). In situations where speakers do not share a common first language, they utilize different nonverbal codes of communication, e.g. proxemics or politeness principles, and they rely – most often unwittingly – on a stereotyped picture of both self and others. The latter is particularly noticeable when one takes into account the multiple identities that each interlocutor normally represents. Based on a person's gender, age, social class, ethnicity or nationality (Byram & Fleming 1998), they define how one relates to the people that they socialise with. In intercultural/international contacts, where two foreigners are involved, what people naturally select to concentrate on is national identity because the national constitutes the most evident definition of the person that they meet (Byram & Fleming 1998).

Morgan (1998) focuses on face-to-face interaction and discusses the factors which determine success in intercultural encounters as: (i) situational, (ii) affective and (iii) cognitive.

(i) Situational factors embrace the very situation in which one finds oneself, the people involved, their goals, status, time, and individual vs. group relations. To Furnham and Bochner's (1986) mind, intercultural encounters most often occur as part of some form of migration, for which people are either selected by others or self-selected. This has a consequence for the rate of success that migrants have in intercultural situations, as this pre-selection may be viewed as a selection of the fittest. It must be reiterated here that intercultural encounters may happen outside the context of migration, e.g. in the foreign language classroom, or they may be a random meeting with a foreigner or a foreign artefact in one's home country.

Interaction in intercultural encounters may also be facilitated by the goals of their participants. Morgan (1998) suggests that ideally interactants should have superordinate goals in meeting others. In addition, they should also enjoy an equal social status. With respect to time, on the one hand the longer one is exposed to otherness, the more likely one is to come to like it, as Robinson (1988) maintains. On the other hand long encounters may result in "a kind of disorientation with oneself" (Morgan 1998: 20). The last situational factor concerns one's relations with a group in which one functions. For instance, a group can support one in the case of negative intercultural experiences in that it will act as a protective shield that will help one absorb some of the culture shock or frustration which one experiences in the course of intercultural encounters.

(ii) Affective determiners of success in intercultural contacts comprise the physiological, emotional, kinaesthetic and tactile modes of perception of the culture that people experience. What normally happens is that the emotional attitude people develop towards a given situation is conditioned by all the senses through which the situation is perceived. Irrespective of the context of an intercultural encounter and the situation it involves, people naturally experience it through the senses as well as cognition. According to Robinson (1988), the strength with which sensory experience impacts on people's understanding of an intercultural encounter is as vital as cognition, which enables people to rationalise the experience.

(iii) Cognitive factors can be broken down into: salience, consistency and attribution. Salience refers to the degree to which a given intercultural experience becomes memorable to people, which, in turn, seems to depend on the emotions that the experience evokes. In Robinson's (1988) view, negative differences as well as negative evaluations appear to bear more salience, as they are more likely to be memorised.

Consistency refers to the readiness to reconcile difference and achieve success in intercultural encounters that people display when they have a positive attitude towards each other. In such a case, even difference is accepted as a natural element of the mutual relation.

Attribution relates to the degree to which people interpret others' actions in the light of the situation in question or other people's personal traits. In intercultural encounters it is of pivotal importance to attribute the behaviour of a cultural stranger to the socio-cultural context in which it occurred rather than in personal terms. Although this kind of conscious *modus operanti* is conducive to genuine intercultural understanding, it is actually difficult to achieve in real life situations. As Heider (1957) explains, it is a psychological protective mechanism that makes people attribute the actions of others to them rather than specific situations, because it is an easy way in which to avoid accepting responsibility for intercultural/interpersonal failure. However, time seems to have a healing effect on tendencies towards personal attribution and people who have known each other for longer will be more inclined towards situational attribution.

In sum, intercultural encounters are most effectively handled by those who: consciously enter the situation, set themselves superordinate goals with relation to the circumstances; share their social status with their interactants; have experienced similar situations before; can count on the support of their social group: do not focus on negative experiences; and are ready to seek consistence and social attribution.

Intercultural encounters have been illustrated by Weaver (1986), who proposed the iceberg metaphor of culture, and Morgan (1998), who expanded Weaver's model by adding a language component to it in order to underline the interaction between language and culture that is involved in intercultural communication. In the light of the metaphor, when representatives of different cultures interact with each other, their cultures clash like two icebergs. However, what is most salient then are the tips of the icebergs, i.e. the most tangible aspects of culture such as language, behaviours and beliefs. At the same time, what escapes notice is the tacit component of culture, i.e. the implicit beliefs, values and thought patterns which motivate actions. If the participants of an intercultural encounter are oblivious to the other person's implicit reasons for a given behaviour, they are likely to misinterpret and stereotype otherness.

The importance of values in intercultural encounters is underlined by Lustig (1988), who explicates that they are so intricate that they differ not only between individuals but also within them. Thus, occasionally a person may experience a kind of internal conflict of values which may simultaneously urge them towards two conflicting courses of action, e.g. helping others and competing with them. Nadler et al. (1985) add that when two cultures meet values conflict between individuals, and the outcome of the situation is determined by: what interactants bring to the conflict, how they negotiate the conflict as it arises, and what modes of conflict resolution they select.

According to Winter, there are three possible interaction patterns and resultant perspectives that participants display within intercultural encounters: "(i) egocentric, declarative dominant distortion of target language culture", (ii) "inductive, overresponsive total acceptance of target language culture", and (iii) "stable self images" (Winter 1986: 326-327).

(i) Egocentric distortion resembles Schumann's (1986) *preservation* – a pattern of integration that he describes in connection with social distance, which develops between an immigrant acquiring a foreign language and the target culture. This kind of interactive attitude is egocentric in outlook, and makes a person view the culture that they experience through intercultural encounters in a negative light, even contrary to the evidence they obtain. In effect, through the negation of the target culture the person's view of their own is enhanced.

(ii) Inductive acceptance resembles Schumann's (1986) *assimilation* in that this pattern makes a person overenthusiastically and uncritically accept the newly experienced culture, to the detriment of their view of own culture.

Finally, (iii) *stable self images* might be viewed as a counterpart of Schumann's (1986) *acculturation*, i.e. a situation in which a person rationalises the observed differences between the target culture and their own, and accepts both cultures without any change to their self-image.

A slightly different pattern of responses to intercultural encounters has been proposed by Bochner (1982), who distinguishes four possibilities: (i) a passing response, where a person involved in an intercultural encounter rejects their own culture; (ii) a chauvinistic response, which makes a person reject the target culture; (iii) a marginal response, which results in a person hanging between the target culture and their own; and (iv) mediating, which leads to a person synthesising both cultures involved. In the latter case, a participant of an intercultural encounter becomes a mediator between two cultures, and acts as one.

3. Intercultural competence

As Lustig and Koester (1999) maintain, intercultural communication requires interaction which would permit its participants to cooperate as well as establish relationships. Only then is it possible to resolve culture clashes and attain mutual understanding. Therefore, it may be stated that effective intercultural communication necessitates intercultural competence, or intercultural communicative competence.

Both terms are frequently used interchangeably, although their scope is different. Intercultural competence refers to the ability to explore and analyse intercultural differences as well as one's own culture, which may serve as a means of increasing one's cultural self-awareness, while intercultural communicative competence additionally covers the ability to handle communication in intercultural encounters (Aleksandrowicz-Pędich 2005).

3.1 Byram's intercultural communicative competence

The concept of Intercultural Communicative Competence (ICC) was introduced by Byram (1997), who sees it as an amalgamation of two, otherwise separate, notions: communicative competence and intercultural competence, which can be developed independently of each other. Hypothetically speaking, a monolingual native speaker of English could work on his intercultural competence without actually having to learn a foreign language at all. Consequently, it seems that intercultural development may be developed even outside a foreign language learning context. However, by combining both types of competence teachers can create opportunities for learners to improve their language/communication skills as well as develop intercultural competence.

When it comes to the composition of intercultural communicative competence, different suggestions have been offered. For instance, Humphrey (2007) perceives it as a combination of language proficiency and the components of intercultural competence, i.e. attitudes, knowledge, skills and awareness.

Byram (1998) has presented a more complex image of the notion, where communicative competence embraces linguistic competence, sociolinguistic competence and discourse competence. Linguistic competence permits correct spoken and written language performance, including message interpretation and production, based on one's knowledge of the target language rules.

Sociolinguistic competence signifies the ability to induce, through the negotiation of implicit and explicit meanings, one's interlocutor's intentions from the language that they produce.

Discourse competence covers the ability to construct particular types of text, e.g. a dialogue or a public speech, in keeping with the conventions of the target language. This competence could also help intercultural mediators construct a new text type in lingua franca communication, whereas Gałkowski (2006) assumes, they may need to creatively negotiate intercultural understanding.

Byram's (1997) intercultural competence consists of four constituents: (i) affective (attitudes), (ii) cognitive (knowledge), (iii) action-oriented (skills); and educational (critical cultural awareness).

Attitudes of curiosity and open-mindedness are supposed to underlie intercultural learning. However, if intercultural competence is supposed to be develop effectively, the attitudes must be accompanied by learners' readiness to shift perspectives and cope with otherness.

The knowledge of social groups, cultural products and practices is another prerequisite for successful intercultural exploration. Yet, it must be expanded to cover the learner's familiarity with the processes involved in interaction between individuals and societies.

Byram (1997) delineates two groups of intercultural skills. Skills of interpreting and relating enable learners to interpret documents or events from other cultures and relate them to their native culture counterparts; Skills of discovery and interaction empower learners to acquire knowledge of cultural products and practices, but also apply one's attitudes, knowledge and skills to genuine intercultural communication.

Finally, cultural awareness, which permits learners to evaluate material culture, behaviours and outlooks on the basis of explicit criteria, is also referred to as political education (Byram 2008). It helps learners anticipate and resolve intercultural conflicts as well as accept otherness in real time.

Here is a detailed presentation of the intercultural competence, as originally envisaged by Byram:

> "1. Attitudes of curiosity and openness, readiness to suspend disbelief about other cultures and belief about one's own,
> 2. Knowledge of social groups and their products and practices in one's own and in one's interlocutor's country, and of the general process of societal and individual interaction,
> 3. Skills of interpreting and relating: ability to interpret a document or event from another culture, to explain it and relate it to documents from one's own,

> 4. Skills of discovery and interaction: ability to acquire new knowledge of a culture and cultural practices and the ability to operate knowledge, attitudes and skills under the constraints of real-time communication and interaction,
> 5. Critical cultural awareness/political education: an ability to evaluate critically and on the basis of explicit criteria perspectives, practices and products in one's own and other cultures and countries" (Byram 1997: 50-63).

Byram (2008: 230-233) breaks each of the five components of intercultural competence presented above into specific objectives which learners are supposed to fulfil. In consequence, he defines attitudes as:

> "• willingness to seek out or take up opportunities to engage with otherness in a relationship of equality this should be distinguished from attitudes of seeking out the exotic or of seeking to profit from others;
> • interest in discovering other perspectives on interpretation of familiar and unfamiliar phenomena both in one's own and in other cultures and cultural practices;
> • willingness to question the values and presuppositions in cultural practices and products in one's own environment;• readiness to experience the different stages of adaptation to and interaction with another culture during a period of residence;
> • readiness to engage with conventions and rites of verbal and non- verbal communication and interaction;" (Byram 2008: 230).

Byram (2008) explicates that attitudes conducive to the development of intercultural competences, i.e. those of genuine openness to otherness, may be displayed by learners in the foreign language classroom, learners on a school trip to a foreign country and students residing abroad for study purposes. Simultaneously, he contrasts such attitudes with those of tourists, driven by a leisure-driven desire for the exotic, and those of businessmen, whose interest in otherness is motivated solely by profit. According to Byram (2008), tourists' and businessmen's attitudes will not facilitate intercultural development.

Knowledge refers to the:

> "knowledge about/of:
> • historical and contemporary relationships between one's own and one's interlocutor's countries;
> • The means of achieving contact with interlocutors from another country (at a distance or proximity), of travel to and from and the institutions that facilitate contact or help resolve problems;

• the types of cause and process of misunderstanding between interlocutors of different cultural origins;
• the national memory of one's own country and how its events are related to and seen from the perspective of one's interlocutor's country;
• the national memory of one's own country and the perspective on it form one's own;
• the national definitions of geographical space in one's interlocutor's country and how these are perceived from other countries;
• the national definitions of geographical space in one's interlocutor's country and how these are perceived from one's own;
• the processes and institutions of socialisation in one's own and one's interlocutor's country;
• social distinctions and their principal markers, in one's country and one's interlocutor's;
• institutions, and perceptions of them, which impinge on daily life within one's own and one's interlocutor's country and which conduct and influence relationships between them;
• the processes of social interaction in one's interlocutor's country;" (Byram 2008: 231).

In Byram's (2008) view, knowledge is composed of two types of it: (i) the knowledge of e.g. one's own or other countries and the relations between them that one has absorbed in the course of socialisation, i.e. the process of acquainting oneself with culture through observation, experience, social interaction or explicit parental/school education; and (ii) the knowledge of the nature of socialisation, its mechanics and its influence on one's culture-determined perception of seemingly objective reality. This explanation brings forward two important implications about the nature of culture. Firstly, culture is not natural, because people acquire it in the course of their lives. Secondly, a person's culture distorts their ways of perception and blinds them to other possible interpretations of reality while being taken for granted.

Skills of interpreting and relating cover the:

"ability to:
• identify ethnocentric perspectives in a document or event and explain their origins;
• identify areas of misunderstanding and dysfunction in an interaction and explain them in terms of each of the cultural systems present;
• mediate between conflicting interpretations of phenomena" (Byram 2008: 232).

Skills of interpreting are supposed to equip intercultural mediators with the ability to decode culturally encoded documents from other countries as well as other people's behaviour so that they can objectivise and interpret the reality that they face. This kind of skills is vital to a better understanding of reality, but they may also be useful in intercultural communication, as the awareness that they result in helps one do away with the negative effects of ethnocentrism which hinder intercultural understanding (Byram 2008).

Skills of discovery and interaction include:

> "(...) ability to:
> • elicit from an interlocutor the concepts and values of documents or events and to develop an explanatory system susceptible of application to other phenomena;
> • identify significant references within and across cultures and elicit their significance and connotations;
> • identify similar and dissimilar processes of interaction, verbal and non-verbal, and negotiate an appropriate use of them in specific circumstances;
> • use in real-time an appropriate combination of knowledge, skills and attitudes to interact with interlocutors from a different country and culture, taking into consideration the degree of one's existing familiarity with country and culture and the extent of difference between one's own and the other;
> • identify contemporary and past relationships between one's own and the other culture and country;
> • identify and make use of public and private institutions that facilitate contact with other countries and cultures;
> • use in real-time knowledge, skills and attitudes from mediation between interlocutors of one's own and foreign culture" (Byram 2008: 233).

Byram (2008) sees the skills of discovery and interaction as the survival tactics that are supposed to be used by a person who suddenly finds themselves in new cultural circumstances, be it on purpose or by chance. A situation of this kind necessitates action of two-fold nature: on the one hand it is necessary to be able to explore the implicit rules that underlie the new milieu and its representatives; on the other hand it is crucial to be able to utilise the knowledge collected in the course of such exploration immediately in order to be able to successfully function within the new culture. Byram (2008) compares this context to the situation of a foreign newspaper/television correspondent on the job or an ethnographer at work.

Critical cultural awareness/political education comprises the:

> "ability to:
> • identify and interpret explicit and implicit values in documents and events in one's own and other cultures;
> • make an evaluative analysis of the documents and events that refers to an explicit perspective and criteria;
> • interact and mediate in intercultural exchanges in accordance with explicit criteria, negotiating where necessary a degree of acceptance of them by drawing upon one's knowledge, skills and attitudes" (Byram 2008: 233).

By critical awareness Byram (2008) means the ability that learners ought to possess to critically evaluate both the new culture under observation as well as their own so that they can judge cultural phenomena consistently, irrespective of whether they originate from their own culture or another. In addition, learners ought to be able to demonstrate the criteria on which their judgement is based so that the same benchmark is applied to what is perceived as familiar and strange. The ultimate goal here is to ensure judgmental objectivity.

Alternatively, Byram (2008) has also described intercultural competence in terms of *savoirs*: *Savoir être* (attitudes), *Savoirs* (knowledge), *Savoir comprendre* (skills of relating and interpreting), *Savoir apprendre/faire* (skills of discovering and interacting), and *Savoir s'engager* (critical cultural awareness). As Komorowska (2006b) observes, Byram's savoirs match the overall goals of European education, as set out by the Council of Europe, and encompass three aspects of a person's development: affective, cognitive and social.

What is worth highlighting is that Moran's (2001) *cultural knowings* overlap with particular elements of Byram's (2008) *intercultural competence*, at least to a certain extent. For example, Moran's (2001) *knowing why* relates to Byram's (2008) skills of interpreting and relating; *knowing how* corresponds to skills of discovering and interacting; *knowing about and knowing self* can be assigned to knowledge of self and other; while *knowing self* seems to have a common denominator with attitudes in that the latter notion involves relativising self. Consequently, Moran's (2001) *cultural knowings* appear to function as guidelines for teachers who would like to bring their teaching objectives, content and classroom practices in line with Byram's conception of intercultural competence.

Another implication of the model of intercultural communicative competence, viewed as the goal of intercultural language teaching, relates to the profile of an intercultural teacher. In Byram and Fleming's (1998) mind, a teacher who is to develop this kind of competence in their students is no longer required to be a native speaker, who once seemed perfectly fit for developing learners' native-like command of the target language in the foreign classroom. In the light of intercultural communicative competence, it is visible that the teacher must have insight into much more than the target language itself: applied linguistics and psychology. Besides, a native speaker may not be sufficiently intercultural in their experience and attitude. Andrews (1998) testifies to this by stating that neither a perfect knowledge of the target language culture, the attainment of which he questions, nor a perfect command of the target language guarantees intercultural success.

Recently, Byram (2008) has proposed that a new goal of intercultural language teaching ought to constitute a kind of transcendence beyond the development of intercultural communicative competence. Opportunities should be created for learners to utilise their intercultural know-how not to transform into mere intercultural speakers, but rather *intercultural citizens*, who would effectively negotiate communication with others in order to take social action and attain common goals. For instance, in a globalised and internationalised world, learners could contribute to the development of international communities, e.g. the European Union, or civil societies. As a consequence, intercultural education of that kind will become a vehicle for instilling democratic values in learners; thus, it will foster both *democratic citizenship* (Byram 2008) and *active citizenship*, as one might put it. On a global scale, this kind of education could result in the development of *cosmopolitan citizenship*, which would foster social justice in newly emerging supranational communicative communities, or *transnational citizenship*, which would make people accept nation states as they are while enabling them to obtain full citizenship in the countries that they choose to identify with.

The transnational dimension of contemporary intercultural language teaching has also been endorsed by Risager (2007), who sees its goal as the development of learners' *intercultural competence of the world citizen.*

3.2 Other conceptualizations of intercultural competence

Other conceptualisations of intercultural competence have been offered by a number of scholars e.g. Ruben (1976), Komorowska (1999), Jandt (2001) or Kohonen et al. (2001).

As early as in the 1970s, Ruben (1976) proposed a list of characteristics of successful intercultural communication, which can at the same time be viewed as his version of intercultural (communicative) competence. His list was summarised as:

"1. **Display of respect:** the individual indicates a deep respect for the worth of others as persons of high potential and worth.
2. **Interaction posture:** the ability to respond to others in a descriptive, non-judgmental manner;
3. **Orientation to knowledge:** the ability to view one's own knowledge and perceptions as personal and not universally valid;
4. **Empathy:** the ability to "put one self (sic!) in another's shoes;
5. **Self-oriented role behaviour:** this dimension refers to an individual's ability to function task and relational roles within a group setting;
6. **Interaction management:** the ability to 'manage' interactions in which one is taking part;
7. **Tolerance for ambiguity:** the ability to react to unexpected or ambiguous situations without excessive discomfort" (Ruben 1976: 339-341).

More recently, Komorowska defined the competence as:

• ability to discern similarities and differences between one's own and target language society's culture;
• ability to analyse new cultural phenomena, including customs and behaviours of the representatives of another society;
• ability to perceive people and issues from the perspective of a cultural insider in order to understand their viewpoint, understand their cultural tradition in contrast with one's own, and release their historical background;
• ability to use the accumulated knowledge to develop a more objective vision of one's own culture, customs, traditions, and thought patterns;
• tolerance towards other cultures and the ability to avoid conflicts in intercultural encounters with their representatives;
• ability to resolve conflicts in encounters with the representatives of other cultural or ethnic groups, including the ability to manage intercultural misunderstandings (Komorowska 1999).

Jandt characterised intercultural competence as:

• extensive verbal and nonverbal communicative competence and the ability to select behavioural styles in consonance with a given context;
• ability to communicate in an unknown cultural environment, and the ability to handle the stress that inevitably accompanies the situation;
• understanding the influence one's own culture exerts on self- perception, as effective communication is preconditioned by the realization of one's own identity, and the resultant reduction in fear of otherness;
• expanding one's knowledge of other cultures, as awareness of the norms and values of other cultures facilitates effective communication (Jandt 2001).

Kohonen et al. (2001) interpreted intercultural competence as:

- respect for one's interlocutor;
- acceptance of other people's ways of expression;
- the ability to participate in verbal and nonverbal communication;
- the ability to suggest solutions to problems which could be resolved in cooperation with others;
- the knowledge of mediation practices and ability to facilitate cooperation;
- the ability to react to other people's behaviour in an unemotional/non-judgmental way;
- the ability to cope with new, atypical situations without embarrassment.

3.3 Risager's extended model of intercultural communicative competence

Risager (2007) has recently extended Byram's (1997) model of Intercultural Communicative Competence (ICC) by appending it with new elements. She believes that the language component of ICC ought to be updated in order to reflect its complexity, and balance it with the culture component. Thus, she posits that it takes into account factors such as: private and inner speech, language varieties, the sociolinguistic characteristics of multilingual speakers and metalingual attitudes. This kind of approach seems to be very sound, particularly when one is cognisant of the fact that Byram's intercultural communicative competence has been largely adopted as part of the general competences which are being promoted by the educational policies of the Council of Europe, e.g. through the publication of the *Common European Framework for Language Reference* (Council of Europe 2001). Risager's (2007) suggestions are supposed to make the notion of intercultural communicative competence more reflective of the plurilingualism and multi-lingualism of contemporary Europe.

Consequently, she introduces the concepts of *languacultural competence* and *discourse*, as components that she deems necessary for educating true world citizens. Risager (2007) substitutes *linguistic competence* for *languastructural competence*, which illustrates her perception of second language acquisition as an extension of one's: lexicon, syntax and morphology; content and language expression; and as process which relates to one's mother tongue and the other languages that one potentially uses (pluri-/multi-lingualism).

Sociolinguistic competence is envisaged by Risager (2007) as a number of *languacultural competences,* which would result from a mixture of languages that the intercultural learner is likely to know. Apart from enabling the learner to interpret text dialogically, negotiate meaning, or distinguish between the semantic and pragmatic aspects of spoken and written language, the new competences additionally empower the learner to communicate interculturally with the use of paralinguistic devices and kinesics. Another two languacultural competences which, in Risager's (ibid.) view, fall into sociolinguistic competence are: the ability to use language creatively and poetically (*poetics*); and *linguistic identity*, which is one's identity that stems from the way one expresses oneself in a foreign language (Risager 2007).

Discourse competence in Risager's (ibid.) version is amended with *languacultural translation and interpretation*, which enables one to mediate meaning and communication in intercultural situations.

Risager's changes are supposed to reflect learners' development as world citizens. Thus, she expands *savoir comprendre* so that it covers the ability to analyse the discourse patterns of the products of "the culture industry" (Risager 2007: 230), e.g. the non-linguistic genres of music or visual creations.

Ethnographic proficiency is Risager's (2007) extension of *savoir apprendre/faire*, which refers to the ability to explore the world's languacultural complexity through ethnographic techniques. Risager (ibid.) proposes that *savoirs* ought to involve *knowledge of language* and *critical language awareness*, which translate as: a global perception of language at international level; an awareness of links between language and identity; a perception of differences between first, second and foreign language learning contexts; as well as an awareness of global issues, e.g. conflicts or terrorism, and the influence that they exert on language teaching pedagogy in particular countries.

Finally, Risager introduces the notion of *transnational cooperation,* which relates to the ability to cooperate with transnational organisations, through which one can construct one's knowledge of the world and establish contacts with the users of other languages.

All in all, Risager's model relates to Byram's (1997) as presented in the table below:

Byram's model of ICC	**Risager's model of ICC for world citizenship**
Communicative competence	
Linguistic competence	Languacultural competence
Sociolinguistic competence	Languacultural competences: semantics and pragmatics; poetics; linguistic identity
Discourse competence	(Languacultural) translation and interpretation
Intercultural competence	
Savoir comprendre	Interpretation of texts and media products (including non-linguistic products e.g. music)
Savoir apprendre. faire	Use of ethnographic methods
Savoirs	Knowledge of language ; critical language awareness
Savoir être	
Savoir s'engager (Critical cultural awareness)	

Table 2-3

3.4 Summary

Irrespective of how intercultural competence is perceived, Byram (2003) indicates that in his view, it does not in itself need to be the actual aim of language teaching. If that was the case, language teaching might be objected to as an attempt to prescribe to learners a specific role which they would have to universally adopt, including the moral standards that it could be associated with, e.g. the norms of human rights. This kind of opposition to intercultural communicative competence as part of EFL instruction would be very likely to surface in Asia, where English is not expected to go beyond the role of a tool for international communication (Parmenter 2003). Thus instead, Byram (ibid.) postulates that learners ought to be given training that will liberate them from any prescription so that they can mediate between cultures, and become intercultural speakers.

Such teaching will also liberate language learners on linguistic level, because they will no longer have to follow the native speaker model of language. With reference to Zarate (2003), he claims that if a learner is not expected to imitate the native speaker but becomes a language partner, it boosts their concept of self. At the same time, he is aware that if learners interpret their status of partners in an extreme way, intercultural mediation will be impossible, as in such a case the participants of intercultural encounters will act totally independently.

One more issue relating to intercultural communicative competence – perceived as an encapsulation of all the awareness, attitudes, skills, knowledge and language proficiency necessary for successful intercultural mediation – is the nature of its development. As Humphrey underlines, it is "an on-going lifelong process" (Humphrey 2007: 31), which is likely to span over an entire lifetime. Consequently, it is hardly possible for anyone working towards this competence to make a firm statement that the process has come to an end and intercultural communicative competence has been fully developed. Byram et al. affirm that "the acquisition of intercultural competence is never complete and perfect" (2002: 11). Although it may sound frustratingly unoptimistic in the context of achievement in foreign language education, it must be stated that total success in intercultural learning is not necessary at all.

A successful intercultural speaker does not need to develop complete intercultural competence and there are a number of reasons for that. Firstly, it would be an elusive goal if a learner was expected to gather all the knowledge that they might need in order to mediate intercultural contacts because cultures are constantly subject to change. They evolve systematically, thus it is impossible to capture those changes within what one learns. Secondly, it is difficult to anticipate what language would be necessary for one to use if they were to negotiate a specific intercultural encounter because various languages are used across countries. Thirdly, every single country is a hub of many different cultures. Fourthly, in practice any language of the world has a potential to become a lingua franca, thus one can never establish what knowledge would be necessary in a given intercultural context (Byram et al. 2002).

One more reason for which it is impossible for one to accumulate all possible knowledge and completely develop intercultural skills is the multitude of identities that can be found within each person. As those identities undergo alterations themselves, it is impossible to expect that in an intercultural situation, which inherently causes a clash of different values, beliefs as well behaviours, one will be prepared for any instance of otherness that they are likely to experience (Byram et al. 2002).

It might be added here that the very incorporation of the s*avoir apprendre/faire* component into Byram's model of intercultural communicative competence is a testimony to his view of the nature of this competence. As the objectives of s*avoir apprendre/faire* indicate, intercultural learners must be prepared for lifelong learning, and they are expected to develop the ability to master new skills, which they would be capable of transferring to new contexts, depending on newly-emerging circumstances. This component is, therefore, an absolute necessity for intercultural learners, because – as Byram et al. (2002) elucidate – neither a model can be set for students to imitate, nor can a native speaker's social identity be mimicked.

CHAPTER THREE

IMPLEMENTATIONS OF INTERCULTURAL TEACHING IN THE EFL CLASSROOM

1. Learner and teacher roles in IC teaching

1.1 The learner as an intercultural mediator

As Byram and Fleming (1998) suggest, in intercultural teaching, the learner is supposed to develop a better understanding of, and a positive attitude towards, the target language society and the culture beyond it as well as to increase their understanding of the native society and culture. Therefore, the goal of intercultural teaching is not only to explore the target culture but also critically assess the learner's culture. This critical assessment of the native culture is necessary for developing an objective cultural perspective, with which to mediate between cultures. It is particularly important when one realises that the learner's familiarity with their own culture blinds them to elements of it which they naturally take for granted, and which – as culturally determined – might appear strange or unacceptable to others in intercultural contacts.

Byram (1998) labels the process through which the learner acquires a new outlook on their culture *tertiary socialisation*, and explains that it is a process of relativisation which accompanies the exploration of new cultures, provided that person who experiences otherness receives proper pedagogic guidance. What Byram (1998) highlights is thus the fact that tertiary socialisation is far from a natural occurrence, and that it may be precluded by one's own values, beliefs and behaviours, which are so deeply-rooted that they may obstruct what might be called *de-perspectivisation*, i.e. a shift in perspective.

In Byram's (1998) view, what tertiary socialisation necessitates is a facilitation of communication and interaction by integrating the learning of language and culture as well as permanent comparison of others and self, which is to enhance reflection on own culture. In effect, tertiary socialisation is likely to result in the afore-mentioned shift in perspective, which allows the learner to distance themselves from their native culture and perceive the target culture without the hindrance of their own cultural perspective. Should this happen, the learner may be able to assume a third place (Kramsch 1993), from which he/she can mediate between cultures. Byram and Zarate (1997) and Byram and Fleming (1998) label such a person an intercultural speaker; Corbett (2003) refers to them as an intercultural diplomat; Irishkanova et al. (2004) use the term intercultural mediator, while the Council of Europe (2008) has proposed the notion of intercultural intermediary.

Gautheron-Boutschatsky et al. elucidate that mediation, which denotes the collective actions of an *intercultural mediator*, is a term deriving from the two meanings of the Latin word *mediare*, which means: "the act of giving, in the sense of obtaining, procuring, bestowing (...) and interposition in the sense of placing between, interposing, interceding" (Gautheron-Boutschatsky et al. 2004: 171). They also see mediation as an implication of conflict and intervention by a neutral person who helps to resolve difference (Gautheron-Boutschatsky 2004).

Irishkanova et al. describe intercultural mediation as the ability to "(..) understand, explain, comment, interpret, and negotiate various phenomena in the target language culture" (2004: 101) which results in "a shared understanding by people of different cultural backgrounds and identities" (Irishkanova et al. 2004: 101).

Byram and Fleming (1998) define an intercultural speaker as a person, knowledgeable of cultures and social identities, who is able to expand the application of this knowledge to intercultural settings for which they have not been directly prepared. The dynamic and heterogeneous nature of culture, as suggested by ethno-linguists, e.g. Riley (2007), calls for generic skills of that kind, which are a far more effective preparation for intercultural contacts than memorised factual knowledge.

Byram (2000a) describes the competencies of an intercultural speaker in terms of communicative competence and intercultural competence, which altogether compose his model of intercultural communicative competence, discussed above. To reiterate, communicative competence involves: linguistic competence, sociolinguistic competence and discourse competence. Intercultural competence encompasses: attitudes, knowledge, skills of interpreting, skills of discovery and interaction, and critical cultural awareness/political education. With the use of these competences an intercultural speaker becomes an intercultural mediator, a self-aware intermediary in their own right, who is fit to face intercultural challenges and does not need to imitate a native speaker for that purpose.

As Bandura (2007) posits, communicative competence may be treated as completely separate from intercultural competence. Hence, a native speaker does not necessarily make a perfect intercultural mediator, unless they have received intercultural training. This role may be taken on with success by a speaker of English as a foreign language, who – with proper competences – will be able to negotiate linguistic and cultural differences in intercultural encounters.

One more characteristic feature of an intercultural mediator is their readiness to act in situations for which they have not been directly prepared. This form of improvisation, which intercultural mediation inevitably involves, requires training which will emphasise learner autonomy (Bandura 2007), and Byram's (2008) intercultural communicative competence is aimed at achieving this goal amongst numerous others.

A round-up of the characteristics of an intercultural speaker is presented by Fantini (2000), who maintains that it is a person who demonstrates readiness to: respect otherness, empathise with others, and act flexibly. At the same time, a mediator needs to display: patience, interest, curiosity, openness, motivation, a sense of humour, tolerance of ambiguity, and readiness to delay judgment. These features overlap with Humphrey's descriptors of an "interculturally successful individual" (Humphrey 2007: 30), which in her view, have been universally incorporated into cross-cultural inventories.

1.2 The intercultural teacher

Interestingly enough, intercultural teaching ascribes the role of an intercultural mediator to both the learner and the teacher (Byram 1997; Damen 1987; Aleksandrowicz-Pędich 2005), which requires a revision of the basic components of a foreign language teacher's professional competence on interpersonal, intercultural and language levels.

On interpersonal level, Kaikkonen (Zawadzka 2004) postulates that if the teacher is to mediate between the learners' native culture and the target culture, they need to display: a relaxed attitude towards the behaviour of others, which would facilitate interpersonal interaction and help them control emotions; readiness to negotiate and cooperate in order to solve problems; empathy, which helps the teacher understand another person's feelings and perspectives; and the ability to act in new situations.

Edelhoff (1997) lists out the intercultural competences of a foreign language teacher in terms of the main three components of Byram's (1997; 2008) intercultural competence: (i) attitudes, (ii) knowledge and (iii) skills.

(i) An intercultural teacher is thus to possess: skills of negotiation; skills of text/media interpretation; teaching skills, which would enable them to handle learner-centred techniques and facilitate learner autonomy;

skills of materials management; and language skills, helpful in the negotiation of meaning.

(ii) The teacher's knowledge is supposed to cover: other societies and cultures, including their own; an awareness of the perspectives of others on their own culture; culture-determined work modes; interpretation of behaviour, and ways of avoiding conflict.

(iii) The teacher's attitudes comprise: readiness to use the target language in order to negotiate interpersonal understanding, reflection, critical cultural awareness, critical evaluation, openness, tolerance and acceptance of otherness.

With reference to the work that the teacher acting as an intercultural mediator is supposed to perform, Gautheron-Boutschatsky et al. (2004) explain that the teacher needs to bring out to learners meanings which are only symbolically represented in the language and behaviour of others. They also have to destereotype the picture of the other by analysing the possible prejudices that exist towards the other culture in the learners' own culture. In addition, the teacher is to demonstrate to learners, and deconstruct, what is relative in culture so that learners are aware of the fact that in order to understand a culture one ought to be mindful of its implicitness and relativity.

It is worth noticing that the complexity of meaning in intercultural encounters is not universally recognised, as illustrated by Gohard-Radenkovic et al. (2004), who cite the definition of mediation activities described by the *Common European Framework of Reference*, where a mediator is viewed only as someone who assists speakers of two different languages in resolving communication problems. At the same time, it is stated that the mediator is not supposed to express any of their own thoughts. In effect, the competences of a mediator are formulated there in purely linguistic terms such as: interpretation, translation, text summary and text reformulation.

In plurilingual societies, which are currently being promoted by the language policies of the Council of Europe, a person who acts as a mediator is given an important pedagogical and social role of "an agent for social cohesion" (Zarate et al. 2004: 230), i.e. a person who facilitates the establishment of a given society's cohesive structure – teachers are very likely to be expected to play such a role in educational systems today.

A very important aspect of intercultural mediation is the need to work with learners not only on samples of the target culture but also the target language as well as the culture of the learners while attempting to ensure that the teacher and learners occupy a central position between the three entities.

Apart from new interpersonal, intercultural and language competences, the role of an intercultural mediator, currently ascribed to the foreign language teacher, requires a shift in the teacher's role in the classroom and their relation to the learner (Zawadzka 2004; Aleksandrowicz-Pędich 2005; Bandura 2007).

Firstly, because of the open nature of intercultural communicative competence, in that it is not a prescribed set of skills, knowledge and attitude, the teacher can no longer be viewed as a *knower*, i.e. a person who is supposed to transmit to the learners a pre-set body of declarative knowledge with a view to obtaining a satisfactory degree of reproduction upon request. Since it is impossible to collect a complete/perfect intercultural knowledge, as Byram (2008) himself admits, the teacher is not capable of doing it either. Therefore, the teacher's task is to engage into situations which create potential for intercultural mediation in a controlled fashion – in the safe environment of the classroom, or outside it – and seek solutions which would help both the teacher and learners collect information, develop skills, and adopt appropriate attitudes.

At the same time, the teacher needs to activate learners (Komorowska 2006b) in order to ensure that they are truly involved in learning. As a consequence, the teacher must be ready to face situations in which they will be puzzled and unable to answer their learners' questions. While assisting learners systematically, the teacher might also need help *from* learners, which is not a realisation that teachers are universally ready to accept; some may treat this kind of occurrence as a case of losing face. At the same time, such a situation is only a natural consequence of the shift in the teacher's role from that of an authority to that of a partner. Teachers must realise that intercultural learning is a lifelong challenge, to them as well as their learners, where full attainment is impossible. Therefore, they become learners themselves, as Barro et al. (1993) propose while discussing ethnographic modes of work in intercultural language teaching.

Secondly, as Bandura (2007) explains, the teacher who acts as a mediator may experience a form of detachment from the role of a foreign language teacher as intercultural teaching involves working not only on the target language but also the sensitive problems of identity, stereotypes and prejudice. Other elements might be added here such as: beliefs, values, and attitudes. This kind of education embraces much more than an average language teacher is prepared for, which has important implications for teacher training.

Byram and Fleming (1998) discuss the role of the teacher as a mediator with reference to the teacher's first language, and they posit that – as has already been indicated – the native speaker's privilege in the foreign language classroom in this specific situation has to be relinquished. What it suggests is not that a native speaker is no longer a suitable teacher, thus, they cannot be disqualified on the basis of their status. It is rather an implication that native speaker teachers, who are not expected to model the target language and its usage, have to shift their role towards mediating and reviewing. Their real task is now to distance themselves from their mother tongue and its culture – re-learn both – while trying to relate to the learners' language and culture. Non-native speaker teachers face exactly the same task, only the relation will go the other way. In conclusion, the status of native and non-native teachers acting as mediators seems to be levelled in the intercultural classroom.

1.3 The intercultural component of teacher education

Proposed models. If the intercultural approach to foreign language teaching is to be effectively implemented in the classroom, it requires teachers who are adequately equipped to put theory into practice. Therefore, intercultural teaching poses a challenge not only to teachers, but also to teacher educators.

It must be noticed that an intercultural teacher is ideally one who possesses and constantly perfects their own intercultural competence. However, as intercultural teaching involves new teacher roles, skills and work modes, it calls for a change in teachers' self-concept, professional qualifications, attitudes as well as skills (Sercu 1998).

Edelhoff (1997) delineates the profile of an intercultural teacher with reference to the three major dimensions of Byram's (1997) intercultural competence: attitudes, knowledge and skills, which might be perceived as the goals and areas of intercultural teacher training.

In terms of *attitudes*, the teacher is supposed to be: involved in intercultural learning themselves; curious about others and themselves; reflective on others' perception of them; seeking to negotiate understanding; ready to share meanings, emotions and experiences with others, including learners; ready to investigate how international peace can be furthered through foreign language education – an element recently highlighted by Risager (2007) and Byram (2008); and ready to adopt the role of an interpreter – or mediator (Byram 1997; Bandura 2007).

As far the *knowledge* component is concerned, an intercultural teacher is meant to be knowledgeable about: the socio-cultural aspects of life in the target language society as well their own; possible applications of the knowledge that they possess for the purpose of interpretation; the mechanics of communication and understanding; the faults of language; foreign language use; and ways to avoid misunderstandings.

The *skills* that intercultural teachers are supposed to master comprise the ability to: perfect their foreign language and communication skills in order to play the role of an intermediary in the classroom and in intercultural contexts outside it; handle authentic language in different kinds of media; and experiment and learn through experience in order to negotiate more effectively.

Andrews (1998) claims that teacher training courses should particularly focus on three aspects of intercultural education: textbook analysis, the use of audio-video materials, and ways of analysing the traits of society with reference to age, class, regional, generational and ethnic differences.

He also stresses that teachers should be taught how to use authentic materials; they should relate Grammar-Translation teaching modes with those of Communicative Teaching; they should also learn how to make use of their learners' culture in the classroom. Overall, he suggests that teachers shift from teacher-centred work to a more balanced approach where the teacher's expertise could be effectively combined with contribution from learners themselves.

Nedkova and Davcheva (1998) propose three components of pre-service teacher training courses for future teachers of language and culture: (i) awareness of the overall concept of intercultural teaching; (ii) practical implementations of the rationale behind intercultural teaching; and (iii) major concepts in the field of intercultural teaching. At the same time, they posit that these be complemented with the development of intercultural communicative competence, as defined by Byram (1997), i.e. including work on teacher trainees' communicative competence (linguistic, sociolinguistic and discourse competence) and intercultural competence (attitudes, knowledge, skills and critical cultural awareness).

As Nedkova and Davcheva (1998) emphasise, intercultural training is supposed to result in the development of not merely language teachers, but rather teachers of language and culture. This implies that apart from a definition of knowledge and skills that teachers should master, also the role of teaching must be clearly defined. Language teaching at large is supposed to reflect the societal context in which it takes place; it is, therefore, to reflect a country's official educational policies as well as the interest of its society. They state that because in Europe today social mobility is a well-established pattern, foreign language teaching should reflect it by facilitating the socialisation of migrants into new communities by preparing both the hosts and the migrants themselves for the challenge.

Nedkova and Davcheva (1998) put forward a proposal for a new, interdisciplinary model of foreign language teacher training which would take into account the needs of contemporary society, and – similarly to Edelhoff (1997) – they model it after Byram's intercultural communicative competence, including attitudes, knowledge, skills, and critical cultural awareness. Interestingly enough, Byram (2000) proposed a similar model himself.

Training with regard to *attitudes* should embrace: attitude formation and attitude change. The former is supposed to raise teachers' awareness of the perceptions of their country through the study of developmental psychology as well as enable teachers to decentre through the study of the psychology of moral development. The latter is to involve social psychology, which could demonstrate how existing attitudes can be influenced.

In terms of *knowledge*, Nedkova and Davcheva (1998) suggest that cultural anthropology should be utilised in order to help teacher trainees realise differences between the beliefs of various social groups e.g. at national and sub-national level. The knowledge component should also cover the teaching of the nature of intercultural communication, with attention to nonverbal aspects, and it should demonstrate intercultural differences through the implementation of behavioural and intercultural psychology.

Skills of interpreting are meant to be developed through the use of comparative text and media analysis, but also cultural studies and other approaches. Work on *skills of discovery and interaction*, which are to help pre-service teachers explore and unravel new facts about other cultures and their own, may potentially involve ethnographic methods of study, e.g. participant observation. This area of teacher training should also create opportunities for trainees to encounter otherness directly, outside the familiar context. In dealing with otherness, and the resultant culture shock, teachers should be supported with social psychology (Nedkova & Davcheva 1998).

Finally, work on *critical cultural awareness*, which boils down to trainees developing a critical attitude towards self, own and other cultures – *politische bildung* in Byram's (2008) terms – should take into account the findings of educational theory within the area of political education, education for citizenship or purposes of education (Nedkova & Davcheva 1998).

An example of a practical teacher training solution is an intercultural teacher training module presented by Guenova et al. (2000), who describes an eight- to thirteen-hour programme whose main goal is to encourage teachers to explore the issue of social identity through learner-focused techniques. The module aims at elucidating to teachers that learners ought to be given a chance to explore own and other cultures autonomously, which may be facilitated by the use of comparative methods.

The module includes four phases which focus on: (I) work on the concept of social identity and identity per se; (II) skills and methods of culture exploration along with examples of class activities; (III) teaching objectives, lesson planning and materials evaluation; and (IV) feedback on the module sessions.

Intercultural training in teacher education in Poland. Aleksandrowicz-Pędich (2005) analyses the components of teacher training programmes at the philological departments of Polish universities, and observes that the courses involve: practical use of English, study of literature, target language cultural studies, linguistics, foreign language teaching methodology, psychology and pedagogy. It might be added that teacher training colleges across Poland, which have also educated foreign language teachers, have followed a similar, albeit somewhat limited, programme.

As Aleksandrowicz-Pędich (2005) rightly observes, it appears that the areas of study that students explore in the course of their university as well as teacher training college studies create vast opportunities for them to engage in intercultural learning. However, as there are no specific guidelines on the incorporation of intercultural components into particular courses, whether intercultural training is a classroom routine or not is at the discretion of the teachers themselves; and even courses devoted to cultural instruction *explicité* most often focus on the teaching of cultural facts.

A similar picture of teacher training in Poland is also reported by Bandura (2007), who – nevertheless – cites a few exemplary exceptions to the rule, e.g. the intercultural projects run by students at the Warsaw University Teacher Training College or the intercultural work that students of German have performed at the Teacher Training College in Toruń.

The conclusion that Aleksandrowicz-Pędich (2005) draws from the status quo is that the degree to which intercultural instruction makes its way into the (teacher training) classroom is largely dependent on the presence of intercultural elements *explicité* in teacher training programmes per se. As studies (Bandura 2007) demonstrate, although European teachers, including Polish teachers, have come across the notion of intercultural teaching and seem to subscribe to the view that intercultural competence does constitute one of the key competences of modern language learners, they rarely practice what they preach, perhaps with a few exceptions, as in e.g. Bulgaria.

At the same time, in her book *Rozwijanie kompetencji interkulturowej na studiach biznesowych,* Aleksandrowicz-Pędich (2006) makes very crucial observations about the possible effects of intercultural training on the their participants, and concludes that even short courses/sessions may have a positive influence on one's ability to communicate in intercultural settings. However, she adds that this kind of training will not result in behavioural and attitudinal change; it will not permit genuine intercultural integration; and it might even have a harmful effect on learners' perception of their own intercultural skills: learners may falsely believe that they are already prepared to handle intercultural encounters. What that implies for teacher training is the realisation that in order to make intercultural training truly effective, one must plan it meticulously as well as make it a permanent feature of a particular course.

Simultaneously, intercultural training appears to be more part of in-service teacher training rather than pre-service education. Therefore, teachers only occasionally are reminded of the need to develop their students' intercultural competence e.g. through: workshops, conferences, and British Council summer schools (Bandura 2007). An example of a larger intercultural teacher training programme was the *COALA* (***Co****mmunication* ***a****nd* ***L****anguage* ***A****wareness among Pre-School Teachers*) project, addressed to teachers from Germany, Malta, Poland, Spain, and Sweden, which promoted the idea of developing intercultural competence in pre-school and early school children (COALA 2007).

All in all, contemporary teacher training must include an intercultural component if it is to produce professional foreign language teachers who would be able to cope with the challenges of FLT pedagogy. Otherwise, intercultural teaching will not commonly become a regular feature of foreign language lessons, which is confirmed by Lázár's (2007) account of the status of intercultural instruction today. She maintains that although the *Common European Framework of Reference* and the national curricula contain recommendations for the introduction of intercultural components into foreign language teaching, most teachers and teacher trainers choose to concentrate mostly on work related to linguistic competence. As Lussier et al. (2007) notice, it might be caused by the fact that intercultural teaching does not actually make a core component of language teaching in the CEFR.

2. Intercultural approaches and techniques

2.1 Various approaches to intercultural content

The ethnographic approach. The use of ethnography in teaching culture has been advocated *inter alia* by Damen (1987), Barro et al. (1998); Sercu (1998) and Corbett (2003). Ethnographic methods, which originate from anthropological research, include: recoding, comparing, translating and explaining experiences. Although Barro et al. (1998) claim that those methods have been traditionally used to explore remote rural communities, they perfectly lend themselves to the investigation of the intricacies of today's intercultural world. An ethnographer studies the lives of others by living with them, collecting and analysing data while directly participating in the world under observation. In other words, he/she is a participant observer (Cooper 1998). This mode of cultural exploration allows a thick description of culture, i.e. a very detailed observation (Geertz 1973).

Ethnographic methods enable learners to unravel other cultures for themselves, as opposed to accepting the image of culture simply transmitted to them by textbooks or the media, which was practised within the British Studies Approach. Naturally, in foreign language contexts, it is difficult for learners to immerse into the target language community and live by its members. Thus, activities which can be used in such circumstances should involve: *textual interpretation*, where text is viewed in a much broader sense than is conventionally the case and covers: cartoons, photographs and posters; *participant observation,* to the degree possible; and e*mpathy-building activities*, through which learners strive to enter other people's minds in order to experience their emotions. Such activities are not supposed to serve as models of target language behaviour but as incentives towards the exploration of the target culture, which, in turn, are supposed to help learners develop the skills of intercultural mediation (Sercu 1998; Corbett 2003).

Corbett (2003) suggests two goals of ethnographic activities: (i) intercultural mediation, which is fostered by *observation with understanding* activities that require learners to take on an outsider's perspective; and (ii) decentring, which is to make learners enter the native speakers' mode of thinking and behaviour. The ultimate goal of decentring is to develop an insider's perspective, i.e. to see the world through the perceptive schemata of a stranger.

In the absence of access to the target language, ethnographic methods may be applied to the learners' own culture in the same way, which is referred to as *home ethnography* (Barro et al. 1993; Roberts 1995). After all, one of the goals of ethnographic work in the intercultural classroom is not to develop factual knowledge but ethnographic skills. In addition, home ethnography helps learners develop a different stance on own culture by "making the familiar strange" (Barro et al. 1998: 84). Such defamiliarisation involves: observing one's own behaviour; describing it; analysing the observation; and interpreting the data obtained. In ethnographic work, it is vital to conclude activities by reflecting on the phenomena observed and relating the observations to behavioural norms, own or strange, depending on the focus of analysis (Barro et al. 1998).

Damen (1987) suggests a number of steps to be taken in the course of *pragmatic ethnography* – which Corbett (2003) calls *practical (amateur) ethnography* – as follows:

1. Choose target group;
2. Choose informant;
3. Do library research on target group;
4. Interview informant (do not name them, ask permission to take notes, do not evaluate the informant on the spot);
5. Analyse data and form a hypothesis;
6. Reflect on own frames of reference/reasoning, try to notice limitations of the evidence used.

Although the above were originally suggested for teacher training, Corbett (2003) maintains that they can also be used in the ELT classroom. In Corbett's (2003) view, the advantages of ethnographic work cover: the acquisition of observational skills, which are essential for intercultural competence; readiness for coping with culture clashes, which learners develop; the discerning of variety in communication patterns; and the development of learners' practical ethnographic independence for the future.

Barro et al. (1998) demonstrate the novelty of the ethnographic/ anthropological approach as compared with the Cultural Studies approach by juxtaposing the two. According to them, in the anthropological approach the learner learns *through* the cultural practices of others, experiences culture, focuses on the palpable, *lives* the target culture and realises that language and culture intertwine. In Cultural Studies the learner learns *about* the cultural practices of others, reads texts, focuses on the cognitive, i.e. tries to understand, and *reads about* the target culture, as if it were an entity separable from language.

Cevasco (2000) demonstrates alternatives to the ethnographic approach proper, which may be very useful in the EFL classroom e.g. analysis of cultural products and practices as signifying practices; the use of semiotics in investigating texts; or second-hand ethnography, where learners may attempt to consider the potential profile of the text audience.

The experiential approach. As intercultural teaching takes a very pragmatic approach to language and culture teaching, and aims not only to increase learners' (inter)cultural awareness and desirable attitudes, but also practical competences that could be used in real-time intercultural communication, it by default places importance on experience. Part of that experience is the ethnographic approach presented above, but experiential learning in the intercultural classroom by far exceeds the boundaries of ethnographic methods.

Teaching culture may reflect the two basic views of education: (i) structuralist (Camilleri Grima & Fitzpatrick 2003) vs. (ii) naturalist (Fenner 2000). Within the *structuralist* framework, teaching boils down to instruction, i.e. transfer of pre-set information from the teacher to the learner. Within this learning mode learners are never offered an opportunity to reflect on the subject matter. In teaching culture this view of education translates into the subject-object relationship between the learner's own culture and the target culture, respectively, which characterized *Landeskunde* teaching (Camilleri Grima & Fitzpatrick 2003). According to Bourdieu (1991), structuralist teaching instils in students a kind of *symbolic power* and imposes on them particular values and perceptions of the world.

Naturalist education, on the other hand, stimulates students' growth by creating an atmosphere in which they can construct their knowledge actively. Ultimately, they are not expected to arrive at a prefabricated picture of the world, but rather create their own reality out of the building blocks and with the use of the tools provided by the teacher. In such circumstances learners enter a dialectic, subject-subject relationship with the foreign culture (Fenner 2000).

Constructivist learning underpins the experiential approach to intercultural teaching in that it requires learners to construct or reconstruct meanings which are implicit in the language that they come in contact with (Kramsch 1993). The same applies to the cultural practices and products that learners may come across. Therefore, it is clear that learners must be actively engaged in intercultural exploration if they are to unravel other people's thinking modes, referential schemata, perspectives and emotions. Yet, if this kind of construction is to occur, experiences must be properly processed. Thus, it is not only important that learners *do*, it is equally vital that they ponder and *reflect* on experience.

Kolb's Learning Cycle (Kolb 1984) can be implemented as a model of how to deal with and explore experience, e.g. in critical incidents which learners may analyse in intercultural EFL lessons.

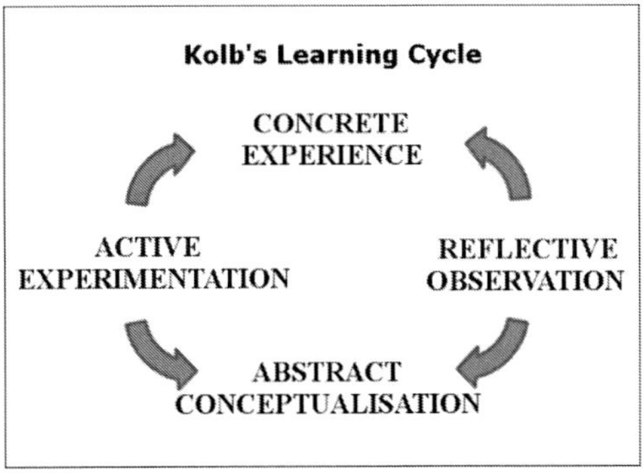

Fig. 3-1

The Learning Cycle involves four consecutive stages through which learners are expected to progress while dealing with any kind of experiential learning task, which seem perfectly suitable for assisting learners in organising and handling intercultural experiences by rationalising them.

The starting point of the sequence is the very experience itself, which learners have encountered, be it through exposure in the classroom or outside it. The following step is reflection, which can be viewed as a stage where by reviewing the experience in question and reflecting on it students can objectivise what has happened and in effect, delay judgment, which is necessary for intercultural understanding. The following step features abstract conceptualisation of the incident, and its aim is to enable students to draw conclusions and truly learn from the experience by expanding their (inter)cultural awareness. The last element of the cycle, active implementation, is the most difficult as in the case of intercultural learning it would boil down to students testing out their freshly gained intercultural knowledge and skills – provided they have been developed over a longer period of time – in practice. This simply means even more intercultural experimentation, which guarantees continuity of intercultural training. Ideally, the testing might happen in the target language country, where learners could try out their intercultural tactics in real life, on the spot.

However, as it may be hard to implement such testing in a general language course run in a school setting, students may alternatively attempt to experiment with their intercultural competence in the safe environment of the classroom, in simulated contexts, where they can additionally benefit from peer and teacher support, and where embarrassment can be alleviated through follow-up discussion and analysis (Kohonen et al. 2001).

Experiential learning represents the bottom-up approach to developing knowledge, where learners are enabled to make cross-cultural comparisons, investigate prejudices, deconstruct stereotypes, and develop intercultural awareness through interaction, whereby they are likely to discern the multi-dimensional meaning of cultural facts (Raw 1998).

Raw (1998) suggests that experiential learning may have different formats: reading tasks, warm-up activities or group/individual research. Thus, it may range from short straight-forward work units to quite elaborate projects. Perhaps, a better exemplification of the nature and types of experiential tasks is the list offered by Kohonen et al. (2001), which embraces: keeping a diary, keeping a portfolio, project work, drama activities, role-plays/simulations, case studies, problem-solving tasks, empathy training, collaborative work or fieldwork. Barro et al. (1993) also add: keeping a fieldwork diary, as different from a private diary, and conducting questionnaires, or making interviews.

Despite the advantages that classroom-based experiential work has, it must be observed that Sercu (1998) emphasises that learners should ideally be involved in fieldwork which enables them to actively participate in direct meetings with representatives of other cultures, where they could engage in truly autonomous learning.

The dialogic approach. The dialogic approach refers to the use of text in the intercultural foreign language lesson, whose aim is to increase learners' awareness of the fact that even literary piece may be a rich source of intercultural information if one analyses it properly. Dialogic analysis is based on the assumption that text construction, i.e. writing, is a manner of encoding a certain cultural perspective or perceptive schema, which is subsequently meant to be decoded by the reader. In consequence, reading is approached here as not only passive reception of universally understandable data, but rather a process of text (re)creation, which is determined by the idiosyncratic perceptive schemata of the reader. If the text writer and readers represent different cultures, the message decoded from the text may be substantially different from the one that was originally intended. Notably, difference in text decoding is also likely to surface even if the writer and readers seem to share their cultural membership as diversity in individuals' referential frames goes beyond the ethnic, or the national, and may be determined by the various sub-cultures that they function in.

All in all, reading takes a very special position in the dialogic approach, and it may be used not only to decrypt cultural codes but also to explore otherness by extracting its implicit cultural background from text. As Caspari (Müller-Hartmann 2000) suggests, intercultural tasks based on literary texts ought to consist of three stages: pre-reading, intensive reading and post-reading.

The pre-reading stage involves activities where learners' curiosity about the text to be read must be raised first. It is also at this stage that learners are meant to be made aware of their own cultural identity, which shapes their position towards the world that they will encounter while reading the text in question.

At the intensive reading stage, learners are required to attempt to decode the text that they read by making effort to see its reality through the eyes of the fictional characters that appear in it. At the same time, learners are supposed to reflect on their original expectations that the text does not fulfil. In effect, they have an opportunity to interpret and evaluate the culture behind the text.

The post-reading activities are supposed to help learners integrate the newly discovered perspectives with their own, which may evoke a shift in the latter.

As Bredella (1997) sees it, altering one's own perspective is not supposed to automatically lead to adapting other perspectives. It is rather an attempt at understanding the intention of one's communication partner, if only partially, and make room for at least certain aspects of other viewpoints within one's own perspective.

Alternatively, learners might change their own perspective completely, but it ought to be underlined that such a change must not be imposed on them within intercultural teaching and, should it occur, it is supposed to happen entirely at the learners' discretion. Therefore, the ultimate goal of the dialogic approach is raising learners' awareness of inescapable differences in perception between cultures.

The comparative approach. The comparative approach, which is one of the signifying differences between intercultural teaching and traditional *Landeskunde* teaching has been advocated by e.g. Byram (1989; 1997) and Edgington (2000). When used instead of monocultural teaching, it may help teachers in counteracting accusations of promoting linguistic and cultural colonialism (Kastendiek 2000). Comparative teaching requires that both the target culture and the learners' mother culture be compared and related to each other. In effect, learners "relativise and contextualise their own culture by experience of another" (Byram 1989: 49). Buttjes and Byram (1991) posit that intercultural mediation requires one to compare cultures a well as transcultural values.

Edgington (2000) enumerates the advantages of the comparative approach as follows: it increases learners' self-awareness as they have to relate what they discover about the target culture to their own. As a result, they manage to decentre, or defamiliarise, what they have so far taken for granted as part of their own culture. It also leads to a shift in learners' cognitive structures, as their perceptions alter due to the differences and similarities they unravel. Finally, it helps learners realise that people's perceptions are determined by the cultures or identities that they represent.

Comparison may follow two tracks: it may focus on either similarities or differences. If the former track is adopted, it is important for the teacher to decide on which perspective, that of the target or native culture, the similarities will be studied from. On the other hand, if the focus is on differences, there is always a danger that learners will develop an image of the target culture that they can hardly relate to. This, in turn, might lead to the development of negative stereotypes, which must be avoided in intercultural language teaching, as it will preclude in-depth exploration of either culture (C1 or C2) and intercultural phenomena (Edgington 2000).

At the same time, if only similarities are analysed, it may evoke in learners the false impression that both cultures (C1 and C2) are congruent to such a degree that no thorough exploration is necessary. Therefore, it appears that the only solution conducive to genuine intercultural learning is a balanced focus on similarities and differences.

With regard to perspectives from which similarities/differences ought to be tackled, it also seems reasonable that two-sided analysis is applied. Otherwise, if only a C1 perspective is adopted, learners may have a feeling that they are unnecessarily learning their native culture to the disadvantage the target culture. On the other hand, if a C2 perspective is used, learners may treat it as excessive concentration on the target culture (Edgington 2000). However, Edgington (ibid.) warns that even when similarities and differences are compared from the perspective of both native and target culture, the problems will not be automatically resolved; they may even be exacerbated. Nevertheless, she deems the comparative approach worth using.

In conclusion, comparing cultures may help students gain precious insight into cultures and develop intercultural awareness, but much depends on how the comparison per se is handled. It is not the question of *whether*, but rather the question of *how* this approach ought to be implemented. One possible alternative to a mere combination of the tactics discussed so far is Edgington's idea that the very issues that arise out of intercultural comparison become subject to scrutiny in the classroom.

Kastendiek (2000) proposes that comparison must not be limited to collecting facts. It is supposed to involve relation of information, interpretation of facts, and analysis of the relevance of the data collected. Byram, Morgan et al. (1994) believe that in the course of cultural contrastive analysis learners are, first of all, to develop awareness of the various value systems and beliefs that cultures implicitly contain. Last but not least, it seems mandatory in the comparative approach to go beyond the national, i.e. depict to learners the multi-tier structure of what is easily generalised as national culture. As Kołodziejczyk et al. (2000) state, in the comparative approach, no master narratives ought to be pursued so that cultures are presented as fragmentary, and difference alone is emancipated.

Collie (1998) perceives the comparative approach as a duality of teaching patterns. On the one hand it is involves collection of factual information, on the other hand it requires interpretation, which involves judgment and analysis, i.e. affective learning. Neither of the two patterns is superior, thus, their position in the classroom is negotiable. In effect, it is supposed to help learners develop a new enriched referential frame which encompasses both other and self, whereby they do not only explore the target culture but also keep a kind of critical distance towards their own culture. This mode of teaching requires the active participation of the learners, who constantly explore, negotiate and discuss the phenomena compared. As a result, they are supposed to develop a better understanding of cultural issues, develop a knowledge which will transcend the limitations of stereotypes and become deeply involved in learning.

What is interesting, Collie (1998) expresses the view that intercultural comparison, through its bi-cultural focus on the target as well as learners' native culture, increases learners' motivation. At the same time, Kastendiek (1998) disagrees and claims that students are in fact seldom incited into learning by the prospect of having to work on both cultures, and in order to evoke and maintain their interest in the long run teachers may need to employ incentives.

Examples of intercultural language teaching activities which illustrate the actual implementation of the four approaches to intercultural training in the foreign language classroom can be found in Kramsch (1993), Tomalin and Stempleski (1993), Corbett (2010) and Huber-Kriegler et al. (2003).

2.2 Intercultural techniques

Overall, intercultural methods and techniques may be divided into those that concentrate on intercultural awareness in a general sense, and those that put particular emphasis on linguistic awareness of culture. The latter group, as the less obvious, does not normally constitute part of intercultural language teaching, however, it ought to find its place in classroom practice, as it does not only help the teacher directly demonstrate the bond between language and culture. It may also be an answer to the concerns of those teachers who decline to incorporate intercultural work into their own teaching on the grounds that they have language work to do. It is exactly through linguistic awareness techniques that culture can be successfully taught even in grammar lessons. What is more, such techniques may prove to provide a source of motivation for students to focus on grammar more in recognition of the fact that grammar indeed encodes culture.

Techniques in teaching cultural awareness. Two exemplary techniques which help learners develop intercultural awareness are *drama* and *reader's theatre*.

Drama. Cooper (1998) advocates the use of *drama* as a method that facilitates the improvement of students' performance skills, which may be particularly useful in real-life intercultural communicative situations. The forms that drama can take in the classroom are: classroom theatre, drama exercises, drama strategies, and role-plays – also advocated by Dunnett et al. (1986).

According to Cooper (ibid.), drama creates the opportunity to develop students' personal qualities by helping them reflect on the performances that they watch and act out in the classroom, which depict both cultural behaviour and content. Drama allows a specific kind of reflection which Cooper (1998) refers to as *active reflection*. Through action it permits learners to ponder on the complexities of human behaviour as well as the world outside. What is worth emphasising is that this kind of reflection is conducive to observing culture from two distinctively different perspectives: that of an actor, i.e. someone directly involved in a given cultural event, and that of an observer, as students performing drama can distance themselves from the actions that they perform. Thus, what they experience is the insider's and outsider's view of culture. As a result, cultural observation is in a sense triangulated, and students' conclusions are likely to be more objective. Cooper (1998) sees this vantage point as the position of a *participant observer*, i.e. a person who benefits from simultaneous engagement and distancing. In addition, she underlines that drama helps the teacher to create contexts which enable learners to practice communication skills in simulated instances of real life. As Gigon (1998) observes, by shifting the focus from language form to communication, drama creates a need for speaking, activates learners and increases their confidence.

Fleming (1998) adds to the advantages of drama used for intercultural teaching by claiming that drama creates situations and contexts that lend themselves to much more scrutiny than real life, as in drama a particular scene may be frozen in time for analysis, or action can be slowed down. There are also a number of modes in which actions can be replayed, e.g. with the use of different intonation or alternative plots of events, through which it is possible to obtain varied outcomes and enrich cultural analysis. One more strength of drama is an opportunity that it creates for students to juxtapose thoughts with actual words. The actors may reveal their thoughts behind their actions in a performance, and the audience can present its own interpretation of what it has watched on stage.

Two techniques for analysing drama that Fleming (1998) suggests are: concealment and distancing. The former denotes situations in which learners attempt to conceal the socio-cultural knowledge that they have in relation to a particular event under analysis so that they can interpret events anew, with a fresh pair of eyes. The latter helps students defamiliarise the reality that they have so far taken for granted by looking at events from a distance.

In sum, Fleming (1998) underlines that in drama activities what really counts is the process of scene analysis and the intercultural outcomes that the analysis results in, not so much the very events. Archer (1986) adds that in order to increase the quality of the follow-up analysis, a role-play may be videoed and transcribed by the teacher. In this way, it will become possible to teach also the language that learners' performances contain; in effect, the learning of both language and culture will be contextualised as well as personalised.

Reader's theatre is a technique which constitutes a combination of the dialogic approach to text with drama. In activities that belong here learners read a passage of text which they are subsequently supposed to script for a performance on stage. By doing so, they have an opportunity to voice their own individual interpretations of the original text, which lies at the heart of dialogic learning. If students participate in the task in groups, which is normally the case, the ensuing discussion reveals to them how differently they perceive the messages that the author of the text encoded, and what different individual codes they utilise while decoding the author's intentions. The value of this kind of activity for intercultural learning is increased by the introduction of texts written by foreign authors (Kramsch 1993).

Dialogic techniques. Other dialogic techniques offered by Kramsch (1993) include: *dialogic role-play*, *the use of film remakes*, *constructing a cultural context* or *behind the looking glass*.

Dialogic role-play is adaptable to numerous contexts and may be utilised in a number of manners, thus, lending itself to numerous purposes. In one of the possible variations learners may be asked to decide how they would describe an aspect of life in their own country to a foreigner while taking into account their knowledge of the target culture. Alternatively, they might be requested to plan the design of a sales stall in order to sell a certain product to the target consumer group from a specific country on the basis of the group's cultural attitudes, preferences and consumer styles (Kramsch 1993).

Constructing a cultural context is a technique in which learners are supposed to read a story without an ending, or a fragment of an unfinished conversation, which they are meant to complete on their own by using the knowledge they already possess about the characters featured. The ending is supposed to be in congruence with the cultural setting of the text. As a follow-up, learners compare their alternative endings with the original and attempt to comment on the discrepancies discerned in the course of the process. This kind of action makes the learners realise how their modes of thinking and interpretative codes differ from those of the author of the text (Kramsch 1993).

Behind the looking glass requires learners to critically assess the contents of official information brochures prepared by the foreign office of a particular country in terms of the imagery intentionally evoked by the authors of the materials. This kind of analysis permits indirect exploration of the values of the target language society as well as the possibility of relating those values to the ones of the learners' home country (Kramsch 1993).

Reflection techniques. Sercu (1998) enumerates a number of techniques, e.g. *cartoons*, *blind maps*, *critical incidents* and *concept investigation*, whose aim is to foster the development of reflection and reflective analysis in intercultural communicative situations. Although originally Sercu (1998) meant the techniques to be used for teacher training, they can also be used, *mutadis mutandis*, with learners in the classroom. After all, as Byram (2008) stated, intercultural development means lifelong learning, involves teachers and learners alike, and it is supposed to be experienced by both parties in the classroom through exactly the same activities.

Cartoons can be analysed by learners with respect to the manner in which they reveal cultural knowledge. For instance, learners can discuss what aspects of culture, including taboos, language issues and values, are depicted in a cartoon image, and decide how they might explain them to a stranger. This technique allows learners to explore their own culture and discover that culture per se is not a collection of information, but rather a body of collectively shared knowledge (Sercu 1998).

In *blind maps* learners receive blind maps of various countries, including their own, and their task is to fill the contours with whatever they associate with the countries in question. As learners complete the task and compare their answers, the following two realisations about culture are likely to surface. On the one hand culture is interpreted individually, as students picture it in different ways; on the other hand culture is very frequently perceived superficially in terms of its explicit manifestations, such as institutions, landscapes, buildings or works of art, while its essence, i.e. thought patterns and mentality, is ignored (Sercu 1998).

Pictures can be used to demonstrate to learners discrepancies between people's descriptions of the reality they come into contact with. As learners receive two versions of the same picture and compare their seemingly objective descriptions of what they can see, they realise that nothing is objective. What picture-based activities highlight is that observation is not an objective act, as it implicitly involves interpretation, and interpretations differ between individuals, as people have a tendency to distort, or filter out, what they see (Sercu 1998).

Critical incidents (Tomalin & Stempleski 1993; Sercu 1998; Corbett 2003) are descriptions of conflicts/situations which are likely to cause offence or embarrassment due to cultural differences between their participants. To Sercu (1998), the value of critical incidents lies not only in the revelation of cultural differences but in the opportunities that this technique creates for students to investigate the reasons for cultural similarities and differences.

Another technique that Sercu (1998) recommends is *anthropological examination of text passages*, through which learners are guided by questions about the reasons for which cultures, presented in intercultural contexts, differ to such a degree that they evoke amazement or irritation. As students attempt to discover the truth about other cultures through a comparison of their own explanations with those suggested by anthropologists, they can potentially notice the difference between their own interpretations of other people's actions and the genuine cultural motives of the agents.

Dunnett et al. propose *stereotypes and prejudices* as the basis of another type of intercultural activity, whose aim is to bring home to learners the truth that the negative stereotypes about the target culture and the positive stereotypes of their own culture that they normally hold do not reflect reality but are an outcome of a cultural bias. Thus, this activity is supposed to assist learners in de-stereotyping the world by demonstrating that a shift in perspective on stereotypes is possible if only one adopts a different mode of thinking. For instance, learners may be asked to look at their negative stereotypes of a foreign culture and attempt to find more positive interpretations of them. By doing so, learners themselves illustrate that untwisting one's subjective vision of the world is relatively simple, and perception depends on the attitude adopted. It is advisable that class discussions on stereotypes are organised, but they have to be led by facilitators who would prepare guiding questions or information on foreign stereotypes (Dunnett et al. 1986).

Ethnographic techniques. Sercu's *concept investigation* is ethnographic in its nature in that within the technique learners can explore culture directly, by investigating cultural concepts, e.g. *café* or *cinema*. What learners are supposed to do is to examine how such concepts are perceived in a given culture, how they are utilized, or what roles they play. While doing so they have to take into account various perspectives e.g. historical, social or economic. This technique permits an investigation of one's own and foreign cultures, thus, it also allows one to compare how concepts function across cultures; it makes learners realize that although concepts frequently appear in different cultures, they may be ascribed different functions and they may evoke disparate associations (Sercu 1998).

Barro et al. (1993) suggest the *ethnographic fieldwork* technique, which is an elaborate extension of *concepts investigation* in that it consists in learners having to spend an amount of time abroad as sojourners in the target language culture in order to explore its culture through daily interaction with the native speakers. This is supposed to enable learners to look at the target culture from the insider's perspective, which Agar (1996) and Hammersley and Atkinson (1995) see as living within a world whose culture one attempts to discover.

Ethnographic fieldwork puts learners in contact with the culture under observation in a fuller way; it systematically exposes them to the target language. In addition, it helps learners verify the realities of the target social group in the light of their own stereotypes. That is likely to sensitise learners to culture-specific elements of life, while in the long run, it may also immunise learners against the consequences of culture shock. Ethnographic work involves: participant observation, interviewing, surveying, and keeping a diary (Barro et al. 1993).

Although investigating other cultures might involve a visit abroad, as it was demonstrated above, it is worth observing that concept investigation may be conducted from a distance, through the use of electronic media, e.g. websites or email, which Carel (2001) and Corbett (2003) name *virtual ethnography*. *Home ethnography*, on the other hand, is the term that Roberts (1995) and Barro et al. (1993) use for fieldwork exercises performed by learners in their home culture, whereby they develop the ethnographic skills which are necessary for them to explore other cultures, e.g. they learn how to ask the right questions, how to elicit informative data, how to unearth anthropological data and how to discover cultural meanings. Corbett (2003), who labels concept investigation as *concept training*, adds that thanks to it, students learn to look at seemingly mundane events and places as culturally significant.

Cultural associations (Corbett 2003) consist in learners juxtaposing and comparing information between their own and other cultures. They can do this in a tabular form, whereby they will list out e.g. food items or meals in selected cultures and compare how they function there. This kind of analysis will depict the occasions on which certain kinds of food or meals are consumed, the places that they are conventionally linked to, and the associations that they evoke within the culture of origin. Although Corbett (ibid.) realises that the information learners manage to collect may be stereotypical, he claims that it will, nevertheless, reveal cultural differences between the cultures concerned.

Negative etiquette (Corbett 2003) is a technique through which learners attempt to devise a list of actions that have to be taken if one wishes to fail in a particular socio-cultural situation. The aim here is not to make students follow the rules that they arrive at in practise, but rather to highlight to them incorrect modes of behaviour. Such a design makes the activity acquire a humorous value, which Corbett views as a motivator. A perfect example of negative etiquette is the book *How to be an Alien* (Mikes 1946). This kind of rule-setting may comprise various aspects of culture, including: national symbols, social conventions, people's beliefs or stereotypes. The creation of rules which would break the socio-cultural norms of a foreign culture may require consultation with a native speaker, but learners may also suggest negative etiquette which would pertain to their own culture.

Amongst other ethnographic techniques, Dunnett et al. (1986) and Hughes (1986) present *culture assimilators*. They are activities which are a more elaborate variation of critical incidents in that apart from an example of a potentially conflicting intercultural situation, they feature a set of multiple-choice explanations, usually four, of the behaviour observed. Learners are expected to read through the explanations and select the one which they believe to be the most adequate, given the socio-cultural context of the incident. At the centrepiece of the activity there is a discussion aroused by the different interpretations offered. The learners are guided by the teacher towards the correct answer only in the sense that the teacher provides them with feedback on the choices made. As Dunnett et al. (1986) add, this feedback must contain detailed information about why their answers are accepted as correct, or rejected as incorrect. That is why Hughes (1986) suggests that such activities ought to be prepared by social psychologists.

Culture bumps resemble critical incidents, but they are accounts of genuine uncomfortable or strange situations encountered by representatives of one culture in contact with another culture. A culture bump occurs when an individual's cultural referential frame/schema makes them expect a particular behaviour on the part of their interactants, and when what they experience mismatches their cultural presuppositions and expectations. In a sense, a culture bump is an instance of culture shock (Archer 1986).

Culture bumps lend themselves to intercultural learning because when they are handled properly, they can foster the development of self-awareness, intercultural skills and the ability to express feelings and emotions, which may, depending on learners' reactions, be positive, negative or neutral.

Archer (1986) proposes a seven-stage scheme for processing culture bumps, which may be treated as a possible structure of a culture bump activity: (a) recall the culture bump in question, (b) define the situation and its context; (c) list other people's behaviours; (d) list own behaviours; (e) analyse and list own feelings at the time of the incident; (f) list expected behaviours in own culture; and (g) reflect on the underlying value(s) that prompt(s) own behavioural expectations.

As can be seen, to Archer (1986), a culture bump essentially involves an interplay of other people's and one's own referential schemata that determine human behaviour. He is also aware of the tacit elements of culture, i.e. beliefs, thoughts and expectations, which underpin people's actions. That is why he advocates a dual-course analysis of one's own and strangers' actions and perspectives.

Since culture bumps are incidents that inevitably involve emotions, in order to be fully grasped, they must be depersonalised. The procedure with which to help learners depersonalise a culture bump and place it within a cultural context is supposed to follow three stages: (a) biased judgemental stage, which embraces a person's own perspective on the culture bump; (b) 'comprehension of other' stage, which involves understanding other people's motives; and (c) self-comprehension stage, within which one is expected to understand why one's own expectations and behaviours differ from those of others. It is vital that in culture bumps learners do not evaluate other people's behaviour and that observable behaviour is separated from personal interpretation. Events are meant to be viewed at cultural level, not personal (Archer 1986).

Culture bumps induce a number of pedagogical problems. Firstly, they are culture-bound themselves in that they are reported by a person who experienced them personally – thus, the account may be biased.

Secondly, teachers must be very cautious about their reactions towards their learners' choice of culture bumps for analysis. The teacher must not belittle students' choice of culture bumps, as perceptions differ from person to person, and what seems trivial to one may constitute a serious trauma to another.

Thirdly, a presentation of culture bumps may evoke the danger of stereotyping another culture by drawing hasty conclusions about it. A possible antidote to that might be requesting students to decide on typical behaviour of their ethnic group in a set context. As it is very likely that learners will find it impossible to agree on a single answer, it may help the teacher demonstrate to them cultural diversity through a hands-on experience (Archer 1986).

Archer (1986) introduces a dramatised variation of culture bumps, which he names *controlled culture bumps*. However, it must be observed that this technique might equally well qualify as an alternative form of a critical incident. In the mode proposed by Archer (1986), the activity does not involve an account of a real life intercultural experience, but a teacher-prepared role-play performed by learners. Subsequently, the role-play situation is discussed under the teacher's guidance so that learners can understand the meaning of the incident and develop tolerance towards other points of view.

Johnson (1979), Dunnett et al. (1986) and Hughes (1986) present an intercultural technique which they name *culture capsules*. A culture capsule is a description of one aspect of life in which two specific cultures differ from each other. Dunnett et al. (1986) suggest that the areas of difference depicted in a culture capsule may cover: race-related issues, family matters, or the social position of women. To Hughe's (1986) mind, a culture capsule ought to be illustrated through visual aids in order to provoke response and incite discussion.

Techniques in teaching linguistic awareness of culture involve references to both verbal and nonverbal modes of communication, thus, bringing to the fore the realisation that culture and language are genuinely intertwined, and intercultural differences can be manifested through: (i) grammar, (ii) vocabulary, but also (iii) non-verbal communication cues and (iv) communicative styles (Sercu 1998). In other words, such techniques demonstrate the practical aspects of what Attinasi and Friedrich (Sercu 1998) as well as Kramsch (1998b) and Fantini (2002) referred to as *linguaculture*, and what Agar (1994) and Risager (2008) named *languaculture*.

(i) An example of a grammar-based technique that Sercu (1998) proposes is an *analysis of language conjunctions, adverbs and particles* in the language of a given culture, which may reveal the speakers' attitude to the concepts or people that they refer to. Sercu (ibid.) suggests that the above-mentioned language elements are not simply grammatical forms but an expression of bias or sympathy. Work of this kind does not have to take the form of analysis exclusively as learners may be asked to create their own sentences with these language forms, and subsequently, they may be asked to explain their train of thought behind the languacultural choices that they will have made.

(ii) *Defining concepts and prototypes* is a vocabulary-based activity that consists in learners relating cultural concepts. However, it differs from concept investigation in that it does not involve direct exploration of concepts. Instead, it requires students to define a specific concept or its prototype on their own, i.e. from a subjective point of view. While students engage in the task they are expected to realise that the manner in which they visualise particular concepts may differ what the concepts actually signify. Therefore, they are likely to discover not only the arbitrariness of concepts that societies live by, but also a tendency that that members of a given culture have to subconsciously stereotype the concepts which they use. Once more, learners will be able to observe here that although concepts may be seemingly shared by cultures, they are interpreted in disparate ways (Sercu 1998).

(iii) Work on *nonverbal communication* may focus on two categories of cues: (i) nonverbal, e.g. signs, body language, proxemics, olfactics, oculesics; and (ii) paralinguistic, e.g. intonation patterns, the use of sound and pitch. Both modify speech and are culture-determined, i.e. they carry cultural information which differs between cultures. In non-verbal communication activities learners may be requested to interpret nonverbal and paralinguistic cues through images that depict them or sentences which describe instances of nonverbal communication in use (Sercu 1998).

One more variation of this technique is modelled after Asher's (1982) Total Physical Response, and boils down to individual students acting out specific signs or body language which the others in the classroom are expected to verbalise; a similar kind of audiomotor exercise is suggested by Hughes (1986).

(iv) The last category of languacultural techniques covers *communicative styles*, which are people's verbal, paraverbal and non-verbal forms of expression, and refer to the way people communicate their messages, e.g. direct/indirect modes of expression, or the overall proportions between verbal, paraverbal and nonverbal communication. Communication styles differ between cultures and may affect intercultural understanding. Thus, learners need to analyse communication styles, e.g. by means of pictures or video footage, and observe what styles people within a specific culture utilise (Sercu 1998).

3. Assessing intercultural competence

Since teaching is administered with a view to making learners acquire new knowledge and skills, it inevitably involves assessment, which provides invaluable feedback for learners and is also a way of validating the teaching procedures used. Additionally, systematic assessment is a formal administrative requirement set by educational systems. Therefore, it is inevitably required within intercultural language teaching. After all, in Byram's words, 'If it isn't tested, it's not taught' (Byram 2000: 8). However, given the nature of intercultural competence, assessment seems a complex issue, and as such is likely to pose a variety of problems.

3.1 Areas of assessment and potential problems

Lussier et al. (2007) propose three potential areas of ICC assessment, which they derive directly from Byram's *savoirs*: *savoirs* (knowledge), *savoir-faire* (know-how), and *savoir-étre.* Byram et al. (2002) also add *savoir comprendre* and *savoir s'engager* and *savoir apprendre* to that.

Savoirs comprises the knowledge of the ways of life, sociocultural context and cultures of the target language communities as well as intercultural awareness. *Savoir-faire* refers to the ability to function linguistically and culturally in intercultural settings, interact with others, and interpret intercultural encounters. *Savoir-étre* denotes the learner's personal identity in terms of attitudes towards otherness, level of motivation, values and beliefs. It requires the ability to redefine self and understand others for more effective intercultural mediation (Lussier et al. 2007). *Savoir comprendre* entails the ability to interpret documents or events from another culture in order to see their cultural foundation, as well as relate them to documents and events from one's own culture. *Savoir s'engager* denotes the ability to explicitly state that criteria on the basis of which one perceives others, and the realisation that these criteria are themselves culture-determined. Finally, *savoir apprendre/faire* involves the skills of acquiring new cultural knowledge and practices and the ability to use them in actual intercultural encounters (Byram et al. 2002). Each of these components of intercultural competence exerts influence on the choice of assessment modes.

As Lussier et al. (2007) posit, if *savoirs* is narrowed down to facts about other cultures, it may be tested conventionally through multiple-choice tasks, short answer quizzes, or matching tasks. One might also add true/false tasks to that. Byram et al. (2002) state that *savoir comprendre* may also be relatively easily assessed through essays where learners have to interpret and relate documents and events between cultures in order to demonstrate not only cultural knowledge but also an understanding of it. Perhaps, essay writing might be successfully used in order to assess *savoir apprendre* as well.

However, *savoirs* additionally covers "the collective memory (...) of culture and civilisations", "diversity in (…) ways of living" and "sociocultural contexts" (Lussier et al. 2007: 27), which are much more difficult to test. *Savoir-étre,* which is existential knowledge – measurable in terms of intercultural differences that learners are familiar with – may as such be tested. Yet, what poses a problem is the dimension of the notion which covers the ability to alter one's own values and integrate the perspectives of others with those one has so far lived by.

The other components are by no means less problematic. *Savoir-faire* signifies the practical skills one needs in order to use the target language in intercultural interactions. This entails the ability to interpret, integrate and adjust to different contexts, and it is this adjustment that may be a challenge to capture through a test. The greatest difficulty lies in assessing *savoir apprendre/faire,* where the process of acquiring cultural knowledge must be assessed as well as the degree to which one successfully puts it into practice in intercultural encounters.

Lussier et al. (2007) demonstrate how a number of elements of intercultural teaching call for a shift in teachers' approaches to assessment. First of all, they draw attention to the fact that developing *savoir-étre* involves the process of selecting and collecting a vast amount of cultural information. Consequently, the very process becomes as essential to intercultural learning as the product that it is supposed to result in. Having said that, Lussier et al. (2007) suggest alternative assessment methods which would involve: "anecdotal records, observation checklists, observation rating scales, documentation of task-related behaviours, attitudes inventories, surveys, portfolios, journals, self-evaluation reports, collection of written products, interest inventories, [and] logs" (Lussier et al. 2007: 29).

3.2 Assessment modes

What transpires from the above is a shift instigated by the nature of intercultural teaching from *summative* to *formative assessment*, which – unlike the former – does not focus on elicitation of declarative knowledge and information, but permits the teacher to observe the process of learning in real-time and diagnose learners' strategies of learning. This mode of assessment furthers the development of the "behavioral, affective as well as cognitive domains" (Lussier et al. 2007: 29) of intercultural development.

As Humphrey (2007) and (Byram 2008) underline, the development of intercultural communicative competence is a *continuous* process – a form of a lifetime challenge. In recognition of that, Lussier et al. (2007) suggest that assessment must be administered systematically in order to capture students' thinking modes, or the capacity to reflect. To that end, they propose the use of a portfolio of learners' works, including: records of performances and projects as well as works prepared by learners.

Intercultural assessment may fall into either of the two ends of the *direct/indirect* dichotomy, which acquires a new meaning in intercultural teaching. Direct assessment is normally viewed as an assessment procedure of which the learner is fully aware, e.g. a class test or an examination. Indirect assessment conventionally refers to situations in which the learner is not aware of being assessed. In intercultural teaching, direct assessment involves techniques which help the teacher observe intercultural learning in progress, e.g. students reflecting on an event; whereas indirect assessment denotes contexts in which what is actually measured is only indirectly indicative of the process of intercultural learning, e.g. knowledge tested through a true/false test (Lussier et al. 2007).

One might propose that direct intercultural assessment focuses on developmental performance, while indirect assessment measures products, which only in part illustrate the learning that has led to their emergence. It must also be added that neither of the two assessment modes should be treated as superior as both help the teacher build a fuller picture of their learners' intercultural achievement. It may be better realised when one remembers that Byram's (2008) model of intercultural competence does not denounce knowledge, but rather builds on it.

Another choice of assessment modes is that of *holistic* and *analytic* assessment. Holistic assessment boils down to synthesising the various aspects of learners' performance in order to obtain a general view of their ability. On the other hand analytic assessment involves a close examination of either the constituent components of competence or that of competence at large (Lussier et al. 2007).

What is worth noticing is that Lussier et al. (ibid.) do not clearly indicate which assessment mode is suitable for intercultural teaching. However, it seems that a combination of both is a reasonable proposition; perhaps, with the caveat that in the case of analytic assessment a close examination of all the possible aspects of intercultural development is physically impossible. Therefore, on the one hand the teacher may need to select particular components for assessment, e.g. for diagnostic purposes, which they can realistically cope with. On the other hand they may need to be able to draw a general, summative picture of their learners' intercultural competence for the sake of end-of-year evaluation.

The last assessment mode choice is that of *teacher assessment* vs. *self-assessment*. The latter, which is conducted by the learner themselves, may be treated as complementary to the former. It indeed seems logical that students do not only rely on the feedback which they receive from the teacher but also build their own inner criteria. This may, in turn, increase their awareness of the developmental processes behind intercultural learning, and activate them so that they take a more active part in the process and systematically monitor the changes to self-perception or attitudes and emotions which they experience. After all, they can best assess what happens within them (Lussier et al. 2007).

Self-assessment may be facilitated by ready-made tools which can be retrieved from Council of Europe materials for intercultural teaching/learning, e.g. the *European Language Portfolio* (EPL 2000; 2004; 2006; 2007) as well as the *Autobiography of Intercultural Encounters* (Council of Europe 2009). Detailed examples of how the *European Language Portfolio* could be used for self-assessment with older learners are provided by Byram et al. (2002), who simultaneously add that their principles may also be applicable to working with younger learners.

Assessment as learning. Byram and Tost Planet (2000) demonstrate that assessment proper does not necessarily need to be the centre point of activities through which teachers may gain insight into their learners' intercultural learning. By referring to the work of Kalnberzina (2000), they demonstrate that assessment is as important as the evaluation of learners' engagement in classroom activities, their response to them and reflection on the actions taken. This kind of approach, very characteristic of intercultural teaching, turns evaluation into a teaching tool, and is also viewed as one more learning mode.

Kalnberzina (2000) engages her learners in project tasks which are assessed through the production of posters, the delivery of poster presentations, essay writing and conference presentations. At the same time, while evaluating the assignments she mostly focuses on: student participation, the degree of empathy towards others and otherness that her learners display, the development of presentation skills, and language use. While assessing essays, she puts emphasis on: the degree to which intercultural information is presented; the scope of information selected; the extent to which learners display understanding of the problems and people that they describe as well as language use.

3.3 Approaches to assessment

The pen-and-paper approach: testing knowledge and information. One of the most obvious aspects of assessment is testing, which in a straight-forward way enables teachers to examine how much their students have learnt. Yet, it must be stated here that tests lend themselves best to verifying fact-based, declarative knowledge, which is only one component of intercultural (communicative) competence. Therefore, those who advocate this means of testing within intercultural teaching must be aware of its limitations.

A representative of this approach to assessment is Valette (1986). She suggests a variety of cultural test tasks which correspond to the four teaching goals and, at the same time, areas of assessment (cf. section 3.1 of Chapter Three) which intercultural instruction involves: (i) developing awareness and expanding knowledge of the target culture; (ii) acquiring a command of etiquette in the target culture; (iii) understanding differences between the target culture and one's own; and (iv) understanding the values of the target culture. Valette (ibid.) proposes a variety of tests which examine the degree to which learners have attained the above goals.

(i) *Awareness and expanding knowledge of the target culture* can be examined through tests on: geographic parameters of the target culture, cultural contributions of the target culture, differences in ways of life, and differences in values and attitudes. Specific examples of testing techniques include activities in which: learners produce lists of target language speaking countries or identify particular spots on blind maps; explain the origin of place names; match famous people's names with their achievements; cite differences that they would be likely to observe in a given foreign country; and select between true/false statements about values and attitudes in other cultures (Valette 1986).

(ii) *A command of etiquette in the target culture* may be tested through activities which focus on knowledge e.g. learners may answer questions about explicit rules of etiquette and their manifestations in real life, or interpret people's behaviour by selecting between multiple-choice prompts. On the other hand the ability to apply rules of etiquette in practice can be tested through activities where learners: describe how they would behave in set situations, e.g. at the table; or what kind of language register (formal/informal) they would prefer to use in a given context (Valette 1986).

(iii) *Understanding differences between the target culture and one's own* can be tested through activities where learners: find set information in culture-specific documents, e.g. timetables, schedules, information grids and relevant newspaper departments; interpret linguistic cultural referents, i.e. culture-specific terms that carry cultural information, by answering multiple-choice questions; or describe how they would perform certain conventional actions in the target culture society, e.g. how they would buy a train ticket, write out a cheque or fill a form (Valette 1986).

(iv) *Understanding the values of the target culture* may be tested by examining how well learners can interpret the behaviour of the members of the target culture or their own. This can be done by: asking students open or multiple-choice questions about people's behaviour in a set situation; or by requesting them to describe situations in which foreigners might experience culture shock (Valette 1986).

It must be reiterated that the mode of testing presented above has serious limitations, which are – interestingly enough – recognised by Valette (1986) herself, who observes that officially established correct answers to test questions may not reflect cultural diversity in that they may not allow for individual differences in thought patterns, thoughts and perceptions.

The portfolio approach: testing attitudes and empathy. Byram (2000b) observes that, aside from knowledge and information, intercultural competence involves the ability to change one's attitudes or tolerance of otherness under the influence of experience, which fosters affective and moral development. At the same time, while he reminds teachers that conventional fact-based tests rely on the quantification of the constructs that they measure, he emphasizes that it cannot – and must not – be done with reference to tolerance. Therefore, he suggests that in this case tests be replaced with the so-called portfolio approach, which would entail self-assessment, and which could be guided by sections of the *European Language Portfolio*. As he illustrates, through the portfolio the learner may record the circumstances in which they have encountered otherness, the feelings that particular situations and events evoked in them, the knowledge they have managed to accumulate, and the actions they took on particular occasions in order to resolve problems or work out cultural differences.

The *ELP* also gives the learner a chance to self-assess their overall intercultural experience with regard to: interest in other ways of life, the ability to change perspective, the ability to cope with living in a different culture, knowledge about another country, and knowledge about intercultural communication.

Irishkanova et al. (2004) also call for utilizing the *European Language Portfolio* in assessing learners' empathy. However, they realize that in order to do this effectively, descriptors need to be proposed which would enable teachers to assess their learners' level of empathy in relation to the language/culture proficiency included within the *ELP*.

Zarate (Little & Simpson 2003) expressed her concern about learners' capacity to self-assess their own intercultural competence. She claims that it may be impossible for learners to adamantly state what they are capable of doing, the more that components of intercultural competence are difficult to describe, due to the lack of sufficient intercultural experiential evidence.

All in all, in Byram's (2006) view, values and attitudes remain the greatest problem in intercultural assessment, both in terms of technical and moral challenges that this kind of assessment involves. However, he does not find all the other components, including knowledge, skills, and the ability to evaluate, problematic to evaluate.

Alternative portfolios for intercultural assessment. Humphrey (2007) presents examples of instruments for teacher- and self-assessment of selected aspects of one's intercultural (communicative) competence which have been designed internationally by scholars and dedicated institutions. Notably, they can by no means be viewed as a remedy to all assessment-related problems in intercultural instruction. Yet, they are an interesting extension of the repertoire of tools that teachers might use in order to diversify their assessment methods, and triangulate the data that they obtain. A number of alternative portfolios are presented below.

The Intercultural Development Inventory is a list of statements which serve as a measurement of one's stage of intercultural sensitivity. It is based on Bennett's (1993) Developmental Model of Intercultural Sensitivity and covers aspects of culture-general difference on national, regional, family or individual levels. As Humphrey insists, it is "a scientifically valid and reliable psychometric instrument" (Humphrey

2007: 40) which is intended to reveal the degree to which one is ready to encounter otherness.

A very interesting suggestion is the INCA (Byram 2008) project, carried out by specialists in intercultural learning theory, diagnostic testing or issues of culture shock. The INCA project has produced a framework of intercultural competence, but most importantly, also a set of assessment tools, including an online module and a portfolio. Although originally the tools were developed for applications in business, where intercultural competence is a vital determiner of success in a globalised corporate world (Humphreys 2007; Aleksandrowicz-Pędich 2006), and where it was supposed to diagnose employees' intercultural and vocational competence, it may at least in part be used by foreign language teachers. The more that it was based on the work of several scholars, including Byram's (1997) *Framework for Intercultural Competence* and research by Kühlmann and Stahl (1998) and Müller-Jacquier (2000).

One more assessment instrument was produced as part of the LOLIPOP (Language and On-Line Portfolio Project) project, developed through the international cooperation of Ireland, Austria, France, Germany, Latvia, Norway, Poland and Spain. It is an electronic, interactive version of the *European Language Portfolio* (available online at http://lolipop-portfolio.eu/index.html) which is supposed to help learners establish the degree of their intercultural development, as well as diagnose the steps that they would need to take in order to develop further. The intercultural competences of the electronic portfolio fall into the categories of: knowledge, attitudes and skills and are described through a set of *can do* statements. Learners' progress can be monitored with the use of the electronic copy of the ELP, but the relevant evidence for it is supposed to be collected within the *Dossier* part of the hardcopy version (Humphrey 2007).

Other approaches: testing culture analysis. Intercultural competence entails more than cultural facts and a knowledge of behavioural patterns. Valette (1986) recognises that and offers a set of three approaches to the testing of learners' ability to analyse the target culture, i.e. the ability to self-learn: semiotic, thematic, and contextual. In the semiotic approach, which was originally advocated by Beajour and Ehrmann (1967), learners are asked to analyse original samples of the target culture, e.g. television/radio programme excerpts or images, and attempt to identify signs which might carry encoded cultural information (Valette 1986).

In the thematic approach, proposed by Nostrand (1967b), learners are required to analyse cultural products, e.g. comic strips or stories, and seek in them themes which would encapsulate the thought patterns that underlie the target culture.

Finally, tests in the contextual mode are modelled after the rationale laid out by Santoni (Valette 1986), who expressed the view that individuals' language reveals their culture. Thus, students are initially asked true/false questions which explain a set of target language statements. While answering the questions, they are expected to justify their choices by citing supporting evidence based on cultural facts, products or other references.

Moral issues in assessment. Byram (2008) discusses the moral issues that are inescapable in the course of intercultural assessment, and indicates that they mostly relate to the assessment of intercultural competences other than knowledge (savoirs), i.e. those that require a change of attitude, values, or readiness to believe or disbelieve what one observes.

One of the key problems is the assessor's criteria on the basis of which an intercultural learner is judged. In case those criteria do not agree with those of the testee, the assessor ought to be ready to present them explicitly as well as reflect critically on them.

Another issue concerns the problem of what is desirable to assess. In some countries it may be inappropriate to critique the values of the learner's social group or their openness to other belief systems. Thus, the very introduction of such assessment may be interpreted by learners as ideological authoritarianism. At the same time, if schooling is perceived as a system of the reinforcement of the values by which a society is expected to be guided, school as an institution has the right to promote e.g. openness and tolerance towards otherness (Byram 2008).

At university level, the problem of value imposition may be naturally counterbalanced by the voluntary nature of tertiary education, which prevents situations where a student would be forced to attend a course whose moral underpinnings clearly went against theirs. However, if intercultural assessment is used within compulsory education, the problem is very likely to surface with might. Tentative resolutions could be, *inter alia*: "careful selection of topics, [or] use of more than one examiner" (Byram 2008: 223). Yet, at present it is all too costly to be deemed realistic; hence, preference towards self-assessment, which may be conducted with the use of portfolios, and constitutes the safer solution for the time being (Byram 2008).

3.4 Summary

This chapter has demonstrated that the most important goal of intercultural language teaching is to incite learners to undergo *tertiary socialisation* (Byram 1998), i.e. empower them to acquire a new outlook on their own culture and ultimately, help them to assume *the third place* (Kramsch 1993), between native and target cultures. In the long run, that is meant to enable learners to act as intercultural speakers (Byram & Zarate 1997; Byram & Fleming 1998), intercultural diplomats (Corbett 2003), or intercultural mediators (Irishkanova et al. 2004).

Interestingly enough, the same role is ascribed to the intercultural teacher (Byram 1997; Damen 1987; Aleksandrowicz-Pędich 2005), who needs to develop adequate interpersonal, intercultural and language skills. According to Edelhoff (1997) and Byram (1997; 2008), the intercultural teacher's competence, alike their learners', embraces: (i) attitudes, (ii) knowledge and (iii) skills, which both groups are expected to use in order to facilitate the establishment of cohesive societies.

If the above-mentioned assumptions are to be realised, the teacher’s role in the classroom and their relation to the learner must be revisited (Zawadzka 2004; Aleksandrowicz-Pędich 2005; Bandura 2007). The native speaker teacher's task now is to distance themselves from their native language/culture and re-learn both while trying to relate to the learners’ language and culture (Byram and Fleming 1998); the non-native speaker teacher will need to do the reverse.

This, in turn, requires appropriate teacher training, which may be problematic to achieve in practice as e.g. in Poland, where university and teacher training college studies create opportunities for intercultural training, specific guidelines on the incorporation of intercultural components into particular courses have not been provided (Aleksandrowicz-Pędich 2005).

When it comes to the methodology of intercultural language teaching and actual classroom practice, teachers now have a repertoire of tools to utilise, including various approaches and techniques.

The ethnographic approach (Damen 1987; Barro et al. 1998; Sercu 1998; Corbett 2003) makes use of ethnographic techniques which include: recoding, comparing, translating and explaining experiences and is based on learning through detailed observation (Geertz 1973), both direct or indirect.

The experiential approach bases on constructivist learning, where – as Kramsch (1993) suggests – learners construct/reconstruct meanings implicitly built into the language that they come in contact with. This approach emphasises experience as much as the reflection which follows.

The dialogic approach (Bredella 1997) refers to the use of text, particularly literary texts, in order to increase learners' awareness of the cultural information implicit in textual data. Dialogic analysis helps learners trace both the process of text construction and decoding. In consequence, reading becomes (re)creation, determined by the culture-bound perceptive schemata of the reader.

The comparative approach (Byram 1989; Buttjes & Byram 1991; Byram 1997) requires a comparative analysis of the target culture and the learners' native culture by relating them to each other. In effect, learners are meant to "relativise and contextualise their own culture by experience of another" (Byram 1989: 49).

Techniques in teaching cultural awareness developed so far comprise: (i) drama (Cooper 1998), which allows students to test their performance skills in situations simulating real-life intercultural communication; (ii) dialogic techniques (Kramsch 1993), which include e.g. dialogic role-play or the use of film remakes; (iii) reflection techniques (Sercu (1998), e.g. critical incidents (Tomalin & Stempleski 1993; Sercu 1998; Corbett 2003), which foster reflective analysis of intercultural communicative situations and equip learners for lifelong intercultural development; and finally, (iv) ethnographic techniques (Sercu 1998; Barro et al. 1993; Corbett 2003), which enable learners to explore culture directly and examine cultural perceptions as well as actions.

Techniques in teaching linguistic awareness of culture focus on: (i) grammar, (ii) vocabulary, but also (iii) non-verbal communication and (iv) communicative styles (Sercu 1998).

However, what currently poses a problem is assessment of intercultural competence. Although areas of assessment have been roughly identified and appropriate assessment modes have been suggested, assessment of intercultural development is believed to bring about moral and practical issues.

Areas of assessment include: savoirs: savoirs (knowledge), savoir-faire (know-how), savoir-étre, savoir comprendre and savoir s'engager and savoir apprendre (Byram et al. 2002; Lussier et al. 2007).

From the discussion of possible assessment modes to date, the following conclusions have been drawn. By and large, *formative assessment*, which permits the observation of the process of learning in real-time, is favoured over *summative* as it is more illustrative of learners' affective and cognitive intercultural development (Lussier et al. 2007).

At the same time, both *direct* and *indirect* forms of assessment are acceptable for intercultural language teaching, depending on the circumstances to which they are applied. What must be born in mind, however, is that in intercultural teaching the direct/indirect dichotomy does not refer to the format of assessment, but rather to the degree to which assessment involves: observation of actual intercultural learning (direct), or examination of knowledge, which may only imply intercultural development (Lussier et al. 2007).

Other forms of assessment include *holistic* and *analytic* assessment and *teacher assessment* vs. *self-assessment.* Lussier et al. (2007) indicate that all the four types of assessment are complementary, but self-assessment is perceived as particularly useful by placing emphasis on learners' independence of the teacher and constituting yet another possible learning mode (Byram & Tost Planet 2000).

On a less positive note, the very idea of assessing intercultural skills incites moral issues which are likely to arise in the course of it. As Byram (2008) explicates, problems mostly relate to: what exactly is selected for assessment in a given setting as well as the assessor's criteria on the basis of which learners are judged. Even intercultural skills, when imposed on learners, may be viewed as a form of ideology, particularly within compulsory education. What is more, assessment of intercultural competence is bound to be subjective, while objectivising it more could turn out to be costly.

Therefore, Byram's (2008) temporary resolution to the above-mentioned concerns is a systematic implementation of self-assessment, which may counteract potential moral dilemmas relating to teacher assessment. In practical terms, such assessment may comprise the use of the following formats: learners' diaries, inventories of attitudes or portfolios.

CHAPTER FOUR

INFORMATION AND COMMUNICATION TECHNOLOGY IN COMPUTER ASSISTED LANGUAGE LEARNING

1. Introduction to CALL

1.1 CALL terminology

Computer assisted language learning may be viewed as part of a broader educational field, referred to as *e-learning*, which Bélisle defines as "(…) integrating the use of digital technology in setting up learning environments" (2007: 4). She goes on to add that "an elearning environment is one where the educational practices are partly or totally based on information and communication technology" (Belisle 2007: 4). Consequently, she distinguishes between different modes in which computer assisted learning can be applied: e.g. presential/distance learning, online/offline learning and solitary/group learning.

At the same time, Bélisle (2007) underlines the important role that learning at school has today, which is not only to equip learners with knowledge, but also teach them how to process the information that is available to them in order to produce even more knowledge. Thus, similarly to other scholars such as: Vygotsky (1978), Kolb (1984), Kramsch (1993) or Wood (1998), she sees learning as not only reception but also knowledge construction through "learning how to think" (Bélisle 2007: 3). All in all, Bélisle's definition of e-learning seems to perfectly encapsulate what modern language education stands for. Although it may focus on language instruction, its goals are more general-educational and they exceed the development of linguistic competence (cf. Chapter One).

The use of computers in foreign language teaching has been referred to through a number of acronyms. Perhaps, the most commonly used name is Computer Assisted Language Learning (CALL). Other terms include Computer Aided Learning (CAL), Computer-Based Teaching (CBT),

Web-Based Teaching (WBT) and Technology-Enhanced Language Learning (TELL) (Carrier 2006).

What merits notice is that particular acronyms refer to different stages in the development of computer assisted language education. For instance, CALL has general reference to computer-based language education, and as such it might be used interchangeably with CBT. CAL is even more general in that it denotes any kind of computer assisted learning, not necessarily language education, however, it puts emphasis on learning rather than teaching. WBT reflects the introduction of the internet into language teaching, and TELL encompasses the use of any modern technology in language education, including desktop computers, notebooks, netbooks, personal digital assistants or mobile phones. Therefore, it seems desirable to distinguish between the meaning of particular terms while using them in order to avoid misunderstandings.

For the purpose of discussing the implementation of computer-based technology in language education the term CALL will be used throughout this publication.

1.2 Computer assisted language learning: a historical overview

According to Warschauer (1996), the history of computer assisted language learning can be divided into three distinctly different periods, reflecting the then-dominant methodology as well as the technology which was harnessed in order to implement educational theories: (i) Behaviouristic CALL; (ii) Communicative CALL; and (iii) Integrative CALL.

Behaviouristic CALL was technologically initiated in the 1950s in the United States of America, where the first mainframe computers were constructed. They were machinery – the term acutely expresses the size and design of the devices – that possessed a number of limitations which precluded their large-scale use. Due to the enormous size of the hardware, which occupied spacious rooms and required intensive ventilation, the first computers could only be used at science laboratories or large universities (Warschauer 1996).

The computers were not only physically large but also complex in operation as they were not equipped with the keyboard or mouse, and – as Gajek (2002a) informs – data had to be fed in with the use of a special perforated tape called *teletype*. The role of the hard disk was played by large spools of magnetic tape, and the graphic user interface did not exist at all. Additionally, mainframe computers had an extremely limited capacity for data processing (Warschauer 1996).

Throughout the 1960s and 1970s large computers appeared at selected American universities, where they were employed in order to facilitate different strands of education, not only language learning. At the same time, foreign language pedagogy was informed by behaviourism, which suggested that language was a system of patterns which could be mastered through intensive mechanical repetition, i.e. habit formation. The teaching procedure thus focused on language drills, where learners repeated selected language chunks until they automatised verbal performance (Warschauer 1996).

As drilling required not only repetition but also systematic reinforcement, be it positive or negative, mainframe computers were used to administer mechanical drills. The computer would display language prompts to learners, whose task was to respond to them by selecting the correct answer. Afterwards, the computer would provide learners with immediate feedback. The computer seemed perfectly suited for the task as it was capable of repeatedly displaying the same language material without deterioration in quality, and it could additionally individualise the learning process by providing personalised feedback (Warschauer 1996).

An example of a complex computer system utilized in the behaviouristic era was the *PLATO* system of the 1960s, courseware developed and implemented at the University of Illinois in order to provide language instruction, practice and testing on a French course (Godwin-Jones 2001; Warschauer 1996). The name meant *Programmed Logic for Automatic Operations* (Gajek 2002a) and, as Ahmad et al. (1985) explain, the system provided learners with not only drilling activities, but also explanations of grammar points. Since both the system itself and the hardware which it required were extremely costly, similar solutions were very few and far between, and they were mostly limited to academic institutions across the USA.

Another project was the 1960s' *Van Campen* programme, run by Stanford University, which consisted in the delivery of a computer-mediated course in Russian at elementary level whose goal was to improve students' basic writing skills in the target language. Within the project the computer was used to display on the screen Russian and English characters as well as generate corresponding sounds (Ahmad et al. 1985; Gajek 2002a).

Perhaps, the most sophisticated project was run by Brigham Young University, which in the 1970s pioneered language teaching through the use of a computer text-based program, tape-recorded audio material and television content within a scheme called *TICCIT* (*Time-Shared, Interactive Computer Controlled Information Television*) (Gajek 2002a).

(ii) *Communicative CALL* emerged in 1970s and continued through the 1980s. Its inception was again related to new developments in both language teaching pedagogy as well as computer technology. The turn of the 1970s and the 1980s saw the introduction of the personal computer, which was sufficiently small in size to be used by individuals at home or school without infrastructural problems. In foreign language pedagogy the behaviourist theory had already crumbled under the pressure of criticism, but *drill-and-kill* software spread even more widely now along with the new computer technology (Warschauer 1996). Even programs published towards the end of the Communicative phase, such as the Polish software *e-Teacher*, followed the behaviouristic pattern (Gajek 2002a), the more that technologically, it no longer posed a sophisticated challenge.

At the same time, the emergence of Communicative Methodology incited calls for technology-enhanced skill practice, which was supposed to engage the learner in deeper interaction with target language samples. The answer to that was the emergence of text reconstruction software, e.g. *Gapmaster* and *SuperCloze*, or programs for paced reading, such as *MacReader*, *Reading Adventure* (Warschauer 1996) or *Storyboard* (Gajek 2002a).

With time, Communicative CALL involved language practice which focused less on form, and more on language use; grammar instruction was replaced with language manipulation; computerised feedback was also limited as accuracy was no longer considered as the major goal of teaching (Warschauer 2000). Ideally, computer software was to create opportunities for learners to create their own utterances in content-focused contexts (Underwood 1984) and expose them to target language input (Kern & Warschauer 2000).

Programs were developed which attempted to imitate real life communication, e.g. Weizenbaum's *Eliza*, which was supposed to give learners a chance to interact with the computer by typing responses to the messages that the program displayed (Osborne 2000). It must be underlined that *Eliza* did not provide any feedback on language quality. Instead, it responded to the user's messages in a manner which was supposed to mimic genuine communication. However, the program's communicative capacity was extremely limited and it could be easily tricked into revealing itself as a poorly-written algorithm for producing verbal responses to unpredictable messages generated by learners.

The major vice of Communicative CALL was that the software used within it only purported to facilitate communicative language practice, and in reality it was too limited to fulfil its role. What is more, it allowed learners to practice isolated language skills, whereas in real communication skills are inevitably integrated. It may be added that while language teaching at the time was meant to be task-based and include problem-solving (Warschauer 1996), Communicative CALL also spawned computer programs which were deprived of any content whatsoever, e.g. word-processing software, e.g. *WordPerfect*, *WordStar* or *Wang*, desktop publishers (Godwin-Jones 2001) or concordancers (Godwin-Jones 2001; Gajek 2002a; Krajka 2007).

(iii) The third CALL phase has spanned since the 1990s until the present day, and it is referred to as *Integrative CALL*. The very name derives from two features that characterize the manner in which computers are currently being implemented in foreign language teaching pedagogy.

One of them is the integration of all the four major language skills: listening, speaking, reading and writing within language practice. As in the communicative phase of CALL it was realised that communicative practice should not involve activities whereby particular language skills would be practised separately, a need appeared for new software which would help teachers and learners assess language skills holistically, ideally through tasks fostering genuine communication. This was possible due to the fact that the computer became a multimedia device, which was capable of displaying text, images, animations, and playing audio/video files. Another technological advancement that facilitated the integration of skills was the introduction of the CD-ROM, which increased the PC's storage capacity (Warschauer 1996).

The then-new technologies, in turn, permitted the creation of elaborate language learning packages, which contained a graphic interface that interconnected various media types through a system of links, menus and sub-menus, e.g. *Tell Me More*, *English+ one p@ck*, or *Euro Plus+ Reward*. Programs of that type also featured artificial intelligence and speech recognition mechanisms which enabled users to participate in conversations with the computer.

Additionally, both the introduction of multimedia and optical discs, led to the development of a number of advanced authoring suites, e.g. *Toolbook*, *HyperCard* and *Macromind Director*, which allowed those who wished to design their own language teaching materials to use hypermedia functionality, a system of clickable links through which various media were interconnected. Simultaneously, word-processing substantially advanced (Osborne 2000; Warschauer 1996).

The other of the two major features from which the *Integrative CALL* phase takes its name is internet access. The internet, which was introduced to language teaching in the 1990s (Alderson and Bachman 2007), has made it possible for learners to engage in real communication with other human beings (Kern & Warschauer 2000). Therefore, communication does not need to be simulated; present-day computer mediated communication (CMC) activities facilitate tele-collaboration, enable learners to publish their own content and offer access to a wealth of information (Warschauer 1996; 2000). E-mail, web forums, blogs and discussion groups allow asynchronous communication, whereas chat rooms and web communicators permit communication in real time.

By and large, it can be stated that modern computers do not only integrate language skills, but they themselves have become integrated into the language learning process. What is more, since international communication is to a large degree mediated by computer technology (Graddol 2006), it is inevitable that communicative practice in the foreign language classroom involves some form of ICT use. In Warschauer and Healey's (1998) view, integrative CALL involves permanent language practice through technology, whereby learners learn the target language communication as much as the technology behind it. However, as Bax (2003) observes, it is not a very common approach yet, and daily foreign language practice is rarely fully integrative.

On hindsight, the history of computer assisted language learning can be presented as a steady progression from accuracy-focused language practice towards genuine communication. In the behaviourist phase, the focus was mostly on language accuracy, the use of mechanical drills and the provision of instant feedback. Bax (2003), who reviewed Warschauer's (1996) version of CALL history, names this phase *Restrictive CALL*, due to the limitations it had in terms of the kind of language practice that it allowed, the roles that it attributed to the teacher and learners involved, and the range of feedback that it provided.

Communicative phase consisted in deep-level language manipulation, the performance of inferential tasks and exposure to input. Bax (2003) calls this phase *Open* CALL as he believes that it opened language practice towards new teacher and learner roles, new software types and new kinds of feedback.

The integrative phase prioritises human-human interaction and access to various discourse communities as the core of language learning (Kern & Warschauer 2000) but, as Warschauer (2000) underlines, it also creates an opportunity for learners to develop social agency, i.e. to produce language content addressed to selected real audiences with the intention to exert some impact on them, e.g. by online publishing. That is why, Kern and Warschauer (2000) re-label Warschauer's (1996) originally proposed CALL phases as: Structural, Cognitive, and Sociocognitive, respectively.

1.3 Typology of CALL software

Gajek (2007) classifies computer assisted language learning (CALL) software within four categories: (i) *language teaching/learning packages*; (ii) *authoring tools*; (iii) *utilities*; and (iv) *virtual learning environments (VLEs)*. However, this list is only a presentation of the major CALL software types, and Gajek (2002a) herself expands it through the addition of: coursebook supplements, electronic dictionaries, interactive stories and parsers.

(i) *Language teaching/learning packages*, also known as language teaching/learning suites or bundles, are sophisticated computer programs, normally distributed on optical discs, CDs or DVDs, which offer language practice in the four major language skills: listening, speaking, reading and writing. They are also attractively designed in that they offer a range of multimedia materials for language education, including: text, still images, animations, videos, audio clips, and web-based features, e.g. access to purpose-built internet forums or chat rooms. Programs of this kind incorporate the latest computer technology, e.g. voice recognition functionalities or artificial intelligence algorithms, which are to increase their educational value. Examples of such programs are: *Euro Plus+ Reward, Tell Me More, English One P@ck, Professor Henry* or *Talk to Me*. What is worth adding is that CALL packages offer complete language courses, organized into units, which are accompanied by review exercises and ready-made tests. Some of them are electronic versions of printed coursebooks, e.g. *Euro Plus+ Reward*, whose name derives from the *Reward* coursebook series by Greenall (1994).

Gajek (2007) explains that such software in the European context is very costly as due to the diversity of teaching and learning needs and objectives on local European markets, it needs to be customized for specific target audiences, which increases costs. In addition, CALL bundles may pose a problem in terms of the requirements that they make towards the quality of the computer hardware on which they are fully operational. In other words, they necessitate the use of good-quality computers, which are also expensive.

Moreover, CALL packages are commercially produced, thus, the features which they are equipped with are frequently superordinate to the educational value that they represent. That is why they have to be carefully evaluated before use (Gajek 2007). To some extent, the problem is alleviated by the system of recommendations which the Polish Ministry of Education officially grants to programs that successfully undergo ministerial verification – such recommended programs may be more trustworthy.

CALL packages can be used by learners on an individual or self-study basis. However, they may also be used in the classroom, even if it is equipped with only a single computer. The programs normally cover a whole range of language proficiency levels, and may be most useful for educational institutions (Gajek 2002a).

(ii) *Authoring tools* are computer programs which do not offer any language teaching/learning content per se. Their function is to provide foreign language teachers, or materials writers, with templates of language teaching/learning activities and tests that can be filled with desirable content. The formats that they embrace are: crosswords, gap-filling tasks, matching tasks, multiple-choice tasks, true/false tasks, short-answer quizzes, cloze reading tasks and others. The usefulness of the programs lies in the fact that even teachers who are not familiar with computer programming languages/scripts can actually author their own computer materials by using a user-friendly interface. The only element that they need to concentrate on is the preparation of appropriate content. Programs of this kind may be available online free-of-charge, as is the case with the Hot Potatoes application, which can be used for free for educational purposes. They may also be used online, as in the case of *WebAuthor*, or they may have to be obtained commercially, e.g. *Testmaker* or *Respondus*. It is easily noticeable that programs of this kind focus on test authoring, thus, they may be used to prepare both online/offline class tests or classroom quizzes whose function would be not so much to assess learners' knowledge but rather to educate them.

At the same time, it must be added that even relatively aged versions of authoring suites, such as Hot Potatoes, permit the incorporation of media other than text into the material authored. Thus, such programs make it possible to prepare not only reading but also listening comprehension tasks, tasks related to pictorial content or even tasks based on video footage (Gajek 2007).

(iii) *Computer utilities* are programs that are not produced for the purpose of language education, but they play an important part in computer assisted foreign teaching and learning. Generally speaking, these are programs that help the user perform various operations, such as text, audio or video editing as well as computations and graph editing (Gajek 2007). Some of these programs may be extremely sophisticated both in format and functionality, e.g. the so-called office suites such as *Microsoft Office*, *Libré Office* or *Star Office*. Others are stand-alone applications, such as web page editors, or software incorporated into the operational system and by default pre-installed on brand-new computers. Examples of the latter would be: *Microsoft Paint*, a basic application for image processing or *Microsoft Windows Movie Maker*, a simple video editor.

Gajek (2002a) states that tasks prepared with and administered in a word processor are basically electronic versions of tasks that are traditionally performed with the use of pen and paper. However, she observes that modern word processors can manage a system of hyperlinks through which text can be easily combined with other media, including audio files, video clips and animations. If that functionality is used by the teacher, a simple text-based activity becomes a multimedia task, which facilitates learning through multi-channel exposure and a combination of skills.

Graphic editors, such as *Paint*, can be used to facilitate teaching a foreign language to children, especially those at the age of 4-12. By implementing colorful graphics for input presentation the teacher diversifies learning, and motivates children, who are given an opportunity to learn through play. This kind of learning is particularly effective in teaching basic language, such as colours and numbers (Gajek 2002a).

Another example of computer utilities may be multimedia presentation programs such as *PowerPoint*, which is part of the *Microsoft Office* bundle or *Libré Impress*, which is a component of the *Libré Office* suite. Programs of this kind help the teacher visualise what is being taught through the use of animated text, symbols and animations, which can be combined with audio and video cues. It is all compiled into a single presentation file which can be played on a computer connected to a multimedia projector. As Gajek (2002a) warns, a multimedia presentation is not interactive in format per se, and much depends on how it is performed. However, if well thought-out and organized, it may be a very helpful teaching aid, which may additionally have a motivational effect on the recipients. It is worth adding that multimedia presentations can be prepared by learners, who – by engaging in the task – can practice not only the target language but also media-related skills (Gajek 2002a).

(iv) *Virtual Learning Systems*, alternatively referred to as Learning Management Systems, are complex learning platforms based on online technology, which are available to teachers, students and learners twenty-four hours a day, and which play the role of an electronic classroom, a database of materials, an electronic school register, a test authoring/administering tool, a communication centre for learners, teachers, school authorities and parents, and a content-sharing medium (Atkinson & Davies 2008).

VLEs can be used in order to run course administration, deliver course content, hold practice sessions based on interaction with materials and people, organise pre-test reviews, test learners and provide feedback. Examples of this kind of software are *WebCT* and *Questionmark* (Chapelle & Douglas 2006) or *Moodle* (Cole & Foster 2007; Gajek 2007). The popularity of virtual learning environments is growing due to increasing interest in electronic course delivery or blended learning courses, where face-to-face instruction is combined with online teaching (Masie 2006; Motteram & Sharma 2009).

The lay-out of VLEs is modular, thus, specific functionalities may either be added to or deducted from what is ultimately offered to the audience involved. VLEs may be managed even without the knowledge of computer programming as they are based on a system of customisable templates. However, most frequently teachers who intend to use them need either proper training or have to self-explore the user's manual; perhaps, with the help of online user forums, where useful information may be obtained from those who operate particular VLEs in their daily practice. Another possibility may be the commissioning of a professional ICT technician who would be responsible for installing and maintaining the platform (Gajek 2007).

The remaining types of CALL software encompass a variety of program types. Coursebook supplements are programs which accompany books and provide multimedia-based activities that enrich the material offered within the coursebooks that they are attached to.

Electronic dictionaries are enhanced with audio clips which supply samples of pronunciation. Besides, thanks to the in-built search engines, they seriously reduce the time that learners need to locate an entry that they are looking for, whereby learners' reading efficiency is increased. In addition, they may be used to look up the meaning of words while typing texts (Gajek 2002a).

Interactive stories are programs that display the text of a story as well as provide its audio version. Thus, they enable learners to read and listen to a text simultaneously. What is more, interactive stories are aleatory stories at the same time in that while reading them learners can take decisions that influence the way in which the stories unfold. This reading mode helps learners create multiple stories out of one core story by following the different action paths available. It may be posited that in such stories the reader interacts with the content. An additional advantage of interactive stories is the presence of audio-visual clues that they are often accompanied by (Gajek 2002a).

Finally, parsers are computer programs that analyse sentence structure and recognise the grammatical functions of particular words by generating derivational trees. Gajek (2002a) cites a program called *Visual Interactive*

Syntax Learning as an example but she adds that the technology behind parsers is rather underdeveloped and the degree to which this kind of software can handle the task that it has been designed for is limited. However, it is an interesting alternative to the blackboard or coursebook with which the teaching of grammar may be enhanced. Parsers visualise grammar and can be more motivating for learners in that they break away from the routine of teacher-centred instruction.

2. ICT-based work modes

2.1 Blended learning: terminology and set-ups

Terminology that is used with reference to the learning modes supported by information and communication technology comprises a number of terms which are either used interchangeably or in separation. As Mason and Rennie (2008) claim, no unanimous agreement has been reached as to the referential scope of particular expressions, hence the discrepancies between the ways in which specific terminology is used.

Computer-mediated learning as such can be named: *distributed learning* (Motteram & Sharma 2009: Mason & Rennie 2008), *distance learning* (Lanham & Zhou 2003), *e-learning* (Reid-Young 2003; Neumeier 2005) and *blended learning* (Silverwood 2007; Slowman 2007; Mason & Rennie 2008), or *b-learning* (Reid-Young 2003).

At first, it must be stated that the above-listed names, irrespective of how they are perceived, are all used in either complete opposition or at least in some form of relation to *face-to-face (f2f) learning*, which is conventional learning that does not involve any use of technology. Neumeier (2005) defines *f2f learning* as "an instructional environment that works in a classroom-based or other setting, without the help of computers" (Neumeier 2005: 164). However, she immediately adds that in today's classroom it is increasingly difficult not to come across any technology. The same appears to have been observed by Heinze and Procter (2004), who imply that e.g. the distinction between *f2f* and *online learning* is blurred by the multiple options that both modes offer.

Distributed learning appears to be the broadest in scope out of the terms listed above as it denotes an interactive and collaborative context where particular learners can increase their learning efficiency by customizing the learning modes that they use in accordance with their preferred learning styles (Tarleton State University 2004).

On the one hand this definition of distributed learning is so broad that it might be inclusive of all the other afore-mentioned types of learning, i.e.

distance learning, e-learning and f2f learning and blended learning. On the other hand Mason and Rennie (2008) observe that in particular circumstances it might, for instance, involve e-learning and distance learning, but exclude face-to-face learning.

Interestingly enough, Tarleton State University (2004) seems to equate distributed learning with the use of technology as it implies that truly varied, learner-oriented learning can only occur if it is supported by technological means.

Distance learning signifies learning modes that give learners opportunities to learn independently, irrespective of time and setting. Distance learning involves dislocation, thus it is possible outside the contexts which have traditionally been associated with education: the classroom, the school library or school at large (Mason & Rennie 2008).

As Gajek proposes, it may happen if the EFL classroom – or school – is not equipped with computer technology. In such a case, learners may use the language lesson only for pre- or post-computer-based work, while the very technology will be implemented outside school, e.g. at home (Gajek 2009).

Krajka (2007) supports this view of Gajek by proposing that this kind of work mode is particularly suitable in contexts where teachers/learners have access to "more advanced learning solutions such as Moodle (…)" (Krajka 2007: 271). *Moodle* is an example of a Learning Management System (LMS), otherwise known as a Virtual Learning Environment (VLE), which allows teachers to transfer in-class activities to contexts outside school via -– *nomen omen* – distance learning. In this manner teachers can make tasks such as: "treasure hunts, reading/listening comprehension activities grammar presentation and practice tasks" (Krajka 2007: 271) available to learners in out-of-class locations.

Should internet connectivity be unavailable to learners outside school, Krajka and Grudzińska (2002) propose that relevant online content is saved and distributed to learners so that they can perform relevant tasks offline. Alternatively, Gajek (2009) suggests that certain tasks might also be performed in ICT lessons at school, provided that the teacher in charge of the subject accepts it. After the computer has been used, learners can report on the work done in a language lesson.

What stems from the afore-cited definitions of distributed and distance learning is that the latter can be perceived as a possible component of the former. In other words, learners may flexibly optimise their work and tailor whatever learning modes they use to their own needs either on the spot (offline) or in distant locations (online) (Mason & Rennie 2008).

E-learning, whose full name is *electronic learning*, denotes any kind of educational context where technology aids the learning process (Tavangarian et al. 2004). It will, therefore, involve the use of: computers; notebooks; netbooks; networking, e.g. local area networks or the internet; personal digital assistants; or mobile phones. However, due to increased access to the internet both in and outside school, more and more frequently e-learning is being paralleled to online learning, despite the fact that it originally meant simply the use of electronics. An extreme example of that stance comes from McDonnell and Connolly (2007), who adamantly discredit the *DynEd CALL system*, which they discuss, as a form of e-learning, simply on the grounds that it does not require permanent access to the internet.

Blended learning can be placed somewhere between face-to-face learning and e-learning in that it is a hybrid learning mode which marries the two approaches. Some scholars view e-learning here as primarily *online learning*, e.g. Mason and Rennie (2008). Others perceive it more generally as the use of computer technology, as illustrated by the definition of blended learning offered by Graham, who states that it is an amalgamation of "face-to-face instruction with computer-mediated instruction" (Graham 2007).

The constituent elements of blended learning can be mixed in different proportions, with f2f tuition being a complement to online learning, and vice versa. For instance, McDonnell and Connolly (2007) have designed a course in Aviation English where 75% of instruction is delivered through e-learning, and 25% is face-to-face teaching.

Bañados (2005) claims that the value of blended learning lies in its adaptability to various teaching/learning circumstances, and any combination of online and f2f learning may be effective, as long as it takes "the individual subjects, contexts and objectives" (Bañados 2005: 164) into account.

Neumeier (2005) states that the level of integration between f2f and online learning may not be pre-set at all, and the proportions may depend on learners' decision during the course. That is why, she distinguishes between high level integration, where the use of technology is obligatory, and low level integration, where e-learning is only a possible option.

To summarise the discussion of various ICT-enhanced learning modes, Mason and Rennie (2008) believe that distributed learning is a mode of education which: involves a variety of media; is learner-centred; and allows learners to study locally or remotely at a selected time. It may also supplement f2f courses, create opportunities for distance education or take the form of online education, exclusively. Hence, the relationship between f2f learning, e-learning, distance learning, blended learning and distributed learning in Mason and Rennie's view is graphically illustrated as follows:

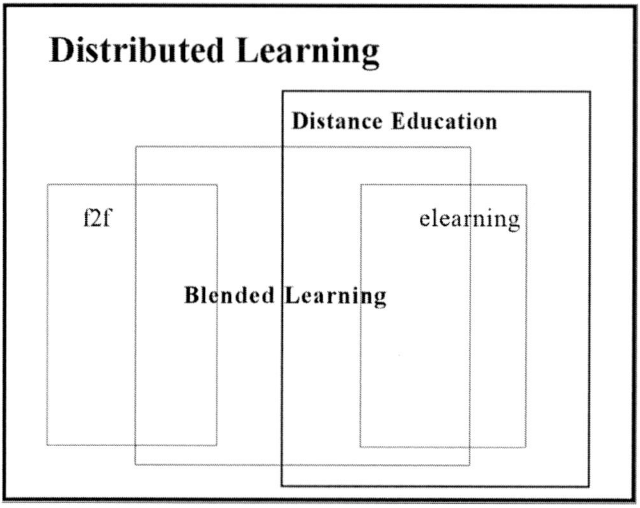

Fig. 4-1

Blend types and approaches to course design. The views of *blended learning* generally fall into two categories: broad and narrow. The broad definition of BL covers the use of technology as such in traditional face-to-face courses. Those who perceive BL in this manner are Salaberry (2001), Claypole (2003) and Mason and Rennie (2008). According to them, blended learning may manifest itself in the use of the tape recorder, the CD-player as well as the computer or the interactive whiteboard.

Other examples of broad definitions of blended learning (BL) are also presented by Neumeier, who sees BL as "any learning context that involves computer assisted learning" (Neumeier 2005: 164); and Bañados, who states that it is "a combination of technology and classroom instruction in a flexible approach to learning that recognizes the benefits of delivering some training and assessment online but also uses other modes to make up a complete training program which can improve learning outcomes and/or save costs" (Bañados 2006: 534).

A narrower view of blended learning reduces it to "blending f2f with web-based learning" (Motteram & Sharma 2009: 91). It appears that this definition in not inclusive of computer-based techniques which do not directly involve the use of the internet, thus, it will not encompass the implementation of CALL packages, computerised quizzes and other applications which can be run from the computer hard drive or within the Local Area Network (LAN).

Motteram and Sharma (2009) review the contexts to which the term has been applied and demonstrate that *blended learning* can refer to three distinct learning blends, each somehow related to technology: (i) f2f and online teaching; (ii) combination of technologies; (iii) real world and virtual world instruction.

(i) *F2f and online teaching* stands for the most common understanding of *blended learning* in modern education as it features the blending of online technology, which normally is utilized to facilitate distance learning and on-the-spot instruction, delivered in the classroom (Frydrychova Klimova 2008). The online technology that is made use of here currently involves VLE (Virtual Learning Environment) platforms, such as Moodle (Modular Object-Oriented Dynamic Learning Environment) (Brandl 2005). As Motteram and Sharma (2009) explain, in the course of online learning, learners typically interact with materials which their teachers post to VLEs. They can also communicate with their colleagues or teachers via synchronous communication tools, e.g. chat rooms, or asynchronous communication channels, e.g. email, forums or bulletin boards.

The two components of the blend may serve different purposes. For instance, classroom time may be used for dealing with problem areas of the target language as well as activities that involve active participation, e.g. fluency-focused, content-oriented tasks. The online component may be used in order to facilitate what Mason and Rennie (2008) defined as distributed learning, i.e. learning where students may need to take individual decisions on the resources and study modes used with a view to increasing learning efficiency. Online tasks can also feature close-ended language tests, where the computer can deliver correct feedback.

(ii) Blended learning can also mean teaching where various technology-enhanced media and tools are mixed to produce the most optimal effect. In this learning mode instruction may be held exclusively online, with course delivery, and teacher-learner communication being realised through relevant technologies, e.g. VLEs and other communication tools (Motteram & Sharma 2009). Mason and Rennie (2008) cite Salmon's term *e-tivities* as an umbrella term for activities that involve this kind of blend. It must be added that Frydrychova Klimova (2008) has envisaged the possibility of expanding the scope of this type of blend by including textbook materials within the media and tools which can be utilised within e-learning environments.

(iii) A relatively recent interpretation of blended learning has been offered by a German teacher working for a language school, whose case is discussed by Mason and Rennie (2008). They state that in this case the teacher runs two complementary lessons on the same topic which differ in terms of the setting in which the learning takes place. They name this approach "real world plus virtual world" (Mason & Rennie 2008: 91) teaching, and explain that the first lesson is a traditional f2f teaching session held in the classroom, while the other is a continuation which occurs in a virtual world created through technology. The latter can be done in Philip Rosedale's *Second Life* – a virtual environment which allows individuals to live a second life by adopting a new identity through the creation of a virtual character, complete with a new appearance, a biography and a network of social relations.

The difference between any other form of online learning and this one lies in the dual nature of the learning process that it entails: it is virtual in two ways: (i) it takes place online, but it also (ii) enables learners to learn while adopting a new identity. This kind of instruction gives learners an opportunity to 'virtualise' themselves (Mason & Rennie 2008).

Blended course designs. Sharma and Barrett (2007) divide blended learning courses into: (i) *dual track* courses, (ii) *integrated* courses, and (iii) courses with *embedded* technology.

(i) *Dual track courses* are characterised by the dual character of the learning process. On the one hand learners receive instruction from the teacher in face-to-face, classroom-based lessons; on the other hand they can follow their own learning path through self-study. Both tracks may either be complementary to each other, or they may be independent.

(ii) In *integrated BL*, learners work with the teacher in the classroom on the subject matter for the study of which they prepare on their own, with the use of technology. Alternatively, they may be requested to perform technology-enhanced consolidation activities after a classroom lesson that they have already participated in (Sharma & Barrett 2007).

(iii) The third possible course design is based on *embedded technology*, i.e. technology which is utilized in the very classroom. The technology itself may vary from relatively obvious tools, such as CD-ROMs, to more sophisticated multimedia solutions. e.g. the use of websites, online communicators or interactive whiteboards (Sharma & Barrett 2007).

Teacher roles in BL. The various roles that teachers may play in blended learning contexts are largely determined by two factors: the degree to which teachers rely on ready-made content, activity formats and platforms for course delivery; and the extent to which they design such products on their own, perhaps with the assistance of ICT technicians.

Bañados (2005) discusses a number of roles which teachers may adopt in BL courses on the *B-Learning English Program*, implemented at Universidad de Concepción in Chile. The roles are not automatically assumed by all teachers involved in BL courses, but they are illustrative of the possible work modes that blended learning may entail. Those roles encompass: (i) *material designer and developer*, (ii) *script writer*, (iii) *manager and producer of media resources*, (iv) *work flow manager*, (v) *online tutor*, and (vi) *manager of the language learning environment*. The first four roles characterize the work that teachers have to perform while preparing BL resources or courseware; the remaining two refer to how they act during a blended learning course.

(i) A *material designer and developer* is responsible for reviewing available computer assisted language learning software in search of inspiration which would help them adjust existing methods and technologies to the objectives of the course that they are intending to design and run. Alternatively, they may take note of new methods or ideas that might be suggested to the technicians who would be responsible for programming and technically managing the BL course (Bañados 2005).

(ii) A *script writer*'s task is to translate the original idea of the course scenario into particular audio and video materials that learners will work with while participating in the course. Scripting video clips and audio recordings will not only involve planning the storyline but also the language items which are supposed to be developed through the scripted activities as well as other areas of knowledge, e.g. culture (Bañados 2005).

(iii) Teachers also need to be active at the production stage, when the scripted multimedia materials are being recorded. In this case teachers function as *managers and producers of media resources*. They have to inform those involved in the production, e.g. the performers, how specific scripts are supposed to be acted out, and the guidelines which teachers may need to supply may include: hints on the behaviour of particular characters, or the quality of the language used. Managing content preparation is a complex process, which means that teachers will inevitably have to participate in the preparation, production and editing of materials (Bañados 2005).

(iv) Before the final product emerges, teachers need to coordinate the project work, e.g. mediate between the teaching team and the designers. Therefore, they play the role of *work flow managers*. The degree to which the intentions of the former group are clearly communicated to the latter affects the quality of the courseware materials that emerge out of the production process. That is why, although Bañados (2005) claims that fulfilling this role may take a long time, the work involved here must be performed with attention to detail.

(v) After courseware has been prepared, the teacher will have to take responsibility for the tuition process per se. Thus, the teacher becomes an *online tutor* (Neumeier 2005). It is important to note that the word *tutor* is very adequate to the role that teachers play in BL courses as their major responsibility is to support learner's independence. Teachers are expected to establish and maintain effective communication with the learners, and offer the necessary support. This work mode will involve the use of electronic tools in order to: guide learners through tasks which they find challenging, incite online communication and motivate learners to perform tasks. A tutor is in addition responsible for assessment, which includes the provision of feedback and reporting on learners' progress. In fact, in BL teachers constantly switch from f2f teaching to online tutoring, with the latter consuming more time than the former (Bañados 2005).

(vi) Finally, teachers can act as *managers of the language learning environment* that they create through blended learning, both online and in the classroom. This means that teachers have to see to their students' work. They have to establish close cooperation with their learners, through which they would be able to identify students' problems, offer suggestions, and facilitate independent learning through the creation of a stress-free atmosphere. However, learner autonomy, which is to be promoted through BL, cannot boil down to the teacher leaving learners to their own devices. Instead, the teacher must actively help learners to successfully follow strategies that they will best benefit from.

If blended learning is indeed to lead to the creation of a learner-friendly environment, conducive to effective learning, it must be well planned and applied with regard to both components that it embraces: e-learning and f2f learning. Thus, the teacher has to ensure that e-learning and f2f instruction mutually consolidate (Bañados 2005).

As Neumeier (2005) adds, a vital element of the interplay between f2f and e-learning is the language teaching methodology selected by the teacher. She notes that f2f teaching is more flexible in that it allows the teacher to use a wide range of teaching methods which have so far been developed. At the same time, she maintains that despite all the technology involved, e-learning is rather restricted as to what can actually be done. Thus, she believes that the teacher is meant to think of ways in which e-learning may be diversified, e.g. through increased use of synchronous communication tools, which permit authentic communicative practice, or by introducing more communication to the f2f component in order to make up for its shortage in online contexts.

Hinkelman (2005) believes that both f2f and e-learning modes can be blended effectively through the creation of a more flexible interactive learning environment which would involve the use of wireless technology and moveable classroom furniture. In such a case, she claims that learners and teachers will be able to engage in "simultaneous online/face-to-face activities" (Hinkelman 2005: 25), based on a wide range of materials.

2.2 In-class work modes

Since modern information and communication technology is versatile with regard to the possible modes of usage which it offers and the purposes which it can serve in language education, computer-enhanced language learning in the classroom may be organized in a variety of ways, depending on the number of computers available and the setting in which they are used. The three basic work modes comprise: (i) *a single computer in class*; (ii) *work in the computer suite*; and (iii) *in-class laptop-based work.*

(i) *A single computer in class.* One of the options is to organize a lesson in which learners make use of only a single computer in the classroom. Gajek (2009) suggests that even one computer can be effectively used in the foreign language classroom in order to facilitate lock-step or group work.

Perhaps the most common way of using a single computer is to connect it to the multimedia projector, whereby it takes on the function of a variety of otherwise separate projected teaching aids, such as: the tape-recorder, the video player, the CD/DVD player; or non-projected aids, e.g. the blackboard or pictorial materials: flashcards, images, maps, posters and charts. This work mode is particularly suitable for the presentation of audio-visual materials other than text as off-screen reading is far from convenient (Gajek 2009).

If it is equipped with loudspeakers, a single computer may serve as an audio media centre, through which listening texts can be played back in the classroom. If it is connected to the web camera and the microphone, it may also be used as a communication tool for synchronous communication, e.g. in telecollaboration projects. Alternatively, it may play the role of an electronic dictionary or a resource centre, particularly when an internet connection is available (Gajek 2009).

A single computer can be connected to the interactive whiteboard. In this way the computer becomes a powerful tool for displaying multimedia presentations as well as an instrument which may be used for activities in which the teacher and learners interact with the content displayed. This kind of set-up may be used with commercially available interactive language learning software or materials prepared by the teacher (Gajek 2009).

One more possibility is to use a single computer as a testing centre, which is permitted by professionally designed virtual testing systems. They normally consist of a set of remote controlled key pads through which learners select and send their responses to questions displayed on a mounted screen. The computer works not only as a test delivery device but also a data processor as it calculates scores, compiles statistics and displays feedback. What is more, it is possible that the computer can select follow-up activities on the basis of the scores obtained by the learners (Gajek 2009).

As Siemieniecki (1997) indicates that an increase in the number of computers at school does not necessarily translate into more effective usage, a single computer in the classroom may, contrary to appearance, facilitate learning more than when a number of computers are being used in a computer suite. It allows learners to work individually, when they take turns to perform specific tasks on the computer, or in groups. The software that Gajek (2002a) recommends for this particular work mode ranges from text processors to CALL packages, web applications, multimedia presentation programs or email clients.

The advantages of language work based on a single computer encompass: the diversification of teaching content through multimedia; increased learner motivation; more teacher control over computer-aided language work; and a reduction in technophobia on the part of those learners who have limited computer literacy (Gajek 2002a).

(ii) *Work in a computer suite.* Teachers my organize CALL lessons in the computer suite, in which case individual learners have the opportunity to work at their own computers. This work mode enables learners to become more autonomous in their learning as they frequently have to take decisions that affect the way their work progresses and the learning strategies that they employ. In other words, their work is highly individualised. The danger inherent in this class arrangement is the fact that particular learners are very likely to work at their own pace, thus, they are bound to complete tasks at different times, which may result in discipline problems (Gajek 2009).

Gajek (2009) warns that the autonomy that learners can enjoy here will not automatically work to their advantage, and especially the less computer literate learners may feel abandoned in a situation in which they may require the teacher's assistance. Gajek (ibid.) maintains that the teacher who works in the computer suite ought to engage learners in cooperation so that they maximize the benefit that they may gain from the presence of their colleagues in the classroom. To that end, learners might be asked to engage in pair work or group work.

As a matter of fact, the student grouping utilised by teachers in the computer suite will, to a large extent, be determined by the classroom arrangement, as discussed by Teeler and Gray (2000), Dudeney (2000) and Krajka (2007). Teeler and Gray (2000) present two examples of the least appropriate lay-outs, which are, nevertheless, traditionally used in the computer suite. One of them involves a U-shaped arrangement of computer stations around the class, with the teacher's computer placed at the open end of the figure. The other one places the teacher's computer in the front of the class, with the learners seated at computer stations arranged in rows in a fashion which resembles the traditional lay-out of desks in the regular classroom. Although both lay-outs might enable the teacher to keep an eye-contact with the learners, they do not stimulate learner-learner interaction, which is crucial to communication. Krajka (2007) believes that for the benefit of EFL learners, human-computer interaction in the computer suite ought to be accompanied by human-human communication and cooperation.

Therefore, both the afore-mentioned classroom lay-outs might be replaced by more pro-communication set-ups, such as the ones offered by Teeler and Gray (2000) or Dudeney (2000). Teeler and Gray's (2000) model has learners seated in small groups around isolated computer stations dispersed across the classroom, with the teacher placed in the front-side corner.

In Dudeney's (2000) first conception, learners are supposed to be seated in pairs round a double row of back-to-back computers located in the centre of the computer suite, with the teacher's computer station placed in the corner at the front of the class. Alternatively, he suggests that learners be seated in pairs at single computers positioned at the walls around the computers suite, with the teacher stationed in either of the front corners and a large work space remaining in the centre of the classroom. While the former set-up is likely to foster group work or pair work, the latter is aimed at stimulating pair work, mostly.

Krajka (2007) proposes another two possible modifications of the lay-outs discussed which would stimulate more human-human interaction in the computer-assisted language classroom. He states that in case of overcrowding, more students can be seated at one computer, with the caveat that each of them is assigned a clearly-defined role and thus remains active. Alternatively, learners can work with a small number of computers in class on a canon basis, where groups of students succeed one another at a computer station while the others are performing tasks which do not require computer access – this solution can also serve teachers and learners in a single-computer-in-class design.

CALL in the computer suite involves the use of either the local area network (LAN) or the internet, and it may be based on the following software: text processors, CALL packages, LAN communication tools, and internet resources, including communication tools used for the purpose of telecollaboration (Gajek 2002a).

(iii) *In-class laptop-based work.* Gajek (2009) differentiates between the computer suite, where learners work on individual computers, and a classroom where each learner is equipped with a laptop connected to the internet. In the latter case the laptop becomes a multi-purpose tool, which every learner can use both in and outside school. Moreover, if laptops are used, no learner is disadvantaged by the lack of access to information and communication technology on a daily basis, because the school laptop can be taken home. According to Warschauer (2002), in such a case learners do not fall victim to the digital divide, and their educational opportunities are levelled.

Laptops can be used as: notebooks; portable resources based on online services; means of communication between the teacher and their learners; electronic registers as well as a course/work books, if the teacher makes use of a VLE platform in order to distribute teaching materials and activities (Gajek 2009).

Out-of-class work. If the EFL classroom is not equipped with computer technology, learners may use a f2f lesson for pre- or post-computer-use work. Thus, they may prepare for the tasks that they will do on a computer in the library or outside school, e.g. at home (Gajek 2009).

As it has been mentioned before, Krajka (2007) posits that out-of-class work may be facilitated by Virtual Learning Environments (VLEs), which permit distance learning. He demonstrates that VLEs offer teachers an opportunity to develop a wide range of tasks which will develop particular language skills, including reading/listening comprehension and grammar activities, as well as tasks such as treasure hunts, which enable learners to complete assignments by integrating the language skills that they already possess.

Out-of-class work may also be understood differently, as work which learners perform largely outside the language classroom, e.g. in other lessons at school – subject to teacher-teacher agreement – and on which they subsequently report (Gajek 2009).

A third option can be implemented if students do not have access to the internet outside school at all, which at present is decreasingly likely. In such a case, they can, nevertheless, perform particular tasks by using computer technology, but they will do it in an off-line mode (Krajka & Grudzińska 2002).

The purposes of ICT in the EFL classroom. Carrier (2006) discusses the concept of digital convergence, which refers to the fact that modern computers are capable of delivering content which has previously required the use of coursebooks, worksheets and video clips. In other words, the multimedia that computers successfully handle today can replace the traditional teaching aids, including: the blackboard, the tape player, the overhead projector or the photocopier.

Gajek (2007) supports Carrier's view as she observes that information and communication technology has developed to such an extent today that it is possible to replace with it any other teaching aid which has hitherto been used in the foreign language classroom. She also lists the purposes for which ICT can be harnessed when it is supposed to facilitate language work, which are: content presentation, knowledge consolidation, documenting learners' knowledge, learning support, communication and testing.

For presentation purposes, web-based content or materials stored on optical discs can be used, including: textual materials, audio recordings, e.g. podcasts; filmic materials, e.g. films or virals; as well as graphics. They can all be incorporated into multimedia presentations, which can also be used to present new language material.

Similarly, consolidation work can include a combination of multimedia, e.g.: text, audio and video, which can be integrated within interactive activities, complete with automated instant feedback.

Learners' knowledge of the target language and culture can be documented through the use of multimedia presentations, text editors, web pages or audio-video files.

Computers may be additionally used to support language learning through the utilisation of electronic dictionaries, encyclopaedias, thesauri, language corpora, concordancing utilities and news reports, delivered by newspaper websites or information agencies.

Computers can also serve as communication tools, which can either permit synchronous communication through chat, audio-video communicators and video conferencing software; or asynchronous communication, which can be conducted through email, discussion forums, virtual learning platforms or discussion groups (Gajek 2007).

Finally, evaluation can be conducted with the use of ready-made testing applications downloadable from the internet, internet-based testing services or tests prepared by teachers themselves with the use of authoring programs.

2.3 Summary

As this chapter has demonstrated, the implementation of information and communication technology within language education has significantly developed since the 1950s, when it was initiated. At the same time, it appears that the afore-mentioned advancement has gathered momentum particularly in the last two decades, in the course of which the computer has been converted into a multi-purpose device, which on the one hand now permits the integration of all the four major language skills while on the other hand is capable of facilitating genuine interpersonal communication (Warschauer 1996).

The significance of the latter lies in the fact that as computer technology currently serves people's communicative needs in real life, it cannot any longer be viewed as an artificial means through which communication skills can be developed in the language classroom. What is more, for example in Europe, ICT has become a primary means of *international* communication (Graddol 2006), which means that it particularly lends itself to facilitating foreign language learning, including its intercultural component.

An additional – albeit equally vital – advantage of the use of ICT in the foreign language classroom is the role that computers may play in learners' overall education by furthering their social agency, e.g. through activities involving online publishing (Warschauer 2000), and by equipping them with professionally useful technology-related skills (Warschauer & Healey 1998).

As it has been discussed, teachers and learners can now make use of a variety of computer-based work modes, both in traditional educational contexts, i.e. at school and in the classroom, as well as outside them (Gajek 2002a; Krajka 2007; Mason & Rennie 2008; Gajek 2009). That has been permitted by the appearance of work modes, such as e-learning or blended learning, which have rendered learners independent of specific settings, in terms of time and location.

On the basis of how computers are being currently used by society, it may be inferred that blended learning is paving the way for future developments in computer-based education. BL has arisen as a new form of integrative CALL and allows the diversification of the teaching/learning process through: face-to-face learning, e-learning as well as distance learning (Mason & Rennie 2008).

What also merits attention is the fact that information and communication technology may at present be used not only in order to design materials (Gajek 2002a) and deliver content but also to assess learners (Chapelle & Douglas 2006). As Chapelle (2001) and Chapelle &

Douglas (2006) report, ICT has multiple applications as a language assessment tool, and it may be used – with varying efficacy – in order to test all the language skills, including even selected forms of free writing or speaking.

However, despite the progress that has been achieved within the area of computer-based testing, the functionalities that have already been offered so far need perfecting in order to attain, e.g.: effective natural language processing, enhanced voice recognition or artificial intelligence.

CHAPTER FIVE

INFORMATION AND COMMUNICATION TECHNOLOGY IN INTERCULTURAL TEACHING

1. The place of ICT in intercultural teaching

1.1 Culture in CALL: a developmental overview

The history of teaching culture within computer assisted language instruction has been, to a large extent, determined by the software and ELT methodology used.

Through the 1960s culture was practically completely absent from computer-based language teaching as the computer was used to administer language drills to students, and value was placed on the accuracy of learner responses as well as the provision of immediate feedback, which was to facilitate habit formation. On the one hand behaviourist methodology did not regard culture as an important element of mechanical learning, on the other hand the computer was not capable of handling more sophisticated tasks, which a focus on culture teaching would have necessitated (Warschauer 1996).

In the 1970s and 1980s, when PCs were introduced, more room for cultural instruction was seemingly created within CALL as sociolinguistic competence was meant to be part of the then-dominant Communicative Approach. PCs themselves were also capable of providing slightly more functionality. Nevertheless, computer-based language practice was based mostly on more sophisticated manipulation of language patterns as computers could not manage much beyond text reconstruction, word mazes and text processing (Warschauer 1996; Godwin-Jones 2001). Even programs created for the purpose of (pseudo-)communicative practice, such as *Eliza,* did not offer learners an opportunity to practise communication. In effect, despite the fact that the source texts possibly contained cultural information, it was largely ignored.

The very end of the 1980s and the beginning of the 1990s saw the introduction of CD-ROM-powered language learning software which gained new functionalities, e.g. voice recognition and the incorporation of multimedia materials.

It is in all probability the stage that Liaw (2006) refers to as the early stage of the history of culture teaching that she discusses – unfortunately, without offering any time frame. In her view, the software which was developed at that time was intended for teaching both language and culture, thus, it contained cultural information and references. Indeed, it was so as the programs utilised featured a multitude of reading and listening texts, accompanied by audio-video illustrative material.

However, in Shaughnessy's (2003) opinion, the programs which were used deformed, or misrepresented, the culture that they were meant to picture through inaccurate content. Therefore, it may be stated that authentic culture was not taught. Liaw (2006) adds that as materials were produced for international audiences, the specificity of the learners' local culture was not taken into account by materials writers, and culture was presented from the ethnocentric perspective of materials writers.

Another stage that Liaw discusses could be placed roughly at the turn of the millennia, i.e. roughly between the 1990s and the noughties of the twenty-first century. It was then that the capacity of computerized networks, including the internet, began to be used on a large scale, including foreign language education. Computer networks became sufficiently sophisticated and functional to enable learners to engage in interactive activities through which they could actively explore other cultures and develop intercultural competence (Liaw 2006).

For instance, online courseware was designed and implemented in order to permit language and cultural exploration through film-based tasks, complete with computerised feedback. Shawback and Terhune (2002), who were the authors of the course in question, underlined the motivational value of the tasks involved in it as well as the role that the latter played in increasing learners' confidence within intercultural activities.

A step further was made approximately in the first decade of the new millennium (in the years 2000-2010, to be more precise), which saw the introduction on a large scale of networked communication projects, launched in order to enable students of English as a foreign language to contact one another by using asynchronous online communication tools such as email or web forums in the so-called telecollaboration. Such e-projects brought learners from different cultures together, thus, permitting true intercultural learning.

For example, Liaw (2006) cites the *Cultura project,* in which American and French students compared and analysed corresponding materials from one another's culture. Corbett (2005) discussed an online forum-based project of his own under the name *Ethnography via a Virtual Learning Environment*. Both e-projects have demonstrated the value of asynchronous communication for intercultural teaching, which in Corbett's view, increases the scope and impact of intercultural dialogue. Rollin and Harrap confirm that by stating that computerised intercultural learning provides learners with an intimate and safe environment in which intercultural learning is "(…) self-paced, the learning also has scope for repetition and reinforcement [and it provides] (…) the opportunity of making one's mistakes in private" (Rollin & Harrap 2005: 4). Other e-projects have been conducted and discussed by Furstenberg et al. (2001), O'Dowd (2003), Belz (2003) or Hanna and de Nooy (2003).

What needs emphasising is the genuine integration of computer technology and language learning that telecollaboration projects have materialised; hence, the name of the CALL era which the technology has supported.

As Liaw (2006) states, practice suggests that network-based communication fosters the development of "foreign language students' understanding of foreign cultural attitudes, concepts, beliefs, and ways of interacting and looking at the world" (Liaw 2006: 51).

The most recent stage in the history of computer assisted culture teaching is the implementation of corpus linguistics and concordancing for the purpose of studying the underlying cultural patterns of a given social group or culture. This kind of teaching relies on learners scouring linguistic corpora of either the target language group or their own, including learner corpora, in search of cultural patterns, value systems and beliefs which language encodes. Due to the availability of ready-made corpora and online concordancers, which search text archives by user-customisable indices, such learning does not pose a great technical challenge any more (Liaw 2006; Krajka 2007).

Scientific evidence, e.g. the study by Leech and Fallon, demonstrates that, by comparing corpora with reference to various senses in which words are used in two cultures, one can detect cultural differences between countries and societies. Corpora can also unravel cultural connotations beyond word use (Liaw 2006). As Partington (2001) maintains, corpora lend themselves to exploring the cultural meaning of not only lexis, but also syntax and discourse.

What is more, they enable learners to compare their cultural patterns with those of the target language by analysing intercultural corpora; learner corpora may be used to that end (Liaw 2006). Yet, despite the fact that corpora-based intercultural research projects were conducted already in the 1990s, and computer assisted concordancing technology was available before telecollaboration projects gained popularity (Osborne 2000), the idea of utilising linguistic corpora in order to teach culture has not yet been adopted by foreign language teachers, which is confirmed by Liaw (2006), who treats this technique in teaching culture as a recent development.

All in all, the history of teaching language and culture with the use of computers could be illustrated as suggested in the table below:

Behaviouristic CALL	**1960s**	**No focus on culture** Mechanical language drills
Communicative CALL 1970s-1980s	**1970s - 1980s**	**No focus on culture** Text reconstruction/manipulation
		Focus on language and culture
Integrative CALL 1990s-2010s	**1980s - 1990s**	TL culture taught through CD-ROM software packages
	1990s - 2010s	**Focus on language and culture** TL culture taught through authentic audio-visuals and interactive LAN-based courseware
	1990s - 2000s	**Intercultural telecollaboration projects** N and TL culture taught through genuine intercultural communication
	Half-2000s - 2010s	**Intercultural concordancing** N and TL culture taught through comparative languacultural analyses of language corpora

Table 5-1

While analyzing the above summary of the history of teaching culture through the use of computers one must be aware of the fact that the time brackets offered are arbitrary and they only depict the time at which particular approaches to culture were dominant. However, it is by no means intended to suggest that e.g. telecollaboration projects are no longer in use, or that they have been replaced by concordancing. It is rather illustrative of the fact that concordancing constitutes a relatively new idea, whereas telecollaboration has been in use for approximately two decades now.

1.2 Rationale for implementing ICT in intercultural education

Information and Communication Technology (ICT) embraces the use of the computer as a stand-alone teaching aid as well as the use of computer-mediated communication, which consists in work online. As the European Centre for Modern Languages (ECML) in Graz interprets it, ICT involves ""'all the technologies in which the computer plays a central role, i.e. Computer Assisted Language Learning (CALL), the Internet, and a variety of generic computer applications" (Fitzpatrick 2003: 71).

The rationale for using the computer in intercultural teaching derives from the nature of the multimedia that modern computers inherently engross, e.g. text, static and animated graphics, audio and video. In general, it can be stated that the use of computers and multimedia is advisable in foreign language education as it: stimulates learners and maintains motivation (Brett 2001; Aleksandrowicz-Pędich 2006; Łyp-Bielecka 2008); produces deeper involvement and generates more focus on the information and knowledge tackled (Brett 2001); and enables learners to follow a variety of learning strategies which best correspond to their learning styles. What is more, the media, including the internet, make language learning authentic (Bandura 2007). Thus, one might state that the introduction of multimedia – i.e. computer technology – into intercultural teaching brings it in line with the assumptions of modern foreign language teaching methodology (Gajek 2002a; Carrier 2006).

The merit of employing technology in intercultural teaching is also highlighted by Aleksandrowicz-Pędich et al. (2003) and Bandura (2007), with the latter expressing the view that foreign language education and the use of information and communication technology are currently at the core of educational reforms. After all, globalisation and European integration call for the creation of a knowledge society, whose interculturally competent members are to be able to communicate across cultures.

The relevance of ICT to intercultural teaching becomes evident when one looks at the characteristics of intercultural teaching enumerated by Bandura (2007): (i) enabling learners to use their knowledge of the native language and culture in the foreign language classroom; (ii) using a learner-centred approach, (iii) creating opportunities for content-based and cross-curricular learning; (iv) engaging learners in problem-solving and task-oriented learning; (v) making learning authentic through the use of original materials; (vi) selecting materials which would promote autonomous learning; (vii) preparing learners for direct interaction with other cultures, e.g. through school exchange programmes or trips abroad; and (vii) stimulating self-reflection on cultural identity.

Potentially, all of the above-listed features of intercultural teaching may be catered for by the implementation of computer-mediated techniques. It is confirmed by Fitzpatrick (2003), whose inventory of the kinds of learning that modern media and technologies facilitate practically overlaps with that of Bandura as it comprises: authenticity, learner-centeredness, learner autonomy, opportunities for real communication, and the use of a plethora of language varieties and information available through technology and media.

The modern multimedia computer serves as a tool with the use of which learners can easily not only explore the knowledge of their own language and culture, but also attempt to present it to members of other cultures, e.g. on internet pages, discussion forums or through video clips and podcasts, which they can create and upload to file-sharing websites such as YouTube. The merit of computer-mediated intercultural learning lies in the fact that on the one hand learners use the computer to discover foreign cultures; on the other hand, as the web is used not only to obtain but also to transmit information, they can learn how to demonstrate their own culture to strangers. As a result, their mother tongue and native culture can be successfully used in the course of intercultural education (Gajek 2007).

Computer-aided work puts the learner in the driving seat. It happens when learners work on individual computers, but it may just as well be the case when students engage in computer assisted pair/group work, where they are mostly expected to interact with their colleagues rather than the teacher. Thus, irrespective of the learning arrangement, learners have an opportunity to assume responsibility for their own learning and become independent of the teacher's authority (Bandura 2007).

As regards content-based and cross-curricular teaching, computers seem to be perfectly suited for this kind of work, as the media that they involve and the internet, which they offer access to, are an unlimited source of information which covers practically any possible aspect of life. Therefore, learning that is facilitated by the media inevitably directs learners' attention to content, subject matter, and not so much language form, especially when the focus of activities is culture (Bandura 2007).

Bandura (2007) sees problem-solving and task-oriented learning in the intercultural foreign language classroom as activities which make learners solve real life problems, frequently through simulation. Due to the repertoire of multimedia that computers can handle, this kind of simulation may be much easier than it was in the communicative classroom. Additionally, computers allow real communication – synchronous and asynchronous – through audio/video communicators, chat rooms as well as email, discussion forums and blogs, respectively. Thus, intercultural problems can be dealt with in real time, issues can be consulted across cultures, and proper solutions may be established jointly with genuine communication partners.

Authenticity is another feature of intercultural learning that computers can cater for in that they enable learners to access foreign cultural products, observe other people's behaviour, enter culturally different communities or even contact native speakers of the target language (Bandura 2007). The power of multimedia in this respect is underlined by Byram (2008), who sees electronic media as a resource that helps learners "discover a range of perspectives and experiences in other countries" (Byram 2008: 86). More acute intercultural experiences can only be provided by face-to-face meetings with otherness; that is why, it may be stated that the computer brings the real intercultural world much closer to the learner than the coursebook or other printed materials. Therefore, it helps the teacher to authenticate learners' experience.

The computer may be very helpful in enabling learners to select materials that best reflect their interests and needs as it potentially offers a vast multitude of not only materials but also work modes in which learners engage. If decisions pertaining to both are delegated to the learners, the outcome is autonomous learning (Bandura 2007).

Heyworth (2003) states that, because ICT puts learners in direct contact with authentic language, "real time information" (Heyworth 2003: 14) and other people, e.g. through forums or chat, it enables them to explore culture on their own, independently of not only the teacher but also school. Consequently, intercultural communication may now be easily practised at home as well.

Bandura (2007) maintains that intercultural teaching is supposed to prepare learners for direct interaction with other cultures, e.g. through school exchange programmes or trips abroad. This kind of preparation is likely to be increased in efficacy if computer resources are utilised in the course of it. The content, communication tools and various access modes which computers offer constitute are a toolset with which to prepare learners for a variety of intercultural situations and contexts.

Intercultural teaching is supposed to stimulate self-reflection on cultural identity. Although it does not immediately transpire how ICT might facilitate reflection of that kind in learners, it seems reasonable to suggest that computers might prove useful here as well. It is possible because computer technology helps learners project themselves, e.g. through an electronic profile that they design for a social networking site or a blog which they write. Such projection may enable learners to distance themselves from who they are, and what they stand for. In effect, it may be easier for learners to perceive themselves through a different pair of eyes, that of a stranger or foreigner. Only this kind of perspective will permit learners to notice the multiple dimensions of their own identity and its complexity at large (Bandura 2007). An example of this kind of practice, where learners truly decentred through an internet exchange in an Anglo-Austrian project, is presented by Penz (2001).

Another argument for using computer technology in intercultural teaching is the genuine intercultural communication which it permits. For instance, email and other internet services allow "an infinite number of potential contacts throughout the world" (Risager 2007: 214).

What is more, the rapid development of ICT has been one of the major causes of international interest in intercultural communication and it per se has created a need for intercultural competence. Thus, intercultural learning based on computer-enhanced intercultural communication seems to be a natural occurrence, which additionally helps learners realise the mutual bonds between language and culture (Risager 2007).

Through the computer, learners can interact with a variety of foreign partners, and if e.g. Polish learners of English communicate with native speakers of the target language, it creates room for intercultural learning on both sides, including mutual language learning. Alternatively, virtual exchanges may involve Polish and other, non-native learners of English, in which case the target language becomes a lingua franca. In consequence, both groups of learners do not merely improve target language skills but also explore how English alters their perceptions and self-expression when it becomes a means of international communication (Gajek 2007).

Although Gajek (2007) draws attention to the fact that computer-mediated communication cannot be equated with face-to-face contacts, as it does not involve the same paraverbal and nonverbal means of communication that people employ in reality, one must be aware that electronic communication is by no means an inferior form of communication, especially in intercultural contexts. It is clearly indicated by Graddol (2006), who maintains that – e.g. in the European context – most international communication in English as a lingua franca takes place through the Internet. Therefore, practising intercultural communication online is as true to life as offline encounters with other cultures.

According to Bandura (2007), the media, including the computer and internet functionalities such as internet pages or email services, constitute the most common source of cultural information which learners can reach outside the foreign language classroom. What is more, she adds that the media do not only function as a source of information but they are, at the same time, a means through which other cultures can be explored. She goes even further and associates intercultural teaching with media-based work, which she sees as a distinctive feature that differentiates it from the communicative approach – largely characterised by learning in artificially simulated contexts.

ICT can also constitute a supplement to what is offered by cultural materials contained within coursebooks. As Byram and Zarate (1996) note, coursebook content ages rapidly and materials may become outdated already at the time of publication. Moreover, they suggest that the most useful resources that lend themselves to (inter)cultural analysis are *inter alia*: tourist brochures, national anthems or jokes, which is precisely what web pages are abundant in. Thus, Byram and Zarate's (1996) suggestions are perhaps an implication that the internet is a rich source of up-to-date materials for intercultural teaching.

Peck et al. (2007) maintain that by using media technology, e.g. filmic materials, songs but also text (literature), teachers present the target language in context, through which "learners are simultaneously sensitised to language (grammar, syntax, vocabulary) and to culture/Culture" (Peck et al. 2007: 21). They believe that the benefits of media-aided culture teaching are three-fold: (i) learners develop communicative skills by practising the target language; (ii) they develop the ability to cope with intercultural difference; (iii) and they have their motivation raised.

On the basis of Carrier's (2006) claim that today various media are all converging into a single resource – the computer, it may be stated that ICT is perfectly suited for intercultural language teaching.

Ultimately, it may be suggested that ICT-based intercultural language teaching fosters the development of learners' *media competence*, i.e. the ability to make use of, and critically assess, various foreign language sources of information, including ICT resources. Work on this particular kind of competence is suggested by contemporary educational documents which set out the goals of education, e.g. *Podstawa programowa* (2008) in Poland, as well as educators. For example, Camilleri Grima and Fitzpatrick (2003) advocate the development of both *digital literacy* and *web literacy*, which embrace "the ability to use ICT adequately and apply them in a principled way to the subject matter at hand" (Camilleri Grima & Fitzpatrick 2003: 56) as well as the ability to utilize internet resources.

It must be underlined that information and communication technology cannot be seen as an instant solution for intercultural teaching. It cannot be perceived as an intercultural methodology, either. As Pfeiffer (2001) observes, computers are only a teaching aid, but how successfully they are used depends on teachers' and learners' response to computer-mediated instruction. Therefore, the above-mentioned ways in which ICT lends itself to intercultural teaching must not be treated as a set of inherent characteristics of the technology. They are rather to be taken as a potential that ICT undeniably offers.

1.3 ICT in intercultural education: advantages and constraints

The use information and communication technology seems to ameliorate intercultural teaching due to the kinds of knowledge, skills and activities that it involves, which appear to perfectly match the requirements and objectives of intercultural education. The features of ICT that interlock with intercultural teaching have been succinctly summarised by Bélisle (2007) as follows: a combination of intellectual understanding and empathy; learner activation; a learning shift from memorisation to transformation; the fostering of interpersonal relations; and immersion in the foreign cultural context.

ICT provides learners with a chance to genuinely grasp the meaning of what is being taught as it creates an enriched learning environment. Through the implementation of multimedia ICT gives learners a chance to experience phenomena and events more directly. In this way learning is not only more realistic but also involves learners' emotions. Images, videos, and audio clues enable learners to live the experience of others, thus, it permits them to empathise with the subjects of study. As a result, learning loses its purely cognitive nature and is enhanced by the immediacy of the learning context. That, in turn, is conducive to constructivist learning, where learners interact with the knowledge that they are supposed to develop. As the sociocultural context that multimedia deliver is deeper, it is likely to foster the construction of more relevant inferences (Bélisle 2007).

Another advantage of the use of ICT in intercultural teaching is the fact that it promotes interactive learning. It appears that interactive materials lead to interactive learning, which is understood as an opportunity for the learner to actively participate in experiences that increase their understanding. Again, understanding that derives from that kind of interaction is not purely cognitive; it is rather based on lived experience, i.e. performing and trying to solve problems. In effect, learning is not a process in the course of which knowledge is memorised. As a matter of fact, in this learning mode there is no pre-fabricated knowledge to be internalised by learners. Instead, learning is rather a transformation that occurs as a consequence of action and participation, which both involve "risk taking, emotional reactions, spontaneous exchanges and the reflective processes for developing self-awareness and awareness of others" (Bélisle 2007: 5).

ICT-based learning is indeed interactive, but this interaction exceeds the boundaries of learning by doing. As Bélisle (2007) stresses, modern networking technology allows real interaction between human beings. This is particularly relevant to intercultural learning, where meanings are supposed to be negotiated. Such negotiation requires two-way communication, where people's actions evoke responses, which can – significantly – be responded to. The computer per se will never fully imitate this kind of interaction (Bélisle 2007; Gajek 2007) but computer-mediated communication will.

Perhaps, the strongest argument for using information and communication technology for the purpose of intercultural foreign language teaching is the opportunity for cultural immersion that computer media provide. It is this kind of learning environment that will foster the development of the basic components of Byram's intercultural competence. Thanks to immersion learners will not only expand knowledge; they will also develop the necessary skills (*savoirs apprendre/faire and savoir comprendre*), appropriate attitudes which foster intercultural understanding (*savoir être*) as well as critical cultural awareness (*savoir s'engager*). ICT will not only enable teachers to follow Byram's *savoirs* in practice, they will, more broadly, empower them to adhere to the general educational goals set out by the Council of Europe (Bélisle 2007).

It has to be reiterated that ICT can only potentially play a facilitative role in intercultural teaching as the technology itself is not an ultimate teaching solution. One must not lose sight of the fact that ICT is only a means that has to be appropriately handled in order to produce an expected impact on learning.

The value of multimedia for intercultural teaching. Multimedia are a combination of various types of media through which content is demonstrated. As Korhonen (1999) defines them, in the case of computer technology multimedia are a kind of mix of textual materials, images, photographs, animations, video clips and soundbites as well as elements of user interface, e.g. buttons or special effects. At a very general level, Kramsch (1993) distinguishes two modes of work based on the use of multimedia: interactive narratives and interactive documentaries.

In the *interactive narrative* scenario, while working with multimedia, e.g. a video clips, learners can themselves create a new reality in that they have the power to influence the course of events which they watch by interacting with the content. The computer interface enables learners to receive messages to which they respond by typing their own responses, and those determine which alternative video clips are played back as a continuation of the story that learners have been working with. The multimedia character of video material also gives learners access to multiple formats in which they can receive content, e.g. they may watch the filmic material, read the transcript of the soundtrack, or alternatively, watch the film with subtitles on.

In *interactive documentaries* learners are perhaps less active in that they do not create any reality, but rather receive information, broaden their horizons by e.g. learning about the target language country. However, the content that they obtain is varied in format, and it may come as video footage, documents, maps, articles or photos. The experience is, therefore, likely to resemble real life, the more that such a diversity of formats helps the learner perceive reality from a number of perspectives, and it is the learner's responsibility to (re)construct their own picture of the world. This is helpful in encouraging learners to relate facts and events, instead of passively receiving information transmitted through a coursebook (Kramsch 1993).

According to Kramsch (1993), the use of multimedia software facilitates new learning modes, which are: non-linear, context-bound, recursive, constructivist and learner-directed.

Non-linear learning relates to the way in which learners access and interact with multimedia material. On the computer both actions are facilitated by hyperlinks, i.e. text or graphics which serve as clickable links that connect various kinds of media. In effect, learners gain access to a complex network of interconnected media – hypermedia – which incite non-linear learning. In such a case information is obtained through multiple access paths which can be followed interchangeably. As a result, learners can arrange, rearrange and organise information in order to construct, or reconstruct, the knowledge that is ultimately built in the course of the process. Learners no longer passively accept what is transmitted in bulk, but rather have to relate chunks of information, discover regularities and interpret data in order to be able to make generalisations (Kramsch 1993).

It is worth noting that such generalisations will be properly informed by the variety of evidence that learners are actively engaged with. Thus, this learning mode is less likely to cause learners to develop a stereotyped image of the target language culture than when a ready-made representation of culture is being conveyed through a set coursebook text.

Korhonen (1999) maintains that hypermedia create a new learning environment where continuous and individual learning are promoted, and where modern technology supports new pedagogical and educational approaches. The corollary of those new approaches is learning which allows flexibility in the time and place of study as well as access modes. Thus, it is learning characterised by a high degree of learner autonomy, self-directedness and responsibility. Hiltunen et al. (Korhonen 1999) stress that hypermedia and the non-linear learning that they bring about facilitate: problem-solving, knowledge acquisition, memorization as well as understanding. Korhonen (1999) has corroborated the latter claim empirically by reporting that ninety-one percent out of the seventy-eight subjects who had been taught interculturally through computer-based multimedia activities stated that hypermedia made understanding easier.

Context-bound learning is a kind of learning that does not occur in a contextual vacuum but is an outcome of contact with multiple situational contexts in which learners are expected to use the target language. Such contextual diversity refers to the different purposes for which the target language may be used by learners (Kramsch 1993). In effect, culture, which is presented to learners through various contexts, may be better understood. This kind of cultural understanding is likely to go beyond the target language culture itself as through it learners may understand the multi-dimensional nature of culture at large.

Kramsch (1993) sees media-based learning as recursive in that it requires constant manipulation of the content that is being tackled. It might be stated that it is a consequence of the non-linear nature of computer assisted learning. As facts are related, they resurface, appear in totally new contexts, and, therefore, require reinterpretation. This seems to imply is that media-based learning produces a synergy effect, i.e. what is learnt is more than a sum of the particular chunks of knowledge involved – it is a kind of added value that derives from the relational and recursive character of media-based activities.

Computer media also make learning constructivist, which means that culture which is taught through computer techniques is not presented as a set of meanings to be simply unravelled by learners. Instead, it becomes a jig-saw puzzle which is to be individually arranged by learners. Construction is necessitated not only by the variety of materials used, but also by their very nature, e.g. the structure and sequencing of visual materials (Kramsch 1993).

The implication of the above is that the target culture, as constructed by particular learners, is bound to differ from one individual to another. In this sense, each learning experience is unique, as are individual people's perceptions of culture outside the classroom.

Finally, computer-enhanced learning is learner-centred. This results in students having to direct their learning, interpret the phenomena that they come into contact with, and also decide on the priorities they will follow while learning (Kramsch 1993). It is all inevitably stimulated by the non-linear, recursive and constructivist character of computer materials and learning techniques as decisions on particular learning steps to be followed must be taken by the learners themselves.

The European Centre for Modern Languages, the International Certificate Conference and the Centre for Information on Language Teaching conducted a review of European language teaching materials produced for the purpose of teaching the languages of the European Union. The results revealed that most materials did not integrate language skills and they were text-based. What they lacked, with the exception of audio material, was a range of elements which (computer) multimedia can easily provide, e.g.: television and radio content, graphics and video, CALL authoring tools, and reference resources (Fitzpatrick 2003). Consequently, it appears that multimedia can revamp intercultural language teaching by supplementing ELT coursebooks through a variety of formats.

The advantages of computer media types in IC teaching. One of the offline media formats which computers avail for use in intercultural teaching is video, which is a combination of audio and visual cues. As Fowler and Blohm (2004) state, the value of video lies in that it can introduce learners to other cultures in an attractive and attention-catching manner; it can be a substitute for the study of textual materials.

It can also illustrate other modes of culture-determined behaviour; e.g. as Brett (2001) states, video depicts the workings of communication, including its paralinguistic aspects: gestures, dressing codes, appearance and culture-bound actions.

Most importantly, it lends itself perfectly to stimulating intercultural observation. Through replay functionality, events can be screened repeatedly, thus, intercultural analysis is likely to be more detailed.

Additionally, video clips help teachers display scenes and situations which would be difficult to recreate, or role-play, in the classroom. At the same time, they are the closest possible alternative to real life experience. Besides, filmic materials help learners experience other people's emotions, which facilitates affective training – a necessary part of intercultural competence.

Aleksandrowicz-Pędich (2006) adds that filmic materials in intercultural teaching present intercultural conflicts, which may be otherwise difficult to reproduce in the EFL classroom. What is more, they can be used to demonstrate model behaviours to learners in a straight-forward manner. Films can also support a presentation of cultural facts and information in that they effectively illustrate the meaning of what is very likely to be new, or strange, to foreign language learners.

Another role that video materials can play is that of a substitute for text-based materials, which have traditionally been used for presentation purposes. Video-mediated presentations are much more likely to vividly illustrate facts or events and raise motivation levels in the classroom. Finally, videos can be easily used by learners themselves for self-study.

The internet. The most-commonly used computer medium today is the internet. Sanko (Sik 1998) proposes that the internet can be used in two ways: as a source of, and a tool for, collecting information; and a means of communication. When it comes to the ways in which the English language can be utilised online, Sik (1998) notes that one can use it either to learn about the world or to make oneself known to the world outside. As the contemporary internet permits the use of all the major language skills: listening, speaking, reading and writing, it creates opportunities for one to explore cultures by actually entering them in real-time.

The internet has the following characteristics. It is a free medium, and as such, it liberates one from the danger of mental coercion or manipulation. It constitutes a powerful communication tool through which one gains easy access to a variety of cultures. Due to the amount of information and material available online, it offers people access to authentic events and real stories.

Through communication channels, such as web forums, chat rooms or web communicators, one can explore various communities, e.g. those which are part of the target language society. Therefore, the internet enables learners to interact with others and participate in their lives. It could be stated that the internet permits immersion in another culture, whereby it makes it easier to obtain up-to-date cultural information or catch up with cultural change. The diversity of internet-mediated interaction is such that it now permits learning the target language through its culture and vice-versa, i.e. the target culture can be explored through the target language (Sik 1998).

Internet pages (www). Noblitt (1989) observes that the internet revolutionises the way in which learners can learn. It is allowed by the specific structure of online documents, which thanks to hypertext technology, make it possible for learners to access material through different paths. What is more, such access paths may also be created by the learners themselves, who may use hyperlinks to relate various materials to each other and organise them into complex, interrelated wholes.

Noblitt (1989) sees hypertext technology as a pedagogical response to the manner in which the human mind arranges and manages information as the mind's workings also involve comprehensive networks of associations and interconnections. In addition, Kramsch (1993) notes that hypertext offers information presented through a variety of channels, which comprise: text, pictorial materials (static and animated), video clips and audio recordings. This translates into the possibility of engaging in multisensory experience and learning with the use of multiple strategies.

Internet-based learning also offers learners a high degree of autonomy in managing the learning task. It is possible due to the fact that e.g. navigation through the material, access paths or multimedia used are all determined by the learner themselves, which facilitates the development of learners' ability to search for information or explore cultural worlds.

Autonomous learning is enhanced through on-screen help options, which can refer to both the language that learners need to use, e.g. grammar and vocabulary help, as well as the exploration techniques that they utilise. Learners can additionally edit and annotate the materials that they work with, e.g. by accessing selected fragments of video or audio clips, or by adding and comparing notes (Kramsch 1993).

All in all, Aleksandrowicz-Pędich (2005) states that internet-based intercultural learning fosters cultural exploration. It allows learners to venture into other cultures and explore them in depth. Corbett (2003) cites examples of a variety of visuals through which culture can be explored, including images published online. However, it must be stressed that practically all the artefacts from his list can be found on the internet, e.g. adverts, travel agents' brochures, postcards, CD covers or paintings. He also discusses the wealth of cultural information that can be traced in images, which – again – is applicable to images available on the internet.

For instance, the study of images and their history, which is perfectly practicable online, can reveal: how nationalities or particular social sub-groups are represented in pictures; what values the fashion of social groups manifests; or how the values of particular communities have changed over time (Corbett 2003).

Corbett (2003) also adds that the internet extends the channels through which learners may experience otherness and access other cultures. This point of view is shared by Byram (2006), who claims that the internet facilitates intercultural ethnographic experiences. The web is abundant with information about up-to-date cultural events; it provides authentic materials, through which learners may base their intercultural training on real issues. Thus, it may be stated that the internet authenticates intercultural experience.

Internet communication tools. In Ruciński's (1988) view, it is essential to be aware of the fact that interaction with the very computer lacks the features of human dialogue, e.g. mutual perception, trust or acceptance. Gajek (2002a) supports this view by maintaining that the computer will not replace the teacher in relaying emotions and ethical, or cultural, values. However, problems of this kind may be solved by using audio-visual online communication tools, which enable learners to contact and share ideas with members of other cultures.

Aleksandrowicz-Pędich (2005) claims that online communication offers learners an opportunity to join other communities, and even become part of other cultures. It is, therefore, an instrument which provides perhaps the closest substitute for a cultural sojourn, which otherwise involves travelling abroad. This kind of *e-sojourn*, as it might be called, allows learners to *live* another culture by interacting with it, instead of learning about it.

As the internet involves language use, it is a medium that permits learners to learn the target language through its culture and vice-versa. It helps learners formulate opinions about cultures and enables them to develop discourse strategies that may be necessary in communication with strangers. Overall, the internet serves as a tool for discovery and learning about the world, but also as a platform for self-presentation (Gajek 2002a), both of which are crucial elements of intercultural competence.

With regard to computer-mediated communication, i.e. the use of internet forums, chat rooms or communicators, Gajek (2007) observes that implementing computers to teach culture is particularly justifiable in countries such as Poland, i.e. those which are relatively monocultural, and where intercultural contacts on a daily basis are rather limited. This deficiency can be counteracted in two ways: by school exchanges and visits to foreign countries, e.g. those facilitated by the European *Socrates* or *Comenius* programmes, or through the use of information and communication technology within the so-called e-exchange projects or school partnerships, e.g. those mediated through the *Global Gateway* (Shaw 2004; Global Gateway 2010) scheme or the *eTwinning* (Gajek 2007) programme. According to Gajek (2007), due to financial limitations, school exchanges are frequently counted out, but they may be replaced with virtual exchange programmes, which enable learners to explore their own and other cultures in a safe virtual environment. Żylińska (2003) underlines that online communication is genuine; it facilitates the exchange of thoughts, ideas and worldviews. It also promotes holistic learning, where cultural knowledge is developed through a variety of experiences and the use of different information sources. This kind of communication leads to shifts in perspectives; it involves real emotions. As in face-to-face contact, it creates opportunities for learners to experience both their native and target culture; develop their cultural identity; and lead learners to what Kramsch (1993) called a *third place*.

Dudeney (2006) believes that online communication stands out from its offline counterpart in that it is convenient for teachers and learners to arrange. It is also a safer way in which learners can meet the target culture, e.g. negative emotions may be cushioned by the fact that learners can communicate from the comfort of their own home or the foreign language classroom, where they may be supported by colleagues or the teacher. Such communication provides opportunities for learners to negotiate meanings with their interlocutors and arrive at interpretations of the cultural phenomena observed. Finally, as intercultural communication online involves both the learners' native and target culture, it also offers them a chance to reflect on their own culture.

To sum up, all the media which the computer encompasses, be it online or offline, can be used as tools for an anthropological/ethnographic exploration of cultures, which – as advocated by Corbett (2003) and Byram (2008) – is an indispensible intercultural technique. Computer-mediated ethnography can be practised in two different modes. It can be done through *distance ethnography*, also known as *virtual ethnography*, and it consists in learners observing the target culture from their home country, by means of the media, including modern technologies such as: the Internet, email, and computer software (Carel 2001; Corbett 2003).

Alternatively, learners can engage in *joint ethnographic projects*, in which they participate by using tools for online communication as well as resources available on websites (Corbett 2003). An example of this kind of telecollaboration is the English-French email project discussed by Dodd (2001).

Corbett (2003) even suggests that the degree to which technological resources are exploited might be a criterion of intercultural course assessment. Yet, teachers must avoid the temptation "to use the new tools [technology] for what we are already able to do without them" (Fitzpatrick 2003: 72). Instead, intercultural teaching should rather be a case of a balance of ICT-mediated and conventional teaching, which Fitzpatrick labels as '"blended learning", i.e. the use of a combination of different media and forms of interaction' (Fitzpatrick 2003: 75).

Constraints on the use of ICT in IC education. There are a number of factors which impair the implementation of information and communication technology for the purpose of intercultural teaching. Some of them stem from the pedagogical challenges that intercultural education poses, others relate to the very technology that is supposed to be used.

Żylińska (2007) expresses the view that in Poland there seems to be resistance among teachers towards the use of technology at large, despite the fact that an increasing number of schools have already been equipped with computers. Bandura (2007) diagnosed the same problem when she examined how teachers taught culture in foreign language lessons at Polish schools. Neither of the researchers examined the exact reasons for which teachers are generally reluctant to use computers in their lessons but they offered a few possible explanations.

It may be that teachers do not call upon technology in their daily work because: they do not believe in its efficacy; they still lack a proper level of computer/electronic literacy; or they find it hard to access the computers, which only seemingly are available to them at school. Belz (2005) seems to subscribe to the latter argument as he observes that the use of ICT in intercultural teaching poses problems related to administrative and logistical nature. It may be hard for a teacher to gain access to the computer suite, which they normally need in a specific time slot.

Gajek (2009) adds that problems could also be related teachers' ICT skills; teachers may simply find themselves unable to operate the equipment, or be totally incompetent to handle technical and software/ hardware-related problems.

Alternatively, teachers may actually be discouraged from using technology as they do not find it congruent with the requirements their teaching is supposed to meet in the light of the teaching programmes that they follow (Żylińska 2007). What transpires on closer inspection of teaching programmes is that learners are not so much required to contact foreign partners in real time and engage in intercultural exchanges; they are primarily expected to internalise a transmittable knowledge that they must display at examinations. Interestingly enough, this happens despite the fact that examination criteria, e.g. those of the new *Matura* exam in Poland, refer to elements of intercultural competence. Thus, it may be concluded that because intercultural competence is underrepresented in examinations, it fails to be properly recognised by teachers.

The degree to which ICT is harnessed to develop intercultural competence in the EFL classroom may also be reduced by the lack of clear socio-cultural context within electronic materials. This argument is particularly pertinent to the use of online communication for the sake of intercultural exploration. For instance, online communication, be it synchronous or asynchronous, may occur in a setting whose context is not evident to its participants. That may affect learners' interpretation of the meanings which are being communicated to them by their interlocutors. In the absence of such clues, the lack of contextual salience has to be compensated for by acute pragmatic sensitivity on the part of the learner. However, this kind of sensitivity may be a challenge to develop (Levy 2007).

In Crystal's (2001) as well as Ware and Kramsch's (2005) opinion, difficulty in dealing with technology-mediated intercultural communication may also result from its austerity with regard to the absence of paralinguistic clues, e.g. kinesics or proxemics, which are as vital for appropriate interpretation of meaning as situational context. Thus, on the one hand it appears that the validity of online communication for intercultural training ought to be revisited, on the other hand it must be realised that online communication is as common today as face-to-face contacts. Moreover, as it has already been stated, Graddol (2006) maintains that intercultural communication in Europe occurs primarily online.

ICT, similarly to other teaching aids utilised in intercultural teaching, has to be handled with care so that it brings about the intended effects. The teacher must be observant of the fact that mere exposure to other cultures, indirect or even direct, does not automatically lead to the development of intercultural competence. As Byram and Tost Planet (2000) postulated, if computer-mediated intercultural activities are to lead to interactions between people's perspectives, beliefs, values, and practices, learners have to try to perceive and interpret communication as such. Otherwise, they will only superficially experience otherness, and – as Belz (2005) and O'Dowd (2003) warn – they will either confirm for themselves the stereotypes they have so far lived by, or they will develop new ones.

From the pedagogical point of view, teachers utilising ICT in intercultural teaching might also face a challenge from their students, who may falsely assume that their teacher will have all the know-how and skills that it takes to arrange for successful intercultural telecollaboration. In consequence, when failure occurs, as is frequently the case (O'Dowd 2003), the blame may be put on the teacher (Belz 2005).

2. Computerised techniques in IC teaching

Computers enable teachers to implement electronic intercultural techniques that are based on multimedia resources, which are likely to evoke more motivation and learner involvement than pen-and-paper techniques.

Intercultural software tools. One of the possible computerised techniques facilitating intercultural training is the use of purpose-designed software, an example of which is *The Same but Different*, computer courseware which was developed for Finnish polytechnic students (Korhonen (1999). The program was inspired by *The Culture General Assimilator*, a teaching approach developed by Brislin et al. (1986), and it is based on intercultural incidents along with multiple-choice explanations which learners have to select from (Cushner & Brislin 1996).

The Same but Different contains a collection of 25 tasks featuring intercultural incidents, whereby learners develop intercultural competence while analysing the sources of the intercultural conflicts presented, and selecting the right interpretations on the basis of insights into the target culture and their own.

Although the program is an electronic version of the culture assimilator technique, which is used offline, due to the fact that it includes hypermedia, it allows learners to function in ways which would not be easily attainable in a pen-and-paper format. Hypermedia create a new learning environment in which learners learn more autonomously. Thus, *The Same by Different* lends itself to self-study, while also supplementing face-to-face learning (Korhonen 1999).

In hypermedia-based tasks, learners can be more flexible in decision-taking as they act independently. They can also truly explore cultural information as it is not transmitted but rather made available in a non-linear fashion, conducive to multi-tier interpretation. Hypermedia also help learners manage data more easily, e.g. through convenient navigation, and facilitate learning through multiple associations , which they incite.

The wealth of hyperlinked media used within the program also permits the creation of a truer picture of the intercultural incidents which learners work on. Thus, it becomes possible for learners to thoroughly explore problems which are more realistic. It is so due to the fact that the incident descriptions in the program are supplemented with additional information supplied in the form of text or graphics, accessible through clickable links. What is more, the program is appended with an entire section devoted to the basics of the theory of intercultural communication (Korhonen 1999), which allows learners to develop intercultural skills as well as expand culture-general knowledge (*savoirs*).

Concordancers are programs which permit the user to search texts for selected words and or phrases and obtain lists of the words/phrases found in context (Lewandowska-Tomaszczyk 2000). As Lewandowska-Tomaszczyk (2000) demonstrates, concordancers can be utilised in order to conduct computer-enhanced analyses of language corpus data, which may reveal much more than mere linguistic discrepancies between particular language systems. Such programs can also be applied for the purpose of comparing how particular, seemingly equivalent, language concepts differ between two languages in terms of their actual conceptualizations and possible extensions of use. This may, in turn, help foreign language teachers and learners investigate how selected entities are categorized by representatives of different cultures, both between national groups as well as within them.

Lewandowska-Tomaszczyk (2000) presents the manner in which it may be investigated how gender is perceived by representatives of particular communities, e.g. journalists. Such analysis can yield valuable insight into various cultures and can be helpful in discovering the perception modes that mould learners' views of what might be mistakenly considered as universally shared concepts.

The value of concordancers as a tool for intercultural learning derives from the fact that the language samples which they return in response to a set query are provided within the context of the text from which the samples originate. Therefore, it is possible for EFL learners to explore the socio-cultural and situational context in which certain expressions are likely to appear in a given language, including text and discourse type as well as authorship and target audience. This may additionally increase learners' sensitivity to the role of new, vital skills, such as media competence, in today's information/knowledge society (Schulte 2000).

Interestingly enough, Liaw (2006) observes that intercultural learning stimulated by the use of concordancers does not necessarily have to follow the teacher's plan. In a project she describes, a concordancer was originally supposed to provide the participating students with a chance to learn culture through lexical, syntactic and textual analysis of meanings. However, as it was concluded, the students used the data obtained from the concordancer as a source of reading texts which they voluntarily read in order to expand their cultural knowledge. Although the effects of such a mode of (inter)cultural learning were not measured, the study demonstrated that concordancers can have wider applications to intercultural teaching that go beyond their primary functions (Liaw 2006).

Computer techniques in intercultural teaching can also involve the use of the internet, as is the case with: telecollaboration projects, email tandems, webquests, e-journals, literature web projects, chat and, videoconferencing.

Telecollaboration projects involve students in genuine communicative exchanges with other people who are in a distant location. This definition is en elaborated version of Osborne's definition of computer-mediated collaboration, which in the past was carried out in a local context, where students from the same classroom cooperated with one another via networked computers e.g. in order to collaboratively tell stories, engage in role-play or compare spoken texts (Osborne 2000). The internet has turned computer-based collaboration into telecollaboration projects, which – as Warschauer (1997) reports – are particularly useful for intercultural learning because, when positive emotions are involved, electronic exchanges increase learners' confidence and encourage participation.

Telecollaboration projects can take two basic forms: collective collaboration and one-to-one collaboration, which is referred to as tandem work. Telecollaboration projects in which groups of students come into contact with one another involve: (i) cooperation between students within their own institution, (ii) cooperation between individual students or sub-groups between different institutions, and (iii) collective collaboration, where all the project participants are simultaneously involved. Examples of the pioneer telecollaboration projects include: the pan-European project *Open to Europe,* conducted within the Socrates programme, and the English-Spanish-French *Leverage project* (Osborne 2000). More recent examples are *eTwinning* (Komorowska 2006a) and *Odyssee* (Czaplikowska 2007).

One-to-one telecollaboration is realised through *E-mail tandem projects*, which are arranged with a view to creating a context in which students would interact with their peers from abroad over a longer period of time. The very exchange normally happens outside the classroom, where the students are relieved from teacher-induced pressure, and where they are less constrained by the time available for email writing.

Osborne (2000) defines email tandems as "(…) a form of open learning, whereby two people with different native languages work together in pairs in order:

"• to learn more about one another's character and culture.
• to help one another improve their language skills.
• to exchange additional knowledge – for example, about their professional life." (Osborne 2000: 61).

The procedure of an email tandem covers: selection of partners, mutual introduction, interaction proper, data analysis and conclusion, which consists in learners producing a summary of the project in the form of an essay, poster, chart or a multimedia presentation.

In the case of a series of email tandems described by Penz (2001), the participants were Austrian students of English from Graz University and American students of German from the University of Little Rock, USA. Within the Austrian-American projects, the participants were each paired with a partner that they corresponded with by email both in German and English. Such a working mode meant that the students involved could use their mother tongue as well as the target language.

In email tandems international partners exchange email correspondence in an attempt to collect information which could be significant for language and culture learning. In the afore-mentioned projects, two groups of the Austrian students were supposed to gather samples of American slang which they were to write an essay about. The other groups collected linguistic data pertaining to sexist language and politically correct language through questionnaires. They also analysed their own email exchanges with regard to speech acts, discourse analysis or learner errors. The American participants used the email exchanges for the purpose of learning the German language and Austrian culture; the projects involved email interaction over a period of six weeks (Penz 2001).

The teacher's role was reduced to assistance in case the interactants faced problems. The e-mail messages produced by the participating students contained personal information as well as project-related subject matter. The intensity of particular exchanges varied as the participants produced two to fifteen e-mails per person. Consequently, the degree to which the final products, e.g. essays or slang lists, were elaborated also differed. In addition, it was observed was that apart from the information that the participants were supposed to collect for the sake of the project, vast amounts of other information, both linguistic and cultural, were exchanged. Therefore, it can be stated that the projects involved even more intercultural learning than had been planned (Penz 2001).

What is worth stressing, the students' feedback on the email tandem work was generally very positive, however, it was determined by the degree to which particular tandems displayed readiness to cooperate. The participants appreciated the inherent advantages of asynchronous intercultural communication that email offered them as a medium. They especially relished that fact that they could afford to delay their responses, thanks to which they had time to reflect on their partners' writing. As a result, they felt safer and more confident than they would have done, had they met their partners in person (Penz 2001).

Penz (2001) stresses that the Austrian students, whose priority was language work, nevertheless, experienced cultural learning. He also observes that the participants were able to perceive each other's perspectives and needed to engage in intercultural negotiation and interpretation.

Webquest was originally developed by Bernie Dodge of San Diego University. It is an internet-based technique which involves learners in interaction with information on the basis of which they are supposed to construct their own knowledge (Dodge 1995). The webquest task usually involves a set of annotated links to pre-selected websites which the learner visits in order to extract the information that he/she needs in order to solve a problem or find an answer to a given question. Therefore, any webquest task is learner-centred, query-driven, process-oriented and interpretative in nature.

As Kurek (2004) posits, webquests help learners develop the so-called *multiliteracies*, which encompass: academic literacy, critical literacy and electronic literacy. Practically, all of them are necessary for successful intercultural mediation as: academic literacy allows one to read and appropriately respond to foreign language texts in varied fields; critical literacy is the ability to critically assess text credibility and draw conclusions from the information obtained; and electronic literacy is the ability to use information and communication technology for communication per se, but also for materials preparation/publishing and self-study.

Dodge (2000) envisages the webquest as a clearly structured activity, which consists of the following stages: introduction, task, process and evaluation.

At the introduction stage, the learner is introduced to the theme of the webquest along with the necessary background information and any vocabulary that they have to be familiar with before they embark on the task.

The task stage involves a presentation of the very problem, or task, that the learner will have to deal with. Dudeney (2006) explains that, at best, a webquest task ought to concern an issue relating to real life which at the same time ought to arouse learners' interest. The context of the task must be clearly drawn up so that learners feel sufficiently engaged in it; the context itself frequently assigns the learner to a role that they have to fulfil while working on the task.

The process stage is the actual webquest work that the learner is meant to perform. This is done by the learner following a host of links to websites, pre-selected and described by their teacher. It has a very motivating effect on the learner if the webquest is concluded with a final product, e.g. a multimedia presentation, a grid to be filled in with information, an information chart or a role-play to be staged. Therefore, the process stage comprises not only web searching, information gathering and processing, but also the preparation of the final product (Dodge 2000). Webquests may be considered as a tool for testing learners' *savoir apprendre/faire*.

Finally, the webquest requires a form of evaluation, which may either be realized as self-evaluation, where learners compare what they have arrived at with their colleagues, or evaluation conducted by the teacher.

Webquests can focus on intercultural issues, but they may also have a linguistic focus. However, as language and culture are interrelated, even linguistically-driven webquests can be conducive to intercultural learning, if properly handled. Examples of intercultural webquests, which might be labelled *culture quests*, have been presented by Buchowska (2004) and Marczak (2004). It is worth mentioning that webquests can be used in a reverse mode, i.e. learners may be requested to prepare webquest tasks themselves, either for their colleagues or foreign partners.

E-Journal is a technique which may serve as a replacement for the reading of coursebook texts, which frequently do not meet learners' expectations and interests. The very name refers to a Finnish educational online project which allows international learners to upload their own text, but also multimedia materials, to an internet page, off which they can be read by others. The *E-Journal* website is also an intermediary between learners who are seeking a communication partner with whom they would like to discuss issues of mutual interest. The selection of partners is age-motivated, but it can also depend on a given learner's language proficiency (Żylińska 2003).

The topics which may be discussed on e-journals cover issues such as graffiti, school life and worries. Texts can be richly documented through images, videos and audio files, and that is what makes e-journals suitable for intercultural learning as the very choice of topics may be an intercultural issue in itself.

What is more, the problems tackled are not dealt with superficially as the multimedia which are utilised help learners build a detailed picture of an aspect of their own culture, which will allow their partners to explore it more thoroughly (Żylińska 2003).

Żylińska (2003) claims that this kind of technique is very involving for learners as they become self-motivated to participate in the exchange. That is demonstrable by an analysis of the length of an average text on the *E-Journal* website that she describes and the relatively good language quality of the texts which have been uploaded.

It appears that e-journals can facilitate the intercultural learning of people beyond those directly involved in them, i.e. the very text authors. Such websites might also serve as an interesting source of materials for intercultural analysis to those who are only visitors. Comparing texts written by representatives of different age, interest, ethnic or national communities might yield invaluable information about people's identity, approaches to life, attitudes to particular problems, outlook on foreigners or self-perception, which includes views of one's own culture or self-identity.

As the *E-Journal* materials are available online, this technique might be optionally combined with a webquest, whereby learners could unravel information about other cultures on the basis of a range of structured resources, with a view to concluding this intercultural exploration by a presentation or role-play.

Literary web projects can also be used to develop intercultural competence in foreign language learners, which has been illustrated by Müller-Hartmann (2000), who wrote about a project based on the American novel *The War between the Classes* by Gloria Miklowitz. The very novel is an interesting material for intercultural learning as it presents a distorted image of American society; i.e. it contains data which could be culturally analysed. In the afore-mentioned project two groups of German learners telecollaborated with a group of Canadian colleagues. The project consisted in the learners reading the novel and interpreting it jointly. The theme of the project was the status of various ethnic groups in Canadian and German society. Both parties involved in the project requested their project partners to provide them with information about their own society.

Interestingly enough, the questions asked within the project were addressed to individual learners, which created opportunities for examining varied points of view on the same issue. The project work revealed not only intercultural differences between the societies in question, but also internal divergences which occurred between different ethnic groups within the same national society. Therefore, it may be concluded that the learners were given a chance to decentre from both cultures and develop new perceptions towards them, i.e. they entered a *third place*.

Literary analysis can be conducted in the classroom, without the participation of the learners' foreign colleagues. However, this kind of discussion is less likely to develop into intercultural learning, unless it is meticulously planned and properly guided.

Yet, when literary texts are analysed in an intercultural context, through telecollaboration – where learners interact with representatives of other cultures – intercultural learning may occur. As Żylińska (2003) maintains, it is also much more motivating because it is heavily learner-centred. In this manner learners engage in education which relates to issues of immediate interest to them, and which is pragmatically useful for them at the very moment at which the learning happens. Thus, learners do not have to be coerced to involve in it.

The value of the use of literary texts for intercultural learning lies in the fact that literature enables learners to redefine, or reinterpret, the value systems and beliefs that underline their own culture by contrasting those with the values, beliefs and assumptions of others, which literary pieces are saturated with (Thanasoulas 2001).

Interestingly enough, this kind of analysis does not need to concern literary texts exclusively, if one bears it mind what Corder (1968) suggested over four decades ago. According to him, literature – in a broader sense – can alternatively be viewed as other media, e.g. film and television, which depict the target language in situational context and help the teacher contextualise learning more thoroughly. Consequently, one might posit that filmic materials which are properly analysed may also foster the teaching of culture.

Genuine internet forums. Levy (2007) discusses the implementation of genuine internet forums, i.e. those originally intended for native speakers, in intercultural teaching. He states that, as learning environments, forums are by definition less safe psychologically for students who decide to participate in them, since learners are not sheltered there in the manner in which it happens in email tandems. He emphasises the authenticity of internet forums which stems from the fact that they are platforms where native speaker users reveal their cultural norms and behavioural patterns through participation in the discussions held. When a non-native speaker joins a forum of that kind, he/she must be prepared for culture clashes and potential cultural conflicts in a setting where no allowances will be made for their non-native cultural origin.

Levy (2007) accounts a forum-based project run by Hanna and de Nooy (2003), in which four English students of French joined the French newspaper *Le Monde* forum by sending their messages to it. As it occurred, those learners who used English on the forum and displayed interest in the topics discussed were tolerated by the native speakers of French more than those who used French and explicitly admitted that they were merely trying to practice the target language.

In other words, according to the project authors, the new participants of the forum had to follow the underlying principles of its primary users in order to be accepted as members. They did not have to adopt French as their language, as long as they obeyed the rules of forum use (Hanna and de Nooy 2003).

Levy (2007) observes that while participating in a discussion forum one can easily notice whether they are being accepted by its community or not, and the very acceptance depends on a code of conduct established by its authors and senior users.

What may be an interesting challenge for intercultural learners is an attempt to join such a forum in order to test their intercultural knowledge, attitudes and skills in an authentic setting. However, teachers must be warned that despite intensive preparation, which such participation requires, it ought to be considered as an option for advanced learners. It will be especially suitable for those who have a readiness to conform to the rules that underpin forum interaction.

Yet, the very readiness may not suffice, as although certain rules may be salient when expressed through the netiquette of online interaction, the code to be adhered to is frequently implicit and needs to be discovered (Levy 2007). Nevertheless, the idea of learners participating in authentic online forums seems to be educationally valid. It permits learners not only to examine how the gate keeping practices of "digital cultures" (Levy 2007: 109) operate in practice, but also to perform socially in a real context, which might be a way of assessing intercultural skills.

As a form of pre-participation practice, a fake online forum can first be designed by the teacher, which would allow learners to experience rule-setting and rule-enforcing practices of an imaginary community in a controlled – thus a much safer – setting (Levy 2007).

Internet chat is an example of a technique in intercultural teaching which involves synchronous communication, i.e. text-based communication in real time. Toyoda and Harrison (2002), who conducted an intercultural chat project, maintain that live communication online creates a context in which intercultural skills can be tested in practice; however, this work mode requires much practice.

The afore-mentioned project involved learners of Japanese who conversed via online chat with native speakers of the language. As Levy

(2007) notes, although the project itself was not interculturally-oriented, it, nevertheless, resulted in intercultural learning. He maintains that, while learners engage in chat conversations and decipher meanings, they inevitably need to rely on their culture-bound conventions and norms.

What Levy (2007) highlights is that what is determined by culture in intercultural chat-mediated communication is not only how learners interpret meanings, but also how they interact and what roles they adopt. All of those components add up to create a context in which co-communicators interact. The more meaningful the context, the easier it is for effective communication to be established. Otherwise, intercultural chat is bound to be problem-ridden.

Levy (2007) observes that on many occasions communication breakdowns between the learners of Japanese and the native speakers involved in the Toyoda and Harrison project occurred simply as a result of intercultural differences in the participants' interpretation of the context in which the conversation took place. As he concludes, interpreting contextual meaning successfully is more demanding in chat conversations because native speakers frequently produce incomplete or abbreviated sentences, which leads to semantic misinterpretations.

Synchronous communication that is allowed by online chat technology does not make intercultural understanding easy because it affects the language that is used by conversation partners. For instance, brevity of expression necessitates the use of incomplete or abbreviated utterances. What is more, chat deprives interactants of access to nonverbal clues, which normally facilitate face-to-face communication; it also causes problems related to turn-taking practices (Levy 2007).

Simultaneously, it must be admitted that if chat conversations are organized in the form of principled intercultural activities, they may yield a multitude of cultural information which may be used to facilitate learners' intercultural communication in the course of time. Technically, it is permitted by modern chat software, which allows users to save the conversation that they have as a text file, as is the case with *Skype*'s chat function. By saving their conversation, learners give themselves an opportunity to analyse asynchronously, i.e. in a delayed manner and in the comfort of privacy, the culturally-determined discourse patterns and interpretations of meanings that may either facilitate or interfere with intercultural understanding. In such a case, the chat itself becomes an evidence-gathering activity and a ground for the practice, or even assessment, of one's intercultural skills. True intercultural learning will occur at the time of the ensuing analysis and discussion of the data collected.

As Osborne (2000) suggests, another possible technique in synchronous telecollaboration is the use of *videoconferencing* software. Examples of software which could be used for that purpose are cited by Gajek (2009), e.g. *Skype*, *zoho*, *ooVoo*, *dimdim* or *megameeting*.

Żylińska (2007) describes an exemplary Polish-French project of that kind, in which teacher training college students, i.e. pre-service teachers, communicated by using the *Skype*, *Microsoft Messenger* and the *Marratech* videoconferencing software in order to discuss issues of generation gap, inter-generation relations, conflicts and their resolutions in both French and Polish society. The three videoconferences held within the project in the years 2004-2005 were supposed to only complement – through the audio-visual channel – other forms of text-based communication. A combination of various telecollaboration formats is, thus, yet another possibility which adds to the repertoire of technology-mediated techniques in intercultural teaching.

ICT-mediated culture teaching in a monolingual setting. As Gajek (2007) suggests, the importance of information and communication technology in the development of foreign language learners' intercultural competence dramatically increases in a monolingual setting, where learners' contact with other cultures is limited, or close to none. Poland may be cited as an example of a country where intercultural teaching occurs in this kind of relatively sterile cultural environment, with the caveat that even here – as Aleksandrowicz-Pędich (2005) observes – intercultural contacts are indeed possible. However, it must be noted that if a specific culture is targeted, opportunities for intercultural learning may be limited, or impossible.

Nevertheless, Gajek (2007) claims that in a setting where access to other cultures is limited, even if telecollaboration is not possible, ICT plays a number of vital functions. Firstly, it helps teachers provide learners with authentic materials. It is interesting that online materials are likely to be more representative of various social communities than their offline counterparts, because particular sub-cultures are easier to locate on the internet than within the target language society.

In addition, the authenticity of online materials may stem from the fact that they are likely to contain cultural data which otherwise might be much more difficult to obtain. Suler explains the reason for that through the concept of "the online disinhibition effect" (Suler 2004: 321), which makes people more outspoken online than in offline contexts.

ICT also serves as a source of up-to-date information about the target language country, which may be otherwise unattainable through other media. As a matter of fact, it frequently happens that breaking news makes it to the internet before it appears on the radio or television, let alone on newspaper pages.

Computer technology is also very likely to arouse learners' interest in the target culture due to the vividness of the cultural materials that it offers and the number of multimedia through which the target culture is represented. Electronic content, supplemented with audio-visuals, stimulates learners and increases their participation in a lesson – if only because of the fact that it is natural for learners to demand the presence of technology at school as it has already become part of their everyday lives (Carrier 2006).

By expanding learners' contact with other cultures in a monolingual setting in a manner that learners may find motivating, technology is likely to foster tolerance towards cultural otherness. At the same time, it must be underlined that the very exposure to other cultures will not automatically translate into openness and tolerance, as illustrated by O'Dowd (2003) and Belz (2005). In intercultural encounters, even indirect, what meets the eye is difference, and, as Bennett (1998) presents, people have a tendency to react to it with distrust, suspicion, prejudice, or even aggression. Thus, the success/failure of an intercultural experience may simply depend on the intensity of the affective experience that it involves.

The implementation of ICT for the purpose of intercultural learning in monolingual contexts creates an environment where learners experience otherness in a more controlled manner than in reality. Moreover, computer-mediated intercultural contacts may not directly involve other people, thus, negative emotions are more likely to be suppressed. In effect, learners may find it easier to detach from the phenomena observed, which promotes a non-judgmental attitude towards others and culture per se.

Last but not least, if learners contact representatives of other cultures only through ICT, they may be requested to present their own local/national identity to foreigners. While doing so, they need to reflect not only on what to display, but also how to present information so that it is comprehensible for strangers. Therefore, on the one hand they need to detach from their own culture, on the other hand they have to change their perspective into that of a stranger.

This kind of learning brings intercultural instruction closer towards the ideal of Risager's (2007) languacultural education as, while communicating their culture to others through English, learners will need to consider how the target language, which is a culture-bound system itself, may affect the message that they ultimately convey.

3. Evaluation of computer-mediated (intercultural) materials

3.1 ELT materials evaluation

Types of evaluation. On a very general level, McDonough and Shaw (1993) distinguish two modes of materials evaluation: external and internal.

External evaluation concerns the evaluation of materials on the basis of what the very authors or publishers explicitly state about their product. Therefore, it is a check of the claims that materials make about themselves. McDonough and Shaw (1993) suggest that this kind of analysis may be the first step of a more complex evaluation procedure, which can help evaluators pre-select materials for a comprehensive analysis.

External evaluation focuses on the blurb description of materials as well as the introduction and the table of contents, which may be analysed with reference to: the intended audience, proficiency level, teaching context, presentation of contents, and the methodology involved. Such an analysis may also include culture-related issues, e.g. the degree to which materials are biased/unbiased culturally, or the extent to which they present "a balanced picture of a particular country/society" (McDonough & Shaw 1993: 74).

Internal evaluation is an in-depth analysis of what materials genuinely offer, and it may be viewed as a verification of the outcome of external evaluation. It may focus on the manner in which language skills are presented in materials, the way in which content is graded and sequenced, authenticity of language, language practice procedures, motivational value or correspondence to learner needs (McDonough & Shaw 1993).

Cunningsworth (1995) cites a classification of evaluation methods which contains: an impressionistic overview and an in-depth evaluation. He maintains that when coursebook evaluation is conducted in an impressionistic mode, it is based on the face value of the coursebook under examination, i.e. the layout or the visual materials. In contrast, he explains that in-depth evaluation is guided by a set of referential criteria, i.e. a checklist.

Ellis (1997) makes a distinction between predictive evaluation and retrospective evaluation. While the former is performed in order to select appropriate materials before a course, the latter is based on either the teacher's impressions (impressionistic evaluation) or information gathered as materials are actually being used (empirical evaluation). He states that predictive and retrospective evaluation modes are not mutually exclusive, and teachers can verify predictive evaluation through a retrospective analysis after a period of use.

Łuczak-Łomża and Metera-Debaene (2002) list out another two types of materials evaluation: revision evaluation and summative evaluation. The former may be conducted in the middle of a language teaching course, when one intends to introduce the necessary modifications to the materials being used. The latter is implemented when materials that have already been in use for a period of time are being evaluated in terms of the learning outcomes that they have brought about.

Simultaneously, Łuczak-Łomża and Metera-Debaene (2002) declare that predictive evaluation, which they call *preliminary evaluation*, is the dominant type, and they also see it as based on a set of criteria, or checklists, which guide the process.

Tomlinson (2003) refers to predictive evaluation as *pre-use evaluation*, and he labels retrospective evaluation as *post-use evaluation*. At the same time, he adds that teachers might also conduct whilst-use evaluation, which is performed as materials are being utilised.

As it has been demonstrated, the idea of predictive evaluation has been widely accepted by methodologists; most recently it has been endorsed by Tsiplakides (2011). However, its drawbacks have also been highlighted.

For instance, Sheldon (1988) expressed the view that predictive evaluation is by default subjectivity-ridden, and even if teachers who undertake it utilise ready-made checklists, they cannot escape the problem. Ellis (1997) also recognised the issue of the subjectivity of predictive evaluation but, to some extent, he counteracted Sheldon's concern by observing that if checklists are implemented, they make materials evaluation at least more systematic.

Tomlinson (2003) maintains that all types of evaluation are by definition subjective as properly worded evaluation criteria are judgmental in character, and he contrasts evaluation with more objective *materials analysis*, where materials are judged in terms of the features that they contain or lack. He also adds that the objectivity of materials evaluation may be increased when it is carried out by a team of evaluators.

Interestingly enough, Inal (2006) endorses the implementation of checklists on two merits; on the one hand they are grounded in classroom experience, on the other hand they are frequently piloted before application. At the same time, Inal (ibid.) notices that, generic as they may be, checklists need to be adapted so that they correspond to the specific contexts in which they will be used – a point of view also shared by Łuczak-Łomża and Metera-Debaene (2002).

Evaluation criteria. A whole range of evaluative criteria has been proposed by scholars to date. The lists produced have varied from relatively short ones, which focused on a set of general criteria to be particularised by individual evaluators, to very detailed, comprehensive inventories. Examples of such lists are cited below.

Hutchinson and Waters (1987) put forward a relatively detailed list of criteria, the most characteristic of which were: (i) the target audience of the materials to be evaluated, including factors such as age, gender, nationality, course of study/occupation or interests; and (ii) aims, which referred to the aims to be achieved within a given course of study, or stage of education, in relation to the materials under examination. The remainder of Hutchinson and Waters' (1987) criteria overlapped with lists produced by other scholars, which are discussed underneath.

McDonough and Shaw (1993) offered a more general set of four criteria for materials evaluation: usability, generalizability, adaptability, and flexibility. Usability denotes the degree to which materials can function as the core, or supplement, of a language course; generalizability refers to the extent to which materials might be useful to larger target audiences; adaptability means the extent to which materials could be supplemented, extracted or adapted; and flexibility signifies the degree to which materials could be variously arranged/re-arranged or sequenced and graded anew in order to meet particular needs.

A comprehensive list of evaluation criteria has been recently proposed by Hanušova (2006), who provides an overall framework of coursebook evaluation, which on a macro level covers the following major aspects of language teaching materials: coursebook organisation, language content; topic, subject, social values; methodology; visuals; and study skills. Evaluation based on this list will involve a scrutiny of an array of micro-level components of teaching materials.

Coursebook organisation pertains to: recycling/reinforcement techniques, reference sections, vocabulary lists, the suitability of the material for self-study and unit length.

Language content can be analysed with reference to (a) grammar, e.g. the items covered, the correspondence of the grammar to learner needs, the size of the grammar unit, balance between the focus on language form and use; (b) vocabulary, e.g. the principles of vocabulary selection, the distinction between active/passive vocabulary, the reflection of the specific/local needs of learners, the presentation of semantic and formal relationships as well as collocations in order to illustrate the structure of the lexicon taught; (c) phonology, e.g. the presentation of a variety of phonological aspects such as sounds, stress, sentence stress and intonation; the reflection of the specific/local needs of learners, the integration of pronunciation work with other skills and the availability of audio material for pronunciation practice; (d) style, i.e. the presentation of specific language styles in appropriate situations and the presentation of a variety of English dialects; (e) language skills, i.e. practice in all four language skills, balance between the skills, omission of skills, authenticity of reading and listening tasks, the nature of comprehension check questions (concept vs. display questions)as well as the balance between accuracy and fluency work in speaking/writing and controlled/communicative exercises (Hanušova 2006).

Topic, subject, social values denote: the real/imaginary character of the topics tackled, the presentation of underlying social and cultural values, stereotyping, the presentation of social diversity through references to people's ethnic origin, occupation, age, social class and disability as well as the presentation of characters in various social contexts, such as family, peer group and workplace (Hanušova 2006).

Methodology refers to: learner needs, i.e. the degree to which the material discusses/ identifies needs and is responsive to the learning needs of the learners targeted, the principles and approaches adopted by the material, e.g. deductive/inductive, the balance between accuracy and fluency work, opportunities for creative language use, the treatment of errors and the status of the learners' native language (Hanušova 2006).

Visuals entail the degree to which visual aids are integrated into teaching as well as their decorative value and the level of quality/attractiveness that they display.

Finally, the *study skills* criterion concerns the presence of opportunities for reflection on study techniques, advice on the development of study skills, the creation of incentives which would encourage learners to take responsibility for their own learning and the presence/absence of materials for independent work (Hanušova 2006).

Checklists, such as the ones discussed above, can be used in two different manners. The more straight-forward way consists in the evaluator examining e.g. a coursebook with reference to each of the checklist criteria and establishing which of them are met and which ones are not.

The other possible way is the subjective/objective evaluation, where the evaluator first subjectively analyses the *language course* for which materials are being selected against a checklist of criteria so that the profile of required materials is produced. Subsequently, the *materials* under examination are objectively evaluated in the light of the original checklist in order to establish which of the desirable features they actually possess, and which they do not. Finally, answers to the questions asked in the two previous stages are compared so that it can be stated to what extent the materials match the teacher's expectations (Hutchinson & Waters 1987).

3.2 Evaluating intercultural materials

More pertinent to the present discussion of materials evaluation for the purpose of intercultural language teaching is an analysis of exemplary checklists which focus on the presence of culture in teaching materials.

It is possible to distinguish between two categories of evaluation checklists pertaining to the cultural component: (i) lists which happen to contain culture as one of the numerous other aspects of teaching materials that they are supposed to examine; and (ii) lists which focus specifically on culture.

Only a small number of scholars have included the cultural components of language teaching materials in the generic evaluation checklists that they have proposed. One of them is Cunningsworth (1995), who incorporated social and cultural values into his checklist by concentrating on how learners are supposed to interpret the cultural contexts which they encounter in coursebooks. His checklist features the following questions:

> "• Are the social and cultural contexts in the coursebook comprehensible to the learner?
> • Can learners interpret the relationships, behaviours, intentions etc. of the characters portrayed in the book?
> • Are women given equal prominence to men in all aspects of the coursebook?
> • What physical and character attributes are women given?
> • What professional and social positions are women shown as occupying?
> • What do we learn about the inner lives of the characters?
> • To what extent is the language of feeling depicted?
> • Do the coursebook characters exist in some kind of social setting, within a social network?
> • Are social relationships portrayed realistically?" (Cunningsworth 1995: 92).

Another scholar whose checklist contains a cultural element is Pfeiffer (2001), who estimates that teaching materials may, amongst others, present cultural knowledge, by which he understands: (i) the knowledge of material culture; (ii) the knowledge of geography and institutions; (iii) awareness of the target culture customs, traditions and appropriate behaviour; as well as (iv) the knowledge of 'big-C' culture, i.e. the arts.

As an aside, a curious discrepancy exists between the ways in which Pfeiffer (2001) and Byram (1997; 2003) view the outcomes of intercultural language learning. While Pfeiffer (2001) maintains that familiarity with the target language culture automatically results in the defamiliarisation of one's native culture and respect for otherness, Byram (1997; 2003) views the former outcome as a skill that must be developed and the latter as a shift in one's attitude, which requires effort.

A far more comprehensive analysis of the cultural component of language teaching materials is affordable when purpose-designed checklists are implemented. It must be admitted that a large number of such checklists have been produced.

One such list has been provided by Huhn (Byram 1989), who presents criteria for assessing the presence of cultural content as:

- inclusion of factually accurate and up-to-date cultural information;
- avoidance or relativisation of stereotypes, aimed at making learners stereotype-conscious;
- presentation of a realistic picture of the target language society, without creating the false impression that it is free from problems;
- learners' freedom in questioning the ideological tendencies implicit in the material – learners should be able to question the dominant image of the target language or their own society e.g. through comparison;
- presentation of cultural phenomena not as isolated facts but in structural or functional contexts; learners should also be able to verify the impact of the model of cultural analysis that they adopt in order to analyse culture;
- explicit elucidation of the relevance of historical materials to understanding contemporary society;
- presentation of historical materials through personalities whereby the latter are portrayed as moulded by their age.

According to Andersen and Risager (Byram 1989), coursebook analysis with regard to intercultural components should cover the following aspects of the content:

- spheres of activity and consciousness of the people involved, e.g. the subjects of conversations, norms and values;
- verbal and nonverbal interaction patterns, i.e. the nature of social relationships, gender and generation-based roles;
- explicit information about countries, including: geographical and social level, as well as historical information and a contemporary view;

• different varieties of language representative of the range of social groups that society is composed of.

Byram (1991) cites four elements of intercultural materials to be scrutinised:

• "analysis at the macro-social level of the social identity of textbook characters";
• "analysis at the micro-social level of the socio-economic, geographic and historical representations";
• "analysis of the viewpoint taken by the author";
• "analysis at the intercultural level of mutual representations of foreign and native cultures" (Byram 1991: 173-184).

Byram, Morgan et al. (1994) also present a coursebook evaluation checklist through which the intercultural component may be analysed with regard to the extent to which the following aspects of culture are dealt with:

• "social identity and social groups: class, regional;
• social interaction at differing levels of formality;
• belief and behaviour: daily routines, and moral, religious beliefs;
• socio-political institutions: state institutions, health care, law and order;
• socialisation and the life cycle: families, schools, employment, religion;
• national history: historical and contemporary events as markers of national identity;
• national geography: geographical factors seen as being significant by members of the target language community;
• national cultural heritage: cultural artefacts perceived as emblems of the national culture;
• stereotypes and national identity: symbols of national stereotypes" (Byram, Morgan et al. 1994: 51-52).

Edelhoff (1997) suggests that intercultural materials be assessed with regard to the four criteria: (i) content quality, (ii) characters presented, (iii) language and (iv) learner involvement.

(i) Content should be evaluated in terms of whether it is realistic, up-to-date and representative of the intercultural character of the target language society. This could be expressed through the following questions:

• To what extent is the image of culture presented smooth or realistic?

- Is the tourist point of view presented or are also the values and opinions central to the target language society demonstrated?
- Are everyday life situations and ordinary life featured?
- Are negative/problematic social aspects presented?
- Is the multicultural character of the foreign language society reflected?; are cultural incidents presented?
- Are all nationalities from the target language society represented?
- Is the nod between language and culture ever tackled?
- Are the teacher and their students encouraged to refer to other materials?
- Do the materials include texts written by different nationalities of the foreign language country or is only the white male point of view presented?
- Are the mentality, values, and ideas of the target language society presented?
- Are phenomena presented in historical perspective?

(ii) The characters presented are to be examined in terms of whether they are depicted as:

- representatives of the different age, gender, mentality, interest, class and family groups?
- in situation where they meet representatives of other nationalities/foreigner?
- through behaviours which would be linked with their society?
- as ordinary people?
- in different moods?

(iii) The target language is supposed to be analysed with reference to whether it is presented:

- along with the implicit value judgments and opinions it carries?; and negative connotations?
- through any instances of derogatory, 'coloured' usage?

(iv) The role of the learners is to be examined through the following questions:

- What are they asked to do?

• Are alternative cultural perspectives presented so that learners can choose and justify their choice?
• Are they encouraged to compare and judge materials, or understand people's mentality?
• Are they invited to adopt the foreign language perspective?
• Are they prepared to behave adequately in intercultural encounters?
• Is learners' essential knowledge checked before they are encouraged to express opinions?
• do they engage in discussion, which would enhance true understanding?
• Are they given a chance to alter the insights that have previously gained?

Skopinskaja (2003) has proposed a checklist which contains six areas to be evaluated: (i) rationale behind language teaching materials; (ii) cultural content; and the presentation of content through: (iii) cultural knowledge, (iv) attitudinal perspective (v) intercultural perspective, and (vi) culture-and-language perspective, which she presents as:

> "• rationale behind FL teaching materials' design, namely correspondence between the aims and goals of the TM and the students' conceptual framework; correspondence between the aims of the TM and the students' needs and goals; topics suitability as determined by students' age, gender, environment and social setting; and explicit/implicit statement of the goal of cultural instruction;
> • cultural content of the TM, that is culturally sensitive versus tourism-oriented portrayal of the cultural character of the foreign society; integration of the cultural content into the FL course; and the nature of the TM character representation with regard to its age, social class, interests, mentality and family situation;
> • presentation of content through cultural knowledge, that is inclusion of the historical, geographical, political, ideological, religious and creative arts perspectives to explain the national identity of the target language community; portrayal of different ethnic origins and sub-cultural groups; presentation of socio-political problems, socially acceptable or taboo topics as well as cultural/racial/gender stereotypes; and reference to the learners' own culture.
> • presentation of content through attitudinal perspective, that is development of tolerance and empathy towards otherness as well as a feeling of the national identity; challenging the learners' existing stereotypes; arousing curiosity about otherness; and preparing students for an adequate behaviour in the target language;

- presentation of content through intercultural perspective, that is encouraging learners to compare the foreign culture with their own; and offering mutual representations, images and stereotypes of the students' own and the foreign culture;
- presentation of content through culture-and-language perspective, that is development of students' linguistic as well as paralinguistic awareness; teaching appropriate register; and authenticity of the material used in the texts, exercises, tapes, etc" (Skopinskaja 2003: 46-47).

Kilickaya's (2004) checklist reflects the assumption that intercultural language learning is supposed to increase learners' awareness of a range of cultures and develop their transferrable intercultural communication skills. Bearing that in mind, she proposes the following guidelines for the evaluation of cultural information contained within a textbook:

"1. Does the book give any information, instructions or suggestions about how the book may be used and how the cultural content may be handled?
2. Does the book address specific learners or are there any characteristics of the learners that the book addresses to?
3. Does the book suggest any role that the teachers using it should have?
4. Do they include a variety of cultures or just specific ones such as British or American culture?
5. Do they represent the reality about the target culture or the author's view?
6. Where is the cultural information taken from? Author's own ideas or empirical research?
7. What subjects do they cover? Are these specific to the target culture? Are there any topics that might not be culturally suitable for the learners in class?
8. What cultural and social groups are represented? Is this adequate coverage of a variety of people or is this limited to a chosen people? If so, what kind of people are these? Are there any stereotypes?
9. Does the book include generalizations about the culture? Does it inform the audience of the fact that what is true of the parts is not necessarily true of the parts?
10. Is the cultural information presented with comments such as being good or being bad? Or is it presented without such comments?
11. Are there illustrations? If so, are these appropriate to the learners' native culture? Would additional information be necessary to explain them or are they self-explanatory?
12. What are the activities asked of the learners? Are they familiar to the learners?
13. Would a teacher using this book need specialized training to be able to use it or is there enough information given?

14. What are the learners supposed to do with the cultural information such as using actively or just be aware of it for a better understanding of the target culture?
15. What is your overall view of the textbook?" (Kilickaya 2004).

Finally, Bandura (2007) posits that intercultural coursebooks ought to feature content including:

• authentic, thought-provoking texts, different styles and perspectives, which would incite knowledge construction, without promoting stereotypes;
• texts about the impact of cultural knowledge on the effectiveness of communication;
• activities fostering learner autonomy by involving learners in an analysis of varied sources, e.g. media, the web or project assignments (home ethnography/virtual ethnography);
• activities stimulating intercultural comparisons;
• content based on learners' knowledge, experience and interests (selected through learner interviews and reviews of teaching programmes as well as coursebooks in non-ELT subjects).

3.3 Evaluation of CALL materials

Davies (2009) raises the point that the evaluation of computer software designed for the purpose of language teaching and learning is more difficult than the evaluation of printed coursebooks. He claims that the challenge of the former type of evaluation stems from the nature of computer software and its Graphic User Interface (GUI). For instance, screen design, the degree to which a program is user-friendly, the software-human interaction that it incites as well as the lack of linear navigation routes may all obscure sections of the program from the evaluator. Moreover, portions of content may be accessed through alternative routes, which can only be discovered in the course of extensive exploration.

A complete checklist for CALL software evaluation has been designed Gajek (2002b), who proposes a very detailed set of criteria which to use when evaluating computer language teaching/learning programs on optical discs – originally, CD-ROMs. Her evaluation criteria comprise the following elements which determine the rate of success in CALL: (i) the teacher; (ii) the learner; (iii) the language content; (iv) computer assisted instruction modes; (v) technical issues; and (vi) the cost.

After conversion, Gajek's (2002b) list can be verbalised through the following check questions:

(i) The teacher's perspective embraces the following criteria:

- Does the software description match the language content of the activities provided?
- Is the language content relevant to the curricular and personal needs of the learners or the educational institution?
- Do the audio-visuals incorporated into the program truly enhance language education, without being merely a marketing trick?
- Are the language skills which are supposed to be developed by the program are easily identifiable?
- Are the learning styles and strategies that the activities and content presentation modes involve are easily identifiable?
- Are the content and work modes featured in the activities not pedagogically harmful to the learner?
- Does the program feature teachers' notes (electronic or printed) providing methodological guidelines on program use?
- Are the criteria of speech recognition explicitly stated (if speech recognition is part of the program's functionalities)
- Is it possible to make save electronic copies or make print-outs of activities for the purpose of homework assignments?
- Does the program enable learners to cooperate/compete?

(ii) The learner's perspective comprises criteria that can be expressed through the following questions:

- Do the program goals state what it enables the learner to do, and not what the program itself is capable of?
- Is the language content clearly organized?
- Is the target age group clearly stated?
- Does the program cater for the needs and interests of both genders?
- Are activity instructions additionally accompanied by examples?
- Is the navigation intuitive?
- Are the navigation options always available?
- Does the program enable the learner to select between varied learning strategies?
- Can the learner select activities according to learning goals?
- Are the activities involving?
- Do the graphics enhance learning?
- Does the learner obtain immediate feedback?
- Can the learner search the program content by key words?

- Is program help available?
- Does the program provide a variety of language tests?
- Does the program enable learners to cooperate/compete?

(iii) Language-related criteria of evaluation cover the following questions:

- Is the language featured by the program correct?
- Is the language presented in clear situational and cultural context?
- Is the language level precisely stated?
- Is it possible to induce grammatical rules from the language samples provided?
- Does the program accept alternative language forms/expressions appropriate in a given situation.
- Are the audio-visuals attractive and do they correspond the language content?
- Are the language goals of the program and its activities accurately stated? E.g. developing language competence, communicative skills or examination skills.

(iv) Criteria related to computer assisted instruction comprise the following questions:

- Is it possible to set a time limit for the activities?
- Are the activities doable in the time allocated by the program?
- Does the program add enhance instruction through the multimedia and interactivity it offers?

(v) Criteria related to technical issues are as follows:

- Is the technician's assistance necessary?
- Does the program inform how it can be updated?
- Are the colours comfortable to the eye?
- Are the font characters clear to read?
- Do the text and graphics not interfere with each other?
- Is the navigation system intuitive? E.g. through the use of icons.

(vi) The cost is determined by:

• Does the price reflect the usefulness of the program for the learner and teacher?
• Are the program functions useful socially, apart from the technical possibilities they create?
• Does the program mostly contain: language content, graphics, audio clips, animations and tools that serve the purpose of language teaching and learning, without too many gadgets of marketing value only?

The National Center for ESL Literacy Education (NCESLLE 2003) has suggested the following criteria for evaluating CALL software:

"• Is the program compatible with your computers and/or network?
• Is technical assistance readily available via phone or email?
• Is an informative and comprehensible guide provided with the software program?
• Does the program encourage communicative practice and cooperative learning?
• What skill areas does the software address: Listening, speaking, reading, writing, pronunciation?
• What kind of activity is the program presenting: Writing practice, reading comprehension, vocabulary development, pronunciation practice? Does the software offer a variety of activities?
• What levels of proficiency is the program designed for?
• Are the interface navigation, and the directions clear and logical?
• Are the vocabulary and cultural assumptions – in the directions as well as the program—likely to be understood by English language learners?
• Does the software program assess learner progress in the skill the learner is working on? For example, if a pronunciation program only requires a learner to repeat a word or phrase and then compare with the program, there is no information about whether or not the learner is benefiting from the activity.
• Does the software program allow the teacher to author her own lessons tailored to the needs of the class or individual learners?
• Do the individual program lessons fit within the time constraints of class or lab sessions so that a learner can finish a lesson in one setting?
• Are there supplementary materials included for class or homework follow-up?" (NCESLLE 2003).

Finally, Davies (2009) proposes his own checklist, which is supposed to be used for evaluating software intended to be used offline, i.e. operated either directly from the computer hard disk, the local area network, or from the optical drive, e.g. the DVD-ROM. However, this list is a versatile tool, suited for practically all contexts in which CALL software can be used at present, and can be applied to online applications as well. It embraces the following questions:

"• Is the level of language that the program offers clearly indicated?
• Is it easy to start the program?
• Is the user interface easy to understand? (For example, is the screen layout clear and easy to interpret?)
• Is it easy to navigate through the program?
• Are icons that are used to assist navigation (e.g. back to the homepage, exit) clear and intelligible?
• Is it always clear to the learner which point s/he has reached in the program?
• Does the program include scoring?
• If a scoring system is used, does it make sense?
• If a scoring system is used, does it encourage the learner?
• Is the learner offered useful feedback if s/he gets something wrong?
• If the learner gets something right purely by chance, can s/he seek an explanation in order to find out why the answer is right?
• Can the learner seek help, e.g. on grammar, vocabulary, pronunciation, cultural content?
• Does the program branch to remedial routines?
• Can the learner easily quit something that is beyond his/her ability?
• Are the grammar and vocabulary used in the program accurate?
• Does the program offer cultural insights?
• If the program includes pictures, are they (a) relevant, (b) an aid to understanding?
• If the program includes sound recordings, are they of an adequate quality?
• If the program includes sound recordings, are they (a) relevant, (b) an aid to understanding?
• If the program includes sound recordings, is there a good mix of male and female voices and regional variations?
• Can the learner record his/her own voice and play it back?
• Does the program make use of Automatic Speech Recognition (ASR)?
• If the program makes use of ASR, is it effective?
• If the program includes video sequences, are they of an adequate quality?
If the program includes video sequences, are they (a) relevant, (b) an aid to understanding?
• Is the program relevant to your national/regional/departmental programme of study?" (Davies 2009).

3.4 Guidelines for evaluating the intercultural component of CALL software

Content-related criteria. All in all, materials evaluation checklists contain evaluation criteria which can be categorised as: (i) cultural content; (ii) cultural perspectives; and (iii) learner activity.

(i) *Cultural content* refers to: (a) material culture (Pfeiffer 2001); (b) socio-political realia (Pfeiffer 2001), including institutions (Byram, Morgan et al. 1994); as well as (c) behaviour and practices (Pfeiffer 2001; Byram, Morgan et al. 1994; Edelhoff 1997).

The other elements of cultural content are: (d) thought patterns, cultural norms, values, verbal/nonverbal interaction patterns, and social relationships (Andersen and Risager, cited in Byram 1989); (e) stereotypes (Byram 1994; Bandura 2007); and (f) languaculture (Edelhoff 1997).

(ii) *Cultural perspectives* concern the different angles at which culture can be tackled: attitudes (Cunningsworth 1995; Skopinskaja 2003; Edelhoff 1997), past/presence (Huhn, cited in Byram 1989; Skopinskaja 2003), society (Huhn, cited in Byram 1989; Cunningsworth 1995), realism (Edelhoff 1997), heterogeneity (Byram 1994; Edelhoff 1997; Skopinskaja 2003), and generalisation/particularisation (Kilickaya 2004).

(iii) *Learner activity* refers to the tasks through which learners explore culture, including: selecting perspectives, discussion, an analysis of the impact of materials on the quality of cultural exploration, dealing with a spectrum of resources, judging/comparing materials (Edelhoff (1997), autonomously interpreting cultural phenomena(Cunningsworth 1995; Bandura 2007), constructing knowledge (Kramsch 1993) as well as learning through experience (Bolt 2001), comparing native language and culture with their target counterparts and self-assessing intercultural competence (Bandura 2007).

Technology-related criteria. From CALL software evaluation checklists three groups of features which are likely to stimulate intercultural learning may be synthesised: (i) navigation; (ii) multimedia; and (iii) additional functionalities.

(i) *Navigation* refers to tools which permit learners to explore program content (Davies 2009) independently and with ease, which may be facilitated by advanced search options (Gajek 2002b).

(ii) *Multimedia* cover audio/video content, which must be relevant and sufficiently clear (Davies 2009) so that it increases learners' understanding of intercultural issues being examined.

(iii) *Additional functionalities* regard tools which would be particularly useful for intercultural exploration, e.g. functionalities providing learners with relevant explanation at the time of need (Davies 2009). Another helpful option could be an annotation tool, which would permit learners to record emotions or append content with their own remarks.

Intercultural learning would also be fostered by tools which would enable learners to interact with other human beings (NCESLLE 2003) , e.g. in order to practice intercultural communication.

What would further foster autonomous intercultural learning is a collection of supplementary materials (NCESLLE 2003), which could potentially encourage learners to extend their intercultural work to work settings beyond the classroom, e.g. home.

Last but not least, additional functionalities could empower teachers to design their own activities, or create entire lesson units (Gajek 2002b), which would open new learning paths, or engage learners in new learning modes.

A checklist for the evaluation of software in intercultural language teaching settings. In the light of the content-related and technology-related evaluation criteria analysed above, an exemplary CALL software evaluation checklist has been compiled for use in intercultural language teaching settings.

The list is open to re-construction, depending on the needs of particular evaluators. However, as it stands, it features criteria pertaining to: (i) cultural content and work modes, aligned to the major components of Byram's (1997) intercultural competence, i.e. attitudes, knowledge, skills of interpreting and relating, skills of discovery and interaction, and critical cultural awareness; and (ii) computer functionalities useful for intercultural learning.

	EVALUATION CRITERIA
WORK MODES/CONTENT	**ATTITUDES** (Do learners …)
	question stereotypes?
	explore culture through multiple perspectives?
	KNOWLEDGE (Does the culture taught cover…)
	material culture?
	socio-political realia?
	behaviour/practices?
	thought patterns/values?
	languaculture?
	SKILLS OF INTERPRETING AND RELATING (Do learners …)
	interpret cultural phenomena?
	compare L1/C1 with L2/C2?
	SKILLS OF DISCOVERY AND INTERACTION (Do learners …)
	consult varied sources?
	do project work?
	engage in intercultural communication?
	self-assess own intercultural skills?
	CRITICAL CULTURAL AWARENESS (Do learners …)
	compare and judge materials?
	explicitly discuss their criteria of cultural analysis?
TECHNOLOGY	**COMPUTER FUNCTIONALITIES** (Does the software feature...)
	alternative navigation routes?
	advanced search options?
	insightful audio-visuals?
	cultural explanation?
	annotation tools?
	online communication tools?
	supplementary cultural materials?
	task authoring tools?

Table 5-2

3.5 Summary

Historically speaking, the implementation of information and communication technology in teaching culture in the foreign language classroom has been increasing simultaneously with advancements in technology and ELT methodology.

In the 1960s-1980s ICT served purposes other than culture teaching, e.g. it was used to deliver mechanical language drills or text reconstruction tasks. The presence of selected observable elements of culture increased within computerised ELT software towards the beginning of the 1990s, where the focus was on both language practice as well as cultural education. As multimedia were being introduced to the computer, so were media-enhanced cultural activities being added to CALL packages or network-based courseware.

The turn of the millennia saw a shift from the use of computers in teaching about culture to teaching culture experientially through ICT-mediated telecollaboration, which permitted genuine intercultural communication. Most recently, intercultural concordancing has enriched the repertoire of computer-based techniques in teaching culture, which allows a comparative languacultural analysis of language corpora.

The very idea of utilising ICT for the purpose of intercultural teaching is justifiable in the light of the kinds of learning which it promotes. As Fitzpatrick (2003) reports, ICT-enhanced learning is characterised by: authenticity, learner-centeredness, learner autonomy, communication-oriented and multimedia-based. Hence, it may be stated that ICT promotes exactly the kinds of learning modes which are most desirable features of intercultural training, as proposed by Bandura (2007). The usefulness of computer technology for intercultural learning has also been corroborated by Heyworth (2003), Corbett (2003), Aleksandrowicz-Pędich (2005), Bélisle (2007), Gajek (2007) and Byram (2008).

Bélisle (2007) additionally posits that, quite significantly, ICT combines cognition with empathy, shifts memorisation work towards transformation, promotes interpersonal relations, as well as helps learners explore foreign cultures from within.

A vast array of computerised techniques have already been developed to facilitate intercultural language learning, for instance: purpose-made intercultural applications (Korhonen 1999), concordancers (Liaw 2006), telecollaboration projects (Osborne 2000; Komorowska 2006a; Czaplikowska 2007), webquests (Dodge 1995; Kurek 2004); e-journals (Żylińska 2003); literary web projects (Müller-Hartmann 2000); and online forums (Hanna and de Nooy 2003; Levy 2007).

As this chapter has already demonstrated, foreign language teachers who wish to deliver intercultural training in their own classroom will not find it problematic to access the relevant professional literature through which they would be able to familiarise themselves with the necessary rationale and the possible work modes, techniques or examples of classroom practice.

However, what may pose a problem is the process of selecting appropriate computer-based materials for intercultural language teaching out of what is available on the market. Although numerous evaluation lists have been proposed for the predictive evaluation of non-CALL (inter)cultural materials as well as computer assisted language learning materials as such, no checklists are available specifically for the evaluation of ICT-based intercultural materials, which is likely to either cause confusion to teachers who would like to develop their learners' intercultural competence, or – at best – leave them to their own devices.

Therefore, it may be concluded that the provision of such checklists might fill an important gap, and enable teachers intending to use ICT for intercultural training to take informed decisions about the choice of actual materials which they would wish to trial and systematically use. An exemplary checklist has been proposed in this chapter.

CHAPTER SIX

RESEARCH MODULE I: INFORMATION AND COMMUNICATION TECHNOLOGY IN THE TEACHING OF LANGUAGE AND CULTURE – THE TEACHERS' PERSPECTIVE

Chapters Six and Seven are an account of a bi-modular research study conducted in April-June, 2011, whose aims were: (i) to investigate to what degree and in what manner Polish EFL teachers implement information and communication technology in language/culture teaching, and what attitudes they display towards CALL (Module I); as well as (ii) to evaluate CALL software, available on the market, in terms of (inter)cultural components (Module II), i.e. features promoting (inter)cultural learning.

This chapter is a report of the research administered within Module I. The preparatory procedure that led to the study began in August, 2010, with the preparation of the research questions. This stage comprised: the preparation and consultation of the first draft of the questionnaire, the piloting of the study, and a revision of the questionnaire in the light of the feedback received. The data gathered were analysed quantitatively in June-July, 2011.

1. Research aims

Module I of the study qualifies as a **focused description** (Larsen-Freeman & Long 1991) in that it was descriptive in nature. The scope of the research was narrowed down to a set of variables relating to the Polish EFL teachers' attitudes/believes towards the use of information and communication technology in the EFL classroom and the degree to which they implement it in order to teach the target language as well as develop learners' intercultural skills.

Consequently, the structured questionnaire which constituted the research instrument contained pre-conceived categories of teachers' behaviour and attitudes/believes against which the respondents' answers were analysed. In the light of Seliger and Shohamy's (1989) delineation of the parameters of research, this study can be regarded as **deductive research**.

On the qualitative/quantitative continuum proposed by Larsen-Freeman & Long (1991) a focused description is placed towards the quantitative end. However, the research conducted within Module I was both qualitative, in that it described naturally occurring phenomena, as well as quantitative, since the data obtained were quantified and analysed statistically. At the same time, it must be admitted that the emphasis was placed on **quantitative data analysis**. This is corroborated by the research **cross-sectional research** (Cohen et al. 2007) design of the study, which is typically associated with the quantitative paradigm (Larsen-Freeman & Long 1991).

Module I did not involve the researcher's artificial intervention into the phenomena under investigation, therefore, it must be viewed as non-experimental (Seliger & Shohamy 1989).

The research was also **analytical** (Seliger & Shohamy 1989) in approach as it analysed the phenomena observed into constituents without distorting their nature. Therefore, it required clearly stated operational definitions of the phenomena observed, which were provided within the research questions that the study was driven by.

In general terms, the research conducted within Module 1 was guided by two main research questions:

1. To what degree and in what manner do Polish EFL teachers implement information and communication technology in order to teach the target language?
2. To what degree and in what manner do Polish EFL teachers implement information and communication technology in order to teach culture and develop their learners' intercultural skills?

The main research questions were further broken down into the following specific questions, illustrative of the aims of the research, in order to examine particular aspects of the issues under investigation:

- In what technological conditions and circumstances do Polish teachers of English work at school? (Research question 1);

- What attitudes do Polish EFL teachers display towards information and communication technology? (Research question 2);
- What kinds of computer skills and qualifications do Polish EFL teachers possess? (Research question 3);
- Do Polish EFL teachers use information and communication technology in their teaching; what kind of information and communication technology do they utilise, and in what manner do they utilise it? (Research question 4);
- Do Polish EFL teachers use information and communication technology in order to develop learners' intercultural competence? (Research question 5);
- What are the potential deterrents which discourage Polish EFL teachers from implementing information and communication technology in the EFL classroom? (Research question 6).

A tabular overview of research conducted within Module I, including its aims, methods, techniques, subject sample and type of data analysis, is presented in Appendix A.

2. Research methods and techniques

In order to gather data within Module I, a purpose-prepared, structured questionnaire of a high degree of explicitness (Seliger & Shohamy 1989) was designed which mostly contained closed-ended questions (Dawson 2002). However, in particular cases open-ended questions were added in order to elicit more detailed information from the respondents. Consequently, the respondents predominantly selected responses from the pre-set options provided by the research author; only in places did they have to answer questions in their own words.

The questionnaire was self-administered, i.e. each respondent filled in the questionnaire paper on their own, without the researcher's assistance. The questionnaire papers were delivered to the respondents in printed format either in person, by post or via email.

As the questionnaire pertained to the use of information and communication technology, which inherently involves techno-jargon, simple, non-technical language was used throughout in order to ensure question clarity.

Two filter questions were used in order to refer the respondents to the relevant sections of the questionnaire paper, with a view to reducing the administration time, encouraging the completion of the questionnaire, and limiting the possibility of the respondents having to answer questions irrelevant to their circumstances.

The questionnaire opened with an introductory note from the author of the research which informed the respondents about the nature and aims of the study. It must be added here that precautions were taken in order to present the aims of the questionnaire to the respondents only in general terms, and reduce non-random variance in the data collected, which might otherwise have been caused by *approval motive* and *self-flattering* (Larsen-Freeman & Long 1991), i.e. the respondents trying to win the administrator's approval, or produce a positive self-image, respectively.

Question types. Since the questionnaire was administered in Poland, and to Polish EFL teachers exclusively, it was produced in Polish, including the administrator's introductory note, the questions and a thank-you note at the end.

The questionnaire contained a mixture of the following types of closed-ended questions: (i) **Likert-type scale** questions (Larsen-Freeman & Long 1991; Cohen et al. 2007), where the respondents had to select their answer from a range of responses, with *strongly agree* and *strongly disagree* options at either end of the response range and intermediate alternatives in between; (ii) **numerical scale questions**, where the respondents selected one of the alternative responses which expressed the frequency of certain actions or occurrences; (iii) **multiple-choice questions**, where the respondents selected one of the two alternative responses provided; (iv) **ranked/interval questions** (Cohen et al. 2007), where the respondents ordered a set of given response categories by arranging them in order of preference; and (v) **hidden response questions**, i.e. those where only one specific answer could be supplied, but it was not pre-determined.

Selected close-ended questions were appended with open-ended response categories, e.g. *others*, which included an additional space for more detail. In particular cases, close-ended questions were followed by open-ended ones in order to elicit more detailed data, or to allow for responses beyond those preset by the questionnaire administrator.

Categories of questions. All in all, the questionnaire contained 71 questions, which were grouped into eight categories from A to G, corresponding to specific aspects of the phenomena under examination.

Section A (9 questions) aimed at establishing the profile of the subjects participating in the study, and it was meant to elicit: the respondents' personal data, including gender, age; professional qualifications, professional position with regard to the Polish professional development scheme; the length of professional experience in ELT; the type of school at which the respondent worked (nursery, primary, lower secondary, upper secondary or teacher training college (post-secondary); the sector of education (public or private); and the weekly workload, i.e. the number of lesson units taught per week.

Section B (9 questions) entailed questions about the information and communication technology infrastructure available at the respondents' school, including: access to computers and internet connectivity as well as the type and age of computer hardware/technologies available.

Section C (13 questions) examined the respondents' attitude towards the idea of computer assisted language learning and the computer as a tool.

Section D (3 questions) elicited data on the respondents' computer literacy with reference to: ICT skills, including the ability to operate computer software, and formal ICT qualifications.

Section E (32 questions) covered questions relating to the degree to which the respondents implemented information and communication technology in language teaching in and outside the EFL classroom, as well as the manner in which they did it. The questions focused on: types of the teachers' activity, computer software and media resources; the amount of time devoted to computer-assisted language learning instruction (CALL); work mode; and purposes for which the respondents used computers in their teaching.

Section F (7 questions) embraced questions investigating to what degree and in what manner the respondents utilized ICT while developing their learners' intercultural competence. The data obtained comprised: the types of media resources used, the aspects of culture taught, the types of cultural activities learners used, the communication tools utilised, the purposes for which the communication tools were implemented, and the internet-enhanced techniques employed.

Finally, Section G (1 question) focused on potential deterrents which might have discouraged the teachers from applying information and communication technology to foreign language teaching at large.

Before the questionnaire was administered, it was piloted (Seliger & Shohamy 1989; Dawson 2002; Cohen et al. 2007) on a group of 10 teacher trainers as well as primary, lower secondary and upper secondary school teachers. The pilot study took place in March-April, 2011, and helped the administrator revise the questionnaire in terms of inconsistencies and lack of clarity in the instructions, questions as well as the lay-out. On the basis of the feedback obtained a number of changes were introduced to the questionnaire paper.

Firstly, the questionnaire size was reduced from 6 A-4 format pages to 3 in order to reduce the risk of causing fatigue to the respondents, which might have resulted in a very low return rate. The researcher shortened the questionnaire by collapsing particular questions, deleting questions whose scope overlapped with others, amalgamating several response categories, reducing the font size and rearranging the lay-out.

Another change introduced concerned question clarity and was aimed at ensuring that all respondents would understand the questions relating to computer-enhanced technologies in the same manner. This was achieved in two ways: questions pertaining to the respondents' ICT skills were reformulated as *can-do* statements in order for the respondents to be able to state which skills they had and which ones they lacked, without them having to interpret the technical jargon originally used.

Moreover, as it occurred that questions which involved terms labelling specific computer-based technologies in Polish could be potentially confusing for the respondents, e.g. (*wyszukiwanie informacji w internecie* vs. *przeglądanie stron internetowych*) [*searching web content* vs. *browsing web pages*, My translation], a simplification was introduced. On the grounds of the assumption that teachers might be able to use computer applications without necessarily being able to name them properly, questions referring to particular technologies were appended with examples of specific computer programs, or web applications, which the respondents were likely to be familiar with. The following questions exemplify the case with regard to the afore-mentioned terminology (My translation):

Tick of the software-operating skills which you have. I can:
❑ *browse internet pages (e.g. in Internet Explorer, Firefox, Google Chrome)*
❑ *search web content (e.g. in the Google search engine)*

As far as instructions are concerned, it was necessary to specify them in order to avoid the respondents' confusion. For instance, the instruction: *Ponumeruj poniższe media od 1 do 7 wg częstotliwości z jaką je wykorzystujesz* [*Number the following media resources according to the frequency at which you use them* (My translation)], had to be altered in order to allow for teachers who did not use the media listed at all. It was also necessary to indicate which end of the 1-7 spectrum was positive/negative. This was done by inserting one more sentence into the instruction: *Media, z których nie korzystasz wcale oznacz cyfrą 0* [*The media which you do not use at all should be numbered as 0* (My translation)].

Minor changes included the addition of a null option to certain multiple-choice questions, e.g.: ❑ *żadne* [❑ *none* (My translation)]. The final copy of the questionnaire was prepared in two versions: the researcher's copy (cf. Appendix B), which contained section titles indicating what was supposed to be measured within each, and the respondents' version (cf. Appendix C), which was ultimately implemented in the course of the research. The omission of section titles in the respondents' copy was determined by the need for brevity as well as the necessity to avoid non-random variance in the data collected.

The revision process was completed in April, 2011.The questionnaire was subsequently re-examined against the research questions which guided the study within Module I and administered to a group of 105 (N=105) EFL teachers from Poland in April-June, the same year.

Research administration. The questionnaire was carried out in different parts of Poland, including: Białystok, Bydgoszcz, Gdynia, Lublin, Łowicz, Łódź, Sieradz, Skierniewice, Warszawa, Zgierz and Zduńska Wola, and it was mostly filled in printed format. Only one respondent (0.95%) filled the questionnaire in electronic format, as an MS Word document (doc), and returned it by e-mail.

The researcher administered the questionnaire himself at 3 teacher training institutions: two teacher training colleges in central Poland and a higher school in Warsaw. When conducting the questionnaire in person, the researcher did not introduce it to the respondents in a way other than by referring them to the questionnaire paper and the instructions contained therein. It was done intentionally as the researcher wished to render all the administration modes comparable.

The respondents filled in the questionnaire paper on the spot and returned it to the researcher, or they filled it at home and returned, subsequently. One respondent within the group examined directly by the researcher returned the questionnaire by e-mail, having requested an electronic version beforehand. All in all, direct administration turned out to be the most effective, irrespective of where the questionnaire was filled in, with a return rate at the maximum level of 100%.

The questionnaire was also administered by the researcher's colleague teachers and teacher trainers across Poland. In that case, the researcher approached his colleagues by e-mail or by phone and arranged for them to administer the questionnaire in their locations. Printed copies of the questionnaire were posted to the colleagues involved, with an attached lead letter in a self-addressed, stamped envelope. The researcher's colleagues who conducted the questionnaire on behalf of the researcher did so at various educational institutions, mostly at teacher training institutions (teacher training colleges, teacher development centres and higher education institutions with postgraduate/diploma courses for in-service teachers). The questionnaires were distributed to the teaching staff of the institutions and their students, teacher-trainees, who were already professionally active, i.e. employed at the level of primary, and lower/upper secondary school.

The questionnaires were handed in to the respondents, filled in, and returned to the person in charge. Subsequently, the copies were posted back to the researcher, or handed over by the colleague teachers in person. The return rate differed from case to case, but on average it equalled to 58%, ranging from 0% to 66%.

3. Subject sample

The research subjects examined within Module I of the study (N=105) were in-service teachers of English, who represented various types of educational institutions, including: primary schools, lower secondary schools, upper secondary schools, language schools and teacher training colleges. The respondents were selected by means of convenience sampling, otherwise referred to as accidental or opportunity sampling (Cohen et al. 2007), in combination with snowball sampling (Miles & Huberman 1994; Cohen et al. 2007).

The subject sample was recruited in a non-random fashion as the respondents volunteered to participate in the research study after they had been invited to do so.

The profile of the subject sample. The subject sample was composed of teachers employed within both the state and independent (private) sectors of education. A vast majority of them were females, and they varied in age from under 30 to over 40 years. Their professional qualifications ranged from no formal teaching qualifications to a PhD degree, while their teaching experience spanned from 1-5 years to over 10 years, with a majority of more experienced teachers. Most of the subjects within the sample held the professional status of EFL teachers, however, roughly one-third were teacher trainers.

The subject sample is described in greater detail below, including variables such as: gender, age, professional qualifications, professional position with regard to the Polish professional development scheme, length of professional experience in ELT, type of school, sector of education, and weekly workload.

Gender. All in all, 105 (N=105) respondents took part in the study within Module I. 16 subjects (15.2%) did not indicate their gender, thus, the data obtained with regard to this variable is based on responses from 89 subjects (84.8%), out of whom 65.7% were female and 19% were male.

This might suggest that female teachers were overrepresented in the research study. However, as the teaching profession seems to be strongly feminised, the disparity between the two gender groups is reflective of general trends in education.

Age. A majority of the respondents (45.7%) fell into the 30-40 age bracket, 20.9% were under 30 years of age, and 28.5% were over the age of 40. It must be observed here that 5 subjects (4.8%) did not indicate their age, thus, the data presented above are valid for 100 (N=100) subjects (95.2%). The two extreme age groups, the under-30's and over-40's, were slightly underrepresented in relation to the 30-40 age group, which constituted a clear majority.

Professional qualifications. The subjects' professional qualifications ranged from a teacher training college diploma through a *licencjat* (an undergraduate degree equivalent to a Bachelor's degree) to a PhD degree. A vast majority of the subjects (80%) had obtained a Master's degree, including 74.29% of the overall sample who held a Master of Arts degree and 5.71% of all the subject sample who had an equivalent degree of a Master of Education in EFL teaching. 15.2% held a *licencjat*; 1.9% had a diploma in English language teaching, obtained from a teacher training college; 0.9% (one subject) held the postgraduate degree of a Philosophy Doctor (PhD), and 1.9%, which stood for 2 subjects, possessed a different degree. One of the latter two subjects had obtained a degree of *magister inżynier*, which one can receive at a higher institution specialising in engineering in Poland (politechnika). The other subject selected the response category of *other degrees* as he/she was completing a teacher training college course at the time of the research and had not obtained any degree yet, however, he/she already functioned as a teacher at a private language school.

All in all, it may be stated that 96.9% of the teachers of English who constituted the sample possessed a university level degree. Two subjects had a teacher training college diploma, and one subject was taking a course in teacher training at the time of the research.

Additional qualifications. 48.5% of the teachers had obtained additional qualifications in the course of their career. Within that group (N=51) 43.1% had completed a postgraduate diploma course; 33.3% had participated in a course increasing their professional qualifications; 23.5% had obtained an international language certificate; and none of them had passed a professional examination, e.g. TOEFL or TESOL.

Professional position. As teachers employed at the primary and secondary level of the public education system in Poland are obliged to participate in the professional development scheme, run by the Polish

Ministry of Education, they hold different professional positions. Out of the sample (N=105), 21.9% were *nauczyciel kontraktowy* (the lowest possible rank), 5.7% were *nauczyciel stażysta* (the second lowest rank), 30.5% were *nauczyciel mianowany* (the second top rank), and 32.4% were *nauczyciel dyplomowany* (the highest possible rank). 9.5% of the respondents indicated that the professional development scheme did not apply to their context, e.g. when they worked for a private language school.

Teaching experience in the EFL classroom. The teachers displayed considerable differences in teaching experience, which ranged from 1 to 41 years. On average, the subjects had been teaching for 13.1 years. The modular response, i.e. the most frequent, was 10 years of teaching.

For the purpose of clarity all the responses were collapsed into 3 subgroups which formed a spectrum of experience: *novice teachers*, i.e. those with experience ranging from 1-5 years; those with an *experience of 6-10 years*, and those with *over 10 years' experience*.

Statistical computations revealed that the vast majority of the sample (59%) were experienced teachers, with over 10 years' experience. Teachers with 1-5 years' experience (21%) and 6-10 years' experience (20%) were fairly equally represented.

Type of school and sector of education. 16% of the subjects declared that they worked at primary schools, 21% stated they were employed at lower secondary schools, 35.2% of the subjects worked at upper secondary schools, 10.5% of the subjects claimed that they worked at language schools, and 33.3% worked at teacher training colleges. None of the respondents worked at a nursery school.

The total percentage score for the subject sample amounts to 116%, which stems from the fact that a number of subjects selected more than one type of school as they were employed at several educational institutions.

For the purpose of the research study the original responses were additionally collapsed into two major categories reflecting the subjects' professional status: teachers vs. teacher trainers. The subjects who worked at primary, lower secondary and upper secondary schools were classified as teachers. Those employed at teacher training colleges were categorised as teacher trainers. In effect, it turned out that 66.6% of the subjects were teachers, 30.4% of the subjects were teacher trainers, and 2.5% subjects were involved in both teaching and teacher training.

Sector of education.13.7% of the subjects were employed in the independent (private) sector, whereas 94.1% worked in the state sector. The total percentage score equals to 107.8% but that is indicative of the fact that 8 respondents selected both options as they worked within both educational sectors.

Weekly workload. The subjects' weekly workload, expressed through the number of hours they taught per week ranged from 8 to 35 hours. On average, the subjects taught 18.8 hours per week, and the modular response was 12 hours.

4. Results of the survey

The data obtained through the questionnaire were analysed quantitatively with the use of PSPP, the statistical analysis computer program. In addition, the spreadsheet application *MS Excel* was used to produce a graphic representation of selected data. The data which emerged yielded by the study were computed with the use of descriptive statistics, i.e. frequency distributions. Below is a discussion of the data obtained.

4.1 The information and communication technologies available at school

Access to computers at school. Only one respondent (1%) stated that no computers were available in his/her school. The remainder claimed their schools offered access to computers in the following places: the learners' common room (3.9%); the school hall (9.7%); the classrooms (48.5%); the administration offices (72.8%); the school library (86.4%); and the computer suite (91.3%).

As the results suggest, computers were mostly available to the teachers, and their learners, mostly in the computer suite and the school library. What is important, the teachers were much less likely to find computers in the regular classroom, and it must be born in mind that foreign language teachers may find it problematic to book a language lesson at the computer suite, which is normally reserved for ICT classes.

At the same time, given the data cited, it seemed possible for the teachers' learners to perform computer-based tasks both in the classroom as well as outside it, e.g. in the library. However, the degree to which self-access is possible usually depends on the actual number of computers at the learners' disposal. Very few schools offered computers to learners in other self-access locations, such as the school hall or the learners' common room.

Frequency of computer access. As the very presence of computers at school does not immediately translate into access, the respondents were asked how frequently they could use the computers (question B2) and the computer suite (question B3), and whether they needed to book the computer suite for a lesson of English in advance (question B4).

The proportion of collapsed positive responses (*always* and *often*) (69.2%) by far outweighed the proportion of collapsed negative responses (*rarely* and *never*) (13.5%). What is more, when the three response categories of *always*, *often,* and *sometimes* were collapsed, it occurred that 86.5% of the respondents could use the school computers with at least a degree of regularity.

Access to computer suite. When the subjects' responses pertaining to their access to the computer suite at school were analysed, the data revealed that the proportions of positive responses (*always* and *often*) (30.7%), neutral responses (*sometimes*) (33.7%) and negative responses (*rarely* and *never*) (35.6%) stood at roughly the same level. Therefore, no definitive conclusion could be drawn from the data obtained.

However, when the three response categories indicating a degree of use (*always*, *often*, and *sometimes*) were collapsed, it turned out that 64.4% of the subjects could use the computer suite at school at least occasionally.

Need to book the computer suite. In addition, the subjects were asked whether it was necessary for them to book a language lesson at the computer suite. It occurred that the proportion of collapsed positive responses (*always* and *often*) (69.2%) was by far greater than the proportion of neutral (*sometimes*) (17.3%) and collapsed negative responses (*rarely* and *never*) (13.5%). All in all, 86.5% of the subjects fairly regularly needed to book the computer suite for an EFL lesson, which implies that even if access to the school computer suite was technically possible, it may have been difficult for the teachers to arrange for a language lesson there. Only 7.7% of the teachers found themselves comfortable enough not to have to reserve the computer suite for their lessons at all.

Access to CALL software. 36.2% of the subjects maintained that computer-assisted language learning (CALL) software was available at the school where they worked. A slightly larger proportion (40%), however, claimed that at their school CALL software was not available at all. A fairly large proportion of the subjects (20%) did not know whether or not CALL software was available at their school.

On the basis of the data obtained, it is impossible to definitively state whether CALL software was available at school to the teachers examined. It may be safely stated that a rather large proportion (40%) of the teachers questioned were deprived of access to CALL programs; the more that the

20% who could not answer the question may have not learnt about the software at their school due to its absence.

Access to the internet. An overwhelmingly large proportion of the subjects (98.1%) maintained that the internet (internet connectivity) was available in their school. Only a single teacher (0.95%) claimed that at his/her school internet connectivity was not available at all. Another respondent (0.95%) did not know whether or not the internet was available at his/her school.

On the basis of the afore-cited data, it may be stated that in the case of the subjects examined it was highly unlikely that the teachers lacked access to the internet at school. However, as the very presence of internet connectivity does not guarantee easy access to teachers, the subjects were asked where exactly the connectivity was available in their school.

Access to the internet (location). The following proportions of the subjects stated that the internet was available in the locations listed: in the learners' club (16.5%), in the common room (18.4%), in the school hall (22.3%), in the classroom (50.5%), in the administration offices (76.7%), in the school library (79.6%) and in the computer suite (89.3%).

Moreover, 26.2% of the subjects claimed that their school was equipped with a wireless connection (Wi-Fi), which – depending on the quality of the hardware installed – might have made the internet available across the school premises. 19.4% of the respondents indicated that the internet was available in other locations in their schools.

20 respondents, out of the subject sample members (N=103) who responded to question B7, indicated that the internet was available in *other places* at their schools. The places that they wrote in included: the teacher's room (90% of the N=20 sub-group) and the dormitory (5% of the N=20 sub-group). Another 5% of the N=20 sub-group did not write in any specific place. The proportion of responses was re-calculated for the overall number of valid cases (N=103) in question B7, which revealed that: to 17.4% of all the subjects within the sample (N=103) the internet was available in the teacher's room while to 0.9% the internet was also accessible at the dormitory; 0.9% did not specify where else exactly the internet was available.

The total percentage of responses in the case of this question (B7) exceeded 100%, and amounted to 399%, due to the fact that the respondents had been able to select multiple responses.

Computer age. When analysing the subjects' responses to the question in which they estimated the age of the computers available at their institutions, the researcher collapsed the age categories of *under 1 year* and *1-2 years* into a *brand-new/relatively new* category; the age categories of *3-4 years* and *5 years* were collapsed into a *aging/relatively aged* category; and the *over 5 years* response was re-labelled as *old/very old.* The computations conducted for the newly emergent age categories revealed that: 5.3% of the subjects believed their school computers were *brand-new/relatively new*; 54.7% of the subjects stated that the computers were *aging/relatively old*; and 20% estimated the age of their school computers as *very old.*.

It may appear that the labels denoting the collapsed *aging/relatively aged* and *old/very old* categories were too stringent in relation to the age brackets which they represented but one must remember that due to the accelerating pace of technological development computer hardware today ages rapidly. As Krajka (2007: 280) observes, "rapid technological progress quickly makes claims about most state-of-the-art equipment invalid".

At the same time, it must be born in mind that computers which fall into the first two categories, i.e. *brand-new/relatively new* and *aging/relatively old.* i.e. those at the age of 1-5, may be fully functional for most purposes in the EFL classroom, which cannot be true of computers within the last category, i.e. those beyond the age of 5.

All in all, in the light of the above considerations and the questionnaire data, it may be posited that 60% of the subjects deemed their computers as EFL-classroom-worthy.

Availability of ICT equipment and peripherals at school. The teachers maintained that the schools where they worked were equipped with the following ICT technologies and peripheral: video digital camera (26.9%), digital still camera (44.2%), combo device (a single device with the functionalities of the printer, scanner and photo copier) (45.2%), scanner (52.9%), interactive board (55.8%), laptops (66.3%), multimedia projector (82.7%), printer (85.6%), desktop computers (91.3%), and other devices (1%). 2.9% of the subjects were not able to state what kind of ICT equipment was available at their schools. Only one subject (1%) indicated that *other devices* were available at his/her school, and he/she wrote in *loudspeakers*.

The total percentage of responses exceeded 100% and amounted to 554.8% but that was due to the fact that in question B9 the respondents had been able to select multiple options.

4.2 Attitude towards the computer/ICT as a tool in the (EFL) classroom

The subjects within the sample revealed their attitude towards computer-assisted language learning, as well as the role of information and communication technology at large in the (EFL) classroom by indicating the degree to which they agreed/disagreed with a series of statements pertaining to both issues. What follows is a description of the data collected.

Attitude towards the computer as a tool in the (EFL) classroom. The teachers expressed their opinions about the statement that *Computer-assisted language learning is more intensive* (than conventional learning). When the positive responses (*strongly agree* and *agree*) and negative responses (*disagree* and *strongly disagree*) were collapsed, it emerged that 73.4% of the subjects approved of the statement, while only 11.4% disapproved of it.

In the case of the statement: *Computer-assisted language learning is more effective* (than conventional learning), none of the subjects selected the most negative response (*strongly disagree*). There was a serious disproportion between the conflated positive responses (*strongly agree* and *agree*) the negative responses (only *disagree* here) as 74.8% of the subjects approved of the statement, and only 6.8% disapproved of it.

The statement *Multimedia facilitates learning as it presents content in context* yielded a serious discrepancy between the collapsed positive responses (*strongly agree* and *agree*) and negative ones (*disagree* and *strongly disagree*) as 85.6% of the subjects approved of the statement, while only 4.8% disagreed.

Another statement that the subjects expressed their views on was formulated as follows: *The computer permits the use of authentic materials.* After collapsing the positive (*strongly agree* and *agree*) and negative (*disagree* and *strongly disagree*) responses, the researcher observed that 96.2% of the subjects accepted the statement, and only 0.95% expressed disapproval.

In question C5 the subjects expressed their views on the following statement: *The computer activates learners, who become more autonomous.* The collapsing of the positive responses (*strongly agree* and *agree*) and negative responses (*disagree* and *strongly disagree*) revealed that 76.9% of the subjects expressed approval of the statement, while only 8.7% disapproved of it.

With regard to the statement: *The computer motivates learners* the collapsed positive responses (*strongly agree* and *agree*) significantly outnumbered the collapsed negative responses (*disagree* and *strongly disagree*). 79.8% of the subjects approved of the statement, and only 6.7% expressed disapproval.

The subjects' responses to the question about the statement: *The computer diversifies learning (it permits the use of various learning styles/strategies)* yielded a serious difference between the two ends of the response spectrum. The collapsed positive responses (*strongly agree* and *agree*) amounted to 94.3% of the subjects, while the proportion of collapsed negative responses (*disagree* and *strongly disagree*) was equal to as little as 2.9%.

The last statement which referred to the computer as a tool in the EFL classroom was worded as follows: *The computer develops skills which learners may find useful in professional/private life.* In this case the conflated positive responses (*strongly agree* and *agree*) amounted to 92.3%, while the negative (*disagree* and *strongly disagree*) ones equalled to 1.9%.

Attitude towards ICT in the (EFL) classroom. In question C9 the subjects were asked to voice their opinions about the following statement: *ICT unnecessarily ruins the teaching/learning routine in the classroom.* The collapsed positive responses (*strongly agree* and *agree*) largely outweighed the collapsed negative responses (*disagree* and *strongly disagree*) as only 6.8% of the subjects approved of the statement, while 83.5% disagreed with it.

In question C10 the subjects expressed their opinions about the statement: *ICT causes chaos and discipline problems in the lesson.* Only 9.6% of the subjects approved of the statement, while 76.9% disapproved of it.

Another statement which the subjects expressed their views about was: *ICT permits only the kind of work that can equally be performed without it.* In this case the conflated positive responses (*strongly agree* and *agree*) constituted a clear minority (13.5%) as a vast majority of the subjects (73.1%) disapproved of the statement.

The subjects' opinions about the statement: *ICT distracts attention from what is being taught*, indicated that only 8.7% agreed with it, whereas a majority of 75.7% expressed disapproval.

The last statement which the subjects were asked to voice their views about was formulated as: *ICT facilitates the teacher's/learner's job.* This time the conflated positive responses (*strongly agree* and *agree*) amounted to 77.9%, while the negative ones (*disagree* and *strongly disagree*) equalled to 12.5%.

4.3 Computer literacy

The computer literacy of the subjects was examined through questions referring to their hardware/software operation skills. For clarity, the questions were formulated as *can-do* statements, and appended with examples of hardware relating to particular skills. In addition, the subjects were also asked about formal ICT qualifications, obtained through e.g. ICT courses or postgraduate diploma studies.

Hardware operation skills. As far the subjects' hardware operation skills are concerned, the following proportions of them maintained that they could: assemble a new computer out of appropriate components (3.8%); replace computer components, e.g. a video card or RAM (Random Access Memory) unit (17.1%); perform basic troubleshooting operations in case of hardware malfunction, e.g. no sound (56.2); connect peripheral devices to the computer (88.6%); power on, reset and shut down the computer (100%); and operate the mouse/keyboard (100%).

The total percentage of responses exceeded the value of 100% and amounted to 365.7%, which was due to the fact that the respondents had been able to select multiple responses.

What was observed here was that a vast majority of the subjects (88.6%-100%) could handle the basic tasks which teachers are likely to face in an ICT-enhanced lesson, i.e. connect peripheral devices to the computer, power on, reset and shut down the computer, and use the controlling devices (the mouse and the keyboard).

Only 56.2% of the subjects were capable of dealing with basic technical problems. At the same time, considerably fewer teachers (3.8%-17.1%) were able to cope with more sophisticated procedures, such as: performing repairs (replacing computer components) or advanced operations, e.g. assembling a new computer.

Out of the three less represented hardware operation skills, troubleshooting appears to be the most desirable in the EFL classroom; the other two (replacing computer components and assembling computers) go beyond the language teacher's responsibility.

Software operation skills. The subjects claimed that they had the software operation skills which allowed them to: write computer programs in programming languages such as *Basic*, *C++* or *Java* (1%); upload web pages to an online server (10.5%); install virtual learning platforms (VLEs) (5.7%); create/master web pages (12.4%); author electronic tests, e.g. with test-authoring software such as *Hot Potatoes* or *QuizMaster* (32.4%); use VLEs (44.8%); use spreadsheets (programs for compiling statistical computations), e.g. *Excel* or *Star Office Calc* (51.4%); create multimedia presentations, e.g. in *PowerPoint* (66.7%); use computer-assisted language learning (CALL) programs, e.g. *Euro Plus+* or *Tell Me More* (70.5%); install CALL software on the computer (71.4%); use online communicators, e.g. *Skype*, *GaduGadu* or *MS Messenger* (82.9%); use basic *Windows* utility applications, e.g. *Notepad*, *WordPad* (simple word processors) or *Paint* (simple graphic editor) (78.1%); search through the contents of optical discs, e.g. *CDs* or *DVDs* (88.6%); search information online, e.g. in the *Google* search engine (97.1%); edit text files, e.g. in *MS Word* or other word processors (98.1%); browse internet websites, e.g. with the use of *Internet Explorer* and *Firefox* (100%); and send/receive e-mail messages (100%).

The total percentage of responses exceeded the value of 100% and amounted to 1011.4%, but it was due to the fact that the respondents had been able to select multiple responses in the case of this question.

The data cited above indicate that a substantial majority of the teachers (66.7%-100%) claimed to have the following computer skills: creating multimedia presentations; installing computer software, including CALL programs; using basic *Windows* applications; searching the contents of optical discs, and text editing.

At the same time, the subjects believed they had the following internet skills: using online communicators, searching information online, web browsing, and sending/receiving e-mails. A smaller proportion of the subjects (1%-51.4%) could handle tasks such as: computer programming; installing and using virtual learning platforms; designing and uploading web pages; authoring e-tests; and using spreadsheets.

A very characteristic pattern can be inferred from the data obtained. Out of the 17 software operation skills included in question D2, 12 referred to searching information or making use of content available in software or online; only 5 skills involved creating content. Yet, out of the latter 5 skills, as many as 3 were the ones that a smaller proportion of the subjects was capable of using. Consequently, it appears that the teachers were content users rather than content creators, which, in turn, implies their predominant reliance on ready-made materials.

Formal ICT qualifications. Responses to question D3 revealed that 21.4% of the subjects possessed formal ICT qualifications, while a substantial majority (78.6%) did not have them.

The researcher collected more detailed data on the ICT qualifications of the subjects. Out of the 22 subjects (21.4%) who stated that they had ICT qualifications, 4 did not specify what kind of qualifications they had obtained. The remaining 17 members of the sub-group (N=22) cited the following qualifications: a certificate in basic computer skills (1 subject), a certificate (of no specified kind) (1 subject); a computer course (of no specified kind) (5 subjects); a *Corel Draw* course (a course in graphic-editing software) (1 subject); postgraduate diploma studies in ICT education (1 subject); a distance learning course in Moodle (1 subject); an ECDL (European Computer Driving License) course (1 subject); an HTML course (a course in webpage design) (1 subject); an OFEC certificate (a course for management staff in education); qualifications of a *Novell* administrator (a course in local area network administration) (1 subject); an SQL course (a course in database management) (1 subject); two Intel courses of no specified kind (1 subject); and WODN (Teacher Development Centre) courses (of no specified number or kind) (1 subject).

4.4 Implementation of ICT in EFL teaching

In question E1 the subjects were asked a filter question worded as follows: *Do you, in any way, use ICT in EFL teaching?* Those subjects who responded positively proceeded through the questionnaire, and those who responded negatively were referred to Section G, which concerned possible deterrents which might have discouraged them from implementing ICT in the EFL classroom.

Consequently, it was assumed that the subjects would have answered the questions in Sections E and F of the questionnaire negatively, and that is how their responses were computed. This procedure aimed at reducing the time it took the respondents to fill in the questionnaire paper.

The filter question *Do you, in any way, use ICT in EFL teaching?* was answered in the following fashion: 93.3% of the subjects claimed they used ICT in EFL teaching, and only 6.7% stated that they did not do so.

The data indicated that an overwhelming majority of the subjects used ICT in the EFL classroom. The questions that followed elicited more details as to how ICT was implemented, what kind of software/media the teachers used, how much of their teaching time they devoted to computer-assisted language instruction, what work modes they most frequently applied, and what purposes ICT served in their classrooms.

The usage of ICT in EFL teaching. The subjects were asked how frequently they prepared teaching materials on the computer. It occurred that the proportion of collapsed responses at the positive end of the response scale (*always* and *often*) (75.2%) by far superseded the proportion of collapsed responses at the negative end (*rarely* and *never*) (10.5%). What is more, when the three response categories of *always*, *often,* and *sometimes* were collapsed, it occurred that 89.5% of the subjects prepared teaching materials on the computer with at least a degree of regularity.

In question E3 the subjects were to state whether they authored e-tests or computer activities for their learners. The proportion of collapsed positive responses here (*always* and *often*) (48.1%) was larger than the proportion of collapsed negative responses (*rarely* and *never*) (31.7%), however, when the three response categories of *always*, *often,* and *sometimes* were collapsed, it emerged that 68.3% of the subjects prepared computerised materials/tests with at least a degree of regularity, as opposed to 31.7% of those who did so rarely, or not at all.

In question E4 the subjects were to state whether they utilised peripheral devices. In this case the proportion of collapsed positive responses (*always* and *often*) (89.4%) outweighed the proportion of collapsed negative responses (*rarely* and *never*) (8.7%) by a large margin. Additionally, when the three response categories of *always*, *often,* and *sometimes* were collapsed, it occurred that 91.3% of the subjects used peripherals with at least a degree of regularity, as opposed to 8.7% of those who did so rarely, or not at all.

Another question elicited from the subjects information on whether they used internet materials in EFL lessons. The collapsed positive responses (*always* and *often*) amounted to 77.1% and surpassed the proportion of collapsed negative responses (*rarely* and *never*), which equalled to (8.6%). Moreover, 91.4% of the subjects used internet materials with at least a degree of regularity, while 8.6% did so rarely, or not at all.

Question E6 asked the subjects whether they created internet materials for learners. It must be observed that none of the subjects selected the response category of *often*, while only 1% of the subjects selected the response category of *always*. In effect, the proportion of positive responses was immensely superseded by the proportion of collapsed negative responses (*rarely* and *never*) (96%). Even when the three response categories of *always*, *often,* and *sometimes* were conflated, it turned out that a marginal minority (4%) developed internet materials for learners fairly regularly, whereas 96% did not create online materials at all, or they did so infrequently.

The responses to this question were congruent with the responses that the subjects gave to question D2, where it was revealed that only 12.4% of them could create web pages. It seems sound to propose that a majority of the subjects may not have created internet materials for learners simply due to the lack of adequate computer skills.

In question E7 the subjects were asked whether they uploaded materials for learners to the internet. The conflated proportion of positive responses (*always* and *often*) (13.7%) was far lower than the proportion of conflated negative responses (*rarely* and *never*) (75.5%). What is more, it occurred that only 24.5% of the subjects uploaded materials to the internet fairly regularly, as opposed to 75.5% of those who did so rarely, or not at all.

All in all, the subjects' responses to this question seem to corroborate their responses to questions D2 and E6; it appears that due to their low computer skills, they created and uploaded internet materials infrequently.

Out of the 42 teachers who uploaded materials, only 10 supplied more details about the exact kind of materials that they uploaded. The answers provided contained 14 different categories of materials: individual assignments for learners to do during the teacher's absence (1 subject); homework assignments (1 subject); information (2 subjects); tests (4 subject); multimedia activities (3 subjects); preparatory materials for language competitions (1 subject); publications (1 subject); bibliographies (1 subject); games accompanying the coursebook (1 subject); authentic materials (1 subject); exercises (1 subject); texts (1 subject); worksheets (1 subject); and answer sheets (1 subject).

When the data were analysed in relation to the entire subject sample for question E7 (N=102), excluding 3 missing responses, it occurred that a fairly small proportion (41.17%) of the subjects ever uploaded materials for learners online.

In question E8 the subjects stated with what frequency they contacted their learners by e-mail. As it was noticed, the proportion of collapsed positive responses (*always* and *often*) (36.2%) was smaller than the proportion of collapsed negative responses (*rarely* and *never*) (44.8%). What is more, even when the three response categories of *always*, *often,* and *sometimes* were conflated, it turned out that only slightly more than half of the subjects (55.2%) contacted their learners by e-mail fairly regularly. 44.8% used e-mail for that purpose rarely, or never. It is worth adding that the modal response category in this case was the most negative answer *not at all*.

Question E9 investigated the frequency with which the subjects used internet chat in order to contact learners. The proportion of collapsed positive responses (*always* and *often*) (3.8%) was very small and was surpassed by the proportion of collapsed negative responses (*rarely* and *never*) (91.3%). A very small proportion of the subjects (8.7%) contacted their learners by internet chat with a degree of regularity. It is worth observing that the modal response category here was the negative option of *never* (81.7%), and a vast majority of the subjects (91.3%) did not use internet chat in contacts with learners at all, or they did so infrequently.

Question E10 measured how frequently the teachers' learners worked with the use of online blogs. None of the teachers selected the most positive response category of *always*. The data obtained indicated that the proportion of collapsed positive responses (*always* and *often*) (3%) was by far outweighed by the proportion of collapsed negative responses (*rarely* and *never*) (84%). Only 20% of the teachers surveyed had their learners working with internet blogs with a degree of regularity. The modal response category here was the most negative option of *never* (77%), and a vast majority of the teachers (84%) did not have their learners working with internet blogs or, even if they did, it happened rarely.

To sum up, the data collected through questions E2-E10 revealed that a vast majority of the teachers within the sample did not use, or rarely used, ICT in order to: create web pages (96%), upload materials online (75.5%), contact learners via chat (91.4%), or engage learners in work based on online blogs (84%). A fair majority of the subjects did not contact their learners via e-mail, or did so rarely (44.8%).

The teachers most commonly implemented ICT in order to prepare materials (75.2%), access online materials (77.2%) and use peripheral devices (89.4%). When it comes to computer-enhanced activity/test preparation, the proportion of central category responses (*sometimes*) (20.2%) was superseded by the bi-modality of positive (*always*/*often*) and negative (*rarely*/*never*) responses (48.1%, each).

Software and media types used in EFL teaching. Questions E11-E20 pertained to the frequency with which the teachers utilised different kinds of computer software in EFL teaching.

In question E11 the subjects were asked how frequently they used multimedia CALL software in their lessons. As it was observed, the proportion of collapsed positive responses (*always* and *often*) (12.9%) was rather small, and it was surpassed by the proportion of collapsed negative responses (*rarely* and *never*) (72.3%). When the response categories of *always*, *often* and *sometimes* were conflated, it occurred that slightly more than a quarter of the subjects (27.7%) used multimedia computer-assisted language learning (CALL) software in their lessons with at least a degree of regularity. The modal response category was the most negative option of *never* (53.5%), while a considerable majority of the subjects (72.3%) never used CALL software in their lessons, or they did so rarely.

In question E12 the subjects were asked how frequently they used virtual learning environments, such *Moodle* or *Librus*, in their teaching. In this case, the proportion of collapsed positive responses (*always* and *often*) (9.2%) was small, and it was superseded by the proportion of collapsed negative responses (*rarely* and *never*) (82.6%). When the response categories of *always*, *often* and *sometimes* were collapsed, it surfaced that only a small proportion of the subjects (17.3%) used virtual learning platforms with at least a degree of regularity. The modal response category was the most negative option of *never* (72.5%), and a vast majority of the teachers (82.6%) did not use virtual learning platforms, or they did so rarely.

In question E13 the teachers were asked how frequently they used electronic dictionaries/encyclopaedias in their lessons. The proportion of collapsed positive responses (*always* and *often*) (43.7%) was less than half of the entire subject sample, and it did not differ dramatically from the proportion of collapsed negative responses (*rarely* and *never*) (34.9%).

In order to reveal a general trend within the subject sample the response categories of *always*, *often* and *sometimes* were conflated, which demonstrated that a majority of the teachers (65%) used electronic dictionaries or encyclopaedias fairly regularly. The modal response category was the positive option of *often* (34.6%), and 35% of the subjects did not use electronic dictionaries/encyclopaedias, or they did it rarely.

In question E14 the teachers indicated how frequently they used electronic supplementary materials accompanying the coursebook. The proportion of collapsed positive responses (*always* and *often*) (47.1%) was less than half of the entire subject sample, and it did not substantially differ from the proportion of collapsed negative responses (*rarely* and *never*) (37.5%). When the response categories of *always*, *often* and *sometimes* were collapsed, the data revealed that a majority (62.5%) of the subjects used electronic supplementary materials with at least a degree of regularity. The modal response category was the positive option of *often* (32.7%), and 38.3% of the subjects did not use electronic supplements, or they did it infrequently.

Question E15 measured the subjects' use of concordancers. The proportion of collapsed positive responses (*always* and *often*) amounted to only 4%, and contrasted with the proportion of collapsed negative responses (*rarely* and *never*) (93%). Even the combined proportions of the response categories of *always*, *often* and *sometimes* yielded a very low percentage (7%). The modal response category was the negative option of *never* (85%), and it was illustrative of the overall of trend within the sample; 93% of the subjects did not use concordancers in their lessons, or did it infrequently.

In question E16 the subjects were asked how frequently they used computer games in their lessons. As it was observed, the proportion of collapsed positive responses (*always* and *often*) amounted to only 9.9%, and contrasted with the proportion of collapsed negative responses (*rarely* and *never*) (83.2%). Even the combined proportions of the response categories of *always*, *often* and *sometimes* produced a very low percentage (16.8%). The modal response category was the negative option of *never* (71.3%), and 83.2% of the subjects did not use computer games in their lessons, or did it rarely.

Question E17 required the teachers to state how frequently they used computerized parsers, i.e. programs for grammatical-linguistic analysis of language samples. The proportion of collapsed positive responses (*always* and *often*) equalled to as little as 1% of the sample, while the proportion of collapsed negative responses (*rarely* and *never*) amounted to 98%. When the proportions of the positive response categories were conflated, it turned out that only 2% of the sample used computerised parsers in their lessons fairly regularly. The modal response category of *never* (90.9%) was indicative of the general trend within the sample, where 98% of the subjects did not use parsers at all, or did so infrequently.

In question E18 the respondents were supposed to state how frequently they used stories with computer-enhanced, interactive content in their lessons. The proportion of collapsed positive responses (*always* and *often*) equalled to 10% of the sample, and contrasted with the proportion of collapsed negative responses (*rarely* and *never*) (76%). The collapsed response categories of *always*, *often* and *sometimes* amounted to only roughly a quarter (24%) of the subject sample. The modal response category of *never* (59%) was indicative of the general trend within the sample, with 76% of the teachers not using interactive stories in their lessons at all, or using them rarely.

Question E19 asked the subjects how frequently they used software for creating multimedia presentations such as *MS PowerPoint*. The combined proportions of positive responses (*always* and *often*) accounted for roughly one-third of the sample (31.1%). At the same time, the combined proportions of negative responses (*rarely* and *never*) amounted to 52.4%. When the proportions of the response categories were conflated, it occurred that less than half (47.6%) of the teachers used software for developing multimedia presentations in their lessons with at least a degree of regularity.

The modal response in this case was *never* (30.1%), but it did not illustrate the general trend within the subject sample as the proportion of those subjects who used presentation software relatively regularly (47.6%) was fairly balanced with the proportion of the teachers (52.4%) who did not use this kind of software, or used it rarely.

In question E20 the subjects stated how frequently they used spreadsheets, i.e. software for mathematical and statistical computations , e.g. *MS Excel*. The collapsed proportions of positive responses (*always* and *often*) equalled to 5.9%. At the same time, the combined proportions of negative responses (*rarely* and *never*) amounted to 86.3%.

When the proportions of the response categories were conflated, it emerged that only 13.7% of the subjects used spreadsheets in their lessons with at least a degree of regularity. The modal response in this case was *never* (70.6%), and it reflected the general trend within the sample as the proportion of those teachers who used spreadsheets relatively regularly (13.7%) was by far superseded by the proportion of those (70.6%) who did not use this kind of software, or used it infrequently.

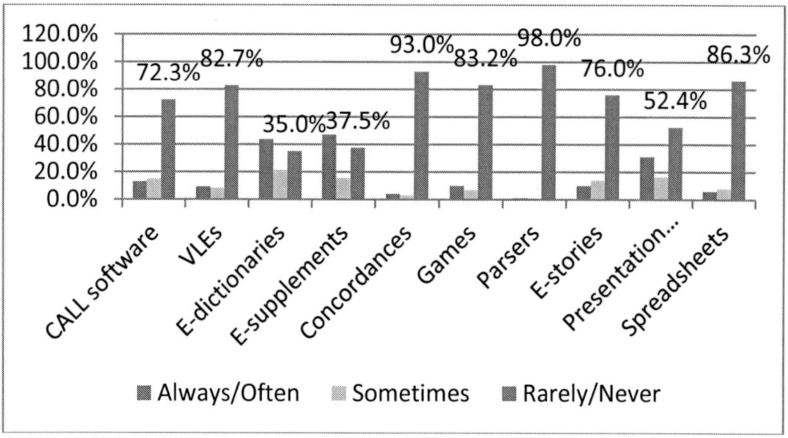

Fig. 6-1

Figure 6-1 demonstrates the proportions of teachers within the subject sample (N=100), excluding five missing responses, who utilised the above-stated types of software in EFL teaching (based on responses to questions E11-E20 of the questionnaire). From the data it was inferred that a vast majority of the subjects within the sample did not use, or rarely used, the following types of software: parsers (98%), concordancers (93%), spreadsheets (86.3%), games (83.2%), virtual learning platforms (VLEs) (82.7%), interactive computerised stories (76%), and CALL programs (72.3%).

A relatively large proportion of the subjects did not use, or rarely used, presentation software (52.4%), but it must be pointed out that of all the software types that the subjects tended to use rarely, or not at all, presentation software was used fairly frequently (*always/often* or *sometimes*) by the largest minorities. The only two types of software that were *always* or *often* used by a slight majority were: computerised coursebook supplements (47.1%) and electronic dictionaries (43.7%).

Question E21 investigated the frequency with which the teachers used various types of media in EFL teaching. The subjects were requested to number each medium listed by the researcher on a scale ranging from 0 to 7. The lowest value (0) was supposed to be ascribed to the medium/media that the subjects did not use at all; the highest value (7) was meant to be assigned to the medium/media that the subjects used most frequently in their teaching practices.

The values assigned to the media were coded as rank orders for every subject, but each item scored as 0 was automatically excluded from the rank as it was not used by the subjects. The coding procedure was not problem-free as particular teachers assigned the same value to several media (giving them an equal status) or, contrary to the researcher's intention, they assigned values which indicated distance between particular media, e.g. medium *a* received 7 points, medium *b* – 5 points, medium *c* and medium *d* – 3 points, etc. In effect, numerous subjects did not apply the full 0-7 point scale.

In order to interpret the responses, the researcher needed to process the data obtained in three stages. In the first stage, rank orders were produced, with disregard to the gaps between the numerical values ascribed to particular items – distance was not important.

In the second stage, each medium was assigned weight points, according the following rule: the item ranking as 1 was assigned 7 points, the item ranking as 2 was assigned 6 points, etc. The weight total for each medium was established by adding the points.

Finally, the percentage of importance for each medium within the entire subject sample was calculated, which was determined by the total rank position of each medium and the number of subjects who included the medium in their rank. The percentage of importance expressed how much of the maximum possible weight total each medium scored within the entire sample. Therefore, the computation procedure for each medium was as follows: *Frequency (%) = Weight total scored * 100/Maximum weight total*. The higher the rank of each medium and the number of subjects who ranked it, the more its weight total increased.

The media were ranked according to the weight totals and percentage of importance, calculated on the basis of the responses obtained from the subject sample (N=104), excluding one missing response. The rank of importance obtained was as follows: (i) text; (ii); audio (iii); photos; (iv) images; (v) video; (vi) maps; and (vii) animations.

As it was observed that the difference in the percentage of importance values for three media, audio clips, images and photographs, were marginal, the researcher investigated the data in greater depth with regard to the rate of inclusion, i.e. the number of teachers who included a given medium in their ranks. The rate of inclusion was congruent with the percentage of importance for the media examined, although the differences between the top-ranking media were marginal, with audio clips, photos and images having been included by exactly the same number of subjects. It was observed that while a considerably large number of subjects included text, audio, photos and images in their rankings (95-97 subjects), a much smaller number of subjects (55-72 subjects) did so with maps and animations (cf. Table 6-1).

Rank	Medium	Weight total	Rate of inclusion	Percentage of importance
1	Text	526	97	72.3%
2	Audio	497	95	68.3%
3	Photos	488	95	67%
4	Images	482	95	66.2%
5	Video	425	89	58.4%
6	Maps	346	72	47.5%
7	Animations	239	55	32.8%

Table 6-1

In sum, it was concluded that text was the most frequently used medium by the subjects. It was closely followed by a cluster of audio-pictorial media (audio clips, photos and images). Video was used to a slightly lesser extent, and the least frequently used media were maps and animations.

The researcher observed that the highest percentage of importance amounted to roughly 75%, thus, he identified 3 potential groups of media within the rank list: (i) the more frequently used media (51%-75%); (ii) the ones used moderately frequently (26%-50%); and the ones used the least frequently (1%-25%). All in all, the more frequently used media were: text, audio-pictorials and video clips; the less frequently used media were: maps and animations; none of the media examined fell into the category of the least frequently used media (cf. Table 6-2).

Category	Rank	Medium	Percentage of importance
I (51-75%)	1	Text	72.3%
	2	Audio-pictorials	67.2%
	3	Video clips	58.4%
II (26-50%)	4	Maps	47.5%
	5	Animations	32.8%
III (1-25%)	-	-	-

Table 6-2

In question E22 the subjects estimated how much time, in percentage points, they devoted to computer-assisted language teaching at large. This question turned out to pose a problem for the subjects as only 80 of them responded to it, with 25 missing responses. The 25 missing responses were not provided by those teachers who claimed that they used ICT in EFL teaching, and who responded to the other relevant questions.

What is more, out of the 80 respondents who used ICT in teaching, 13 subjects claimed that they devoted no time to computer-assisted language teaching. Confusing as the data may be, they seem to indicate two potential problems: either some of the subjects found it problematic to estimate what proportion of teaching time they devoted to computer-enhanced instruction, or they themselves could not clearly decide what kind of work qualified as computer-assisted language teaching.

All in all, the subjects who responded to question E22 (N=80), claimed to devote from 0 to 80% of their teaching time to computer-enhanced instruction. The mean value suggests that on average they practised computer-assisted language teaching roughly within a fifth of their teaching time (19.7%).

Work modes in the use of ICT in EFL teaching. In questions E23-E26 the subjects were requested to state with what frequency they used the four work modes of computer-enhanced teaching: learners working with a single computer in the classroom, learners using a number of laptops in the classroom, learners working in the computer suite, and learners performing computer-based tasks outside the classroom, e.g. at home or in the library.

Question E23 related to the frequency with which the teachers implemented the single-computer scenario. It was observed that the cumulative proportion of the two positive response categories (*always* and *often*) amounted to 38.6%, and was slightly lower than that of the two collapsed negative responses (*rarely* and *never*), which equalled to 44.6%. However, when the response categories of *always*, *often* and *sometimes* were collapsed, it turned out that only a slight majority (55.4%) of the subjects worked with one computer in the classroom with at least a degree of regularity. 44.55% of the subjects did not use this work mode at all, or used it very irregularly. All in all, it was difficult to establish a clear-cut trend with reference to the work mode in question.

Question E24 concerned the frequency with which the subjects used the several-laptops-in-the-classroom scenario. In this case the cumulative proportion of the two positive response categories (*always* and *often*) amounted to only 2%, and was clearly superseded by the two collapsed negative responses (*rarely* and *never*), which were equal to 96%. Even the collapsed response categories of *always*, *often* and *sometimes* yielded a low percentage (4%). The modal response (89%) was indicative of the general trend within the sample as an overwhelming majority (96%) of the subjects within the sample never used the work mode, or used it very infrequently.

It might be hypothesised that this work mode was used by the subjects so little due to the lack of appropriate equipment, despite the fact that in question B9 of the questionnaire 66% of the subjects maintained that they had access to laptops at school. One must be cognisant of the fact that the very presence of laptops may not suffice for teachers to be able to use them in their teaching, because what matters is an adequate number of them.

Question E25 related to the frequency with which the teachers used the computer suite in EFL teaching. The cumulative proportion of the two positive response categories (*always* and *often*) amounted to 16.2%, and was considerably lower than that of the two collapsed negative responses (*rarely* and *never*), which equalled to 62.8%. The collapsed response categories of *always*, *often* and *sometimes* revealed that only slightly more than a third of the teachers (37.1%) worked in the computer suite fairly regularly. 62.8% did not use this work mode at all, or used it very rarely.

Since responses to question B1 of the questionnaire revealed that 91.3% of the teachers had a computer suite at school and in question B3 64.4% declared that they could use the computer suite at school at least occasionally, it appears that the fact that only a third of the subjects actually worked in the computer suite could not have been caused by lack of equipment or access. At the same time, one must remember that responses to question B4 demonstrated that only 7.7% of the subjects did not need to book the computer suite for a language lesson, thus, for the remainder of the sample the obligation to do so might have been a serious deterrent.

Question E26 concerned the frequency with which the subjects made their learners work with the computer outside the classroom. The conflated proportion of the positive response categories (*always* and *often*) amounted to 26.9%, and was slightly lower than that of the two collapsed negative responses (*rarely* and *never*), which equalled to 33.6%. When the response categories of *always*, *often* and *sometimes* were conflated, it turned out that 66.3% of the teachers made their learners use the computer outside the classroom with fair regularity. That was supported by the modal response *sometimes* (39.4%). A third of the subjects (33.6%) did not work in this manner at all, or resorted to it very infrequently.

The purposes of ICT in the EFL classroom. The last batch of questions in Section E (E27-E32) concerned the purposes for which the teachers used ICT in the EFL classroom, including: presenting content, testing, supporting learner autonomy, consolidating knowledge, documenting learners' knowledge and facilitating learner-learner communication.

In question E27 the subjects were asked how frequently they used computers in order to present content to learners. In this case, the proportion of collapsed positive responses (36.2%) was slightly larger than the proportion of collapsed negative responses (27.6%). When the response categories of *always*, *often* and *sometimes* were conflated, it emerged that a majority of the teachers (72.4%) used computers for the purpose of material presentation fairly regularly. The modal response category was the intermediate option of *sometimes* (36.2%), and roughly a third of the teachers (27.6%) did not use computers in order to present material to learners, or they did it rarely.

Question E28 required the subjects to state the frequently with which they used computers for testing. As the data revealed, the proportion of collapsed positive responses (*always* and *often*) (21%) was substantially smaller than the proportion of collapsed negative responses (*rarely* and *never*) (58.1%). The collapsed response categories of *always*, *often* and *sometimes* revealed that only 41.9% of the teachers used computers for testing with a degree of regularity. The latter proportion was, nevertheless, superseded by the collapsed negative responses. What is more, the collapsed responses at the positive end were only marginally larger in proportion than the modal response of *never* (40%) alone. All in all, a majority of 58.1% of the subjects did not use computers for testing, or they did so rarely.

Question E29 investigated how frequently the teachers used computers in order to facilitate learner autonomy. As it was observed, the proportion of collapsed positive responses (*always* and *often*) (27.6%) was smaller than the proportion of combined negative responses (*rarely* and *never*) (37.2%). The collapsed response categories of *always*, *often* and *sometimes* revealed that 62.9% of the subjects used computers in order to facilitate learner autonomy in a fairly regular manner. The modal response category was the intermediate option of *sometimes* (35.2%). At the same time, 37.1% of the subjects did not use computers in order to support learner autonomy at all, or they did it infrequently.

Question E30 examined the frequency with which the teachers used computers for material consolidation. The proportion of collapsed positive responses (*always* and *often*) (21.9%) constituted roughly half of the proportion of collapsed negative responses (*rarely* and *never*) (43.9%). The collapsed response categories of *always*, *often* and *sometimes* produced a majority of 56.2%, indicative of those subjects who used computers for consolidation work with a degree of regularity. The modal response category was the intermediate option of *sometimes* (34.3%), and less than half of the subjects (43.9%) did not use computers in order to consolidate material, or they did it rarely.

Question E31 pertained to the frequency with which the subjects used computers in order to document learners' knowledge. The proportion of collapsed positive responses (*always* and *often*) (32.4%) was surpassed by the proportion of collapsed negative responses (*rarely* and *never*) (50.5%). However, when the response categories of *always*, *often* and *sometimes* were combined, it occurred that nearly half of the teachers (49.5%) used computers for the purpose of documenting learners' knowledge fairly regularly. At the same time, the modal response category was the most negative option of *never* (32.4%), and slightly more than half of the subjects (50.5%) did not use computers in order to document learners' knowledge, or they did so infrequently.

In consequence, it was impossible to conclude which trend was predominant within the sample as it was characterised by a near 50/50 ratio of positive to negative responses.

In the last question in Section E (question E32) the subjects were requested to indicate how frequently they used computers in order to facilitate learner-learner communication. In this case, the proportion of collapsed positive responses amounted to a little as 14.3%, and was by far superseded by the proportion of collapsed negative responses (64.8%). The negative responses were not outweighed even by the collapsed response categories of *always*, *often* and *sometimes*, which amounted to only 35.2% of the teachers. In sum, it turned out that a majority of the subjects (64.8.9%) did not use computers to support learner-learner communication, or did it infrequently, while only 35.2% of the subjects did so fairly regularly. The modal response category was the most negative option of *never* (41.9%).

The data collected through questions E27-E32 indicated that a vast majority of the subjects within the sample did not use, or rarely used, computers in order to test (58.1%) or support learner-learner communication (64.8%). Relatively large proportions of the subjects did not use, or rarely used, computers in order to consolidate material (43.8%) or document learners' knowledge (50.5%), but it must be emphasised that of all the purposes for which the subjects used computers rarely or not at all, material consolidation and documentation of learners' knowledge were always/often or sometimes practised by the largest minorities (21.9%/34.4% and 32.4%/17.1%, respectively). The only end to which a fair majority of the subjects utilised computers was material presentation. In this case, the proportion of negative responses (27.6%) was surpassed by the bi-modality of the collapsed positive (*always/often*) (36.2%) and central (*sometimes*) (36.2%) response categories.

It was also discovered that a relatively large proportion of the teachers claimed that they did not present material through computers at all (16.2%), or they rarely did so (11.4%). The most balanced case was that of teachers supporting learner autonomy through computers. A very small majority (37.1%) rarely did so, or did not do it at all, with a relatively large proportion of positive (*always/often*) (27.6%) and central responses (*sometimes*) (35.2%) at the other end.

Figure 6-2 presents a graphic overview of the manner in which the subjects responded to questions E27-E32.

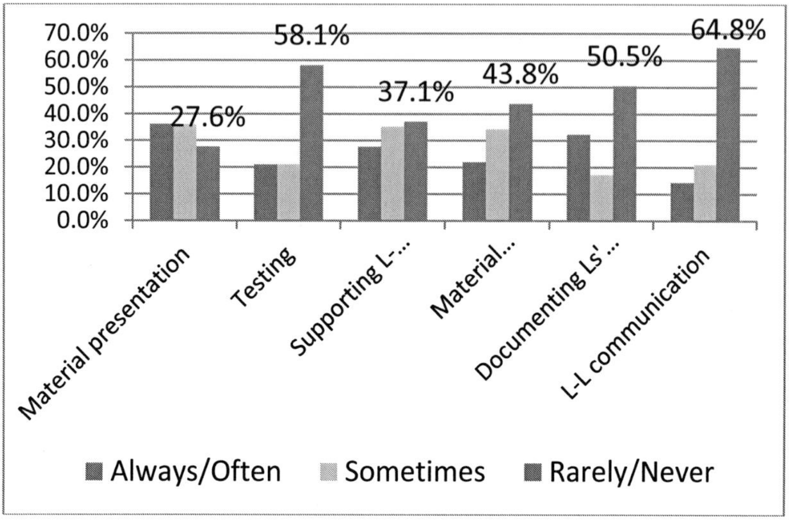

Fig. 6-2

4.5 Implementation of ICT in developing learners' intercultural competence

Section F (questions F1-F7) comprised questions about how and to what degree the respondents utilized ICT in developing their learners' intercultural competence.

Question F1: *Do you use computers in teaching culture?* served as a filter question. Those subjects who responded positively proceeded through Section F, whereas those who responded negatively were referred to Section G, devoted to the possible deterrents which might have discouraged them from implementing ICT in the EFL classroom at large.

Consequently, it was assumed that the subjects who answered question F1 negatively would have responded to the questions in Section F in the same manner, and that is how their responses were computed. This procedure aimed at reducing the time that it took the respondents to fill in the questionnaire paper.

44.8% of the subjects claimed they used computers in teaching culture, while 55.2% stated that they did not. The data indicated that a minority of the teachers used ICT for the purpose of teaching culture. When the data were juxtaposed with the proportion of teachers who used ICT in the EFL classroom at large (cf. question E1), it occurred that out of all the teachers who, in any manner, implemented ICT in language teaching, 48% used computers for cultural training.

The remainder of the questions in Section F elicited the details of how the subjects used computers in order to teach culture, including: the types of media used, the aspects of culture taught, the types of cultural activities conducted, the communication tools utilised, the purposes of the use of the communication tools and the internet-enhanced techniques implemented.

The frequency with which the subjects used various types of media in teaching culture was investigated through question F2, where the teachers were requested to number each medium listed on a scale ranging from 0 to 8. The lowest value (0) was supposed to be ascribed to the medium that the subjects did not use at all; the highest value (8) was to be assigned to the medium that the subjects used most frequently.

The values assigned to the media were coded as rank orders for every subject; each item scored as 0 was automatically excluded from the rank as it was not used by the teachers. The problems that arose from the procedure were equivalent to those faced by the researcher in question E21, i.e. the subjects assigned the same value to several media, thus giving them an equal status, or they assigned values which indicated distance between particular media, e.g. medium *a* received 7 points, medium *b* – 5 points, medium *c* and medium *d* – 3 points, etc. In effect, in numerous cases the subjects did not apply the full 0-8 ranking scale.

The responses collected were processed in the same way as in the case of question E21. Firstly, on the basis of the data obtained, rank orders were produced, with disregard to the gaps between specific media, as indicated by the numerical values ascribed to them.

Secondly, each medium was assigned weight points, according the following rule: the item ranking as 1 was assigned 7 points, the item ranking as 2 was assigned 6 points, etc. The sum of the points yielded the weight total for each medium. The maximum weight total was the number of points that every medium would have scored, had all the subjects ranked it as 1.

Thirdly, the percentage of importance for each medium within the entire subject sample was computed. It was dependent on the rank positions of each medium for every teacher, as well as the number of teachers who included the medium in their rank. The percentage of importance expressed how much of the maximum possible weight total each medium scored within the entire sample. Thus, the following formula was used: *Frequency (%) = Weight total scored * 100/Maximum weight total*. The higher the rank of each medium and the number of subjects who ranked it, the more its weight total increased.

The media were ranked according to the weight totals and percentage of importance, calculated on the basis of the responses obtained from the subject sample (N=104), excluding one missing response (based on responses to question E21 of the questionnaire). The rank of importance obtained was as follows: (i) photos (29.7%); (ii); video clips (28.1%) (iii); images (27.5%); (iv) audio clips (25.5%); (v) text online (24.3%); (vi) maps (21.5%); (vii) hypertext (16.2%); and (viii) animations (9.9%).

The low values of the percentage of importance for all the media stemmed from the fact that 55.2% of the subjects did not implement ICT in teaching culture at all (as question F1 demonstrated). The data depicted that while the percentage of importance for the media which were ranked 1-6 (photos, video clips, images, audio clips, text online and maps) was very small, there was a clear discrepancy between the bottom two items (hypertext and animations) and the remainder of the media up the rank. It was researcher noted that the highest percentage of importance amounted to nearly 30%, thus, 3 clusters were indentified within the rank list: (i) the more frequently used media (21%-30%); (ii) the ones used moderately (11%-20%); and the ones used the least frequently (1%-10%). The media which were used the most frequently were: photos, video clips, images, audio clips, text online and maps. Hypertext was implemented moderately frequently, while animations were used the least frequently (cf. Table 6-3).

The rate of inclusion was congruent with the percentage of importance for the media under study, however, between the media ranking as 1-5 (photos (44), video clips (42), images (43), audio clips (40) and text online (33)), it varied minimally. One can observe that while a considerably large number of subjects included photos, video, images, audio, and text online in their rankings (40-44 subjects), a noticeably smaller number (17-26 subjects) did so with hypertext and animations (cf. Table 6-4).

In question F3 the subjects marked the aspects of culture that they taught with the use of information and communication technology. They either ticked off the aspects of culture provided by the researcher, or added their own responses in the space provided. As the data revealed, the teachers taught the following aspects of culture: cultural events (39%); people (36.2%); places (35.2%); geography (27.6%); institutions (25.7%); links between language and culture (languaculture) (23.8%); stereotypes (21.9%); behaviours (21.9%); material culture (artefacts) (16.2%); and thought patterns, views and values (16.2%). In addition, 3.8% of the teachers claimed that they used ICT in teaching other aspects of culture. The total percentage of the responses exceeded 100% due to the fact that the subjects had been able to select multiple options (cf. Table 6-5).

Rank of importance	Medium	Weight total	Percentage of importance
1	Photos	247	29.7%
2	Video clips	234	28.1%
3	Images	229	27.5%
4	Audio clips	212	25.5%
5	Text online	202	24.3%
6	Maps	179	21.5%
7	Hypertext	135	16.2%
8	Animations	82	9.9%

Table 6-3

Category	Rank	Medium	Weight total	Rate of inclusion	Percentage of importance
I	1	Photos	247	44	29.7%
	2	Video clips	234	42	28.1%
	3	Images	229	43	27.5%
	4	Audio clips	212	40	25.5%
	5	Text online	202	40	24.3%
	6	Maps	179	33	21.5%
II	7	Hypertext	135	26	16.2%
III	8	Animations	82	17	9.9%

Table 6-4

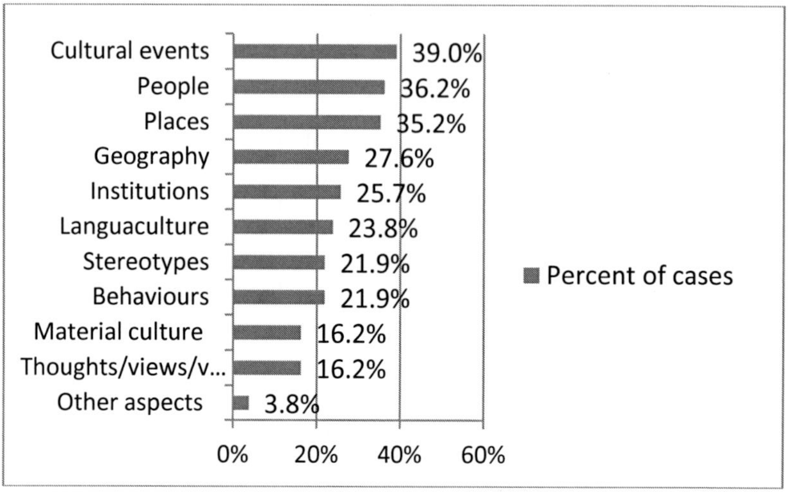

Table 6-5

The other aspects of culture, written in by 3.8% of the teachers covered: art, history and media, latest social-political news, and songs – each of the responses was added by a single teacher. It is worth noticing that the aspects of culture suggested by the respondents themselves appear to be instances of the aspects provided by the researcher. For instance, art may easily qualify as material culture; history will inevitably involve teaching about people, places and events; media may cover material culture and institutions; socio-political news may embrace people, places and events; and songs may be treated as material culture. That is perhaps why such a small number of subjects wrote in alternative options at all.

In sum, the aspects of culture most commonly taught by the subjects through ICT were: cultural events, people and places (cited by over 35% of the subject sample). At the same time, the most neglected aspects were: material culture; as well as thought patterns, views and values (cited by roughly 16% of the subject sample), of which the latter response category may indeed be a challenge to teach.

In question F4 the subjects were asked to state what types of computerised cultural activities their learners performed. The respondents maintained that their learners: analysed images and photos (34.3%); observed foreign cultures through ICT, i.e. they involved in virtual ethnography (26.7%); made notes (23.8%); created texts about their own culture (21.9%); communicated with representatives of other cultures

(7.6%); analysed their own intercultural communication (5.7%) and performed other ICT-based tasks (5.7%).

The respondents could specify what other computerised activities their learners performed beyond the types originally featured in the questionnaire. All the 6 subjects who ticked off the option *other activities* provided their own activity types, which entailed: creating multimedia presentations (4 teachers), doing culture tests (1 teacher), and doing activities based on a film clip (1 teacher).

The data collected revealed that the largest proportion of the subjects (over 20% of the sample) used ICT in order to deliver cultural activities where learners: analysed images and photos (34.3%); engaged in virtual ethnography (26.7%); made notes (23.8%) and created texts about their own culture (21.9%). The smallest proportion of the subjects (less than 10% of the sample) arranged activities where learners: engaged in intercultural communication (7.6%), analysed their own intercultural communication (5.7%), created multimedia presentations (3.8%), took culture tests (1%), and completed activities based on film clips (1%). The total percentage of the responses exceeded 100% as the subjects had been able to select multiple options.

In question F5 the subjects were asked what tools for online communication their learners made use of in order to expand cultural knowledge. The largest proportion of the subjects (29.5%) maintained that their learners did not use any tools of online communication for that purpose, which is congruent with responses to question F4, where communication-based cultural activities came at the very bottom of the ranking of the most commonly applied activity types.

The remainder of the subjects maintained that their learners used: e-mail (27.6%); internet forums (18.1%); internet communicators (15.2%); blogs (11.4%); discussion groups (11.4%); internet chat (11.4%); (5.7%) video conferencing tools (5.7%); and video conferencing applications (1%). The total percentage of the responses exceeded 100% as to the subjects had been able to select multiple options.

It must be added that 3 subjects (2.9%) ticked the option of *other tools*, and in the blank space provided specified the exact other tools. However, the answers given did not truly respond to the question asked as they contained the following: a web portal (cited by1 teacher); web pages devoted to culture (1 teacher); and *Wikipedia* (1 teacher). None of the three referred to an online communication tool, which question F5 concerned, therefore, these responses were regarded as invalid.

The data gathered implied that when the subjects arranged cultural activities based on online communication, their learners mostly engaged in asynchronous, textual communication (e-mail: 27.6%; forums: 18.1%; communicators: 15.2%; blogs: 11.4%; and discussion groups: 11.4%). The tools for synchronous audio/video communication, i.e. chat (11.4%) and videoconferencing (1%), came towards the bottom of the hierarchy.

In question F6, where the subjects indicated the purposes for which their learners used online communication tools, the largest proportion (26.7%) opted for the use of online communication in order to exchange thoughts; 15.2% of the teachers claimed that their learners exchanged information; and 10.5% disclosed that their learners presented their own culture to others.

What drew the researcher's attention was the fact that the least common purpose for which the teachers' learners utilised online communicators was the presentation of their own culture. It seems that the online communication of the subjects' learners was limited only to sharing thoughts and information, thus, the potential of web-based communication tools, particularly for intercultural learning, was not used.

Question F7 requested the subjects to reveal how frequently they used typically intercultural internet-based techniques: telecollaboration (online synchronous/asynchronous communication projects), e-mail tandems (e-mail exchanges in pairs), webquests (web-based query-oriented activities), cultural assimilators (tasks based on interpreting culturally-determined behaviour), literature online (text-based activities, including projects, relating to literary and non-literary pieces online), and e-journals (thought- and attitude-oriented activities based on electronic diaries).

A definitive majority (99%) of the teachers did not use *telecollaboration*, or used it rarely, while 1% used it occasionally. Only 2.2% of the respondents often used *e-mail tandems*. The same proportion (2.2%) of the subjects claimed they used the technique sometimes, and another 2.2% of the subjects used it rarely. The data depicted a clear-cut majority (96.6%) of those who never used the technique. The combined negative responses (*rarely* and *never*) produced an overwhelming majority (95.7%) that did not use e-mail tandems or used them rarely.

Similarly to the previously-discussed techniques, the combined negative responses produced a vast majority (87.9%) of those who did not use *webquests*, or used them rarely, whereas the collapsed positive responses amounted to only 4.3%. When the response categories of *always*, *often* and *sometimes* were conflated, it occurred that only 12.1% of the subjects used webquests with at least a degree of regularity.

Culture assimilators. While none of the subjects selected the two positive response categories (*always* and *often*), the collapsed negative responses (*rarely* and *never*) (97.9%) by far surpassed the moderate response of sometimes (2.1%).

In the case of *literature online*, the conflated negative responses (*rarely* and *never*) (81.6%) superseded the collapsed positive responses (*always* and *often*) (8.2%). When the response categories of *always*, *often* and *sometimes* were combined, it turned out that only 18.4% of the subjects used literature online fairly regularly.

As far as *e-journals* are concerned, the collapsed negative responses (92.7%) surpassed the collapsed positive responses (4.2%), while the conflated response categories of *always*, *often* and *sometimes* revealed that only 7.3% of the teachers used e-journals with a degree of regularity. A bar chart was compiled which presents the frequencies with which the subjects used all the techniques examined (cf. Table 6-6).

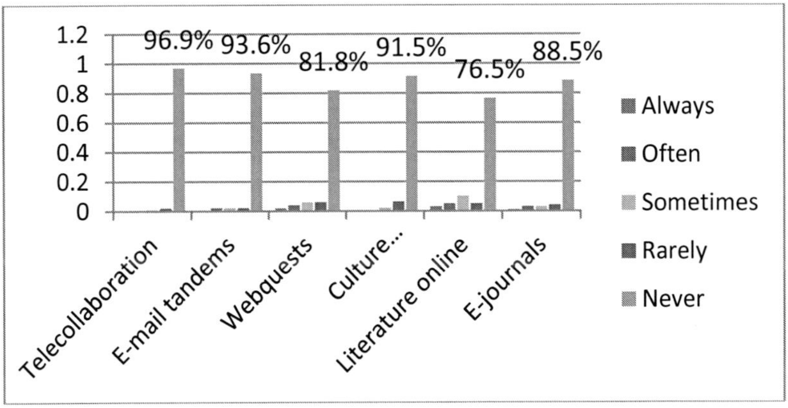

Table 6-6

Table 6-6 clearly illustrates how little the subjects utilised the intercultural internet-based techniques as the number of subjects who never used the specific techniques amounted to: 96.6% (telecollaboration); 93.6% (e-mail tandems); 91.5% (culture assimilators); 88.5% (e-journals); 81.8% (webquests); and 76.5% (literature online).

4.6 Deterrents to applying ICT to EFL teaching

The final question of the questionnaire investigated the possible deterrents to the use of ICT in the EFL classroom. The responses given indicated to what proportion of the teachers surveyed the deterrents listed by the researcher posed a problem.

Particular responses were selected by the following proportions of teachers: technical problems (61.2%); lack of ICT skills (poor computer literacy) (38.8%); lack of orientation in software (31.1%); costs (16.5%); and learners' reluctance towards ICT-based work (3.9%). 26.2% of the subjects suggested that there were other factors that deterred them from using information and communication technology, and 9.7% of the subjects stated that they found no deterrents to the implementation of ICT in the EFL classroom.

Out of the 27 subjects who ticked off the *other deterrents* option, 26 specified what deterrents they meant; there were 37 responses in all as particular subjects added more than one response.

The 37 responses were scoured by the researcher for possible categories, and in effect, the following additional deterrents were identified: lack of access to computers, including the computer suite and other equipment (9.7%); limited access to computers (3.9%); problems with web connectivity (2.9%); lack of adequate equipment (2.9%); lack of adequate software (2.9%); lack of learners' concentration (1%); lack of time (9.7%); poor language competence of the learners (1%); and limited equipment (1.9%).

Out of the deterrents added by the respondents the ones that stood out were the responses which were statistically at least at the level of the lowest-ranking response category from the list of responses originally provided by the researcher in question G1; they were: lack of time (9.7%), limited access to computers (9.7%), and lack of access (3.9%).

In conclusion, it is worth underlying that only relatively small proportions of the teachers within the sample complained about limited access to equipment (9.7%), lack of equipment (3.9) or ICT-related costs (16.5%). This seems to corroborate the data obtained from question B1, where only 1% of the subjects stated that he/she did not have access to computers at school, and question B2, where 86.5% of the respondents maintained that they could use the school computers fairly regularly.

However, the apparently most serious problems faced by the subjects were: technical issues (61.2%), lack of ICT skills (38.8%), and lack of proper orientation in software (31.3%). Given the fact that only a fifth of the subjects (21.4%) had formal ICT qualifications, it might be inferred that the subjects were in need of CALL training, with the caveat that such training would have to involve ICT skills as well as elements of computer-assisted language instruction.

5. Summary of the findings

- Only a small minority of the subjects could not use computers at school, or could do so rarely.
- Computers were mostly available at school in the computer suite and the school library. It was far less likely for computers to be available in the regular classroom than in the other two locations.
- A majority of the teachers could run EFL lessons in the computer suite fairly regularly, but only a third of the teachers could always/often do so. At the same time, most of the teachers needed to book the computer suite for an EFL lesson in advance.
- Less than 50% of the teachers were aware of the fact that CALL software was available at their schools. An almost equal proportion of the teachers knew that there was no CALL software available where they worked.
- Almost all the teachers had access to the internet at school. Online connectivity was mostly available in the computer suite, the school library, and to a lesser extent, in the regular classroom.
- On average, the teachers estimated the age of the computers they had access to at 3-4 years, that is the hardware was capable of serving CALL purposes.
- A majority of the subjects' schools were equipped with the most basic ICT-enhanced teaching tools: desktop computers, printers and multimedia projectors.
- The teachers displayed very positive attitudes towards the computer as a tool in EFL teaching as well as the role of ICT at large in the EFL classroom.
- A majority of the teachers could operate the computer and handle the most basic tasks which they were likely to face in an ICT-enhanced lesson. However, they would face problems having to perform more complex repairs or advanced operations, e.g. assembling a new computer, which cannot be viewed as the EFL teacher's responsibilities. Simultaneously, over half of the teachers claimed that they would be able to deal with basic technical problems, should they arise.
- Most of the teachers maintained to possess computer skills useful for EFL teachers: creating multimedia presentations; installing software, using basic applications, searching the contents of optical discs, and text editing.

- Most of the teachers believed that they also had essential internet skills: using online communicators, searching information online, web browsing, and sending/receiving e-mails.
- The teachers would struggle with more sophisticated software-relating operations: installing/using VLEs; designing/uploading web pages; authoring e-tests; and using spreadsheets.
- Most of the teachers did not have formal ICT qualifications, and those who did gained their qualifications through ICT courses.
- A vast majority of the subjects implemented ICT in EFL teaching.
- The teachers most commonly utilised ICT in order to prepare materials, use peripheral devices, and access online content. At the same time, a considerably low proportion of the teachers created web pages, uploaded materials online, contacted learners via chat, or engaged learners in work based on online blogs. Therefore, the teachers acted as content users rather than content purveyors.
- The most common computer-enhanced channel of teacher-learner communication was e-mail.
- When working with computers, the teachers mostly used electronic dictionaries and computerised coursebook supplements. The software which they did not use, or used to a rather limited extent, included: CALL software bundles, VLEs, concordancers, games, parsers, interactive computerised stories and spreadsheets.
- The most frequently used media in EFL teaching were: text, audio-pictorial media (audio clips, photos and images) and video clips.
- On average, the teachers devoted roughly a fifth of their teaching time to computer-assisted language teaching.
- When teaching English through ICT, most of the teachers rarely/never engaged learners in work with laptops and work in the computer suite. The teachers were more likely to use one computer in the classroom, or they asked learners to work with computers outside the classroom, e.g. in the school library or at home.
- The teachers were most likely to use computers for material presentation. Very few of them used computers for the purpose of testing or supporting learner-learner communication, and only a slightly larger proportion of the teachers used ICT in order to consolidate material or document learners' knowledge.
- A slight majority of the teachers declared that they used computers for teaching culture in the EFL classroom.
- The most commonly used media in teaching culture through ICT were: photos, video clips, images, audio clips, text and maps.

- The aspects of culture most commonly taught by the teachers through ICT were: cultural events, people and places. At the same time, the most neglected aspects were: material culture, thought patterns as well as views and values.
- The largest proportion of the teachers used ICT in teaching culture so that their learners could: analyse images and photos; engage in virtual ethnography; make notes; and create texts about their own culture.
- When the teachers arranged cultural activities based on online communication, their learners mostly engaged in asynchronous, text-based communication.
- The online communication activities in which the teachers' learners normally participated were mostly limited to sharing thoughts. To a lesser extent, the learners exchanged information. The least frequent purpose for which the learners used online communicators was the presentation of their own culture.
- An overwhelming majority of the teachers never used, or used infrequently, typically intercultural internet techniques such as: telecollaboration, e-mail tandems, webquests, culture assimilators, literature online and e-journals. The most frequently used of these techniques was literature online, but it was utilised by a very small proportion of the teachers.
- Lack of proper orientation in software, lack of ICT skills and technical problems were the most often cited deterrents that discouraged the teachers from using ICT in the EFL classroom. It emerged that the teachers were in need of CALL training, which ideally should involve ICT skills as well as elements of computer-assisted language instruction.

CHAPTER SEVEN

RESEARCH MODULE II: CALL SOFTWARE EVALUATION WITH REGARD TO COMPONENTS OF INTERCULTURAL COMPETENCE

The research study within Module II was administered in July-September, 2011. The preparatory procedure began in August, 2010 and continued until April, 2011, comprising: the formulation of the research questions, the preparation and consultation of the first draft of the software evaluation checklist as well a revision of the checklist against the feedback obtained. The data gathered were analysed quantitatively and qualitatively in July-September, 2011.

1. Research aims and methods

Module II of the study qualifies as a **focused description** (Larsen-Freeman & Long 1991) due to its descriptive character. The scope of the research was narrowed down to a number of variables relating to the components of intercultural competence that selected CALL programs permitted learners to develop through the content and technological functionalities which they featured.

The research involved **predictive materials evaluation** (Ellis 1997; Tsiplakides 2011), also known as **preliminary evaluation** (Łuczak-Łomża & Metera-Debaene (2002) or **pre-use evaluation** (Tomlinson 2003), whose aim is normally to help teachers select appropriate materials. The evaluation consisted in the researcher reviewing the content of the programs, the activities provided as well as the technological functionalities and user utilities available within the software.

Cunningsworth (1995) labelled this kind of evaluation **in-depth evaluation**, and explained that it is typically based on a set of criteria, or checklists, which guide the process. According to Tomlinson (2003), the procedure used might also, at least in part, be referred to as **materials**

analysis, because e.g. the technology-related criteria utilised were not judgementally worded, and they only referred to the presence, or absence, of specific features within the software under scrutiny.

As the research instrument was a checklist of evaluation criteria, according to Seliger and Shohamy (1989), this kind of study qualifies as **deductive research**.

Although Larsen-Freeman and Long (1991) placed a focused description towards the quantitative end of the qualitative/quantitative research continuum, the position implies that, to some extent, it shares the features of both research modes. The research conducted in Module II was qualitative on the one hand, as it relied on description of naturally occurring phenomena, and quantitative, on the other hand, as the data collected were quantified and analysed through simple statistical methods. Therefore, this study bore the features of both qualitative and quantitative research, including **quantitative data analysis**.

With regard to design, this study was **cross-sectional research** (Cohen et al. 2007; Larsen-Freeman & Long 1991), as the CALL programs involved were analysed on a single occasion. The research conducted within Module II did not involve any artificial intervention of the researcher into the phenomena under investigation, therefore, it was not experimental, but **analytical** (Seliger & Shohamy 1989) in approach.

Module II of the research study was in principle motivated by the question below:

> Does CALL software targeting lower/upper secondary school level audience available in Poland permit the development of learners' (inter)cultural competence, and which components of intercultural competence does it address?

However, this general question was further broken down into specific research questions posed at the onset of the research, which were as follows:

- Does CALL software targeting lower/upper secondary school level audiences available in Poland permit learners to work on the major components of intercultural competence such as: attitudes, knowledge, skills of interpreting and relating, skills of discovery and interaction, critical cultural awareness? (Research question 7);
- Does CALL software targeting lower/upper secondary school level audiences available in Poland feature technological functionalities

which facilitate intercultural learning, such as: advanced search options, task authoring tools, cultural explanation, insightful audio-visuals, annotation tools, supplementary cultural materials and online communication tools? (Research question 8).

Research administration. Each of the programs studied was examined against the criteria featured within a checklist which had the form of a tabular evaluation sheet. However, while progressing through the evaluation process, the researcher also compiled notes about the content- and technology-related features of the software contained within the evaluation checklist. The notes were made in electronic format, with the use of the *MS Excel* program. The researcher prepared a file which contained 6 different data sheets, each named after one of the programs examined. The data sheets included a copy of the researcher's software evaluation checklist, each, which was subsequently filled in with the researcher's notes about the qualities of the software; the notes took the form of commentaries corresponding to particular aspects of the software, comprised by the evaluation checklist.

As the researcher did not intend to quantify the extent to which each of the evaluation criteria were fulfilled by a given program, if a specific criterion was met at all, the numerical value of 1 was assigned to it on the evaluation sheet. If a feature was absent from a program, it was assigned the numerical value of 0.

Finally, the numerical values were transferred into a collective software evaluation form as a series of dots which symbolized either the presence (•) or absence (○) of a particular (inter)cultural element within each program.

A tabular overview of the research conducted within Module II, including its aims, methods, instruments, sample and type of data analysis, is presented in Appendix D.

2. Research instrument

The study was conducted with the use of an evaluation checklist against which the content and functionalities of the CALL programs under study were analysed. The evaluation checklist needed to be custom-designed because despite the large number of materials evaluation checklists for EFL coursebooks, intercultural evaluation checklists for CALL programs did not exist.

Besides, it was also done in recognition of Inal's (2006) claim that ready-made checklists used on an *as-is* basis may not be applicable to all contexts and need to be adapted so that they match the specific circumstances in which they are supposed to be used.

The checklist contained 21 evaluation criteria in total. It consisted of two major sections: (i) content-related features of software, which contained 13 evaluation criteria pertaining to the components of intercultural competence that the content of the CALL software addressed; and (ii) technology-related features, which comprised 8 criteria regarding the functionalities of the CALL software that could facilitate intercultural learning.

The content-related section of the evaluation checklist was based on Byram's (1997; 2008) components of intercultural competence, as he described them within his model of intercultural communicative competence. The researcher decided to model the evaluation checklist after Byram's intercultural competence due to a number of reasons:

(i) The focus of the research was not on fostering intercultural education per se, but rather on the possibility of developing elements of intercultural competence as part of EFL instruction, to which Byram's model applies.
(ii) Byram's model contains a very detailed break-up of the components of intercultural competence that EFL teachers might wish their learners to work on.
(iii) The model is compatible with educational documents shaping contemporary European language education, e.g. the *Common European Framework of Reference for Languages: learning, teaching, assessment* (CEFR) (Council of Europe 2001) as well as practical instruments for teachers to use in language/culture teaching, e.g. *the European Language Portfolio* (Council of Europe 2004) and *the Autobiography of Intercultural Encounters* (Council of Europe 2009).
(iv) In addition, by following Byram's model, the most essential assumptions lying at the core of the research were brought in line with the underpinnings of other European research projects focusing on language learners' intercultural development – endorsed by the European Centre for Modern Languages in Graz within the *Languages for social cohesion: Language education in a multilingual and multicultural Europe* (ECML 2004-2007) research programme – which were informed by Byram's concept of intercultural competence.

The evaluation criteria of the content-related features of the software to be evaluated were worded in the form of 13 questions which fell into 5 distinct categories that covered the major components of intercultural competence, as proposed by Byram (1997; 2008): (i) attitudes, (ii) knowledge, (iii) skills of interpreting and relating, (iv) skills of discovery and interaction, and (v) critical cultural awareness.

(i) *Attitudes*. Question 1: *Do learners work on their attitudes?* examined whether the software fostered work focused on learners' attitudes, i.e. work which would help learners develop a more positive attitude towards difference and otherness at large, or which would allow learners to shift perspective and perceive cultural phenomena from a less self-centred perspective. This question embraced activities which would facilitate the development of learners' empathy.

(ii) *Knowledge.* Question 2: *Does the culture taught comprise material culture*?; question 3: *Does the culture taught comprise socio-political realia?*; question 4: *Does the culture taught embrace behaviour/practices?*; question 5: *Does the culture taught include thought patterns/values?*; and question 6: *Does the culture taught include languaculture?* measured which aspects of cultural knowledge the software enabled learners to develop.

Material culture was understood here as: the geography of a given area/country; tourist attractions and places of interest; artefacts, including objects of daily use (e.g. tickets, brochures, newspapers, means of transport) and works of art (painting, music, sculpture, literature, photography, etc.). Material culture also included famous people, e.g. artists, politicians and other figures of public life.

Socio-political realia were defined as the state institutions (government, administration), welfare and health care services, legal institutions of a given culture, social units: families, schools, professional, religious groups as well as gender groups and their roles in society. Socio-political realia also included historical background, i.e. important events underlying a particular cultural community.

Behaviour and practices were operationalised as culture-determined: customs and traditions; appropriate behaviour in given social contexts, both formal and informal; as well as elements of nonverbal interaction, e.g. gestures, body language, or facial expressions.

Thought patterns and values denoted the nature of relationships between various social groups and people's views of gender and generation-based roles in society. They also referred to beliefs about what is true or false, right and wrong, or moral and immoral to do.

Languaculture was understood as the manner in which language and culture interweave, including: texts explicitly raising learners' awareness of the importance of (inter)cultural knowledge for effective communication; illustrations of language-coded value judgments, positive and negative connotations of words, instances of derogatory language use; and other culture-determined aspects of verbal behaviour.

(iii) *Skills of interpreting and relating*. Question 7: *Do learners interpret cultural phenomena?*; and question 8: *Do learners compare L1/C1 with L2/C2?* focused on the manner in which the software made learners interpret and relate the instances of culture that they came across when working with the software. It must be added that while *L1/C1* denoted the learners' mother tongue and native culture, *L2/C2* did not signify only the target language/culture, but more broadly, any other/foreign languages/cultures.

(iv) *Skills of discovery and interaction*. Question 9: *Do learners consult varied sources?*; question 10: *Do learners do project work?*; question 11: *Do learners practice intercultural communication?*, and question 12 *Do learners self-assess own intercultural skills?* referred to the ways in which the software permitted learners to learn and interact with cultural phenomena.

(v) *Critical cultural awareness*. Question 13: *Do learners compare/judge materials?* examined whether the software required learners themselves to compare, or judge, the materials that it involved in terms of their informative value, interest, or origin, as well as the potential to development (inter)cultural competence.

The technology-related section of the evaluation checklist contained 8 criteria (criteria 14-21) pertaining to particular technological functionalities of the software which could be useful for teachers and learners working on intercultural competence. The criteria were founded on an overview of checklists for the evaluation of CALL materials (cf. Chapter Four), including: (i) alternative navigation routes, (ii) advanced search options, (iii) task authoring tools, (iv) cultural explanation, (v) insightful audio-visuals, (vi) annotation tools, (vii) supplementary cultural materials, and (viii) online communication tools.

(i) *Alternative navigation routes.* Criterion 14 pertained to the number of navigation routes through which learners would be able to access various elements of the content offered within the software. For instance, whether the software allowed learners to reach the same material through the main content menu, learning paths or thematic course exploration tools. When at least more than one of these options was available, it was assumed that alternative navigation was possible.

(ii) *Advanced search options*. Criterion 15 examined whether learners would be able to search the content of the software by using an in-built search utility, similar to a search engine which allows users to scour the content of the internet. Advanced search options were supposed to go beyond a simple word search, which is only an electronic version of a glossary/dictionary. They were defined as search functionalities which would permit learners to establish the exact location of words within the program, but also as tools which would help learners find: relevant vocabulary organised in thematic sets, or relevant media, e.g. images (photos, drawings), maps, audio/video clips and reading passages.

(iii) *Task authoring tools*. Criterion 16 referred to utilities which would enable teachers to design new tasks for learners, either out of the content available in the software, or ideally, out of alternative content, e.g. accessible online, through which learners would be capable of developing attitudes, knowledge, skills, critical cultural awareness and (self-) assessment skills.

(iv) *Cultural explanation*. Similarly to the help options commonly available in CALL software which assist learners in operating the programs, cultural help utilities could enhance the development of intercultural competence. Criterion 17 referred to pop-up messages with explanation of the cultural phenomena depicted through the program content as well as clickable links with additional cultural information which would accompany reading, listening and video materials, or language-focused tasks.

(v) *Insightful audio-visuals*. Criterion 18 pertained to the quality of drawings, photographs, or audio/video clips used in the programs under evaluation in terms of informative value. It was assumed that if the afore-mentioned media carried information which would help learners expand their cultural knowledge, or understand the cultural phenomena under observation, they could be viewed as insightful.

For instance, an insightful photograph would present people or places in a broader context, whereby learners could discover the exact location of a cultural event, the time of year, the time of the day, the participants and their actions.

(vi) *Annotation tools*. Criterion 19 signified annotation tools, which were understood as functionalities which could serve as an electronic diary, with the use of which learners could annotate particular reading texts, images, audio/video clips, or new words and phrases. It would be useful for intercultural learners not only for gathering and storing information but also for recording emotions, or making intercultural commentary, e.g. in order to highlight intercultural similarities/differences.

(vii) *Supplementary cultural materials*. Criterion 20 referred to supplementary cultural materials, defined as content permitting learners to increase their intercultural competence, which were supplied outside the mainstream teaching materials featured within the software. Such added content might – but would not have to – relate to what was supposed to be taught through the software examined, and might be available as online materials accessible from within the program, e.g. in the form of cultural texts, audio/video clips, activities (cultural quizzes), or communication tasks.

(viii) *Online communication tools*. Criterion 21 aimed at examining whether the software offered learners asynchronous or synchronous communication utilities which would permit genuine, text, or voice-based, communication with representatives of other cultures. Such tools would typically comprise: an online forum, a chat room, a voice communicator or an e-mail application.

Before the evaluation checklist was utilised, two draft versions of it were prepared and subsequently consulted with 10 independent judges who expressed their opinions concerning the design of the instrument as well as its content. On the basis of the feedback obtained in the course of the consultations several changes were introduced to the instrument.

Both versions of the draft differed in the content-related criteria. In draft 1 the content-related criteria constituted a macro-level checklist (Cunningsworth 1995) which drew directly upon Byram's components of intercultural competence (Byram 1997; 2008), reformulated as the following 5 questions: *Do learners work on attitude towards otherness?*; *Do learners work on intercultural knowledge and themes?*; *Do learners develop intercultural skills?*; *Do learners develop critical cultural awareness?*; and *Do learners develop their independence as cultural explorers?*.

After the consultations, it was decided that the macro-level version of the checklist was too general and it would be particularised by breaking Byram's (1997; 2008) elements of intercultural competence into more specific questions. In effect, the second draft version was prepared, which classified as a micro-level checklist (Cunningsworth 1995), with 13 criteria grouped into 5 categories corresponding to the areas of intercultural competence originally featured within draft 1: attitudes, knowledge, skills of interpreting and relating, skills of discovery and interaction, and critical cultural awareness. This time the questions were derived from Byram's (2008: 231-133) comprehensive presentation of the sub-skills of intercultural competence as well as an overview of evaluation checklists for (inter)cultural materials (cf. Chapter Five).

In sum, the changes introduced after the consultations involved the transformation of the original macro-level checklist into a more specific micro-level list, where the more detailed questions were gradually eliminated up to a point at which the list appeared to be sufficiently specific, but the same time, relatively short. The latter was born in mind in accordance with Cunningsworth (1995), who warned that lengthy evaluation checklists might turn out difficult to handle, and they might disorientate potential evaluators.

The final version of the evaluation checklist utilised in the course of the research in Module II is demonstrated in Appendix E.

3. Research sample

The research sample was compiled in a non-random manner, by means of convenience sampling, otherwise known as accidental or opportunity sampling (Cohen et al. 2007) as the researcher selected the programs to be examined on the basis of availability at the time of the study. 6 multimedia CALL software packages, addressed to lower secondary and upper secondary school learners, were selected:

- *EuroPlus+ Reward,* which was addressed to older primary, adolescent and adult learners (lower/upper secondary school level);
- *Tell Me More Junior 13-15,* for lower secondary school learners;
- *English+ one p@ck* for adolescents (lower/upper secondary school level);
- *Tell Me More Special Edition 1000h,* dedicated to a general audience, including lower/upper secondary school level;
- *Język Angielski. Profesor Henry Megapakiet. Wersja 6.0,* for a general audience, including lower/upper secondary school level;
- *New Reflex English,* for adolescent and adult learners, including lower/upper secondary school level.

The programs were released in Poland, but they were licensed versions of software available worldwide. All the software packages constituted independent CALL courses in English, with the exception of *EuroPlus+ Reward*, which had been published as material accompanying Simon Greenall's internationally acclaimed coursebook series entitled *Reward.*

4. Results of CALL software evaluation

The results obtained in the course of the evaluation are presented on a program-by-program basis, with each CALL software package under examination discussed with regard to its content and technological functionalities analysed against the 21 criteria of the CALL software evaluation checklist implemented. In each case, an overview of the program in question is also initially offered.

4.1 English+ one p@ck

Program overview. It was the oldest CALL program contained within the research sample. The multimedia language course was released in Poland by Optimus Pascal S.A. under a license from Edusoft. The program was published in the years 1995-1998 on 10 CD-ROMs. The language proficiency levels that the software targeted, as described by the manufacturer, were: Basic level (3 CDs), Intermediate level (3 CDs), and Advanced level (4 CDs).

The program is addressed to adolescent learners, including lower/upper secondary school learners, and focuses on the development of the four major language skills: listening, speaking, reading, writing. The language areas to be developed through it are: grammar, vocabulary, and business English.

The course contains: 3,500 expressions, 1000 hours of activities, 280 lessons, and permits language practice in 3 learning modes: (i) Open Mode, where the user can explore content and activities on their own; (ii) Routes Mode, which takes the user through the language course along preset learning paths; and (iii) Adventure Mode, where the user can practise, or consolidate, language knowledge and skills by taking part in an adventure game, in which he/she enters a city in an English-speaking country, e.g. New York, Vancouver or London, in order to find an object hidden there. The task can be completed by using English and interacting with the characters featured and consulting the reference resources, which are books with information about: the tourist spots, places of fun and entertainment, famous buildings as well as famous people.

The Polish Ministry of Education has officially recommended the program as a teaching aid for use at primary, lower secondary and upper secondary school.

User's manual. English+ one p@ck is accompanied by a printed user's manual, which introduces the user to the learning goals of the program, discussed with regard to 3 language areas: language, viewed as a system of grammar; vocabulary; and the four fundamental language skills: listening, speaking, reading and writing. There is no mention of culture in the manual, nor is there any reference to the development of intercultural competence.

Content overview. The content of the program is categorised as: *Language*, *Reading*, *Vocabulary*, *Speaking*, *Writing*, and *Listening*. The *Language* category focuses on grammar and involves typical language practice, with very little context provided. Although various aspects of grammar are presented in sentences accompanied by drawings, the sentences are isolated examples of language usage, and images do not explain the context of the language presented.

The *Reading* category carries very little cultural information. The focus of the reading passages is mostly on language practice. In particular texts there is an obvious need for cultural explanation, or more cultural information, which would help the learner understand the context of the content, but neither of the two is supplied.

Learners will work on the reading passages by reading mother tongue translation or listening to the text. The language focus of the readers is clear when one looks at the language-oriented information displayed by the program in each reading section: the main idea of the text, connectives, reference words and key words.

In the *Vocabulary* category, at the Basic level, the program displays on the screen a list of unrelated words. At Intermediate and Advanced levels the vocabulary lists are arranged into themes, e.g. *Families in the 90s*. The learner can listen to the pronunciation of each word and access an on-screen dictionary-like entry about each word, including exemplary sentences, but no cultural information. The learner can also see the Polish translation of each vocabulary item. The vocabulary presented is practised in gap-filling activities and crosswords, and can be tested in gap-filling activities.

The *Speaking* category contains drawings illustrating scenes from which the learner can select the characters to whom he/she is initially supposed to listen; While listening to a short dialogue the learner can access the transcript of the text and the Polish translation. What is presented as speaking practice is actually mechanical practice in reading aloud as the learner can record himself/herself reading each dialogue and listen to his/her own recording afterwards.

The drawings accompanying the speaking activities scarcely illustrate the scene, and no broader context is provided; the background of the drawings is limited, and frequently only the characters themselves are visible.

The *Writing* category allows the learner to read examples of pieces of writing, or documents, e.g. a cheque, a letter and a postal order form, with a view to exploring their layout. The learner practices writing by filling the gaps with appropriate text, which is provided by the program; the activity does not involve actual typing.

In the *Listening* category the user will listen to short texts, and while listening he/she can have the English transcript or Polish translation displayed. Afterwards, the learner can record and listen to himself/herself. Additionally, the user can also practice language by filling the gapped transcripts of the recordings. No cultural explanation accompanies the texts, and the focus of the activities is language-oriented.

The affective component (attitudes). Within this program learners do not work on their attitudes towards the target language culture, or any other culture. Neither do they engage in tasks which would make them reflect on their attitudes towards their own culture. Therefore, it may be stated that learners do not develop a more positive attitude towards difference and otherness in general, and they are not given an opportunity to shift perspective and observe cultural phenomena from a less self-centred perspective.

The cognitive component (knowledge). Learners can develop the following five elements of cultural knowledge: (a) material culture, (b) socio-political realia, (c) behaviour/practices and (d) thought patterns/values, and a single element of (e) languaculture. Below are selected examples of the kinds of cultural knowledge featured within the program.

(a) *Material culture.* At the basic level learners can see a number of artefacts: a car advertisement for a second-hand Corvette, a job advertisement for computer sales people, a meet-me ad, a pet ad; and an American home add. In the writing tasks they see examples of: a cheque, a short informal letter, or a postal order form. The reading text titled *New Mexican Restaurant Open in Soho* features items of Mexican food: tacos with beans and salsa.

A number of places of interest are presented in the listening texts, e.g. The Apollo Theatre or New York. Learners can also listen to a radio broadcast from Cape Canaveral, where a space shuttle is being launched, however, no cultural commentary, or explanation, is offered. The reading texts include information about e.g. New York's Soho, but the place is not clearly introduced and learners may easily confuse the place with London.

Elements of world history are presented in the reading texts, e.g. learners read a text entitled *See Picasso paintings at MOMA*, where they learn that Picasso was a Spanish artist. At the same time, it is not explained where the Museum of Modern Art (MOMA) is, and no information about the painter is provided. In the *Time Traveling Tourist*, learners read about a character who travels back in time while visiting the Tower of London and talks to Ann Boleyn. Yet, the Tower of London per se is not even introduced.

Extensive factual knowledge on important cities, famous people, institutions, places of entertainment, feats of architecture, and places of interest is offered by the *Adventure* learning mode, which is an adventure game where learners enter a city in an English-speaking country with the task to find an object hidden there by using the English that they have learnt with the program.

In order to obtain hints as to the whereabouts of the hide, they have to read about selected famous places in each city and interact with the city's virtual inhabitants by asking them multiple-choice questions in order to receive necessary information. In this manner program users learn extensively about American, Canadian, Australian, English, Scottish, and Irish cities, such as: New York, Washington D.C., Miami, Los Angeles; Vancouver; Sydney; London; Edinburgh; and Dublin, respectively.

In addition, learners can verify the information that they gather by using reference sources available from the adventure game menu, which are books on the: *Fun and entertainment*, *Famous people*, *Famous buildings*, and *Places to see* of the cities in question along with an *Overview* of each. *Adventure* allows learners to collect factual information and develop declarative knowledge about the cities.

The kind of cultural knowledge that learners can acquire through the *Adventure* game is illustrated by a game set in Edinburgh, Scotland, which is available to students at the Intermediate level. The *Fun and Entertainment* book here discusses in greater detail the *Pubs and Distilleries* of the city, e.g. the White Hart Inn, the Waterfront Whine Bar, and the Cafe Royal, and offers photographs of each place. It also covers: the city's museums and galleries, e.g. Canongate Tolbooth, Edinburgh Wax Museum, and The John Knox House; theatres: The Traverse Theatre and The Royal Lyceum; the Edinburgh Zoo; the Waverley Shopping Centre; and the Usher Hall music centre.

The *Famous people* book contains a collection of articles illustrated with drawings of Scottish: actors, artists, athletes, animal trainers, curators, detectives, journalists, royalty, set designers, soldiers, writers and storytellers, historical/legendary figures, musicians, professors, royals, animal trainers, and good citizens.

The *Famous buildings* book includes a collection of photo-illustrated articles on castles, houses and palaces, e.g.: The Palace of Holyroodhouse, Dalmeny House, or Edinburgh Castle.

The *Places to see* book contains a collection of articles on Edinburgh's: banks, churches and cathedrals, clocks, statues, monuments, gardens, streets, towers, and train stations, all accompanied by photographs.

(b) *Socio-political realia*. Examples of socio-political realia presented within the *English+ one p@ck* program are few and far between, and the information that learners receive is mostly limited to a number of isolated facts. For instance, at the Basic level, from the *Postcard-Haiti* reading text, learners find out that the Port au Prince is Haiti's capital city. The *Missing Money – a Mystery at First Bank* reading text features the name of the New York Police Department. Police is also mentioned in the *Follow That Man* text, where a woman is robbed in New York, and she and her companion call a police officer for help.

In a listening radio quiz it is mentioned that the state of Tennessee is located in the USA, but no further information is supplied.

At the Intermediate level, the *Adventure* game permits learners to expand their knowledge of the socio-political realia of Scotland, by familiarising them with basic facts about the city of Edinburgh, its people, and major areas.

(c) *Behaviour/practices*. At all the language levels the software contains numerous examples of culturally-determined behaviour and people's practices.

For instance, at the Basic level, learners learn how people sell second-hand cars, or meet other people through advertising. They read texts about: the changing eating habits of Americans; women's eating habits and increased travel of British businesswomen.

Other reading texts illustrate how to behave in daily situations, including: travelling by train, asking a class colleague out to a restaurant; dealing with a personal robbery; or dealing with a robbery.

The speaking activities present how to: order coffee at a restaurant, book a room at a hotel, or answer a phone call. The writing activities teach learners how to: write a cheque and a short informal letter, or fill in a postal order form.

At the Intermediate level, the reading texts depict the following practices: online dating, arranging marriages; sending a parcel by mail; school exchanges; or expecting a baby.

The First Thanksgiving is a reading text about the origin and celebration (mostly food practices) of Thanksgiving in the USA, and *The Garbage Man* reading tells the story of a man who creates art out of garbage materials. No location is given, and it can only be guessed that the Plaza Art Gallery, which is the setting of the text, is located in the USA.

In the *Adventure* game, the *Fun and Entertainment* reference book offers detailed information about selected Scottish festivals along with illustrative photos. The festivals include: the Scottish International Children's Festival, the Royal Highland Show, the Edinburgh International Jazz Festival, and the Edinburgh International Festival of Music and Drama.

From the listening texts learners find about Thanksgiving and Independence Day celebrations in the USA as well as the Bank Holiday festival in Britain. The writing activities teach learners how to write a formal letter, a memo and a report.

At the Advanced level, the reading texts at least in part illustrate: how to write a letter of complaint to a department store about a faulty product or how to behave at a laundry shop. The texts also demonstrate the lifestyle of celebrities, information-collecting practises of journalists, industrial waste disposal practices, or the impact of inadequate language usage on intercultural interaction.

The text entitled *Culture Crash* explains differences between the language practices of New Yorkers and southerners in the USA pertaining to directness/indirectness of self-expression. The text also contains the author's reflections on cultural differences and misunderstandings caused by them.

The writing tasks instruct learners on how to write a letter of apology or a job application.

(d) *Thought patterns/values* in *English+ one p@ck* are presented only in a small number of materials at the Advanced level.

An example is the reading text entitled *Culture Crash*, which explicitly demonstrates differences between the thought patterns and believes of New Yorkers and southerners in the USA pertaining to directness/indirectness principles which govern interpersonal communication. The text contains the author's reflections on cultural differences and possible misunderstandings that can result from them.

The reading text *Company Dumps Toxic Waste* depicts people's attitudes towards environment pollution, and the *Phone-in* listening text features a radio phone-in programme where people express their opinions about the advantages and disadvantages of the freedom of the press. In the text *Letter to the Editor* opinions are expressed about human endeavours to travel to the outer space.

The listening texts feature: a video about the believes of the Australian Aborigines about the beginning of the world; and an audio clip about the manner in which the Americans stereotype the Mexicans, and how the Mexicans are likely to take it as an offence.

(e) *Languaculture*. Only in one case is an element of languacultural knowledge presented by the program, thus, it may be stated that this component of cultural knowledge is only symbolically present within the software. It happens in the afore-mentioned text *Culture Crash*, where differences between the language practices of New Yorkers and southerners in the USA pertaining to directness/indirectness self-expression are explained. Additionally, the text author expresses his reflections on cultural differences and possible misunderstandings caused by them.

The action-oriented component (skills of interpreting and relating, and skills of discovery and interaction). The program does not allow learners to develop intercultural skills in that it does not offer activities where they would be expected to interpret cultural phenomena on their own ,or compare instances of their mother tongue and native culture with samples of another language or culture. Learners do not collect cultural data from varied sources, and they are not required to participate in project work, whereby they would be able to further their skills of discovery and interaction.

As a matter of fact, the software does not involve intercultural communication and learners derive all their knowledge from the content that they find on the screen.

The only form of assessment in the program is strictly language-based and requires attention to form and accuracy. Cultural knowledge is not subject to assessment, and learners are neither guided towards the self-assessment of intercultural skills, nor are they provided with tools that could serve that purpose.

The educational component (critical cultural awareness). Learners' critical awareness is not developed, as the program does not include activities where learners would compare, or judge, the materials on the basis of which they could acquire (inter)cultural knowledge.

The technology-related features. Only 3 technology-related features which could facilitate the development of intercultural competence are available in the program: (a) alternative navigation routes; (b) supplementary cultural materials and (c) online communication tools. Task authoring tools, cultural explanation and annotation tools are completely absent.

As far as insightful audio-visuals are concerned, it must be noted that visuals in the program are very simple drawings of poor quality, by current standards. They are limited in what they depict, they come with little background, which would have provided context for the characters or scenes shown. For instance, in many cases it is very hard, or impossible, to establish the setting that a given drawing illustrates.

(a) *Alternative navigation routes. English+ one p@ck* allows learners to navigate through the content in three ways. Users can access desired content on the basis of the language areas or skills which they wish to practice by selecting from the options provided in the main program menu: *Language (grammar)*, *Vocabulary*, *Listening*, *Speaking*, *Reading* and *Writing*. In addition, the main menu includes a direct link to the internet resources which supplement the program.

Another navigation option is a miniaturised version of the main program menu, hidden under a road-sign-like icon placed in the left-top corner of the interface screen, which learners can access from any area of the program. Thanks to it, users can call up the features of program at any time without a need to return to the main menu.

Users can also navigate through the content by selecting one of the desired learning routes, e.g. *Listening and Speaking*, *Vocabulary and Reading*, or *Language and Listening*.

(b) *Supplementary cultural materials*. The program is supplemented by a set of online resources, presented as an online magazine called *English Discoveries Online*. The original version of the magazine, which used to be available directly from the program menu is no longer accessible online, however, its updated version – offered by the manufacturer of the program – is available on the internet at http://ed.engdis.com, and is possible to find via internet search engines.

The magazine features monthly editions of news articles from all over the world, categorised under topics, such as: world, business, science and technology, environment, lifestyle, arts and entertainment, sport, health, and general interest, and are regularly updated. The texts are appended with links to authentic websites relating to the topics presented, e.g. links to organisations featured in the text, which gives learners an opportunity for further cultural exploration.

Another feature of the *English Discoveries Online Magazine* is Talking idioms, where learners can learn English idioms, i.e. a linguistic component of culture.

The *In Site* feature of the *English Discoveries Online Magazine* is a section which contains reviews of interesting websites, including websites recommended by learners. Some of the websites there lend themselves to the teaching/learning of culture, e.g. the *NASA Multimedia Gallery*; *Monet at Giverny*, a virtual visit to *Monet's Garden*; *Mexican Modern Art Game*, a virtual visit to an interactive museum; and the *Exodus* website, which features vacation destinations on all continents.

(c) *Online communication tools*. Two text-based forms of communication are permitted by the features of the *English Discoveries Online Magazine*, which supplements the program. However, only one of them was fully functional at the time of the evaluation.

The active tool allows asynchronous communication through an online forum named *Discussion Time*, where learners can contact an international community of language learning colleagues who also happen to be using Edusoft software.

The tool which appeared to be temporarily out of order at the time of the evaluation aimed to permit synchronous, real-time, communication by means of *Web Pals*, an online chatroom. When the feature was accessed for evaluation, an error message was displayed on the screen: "Connection with Global Server is lost", and the site was not operational. In conclusion, it may be stated that at least one online communication tool is available to learners who use the *English+ one p@ck* package.

In sum, the software helps learners develop only the cognitive component of intercultural competence (knowledge), while completely neglecting the remainder of its elements: attitudes, intercultural skills and critical cultural awareness.

Technology-wise, it offers three functionalities which could foster intercultural development: (i) alternative navigation routes, (ii) supplementary cultural materials online, and (iii) two communication tools, one of which is fully operational.

The results of the evaluation of the *English+ one p@ck* program with regard to the checklist criteria are summarised in tabular format in Appendix F.

4.2 EuroPlus+ Reward

Program overview. The CALL software is a multimedia language course manufactured by Young Digital Poland S.A., Poland, currently known as Young Digital Planet S.A. The program was released in 1999 on 8 CD-ROMs, and it targets the following language levels: Elementary level (2 CDs), Pre-Intermediate level (2 CDs), Intermediate level (2 CDs), and Upper-Intermediate level (2 CDs). The age groups that the program is addressed to are: older primary children, adolescents and adults.

The course focuses on the development of the four major language skills: listening, speaking, reading and writing; the target language areas that it gives priority to are grammar and vocabulary. The program content amounts to 600 hours of learning, 16 types of interactive activities and 86 lessons.

The software package originally aimed to accompany the *Reward* (Greenall 1994) coursebook series by Macmillan Heinemann English Language Teaching, however, it can also be used independently. This program has obtained a recommendation of the Polish Ministry of Education as a teaching aid for use at Polish public schools.

The *user's manual* introduces the learning goals of the software as: grammar, vocabulary and language skills, without any reference to culture.

Content overview. The program features 29 units, and the content of each unit falls into lessons, each featuring a number of screens, referred to as pages. In addition, within each unit there is also a *Video lesson* and a *Progress check* lesson.

The grammar activities take the form of: error correction, gap-filling, sentence writing, and multiple-choice assignments. The vocabulary activities involve: drag-and-drop matching, selecting appropriate items, gap filling, and dictionary-based work. The reading tasks are based on: matching headings with fragments of text, (multiple-choice) comprehension check questions, skimming and scanning. The listening comprehension activities take the form of: matching, gap filling, and comprehension check questions. The writing activities involve: rearranging jumbled paragraphs, paragraph writing and matching. The speaking tasks consist in the learner: answering a set of questions; recording the lines of a dialogue; or participating in discussion tasks on the online forum provided within the software.

The affective component (attitudes). The program contains a small number of activities that help learners shift perceptual perspectives or empathise with strangers. An example of this kind of activity appears in Lesson 26 at the Intermediate level, where users read a text entitled *Some rattlin' good recipes* about a rattlesnake cook-book. One of the questions that the text is followed by reads: *Do you eat anything in your country which foreigners might consider strange?* In order to respond to the question learners need to decentre and attempt to perceive their own culture from the perspective of a stranger. This kind of work might sensitise learners towards the issue of culture-bound character of intercultural perception, and in effect make them more tolerant towards otherness.

In Lesson 10 at the Upper-Intermediate level learners read the text *Rules of Law*, which cites controversial laws from all over the world, e.g. Paraguay, UK, USA and Malaysia. Afterwards, they are asked to guess the reasons why the legal rules were introduced. As a follow-up, learners are supposed to formulate legal rules for their own country which would be amusing or strange to others. Similarly to the previous activity, learners here need to perceive their own culture from a stranger's perspective. Therefore, they are offered an opportunity to empathise with representatives of other cultures.

Lesson 14 at the Upper-Intermediate level features an activity where learners listen to texts about the lifestyle of the Amish people in California, USA. Subsequently, they are requested to describe their daily routine as if they had spent a day in the Amish community, which creates room for more empathy development.

In Lesson 4 at Pre-Intermediate level users read a text on positive and negative impressions of Britain and the USA. In an exercise that follows (Exercise 2) they are supposed to state which of the impressions was the most surprising to them. In this manner they need to externalise their, otherwise internal, suppositions about the cultures in question.

It is worth observing that in Lesson 6 at Pre-Intermediate level learners have access to video commentary by the author of the program Simon Greenall, who explains the importance of training in crosscultural awareness in EFL learning. The commentary explicitly highlights the importance of studying: intolerance; people's expectations towards the behaviour of the representatives of other cultures; and the surprise that they feel when their intercultural experience is different from expectations.

The video commentary accompanies an excerpt of Paul Theroux's book *The Kingdom by the Sea*, which presents Britain from the perspective of an American traveller. By reading the text as well as following the video commentary, learners might additionally focus attention on their own attitudes and expectations towards other cultures.

The cognitive component (knowledge). The program helps learners develop all the 5 aspects of the cognitive component of intercultural competence: (a) material culture, (b) socio-political realia, (c) behaviour/practices (d) thought patterns/values, and (e) languaculture.

(a) *Material culture*. Resources featured in the software demonstrate a vast array of examples of material culture: artefacts (consumer goods, personal possessions, objects of daily use, home furniture, works of art and inventions), renowned artists, public figures, institutions, places of interest, and elements of geography.

In reading texts learners read about artefacts such as: a landing card (Elementary level/Lesson 3); a language school brochure (Elementary level/Lesson 4); a school report (Upper-Intermediate level/Lesson 9); a police announcement (Elementary level/Lesson 19); international brands and products (Upper-Intermediate level/Lesson 20); personal possessions (Elementary level/Lesson 5), e.g.: a mobile, a personal stereo, sun glasses, a watch, a comb, and keys; objects of daily use: keys, a paperback novel, a penknife, diary (Intermediate level/Lesson 8); home objects in Britain and Russia, as well as a Scotsman's boat home (Elementary level/Lesson 7); the features of a Japanese home (Pre-Intermediate level/progress check); or the clothing, means of transport and meals of the Amish in the USA (Upper-Intermediate level/Lesson 14).

They also listen to texts about the accessories of a holiday-maker (Pre-Intermediate/Lesson 13) or local produce in Britain (Intermediate level/L 28). The video clips cover: souvenirs from Nigeria, Africa (Intermediate level/Video Lesson B); and consumer goods manufactured by young Britons who own small business firms, e.g. fish tanks and clocks (Upper-Intermediate level/Video Lesson C);

The inventions which learners find out about in the reading texts and videos are: silicon superbrains, artificial intelligence, high-tech gadgetry at a computerised home, means of communication, e.g. email, fax, satellite television or CD-ROM (Upper-Intermediate level/Lesson 13); and the *Eurostar* train (Pre-Intermediate level/Video Lesson D).

Through reading texts learners also acquire information about recognised artists in the following areas: popular music (Whitney Houston, Sting, Elton John); classical music (Mozart); film (Kevin Costner, Jodie Foster); literature (Agatha Christie, William Shakespeare, Doris Lessing and Mark Twain) (Elementary level). Video Lesson 1 at Intermediate level contains an interview with Rhythm and Blues singer Hinda Hicks, and rock band the Little Mothers is introduced through a video interview in Video Lesson D at Upper-Intermediate level.

Literary pieces presented in the program include: Charlotte Brontë's *Jane Eyre* (Upper-Intermediate/Lesson 11); *The Art of Travel* by Francis Galton (fragment) (Upper-Intermediate level/Lesson 11); a poem entitled *Valentine* by Carol Ann Duffy; *Great Railway Journeys* by Lisa St Aubin de Terán; *Sister Coxall's Revenge* by David Muscillo; *The House of the Spirits* by Isabel Allende (Upper-Intermediate level/Lesson 16); or *A Cup of Tea* by Katherine Mansfield (Intermediate level/Lesson 25).

The music that learners explore may be exemplified by *The Girl from Ipanema* (Upper-Intermediate/Lesson16), or *Tender is the Night* by Scott Fitzgerald (Upper-Intermediate level/Lesson17).

The places of interest, or places to go, featured within the program content are, e.g.: Hemel Hempstead, a town located 10 miles north of London (Pre-Intermediate level/Video Lesson B); Broadstairs, Kent (Upper-Intermediate level/Video lesson B); Venezuela (Pre-Intermediate level/Progress check); Crete, Greece (Pre-Intermediate level/Lesson 10); South America (Rio de Janeiro, Lima, The Amazon, Santiago) (Pre-Intermediate level/Lesson 13); Gdańsk, Poland; St Petersburg, Russia

(Pre-Intermediate level/Video Lesson C); Cambridge, Massachusetts, USA; Madrid, Spain (Upper-Intermediate level/Lesson 4); Arizona's geography, topography and tourists' spots; Patagonia, Argentina (Upper-Intermediate level/Lesson 7); Michigan, USA (Upper-Intermediate level/Progress check B); Oxford's tea shops (Pre-Intermediate level/Lesson14); the *Tradewinds*, a gift shop in St Albans whose owner presents the gifts on sale – items from different countries of the world (Elementary level/Video Lesson F); a health club (Pre-Intermediate level/Video Lesson E); or types of restaurants in the USA (Elementary level/Lesson 25).

Folk culture is represented in the program through: a ghost story set in Scotland (Upper-Intermediate level/Lesson 8), or video clips about The Robin Hood Festival at The World of Robin Hood theme park, in which experts talk about the legend of Robin Hood (Upper-Intermediate level/Video Lesson E).

The public figures featured within the program are e.g.: Amy Dacyczyn, the founder of the *Tightwad Gazette* (Upper-Intermediate level/Lesson 17); and Thomas Cook, the man who gave rise to the practice of package holiday tours in Britain (Pre-Intermediate level/Lesson 7).

There are also examples in the program of content depicting cultural products relating to social institutions. One of them appears in Lesson 24 at Intermediate level, where Shelley (an American) talks to Tom (an Englishman) about the media in the USA, including: newspapers, television, radio, and most popular types of programmes. Another instance of that kind of material culture is a video tour of St Giles College, presented in Video Lesson A at Elementary level, where the college staff introduce selected places at the school, e.g. the classrooms, or the library.

(b) *Socio-political realia*. The program content helps learners find out basic socio-political facts about the world, including language and the administrative units of particular areas.

For instance, in the matching activities featured in the program learners match: countries of the world and their cities (Elementary level/Lesson 1), including European locations (Elementary level/Lesson 20). They also recognise and label African countries on a map of the continent; and match the current names of African countries to their old names, e.g. Zimbabwe-Rhodesia (Intermediate level/Video Lesson B).

In an activity at Elementary level (Progress check A) learners are given facts about the English language, including information about the native speakers of the language, the speakers of English as a second language, and the number of words that the English language comprises.

The Upper-Intermediate level/Lesson 18 includes an activity in which students read definitions of political institutions and entities, e.g.: a constituency, the Prime Minister, a councillor, a referendum, a mayor, and a government.

A group of activities carry information about the socio-political realities of life in particular countries of the world, for example: a factfile about Thailand and UK and a listening text about Sweden, from which learners find out about the countries' area, population, armed forces and education systems (Elementary level/Lesson 29).

A listening text at Upper-Intermediate level (Lesson 9) presents a teacher's experience in Sudan, where the conditions of the country's poor schooling system are presented.

Lesson 10 at Upper-Intermediate level features a text, a radio programme and a dialogue-based activity where the legal rules of selected countries from all over the world are presented, including: Paraguay, UK, USA, Malaysia and India. The radio programme introduces issues of law and order in Britain, and the dialogue which learners act out relates to gun laws and other legal regulations in the USA.

Lesson 14 at Intermediate level contains a listening text about Cedar Rapids, Iowa in the USA, which demonstrates an example of a small American dwelling with a large immigrant community from the Czech Republic.

A number of activities in the program pertain to important national institutions which shape people's lives. In Lesson 24 at the Intermediate level there is a dialogue about the media in the USA, e.g. newspapers, television, and radio as well as the control of the media and the most popular types of programmes.

In Video C at Upper-Intermediate level learners watch interviews with young people who run their own small businesses in Britain, in which information about The Prince's Youth Business Trust and its role in supporting self-employment amongst young people is provided.

Lesson 4 at Elementary level contains a video about a language school from Oxford which presents the institution's facilities: a car park, a cafe and a self-study room.

In Lesson 9 at Upper-Intermediate level a reading text about the American space agency NASA and an excerpt from *Boy-Tales of Childhood* by Roald Dahl give learners an account of the author's kindergarten memories.

The socio-political realia depicted in the program also include historical facts about the world, e.g.: important events in UK/USA history (the Battle of Waterloo, the death of Elvis Presley, Christopher Columbus' voyage to America, the human kind's first walk on the Moon, or the sinking of the Titanic are presented in Video Lesson E at Elementary level).

In Lesson 30 at Elementary level learners read a text about the history of the Olympic Games; Lesson 7 at Pre-Intermediate level contains an *Around the World* quiz about important events in the history of travel (the first solo flight across the Atlantic), and holiday-making (the opening of California's Disneyland); and Lesson 19 at Upper-Intermediate level involves a listening text about legendary places in Britain: Sherwood Forest, Holy Island, Stonehenge, Lyonesse; and a reading text about *The Lost Continent of Atlantis*.

(c) *Behaviour/practices. EuroPlus+ Reward* features a myriad of materials that illustrate the behavioural patterns and practices of people from diverse ethnic, national and cultural backgrounds. The forms of behaviour which are presented in the program include: the social practices of today and the past days, the daily routine, travel-related practices, work-related practices, leisure time activities, verbal behaviour as well as traditions or important events in people's lives.

The social etiquette of the past in Britain is depicted through a listening text about changes to social customs in the country over the last fifty years (Upper-Intermediate level/Lesson 2); and an extract from Charlotte Brontë's *Jane Eyre*, where Jane's first day at school is described (Upper-Intermediate level/Lesson 9) as well as a story of deception, included in Lesson 6 at Upper-Intermediate level, which is accompanied by the program author's video commentary, where he explicitly draws learners' attention to the role of women in British society in the 19th century.

Modern-day behavioural norms are presented in a number of materials. For instance, at Intermediate level in Lesson 10 social gaffs from England, Germany and USA are presented, and learners interpret the mistakes of the people described.

At Pre-Intermediate level in Lesson 1 there is a text about international customs of hospitality, and Lesson 31 at Elementary level contains a grid form *When in Rome* about appropriate and inappropriate ways of behaviour in different countries (e.g. China, Japan, Saudi Arabia, Britain and France). At Elementary level in Lesson 31 learners listen to an Australian talking about appropriate and inappropriate behaviour in his country; other countries are tackled in a video documentary in Video Lesson G at Elementary level, while at Pre-Intermediate level (Lesson 18) the text *How to be an American* cites the national characteristics of North Americans.

Pre-Intermediate level contains the reading text *Home Rules*, which pertains to the manner in which people arrange and run their homes in different parts of the world; and Lesson 2 at Upper-Intermediate level features texts on greeting habits in Japan and other countries, e.g. Hungary, Spain, Australia and Timbuktu, Africa.

The daily routine of people from across the world is featured within Lesson 7 at Elementary level in the text *Daily routines around the world,* which concerns people from e.g. USA, Germany, Austria, Greece, France, and Norway.

Expats from USA, Canada and Australia living in the UK talk about their daily routine as well as favourite and most disliked activities in Video Lesson A at Pre-Intermediate level.

At Pre-Intermediate level in Lesson 14, the text *Teatime* describes the daily practice of afternoon tea; at Pre-Intermediate level in Lesson 15, Karen, from Hong Kong, and Pat, from San Francisco, talk about a typical breakfast, lunch and dinner in their countries; and in Lesson 15 at Pre-Intermediate the text *A Nation of Shoppers* presents the shopping habits of the British.

Lesson 25 at Elementary level features the text *Eating out in the USA*, which is followed by an activity where learners extract information on how to behave at a restaurant, e.g. where to sit, how to pay, or how much to tip the waiter. Ordering food at a restaurant is practised in two conversational activities in Lesson 25 at Elementary level; and Lesson 27 at Elementary level offers users an audio clip which demonstrates how to report the loss of property at the Lost Property Office.

Behavioural patterns relating to family life are depicted through: a text at Elementary level (Lesson 6), where users learn about a Senegalese farmer's and vet's life and family; an interview with Corrine, a Frenchwoman who talks about her family life (Pre-Intermediate level/Lesson 9); and a text where Kathy, an Australian, talks about her family (Pre-Intermediate level/Lesson 9).

Travel practices are illustrated by: a dialogue between a customs officer and a visitor to Britain, which users act out in Lesson 23 at Pre-Intermediate level; an activity where three people talk about their travel plans (Intermediate level/Lesson 2); a text where a man and a woman talk about the precautions which they take when going away (Intermediate level/Lesson 31); and texts about what to do to keep healthy on holiday (Elementary level/Lesson 28). Lesson 15 at Upper-Intermediate level also features a text about a family who are picking up father from the Heathrow airport.

Work-related practices are reported by: Dan, an Australian living in England, who talks about his professional and social life (Intermediate level/Lesson 1); and young people featured in a video in which they explain how they launched their own small businesses (Upper-Intermediate level/Video Lesson C).

Leisure activities which the program demonstrates include: forms of relaxation worldwide (Elementary level/Lesson 9); ways to have a perfect day out (Elementary level/Lesson 34) and a perfect weekend (Pre-Intermediate/Lesson 38); listening to music and reading books (Upper-Intermediate level/Lesson 16); entertainment in Japan and Argentina (Pre-Intermediate level/Lesson 16); gambling in Thailand (Intermediate level/Lesson 4); women's football (Intermediate level/Video Lesson F); street music in Paris and New York (Upper-Intermediate/Lesson 16); playing in a classical music orchestra (Upper-Intermediate level/Lesson 16; and dinner parties (Upper-Intermediate level/Lesson 12).

EuroPlus+ Reward also presents forms of verbal behaviour, e.g.: international customs referring to the use of first names and surnames (Pre-Intermediate level/Lesson 1); ways of expressing agreement and disagreement in English and other languages (Upper-Intermediate level/Lesson 3); and verbal practices and social norms in different languages worldwide, as illustrated by an article from *the Independent* (Upper-Intermediate/Lesson 2).

The behavioural patterns and practices that learners can explore within the software also refer to traditions or important events in people's lives worldwide. The traditions include: British weddings and wedding anniversaries (Elementary level/Lesson 22); the lifestyle of religious groups, e.g. the Amish of the USA (Upper-Intermediate level/Lesson 14); folk festivals (a folk festival at Broadstairs, UK or Morris dancing) (Upper-Intermediate/Video Lesson B); St Valentine's Day and the Guy Fawkes Night (Pre-Intermediate level/Lesson 23);

Hindu weddings and the wedding traditions of Moslem countries, China, India and Egypt (Intermediate level/Lesson 3); an English New Year's Eve party (Intermediate level/Progress check A); Christmas in Japan (Intermediate/Progress check X); and the Day of the Dead in Mexico (Pre-Intermediate level/Lesson34). Finally, in Lesson 22 at Elementary level, 3 speakers talk about passing an exam, whereby learners find out how universities in Britain announce exam results.

(d) *Thought patterns/values*. In Lesson 2 at Upper-Intermediate level, program users are requested to speculate about the thoughts that underlie the social norms and verbal behaviour of people in European countries, presented in an article from *the Independent* newspaper.

In the same lesson, a listening text about the changing social customs in Britain over the last 50 years features Mary Davies and her grandson Peter, who talk about expectations towards children and their role in a family, the role of the family head, and the ideal age for getting married.

There is also a reading text there on the greeting practices of the Japanese, which is followed by a task where users are supposed to use the online forum in order talk to others about the reasons for which Japanese bowing may be difficult to foreigners. In other words, learners are meant to explore the thoughts behind people's actions.

The Day of the Dead text from Lesson 34 at Pre-Intermediate level contains information about the thought patterns behind the Mexican holiday, e.g. the Mexicans' view of death.

Lesson 3 at Upper-Intermediate level contains a video commentary which accompanies an activity on expressing agreement/disagreement, where the author of the program explicitly explains that in British and American English it may be rude to disagree directly. It is also suggested there that in some cultures gestures are used, and in others disagreement is verbalised.

The text *Gruezi, Gruezi, Everybody* in Progress check A at Upper-Intermediate level depicts greeting habits in Switzerland, and explains the thoughts and values behind the Swiss greeting patterns.

At Upper-Intermediate level in Lesson 5, an activity contains an audio clip in which five native speakers of English talk about how they feel while watching the sunset. In this manner the speakers' thoughts on life may be inferred.

At Upper-Intermediate level in Lesson 6, learners are supposed to use the online forum and discuss jobs that are better done by men as well as interpret the behaviour of one of the characters from a story which they first read. This activity also gives learners a chance to explore the thought patterns of others, including foreigners.

Other thought patterns that the software allows learners to explore comprise: thoughts on crime and fair punishment (Upper-Intermediate level/Lesson 10); the thoughts of religious groups, e.g. the Amish (Upper-Intermediate level/Lesson 14); international superstitions (Upper-Intermediate level/Lesson 19); the values and qualities symbolised by world-famous brands, e.g. Mercedes (reliability), Benetton (freedom), and Gillette (cleanliness and freshness) (Upper-Intermediate level/Lesson 20); thoughts/values underlying daily actions, e.g. people's thoughts behind football, good/bad news, green spaces in English cities and bus stop queuing in England (Intermediate level/Lesson 12); values in life, such as friendship or love (Intermediate level/Lesson 23); and people's attitudes towards their own education and career (Intermediate level, Lesson 39).

(e) *Languaculture*. The relationship between language and culture is explicitly tackled in the program, and it is brought to the fore by the video commentaries from Simon Greenall, who draws learners' attention to the importance of culturally-determined forms of verbal behaviour, e.g. expressing particular meanings, applying directness/indirectness principles in speech, or using socio-culturally appropriate intonation.

In Lesson 24 at Pre-Intermediate level, learners explore phonological and lexical differences between British and American English. In the video commentary which accompanies the text *Divided by a common language?,* the program author explains the extent to which both the varieties of English differ, and the impact the differences have on communication between the cultural communities beyond the British and American varieties of English.

The same lesson contains a text about the growing importance of the Spanish language as a means of communication in the United States of America as well as other languages used by the country's immigrant communities. In this unit (In Lesson 24 at Pre-Intermediate level) learners are also supposed to reflect on the linguistic diversity of their own country.

In Progress check C at Pre-Intermediate level, the video commentary in the *Sounds* section elucidates how intonation affects the tone of utterances, and how it may make a speaker sound more polite. In addition, the commentary explains that the British attempt to sound as polite as possible even when they are irritated. In addition, Simon Greenall elucidates that in British and American English it is rude to criticise somebody in their face, and warns that transferring the principles of verbal criticism from one's culture into British or American culture may cause offense.

The action-oriented component (skills of interpreting and relating, and skills of discovery and interaction). The program allows learners to develop the following intercultural skills: (a) interpreting cultural phenomena, (b) comparing their native culture with other cultures, and (c) practising intercultural communication.

However, learners are not incited to consult varied sources as they are not referred to materials outside the program; neither are they encouraged to seek cultural resources on their own. The program does not involve any project work, and it does not feature activities where learners would need to reflect on their own intercultural skills.

(a) *Interpreting cultural phenomena*. When working with the software, learners do not only passively acquire cultural knowledge presented through the program content. On numerous occasions they are requested to ponder what they observe and draw their own conclusions. Therefore, learners explore cultures by interpreting them, and the cultural phenomena which are analysed cover: verbal behaviour (literary pieces, utterances; views and opinions) as well as non-verbal behaviour (physical actions, gestures and facial expressions). Examples of the this kind of work are discussed below.

At Upper-Intermediate level in Lesson 2, learners speculate about the thoughts that might underlie what the characters say in an article on social norms and verbal behaviour in European countries from *The Independent* newspaper. In the same unit, learners interpret what kind of article (front page news, latest news, social news, political news, foreign correspondent's diary) a passage from *The Independent* falls into, and they are supposed to justify their responses.

In Lesson 9 at Upper-Intermediate level users are to interpret a girl's school report, and explain what message is conveyed by the teacher's comments about the pupil's school performance.

In Lesson 10 at Upper-Intermediate level learners are encouraged to guess the reasons why particular laws have been introduced in countries such as: Paraguay, UK, USA and Malaysia.

At Pre-Intermediate level in Lesson 3 learners are shown a photograph of a room and they have to judge what function the room has. What is interesting, no ready-made answer is suggested by the program, and it is an open-ended task where learners can follow their own train of thought.

At Pre-Intermediate level in Lesson 18, after reading the text *How to be an American* about the national characteristics of North Americans, learners are asked to state whether they agree with the author's view of the Americans. They are not meant to accept the text author's image of the nation, but attempt to offer their own interpretations of American culture.

In the remainder of interpretative activities, learners: read quotations by British people and try to guess what these people are describing (Pre-Intermediate level/Lesson 4); or think why the woman in the passage *Theroux' Kingdom by the Sea* did not greet the writer – an American visitor to Britain (Pre-Intermediate level/Lesson 6).

At Intermediate level in Video Lesson A, after watching a video where a TV crew meet their new colleague, a sound engineer), learners interpret the meaning of the characters' behaviour, words, and facial expressions; and at Intermediate level in Lesson 10, learners interpret the nature of exemplary social gaffes from international cultures.

Finally, in Lesson 23 at Intermediate level learners read a poem *Valetine* by Carol Ann Duffy and listen to two speakers talking about it.

Afterwards, they attempt to interpret the author's views of love by choosing a phrase which best summarises them, e.g. *Love lasts forever*. In fact, what learners engage in is poem interpretation.

(b) *Learners compare their native culture with other cultures*. The program requests learners to compare both their own language and culture with others. The comparisons incited by the program concern: spoken and written communicative practices, lifestyles, traditions (including legends), thought patterns, opinions and beliefs, personal interests, basic country statistics and social services.

Most importantly, on numerous occasions learners are asked to make comparisons by interacting with an international community of the program users via an online forum. In this manner, learners' intercultural, or even crosscultural, knowledge is likely to reach beyond the information that the program itself provides.

Crosscultural comparison is highlighted as a vital aspect of EFL learning by the very author of the program, who makes a number of comments about it in video commentaries that accompany relevant activities. For instance, in Lesson 12 at Upper-Intermediate level, he maintains that that the socio-cultural training in the program is there to increase learners' awareness of other cultures and, at the same time, increase awareness of their own culture.

In Lesson 39 at Intermediate level, he states that the value of crosscultural comparison does not lie simply in a presentation of two cultures, but is rather supposed to serve as a mirror in which learners can reflect their own culture.

Examples of inter/cross-cultural comparisons practised by learners within the program are provided below.

As far as lifestyles are concerned, learners compare corresponding aspects of their own culture with: a Senegalese farmer's family life (Elementary level/Lesson 8); an old English house (Elementary level/Lesson 6); the daily routines of people from around the world (Elementary level/Lesson 7); the eating habits of the Americans and the Chinese (Elementary level/Lesson 25 and Pre-Intermediate level/Lesson 15); the High Street in Britain (Elementary level/Lesson 14); the home rules followed in different parts of the world (Pre-Intermediate level/Lesson 3); and the dressing codes in Kuwait, Sweden and India (Pre-Intermediate level/Lesson 19).

Numerous comparative activities involve the use of the *EuroPlus+* online forum, where learners can synchronously (in voice mode), or asynchronously (in text mode), communicate with other program users from across the world. Such activities inspire learners to compare: the shopping habits of the British with their own (Pre-Intermediate level/Lesson 14); other program users' family structure with that of their own (Elementary level/Video Lesson B); their own daily routine with that of other users (potentially foreigners) (Elementary level/Lesson 7); the age at which to do things in Britain with the relevant age in their own country (Elementary/Progress check B); and the consumer goods which they buy with those that other program users purchase (Upper-Intermediate level/Lesson 17).

The social services which learners compare include: the healthcare system of Britain with that of their own country (Elementary level/Lesson 28); the USA media with the ones that they use (Intermediate level/Lesson 24); and the education system of their own country with that of the USA and Britain (Intermediate level/Lesson 39).

When learners focus on basic country statistics, they are requested to compare the factfiles about Thailand, UK, Sweden and Brazil with the equivalent statistics compiled for their own country.

The crosscultural comparisons, incited by the software, which focus on thought patterns, impressions, and beliefs concern: people's first impressions when visiting a foreign country (Elementary level/Lesson 30); views of technology (Upper-Intermediate level/Lesson 13); the future of English (Pre-Intermediate level/Lesson 12); tactics in expressing polite/angry complaints (Intermediate level/Lesson 32); and views of typically male sports (Upper-Intermediate level/Lesson 3).

On the online forum, learners also exchange interests, including their favourite film stars, singers, sportspersons, politicians, clubs, TV programmes, films or restaurants (Elementary level/Lesson 10); and favourite bands or types of music (Upper-Intermediate level/video lesson D).

When cross-culturally comparing traditions in the program, learners do so with regard to: wedding customs (Intermediate level/Lesson 3); New Year's resolutions (Elementary level/Lesson 24); and national legends (Upper-Intermediate level/Lesson 19).

Verbal practices which learners have an opportunity to compare in the program cover both written and oral communicative practices. For instance, at Intermediate level in Lesson 2, users compare the layout of a personal letter in English with the equivalent letter in their own language.

In a spoken activity based on the online forum, learners discuss rules for using first names and surnames in their country with an international community of *EuroPlus+* users. In addition, they are supposed to share with others reflections on the situations in which foreign visitors to their country are likely to use English.

In Lesson 12 (Pre-Intermediate level) users read a number of paragraphs containing the word *home* and match them with definitions of the word which correspond to the context of each paragraph. Afterwards, they are supposed to think and state how they would express the same meanings in their own language.

Crosscultural comparisons in the program are justified by the program author, who gives learners a purpose in discovering crosscultural differences by warning them about the dangers of cultural transfer.

(c) *Practicing intercultural communication.* On numerous occasions users of the program are guided towards genuine intercultural communication through tasks relating directly to lesson content, in which they are meant to exchange ideas and compare their own culture with that of the other users. This can be practised synchronously, or asynchronously, depending on whether learners select a text-based forum or a voice connection. Multiple examples of activities which are likely to breed intercultural communication have been cited above. Here are a number of others:

At Upper-Intermediate level in Lesson 11, learners are instructed to use the online forum in order to discuss their opinions on the most important contributions to human lives so far.

At Upper-Intermediate level in Lesson 20, learners are supposed to consult other program users from across the world on the target audience of a series of advertisements for a number of products. In addition, they are to decide the best place in which each advertisement should be displayed.

In Lesson 24 at Intermediate level, learners are requested to use the forum in order to answer questions about the media in their own country. Since learners are instructed to share their answers with others, the activity will inevitably create opportunities for crosscultural comparison.

In Lesson 8 at Upper-Intermediate level, learners read a ghost story relating to Chopin, and as a follow-up, they are asked to discuss with international partners online selected ghost stories from their own countries.

Other crosscultural comparisons include: ways to have a perfect day out (Elementary level/Lesson 34); verbal behaviour: formal and informal ways of addressing people in English and the learners' own language (Upper-Intermediate level/Lesson 2), or confusing notices in English and the learners' mother tongue (Upper-Intermediate level /Lesson 1).

The educational component (critical cultural awareness). The software encourages learners not only to acquire cultural knowledge through the materials with which they work, but also to judge the materials themselves; yet, a comparison of the very materials is not practised.

The elements of materials which learners are encouraged to judge include: the attitude/perspective of material authors, the tone, the informative value as well as the objectivity of the materials. Examples of the techniques through which it is done are cited below.

In Video Lesson B at Pre-Intermediate level learners watch a video about Hemel Hempstead, a town north of London, featuring interviews with visitors to a night club. After viewing, learners are supposed to go to the online forum and evaluate the interviews with other program users on a 10-point scale with regard to: the level of interest the material has generated, the information that it carries, and the insight into life in Britain that it provides. Especially the last two evaluation criteria constitute the kind of reflection on materials that learners with critical cultural awareness need to engage in.

At Pre-Intermediate level in Video Lesson D, learners watch a documentary about the *Eurostar* train, and afterwards, they are to answer three questions about it. One of the questions elicits learners' opinion about the material, which creates room for critical judgement.

In Lesson 36 at Pre-Intermediate level learners read a text about the weather in, and the best time to visit, selected world countries. The text is followed by questions which stimulate assessment of the truthfulness, objectivity and universality of the information provided by the article.

In Lesson 4 at Intermediate level learners read a text about queuing at bus stops in England, and they are to requested to state whether the text overall is humorous or serious. This kind of judgement is vital for critical cultural awareness, because the tone of a cultural text is likely to exert a serious influence on how culture is presented, and the ability to judge it is a prerequisite of intercultural competence.

In Lesson 14 at Intermediate level learners attempt to distinguish facts from opinions while reading a text about Prague; in the same lesson, they judge the attitude of the author of a travel guide for visitors to St Petersburg towards the city. In this manner they can establish the point of view, or perspective, that the guide represents.

A similar activity is included in Lesson 15 at Intermediate level, where learners are instructed to decide the writer's attitude towards the traffic cones presented in the text *Design classic: the traffic cone.*

The technology-related features. *EuroPlus+ Reward* offers users the following functionalities: (a) alternative navigation routes, (b) advanced search options, (c) cultural explanation, (d) insightful audio-visuals, (e) annotation tools, (f) supplementary cultural materials, and (g) online communication tools. However, the software does not feature a task authoring utility.

(a) *Alternative navigation routes*. Different navigation routes through the program can be taken by its users. For instance, the *Table of Contents* gives learners access to particular units, from which individual lessons can be selected.

From the main menu users can also choose the *Course exploration* utility, through which they can access any language component, or topic, within all the units and lessons featured. Users can select desired content from pre-defined indices: *Topic*, *Grammar and function*, *Vocabulary*, *Reading*, *Listening*, *Writing*, *Speaking*, and *Pronunciation*. However, the program does not allow learners to access particular multimedia resources.

(b) *Advanced search options*. A general word search can be performed in the program through the *AZ Vocabulary* tool, a glossary containing words arranged alphabetically along with translations; both English vocabulary and Polish translations can be independently searched.

What facilitates the search is the fact that the program also indicates through colour-coded squares which level a particular word belongs to, and displays the number of the lesson where the word appears. Words can also be searched in *Unit/Lesson* mode, where the user selects a particular lesson that they wish to find vocabulary from.

Additionally, words can be searched in *Word Bank* mode, whereby learners can reach vocabulary arranged by themselves in 30 pre-defined categories, e.g. *Countries and nationalities*, *Customs and traditions*, *Education*, *Food and drink*, *Geographical features*, *Politics*, *government and society*, or *Religion*. Learners can add their own categories as well, which may be particularly useful for intercultural learning.

(c) *Cultural explanation*. The program features cultural explanation in the form of commentaries by Simon Greenall, attached to particular elements of content as video clips. In each case the commentaries help learners expand their intercultural knowledge relevant to the issue in question while, at the same time, clarifying cultural phenomena, which might otherwise be too problematic for learners to understand. The commentaries provide explanation pertaining to: behavioural and social patterns, including culture-determined aspects of verbal behaviour (languaculture); factual information on artefacts, social groups, artists, and cultural phenomena; as well as advice on the intricacies of crosscultural communication.

The behavioural and social patterns explained by the video commentary include: the principles of verbal criticism (Upper-Intermediate level/Lesson 3); ways of expressing agreement/disagreement, including the use of gestures for that purpose (Upper-Intermediate level/Lesson 3); or the role of women in British society (Upper-Intermediate level/Lesson 6).

The languacultural elements tackled through the video commentaries comprise: differences between American and British English (Pre-Intermediate level/Lesson 24); politeness principles relating to the use of intonation in English and rules governing verbal criticism in British and American English (Pre-Intermediate level/Progress check C); as well as the tradition of storytelling (Upper-Intermediate level/Lesson 19).

Factual information on artefacts, social groups, artists, and cultural phenomena concerns: *Guinness* as a national Irish drink (Pre-Intermediate level/Lesson 14); the contents of selected paintings from the National Gallery, London; education systems in the USA and Britain (Intermediate level/Lesson 39); the Amish people and their lifestyle (Upper-Intermediate level/Lesson 14); or Scott Fitzgerald and his writings (Upper-Intermediate level/Lesson 17.

Cultural explanation also includes advice on how to handle the challenges of crosscultural communication. For instance, at Pre-Intermediate level in Lesson 30, users do a questionnaire *Doing things the right way* concerning behavioural norms in their own culture. The author's video commentary which accompanies the activity carries comments on behaviour and customs in Britain and America as well as possible differences that might exist in other cultures. Thus, it may be inferred that the commentary sensitises learners to intercultural difference as such.

In Lesson 6 at Pre-Intermediate level, in the video commentary the program author increases learners' crosscultural awareness by highlighting the importance of studying intolerance for the purpose of crosscultural development. He elucidates the discrepancy between people's expectations towards the behaviour of the representatives of other cultures and the actual experience, which frequently causes surprise. In this manner, learners are mentally prepared for handling otherness in intercultural contacts.

In Lesson 1 at Intermediate level, learners work on a questionnaire on polite requests. The video commentary accompanying the activity focuses learners' attention on politeness principles in English; the program author remarks here that although learners are not supposed to adopt native speakers' customs and behaviours, they must remember that if they do not, in particular situations they may appear to be impolite. The focus of the activity per se is on grammar, but the cultural explanation additionally shifts it towards culture and culture-determined politeness/friendliness principles.

One more example of cultural explanation appears in the same lesson, where the video commentary brings to the fore international customs of hospitality. This time, the author of the program makes learners aware of the fact that rules describing socio-cultural behaviour should serve them as guidelines rather than proper rules, which implies that learners are supposed to manage difference and intercultural challenges independently by using the knowledge and skills that they have already acquired.

(d) *Insightful audio-visuals*. The audio-visual aids available in the program comprise: audio and video clips, and images, some of which provide invaluable cultural information.

Helpful videos are offered in the video documentary series, whose episodes accompany particular cultural activities. The videos present the aspects of culture tackled in a given activity in greater detail; they frequently feature real characters who talk about their lives, e.g. at Elementary level in Video Lesson B, two families, *The Sowerbutts and the Lambs,* talk about the details of their daily routine. The clip is informative as the events described are presented in socio-cultural context; both the audio and video cues are helpful in this case.

Another example is featured within Elementary level in Video Lesson C, entitled *A day in the life of a London taxi driver*. The video constitutes a good opportunity for learners to listen to a London accent, and learn directly from a taxi driver about his job. The video also contains glimpses of London's landmarks as the taxi passes by them.

A culturally insightful a audio clip is a listening text which accompanies Lesson 17 at Elementary level, where users listen to Lisa, who speaks about English breakfast as it is stereotyped, and as it is actually prepared on a daily basis.

The images available in the program facilitate intercultural learning in two ways. On the one hand they assist learners in completing the tasks which they accompany, on the other hand they may provide additional cultural insight. For instance, images of newspaper advertisements for cultural attractions (theatre, gallery, cinema, arts centre) accompany a listening dialogue on the basis of which learners are supposed to decide which of the attractions the couple presented in the dialogue should choose. However, the images do not only help learners respond to the question, they also demonstrate the lay-out of advertisements and the kind of information that they may contain.

(e) *Annotation tools*. The program offers a note-taking tool which allows users to add their own commentary to particular pages of the course lessons. The utility might serve diverse purposes, e.g. it might be utilised as a cultural diary.

In addition, users might use the *AZ Glossary* for annotation as they can add their own words to it. The space available was originally meant for word translations and allows up to roughly 50 characters, but it might permit learners to append particular vocabulary items with brief cultural explanation.

(f) *Supplementary cultural materials*. The program contains supplementary cultural materials in the form of an online news service available from the main program menu. It constitutes an additional cultural resource, and features reading texts based on international news items, tailored to the learners' language level. Yet, what is interesting, the program informs that the aim of the service is to foster the development of reading skills, not cultural knowledge.

As the researcher has found out from the manufacturer's customer service line, the news service has not been updated since 2010, but an entire collection of news articles, dated 2009-2011, is available there. The articles, illustrated by images, fall into the following categories: *Science*, with international news on discoveries, new technologies, natural phenomena and nature; *Culture*, with international news on festivals, traditions, traditional sports, famous artists and religious holidays; and *SportsNews*, featuring famous sportsmen, competitions and sports records.

(g) *Online communication tools*. The program is equipped with an online forum, which permits synchronous communication in two modes: a text-based chat and a voice communication tool, both available to an international community of program users.

Asynchronous communication may be practised through a text-based opinion board named *Tablica opinii* (*Opinion Board*), where users can type their comments on the very program and its features. They can also respond to other users' comments, however, the topic of communication is restricted to the program contents and its functionalities.

A third communication tool is an online *Teacher's Service*, which gives users a chance to send selected open-ended activities, those that cannot be automatically assessed, to a teacher of their own choice via e-mail. It serves mostly language practice purposes and does not allow intercultural learning per se. However, if the teacher happens to be a foreigner/native speaker, the utility could be used for cultural learning.

In sum, the program enables learners to develop elements of the affective, cognitive and pragmatic components of intercultural competence. In terms of technological functionalities, it provides users with an advanced interface which includes a range of seven features, such as: (i) alternative navigation routes, (ii) advanced search options, (iii) cultural explanation, (iv) insightful audio-visual aids, (v) annotation tools, (vi) supplementary cultural materials, and (vii) online communication tools, which at the time of the research were out of order.

The results of the evaluation of the *EuroPlus+ Reward* program with regard to the checklist criteria are summarised in tabular format in Appendix F.

4.3 Tell Me More. Special Edition

Program overview. This CALL software is a multimedia language course, manufactured worldwide by: Auralog, and released in Poland in 2009 by Techland. The program is offered on a single DVD-ROM, and it is accompanied by an Audio CD-ROM, with MP3 recordings for learners to listen to.

According to the authors of the software, *Tell Me More* targets learners at the level of: Beginner, Intermediate, and Advanced; and it is addressed to an unspecified, general audience, including adolescent learners.

The software helps learners develop the four major language skills: listening, speaking, reading, writing, and the target language areas which it focuses on are: grammar, vocabulary and culture. The course offers over 40 types of activities and 1000 hours of language work.

The program permits language practice within 6 streams: culture, grammar, writing, themes/topics, pronunciation and vocabulary. The user can select between 3 learning modes: (i) *Guided Mode*, where the course will be explored by following preset thematically organised paths; (ii) *Free-to-Roam Mode*, where the learner can access the program content at his/her discretion; and (iii) *Dynamic Mode*, where the user initially sets the learning objectives, while the program itself monitors the user's learning progress and selects relevant activities, depending on the level of success the user has had.

User's manual. Tell Me More. Special Edition is accompanied by a comprehensive printed manual, where it is suggested that the learning focus of the software is on the four major language skills: listening, reading, speaking – pronunciation, and writing) as well as culture.

Content overview. The content is categorised into 5 workshops: *Cultural Workshop*, *Lesson Workshop*, *Vocabulary Workshop*, *Grammar*

Workshop, *Oral Workshop* and *Written Workshop*. Lessons in the program can be taken at preset 10 levels of difficulty.

In the *Cultural Workshop*, the learner can find the following elements: *Cultural texts*, *Cultural quizzes*, *Patchworks* and *Mapmania*. *Cultural texts*, 73 texts in total, are arranged in thematic categories such as: *Geography*, *History*, *Traditions*, *Cuisine*, *Literature*, *Art and Architecture*, *Entertainment*, and *Society and Economy*. At levels 1-3 each of the texts is reduced to a single sentence describing e.g. a famous place or a tourist attraction. At the higher levels (4-10) the texts are developed into more informative paragraphs, with links to relevant maps where the position of the places that learners read about are indicated.

The *Cultural quizzes* check only declarative knowledge, not skills, e.g. *What is the public health service of Great Britain? Answer: The National Health Service.*

Patchworks are short pictorial-textual matching quizzes where the user will match the names of professions, famous places, food items or famous people with corresponding images, while *Mapmania* offers map-based quizzes which involve: matching places, or geographical features (lakes, rivers, or islands), with their names.

The *Lesson Workshop* comprises a choice of video dialogues which feature scenes that are to serve the purpose of language practice, exclusively. The dialogues give learners an opportunity to practise speaking and pronunciation by taking one of the roles in the dialogue. The speech recognition functionality allows the computer to interact with the learner during the activity, but what both parties say is, nevertheless, predetermined. The dialogues contain very little context and are followed by language practice activities where language is isolated from context.

The *Vocabulary Workshop* aims at fostering language practice focused on lexis. Within this section learners have access to a word-based glossary. The activities that learners can perform here take a number of formats, which include: picture/word associations; word searches; word associations, i.e. matching pairs of words; multiple-choice sentences; fill-in-the-blanks activities; word/topic associations, where learners can arrange words into thematic groups; mystery phrases, which are a word/phrase-based version of the *Hangman* game; and crossword puzzles, where users will insert into a crossword the words which they can hear.

The *Grammar Workshop* contains a set activities targeting grammatical instruction and practice, that is why learners will find grammar explanations here along with a range of grammar activities: multiple-choice sentences; fill-in-the-blanks activities at sentence level; activities where learners categorise words according to the grammatical functions which the words have in a passage.

There are also grammar practice activities where learners: manipulate grammar items, e.g. articles; read sentences and manipulate selected grammar elements, e.g. they transform object pronouns into personal pronouns; write down the sentences which they listen to (dictation); and perform text transformation.

The *Oral Workshop* contains speaking practice in the form of: video dialogues, role plays, and video-based comprehension activities. In the video dialogues, learners listen to the computer's role in a dialogue and respond by reading aloud one of the 3 answers provided. In the role plays, they watch a fragment of a film and act it out with the computer by taking one of the roles. In the video-based comprehension activities, learners watch a video and answer a number of comprehension questions about it.

The *Written Workshop* comprises video dialogues and video-based comprehension activities, which are followed by: grammar practice activities involving the manipulation of grammar items, e.g. articles; transformation-based sentence practice activities; dictations; and scrambled word activities, where learners drag and drop particular words to the right place in a sentence. Within the *Written Workshop* learners also perform expression activities, in which they describe an image, or a video scene while trying to observe a word limit.

The affective component (attitudes). *Tell Me More. Special Edition* is a program which does not target the affective development of its users. Learners here do not observe, or reflect on, their attitudes towards other cultures. They do not develop a more positive attitude towards cultural difference, and they are not offered opportunities to shift perspectives while dealing with otherness.

The cognitive component (knowledge). 3 aspects of the cognitive component of intercultural competence can be developed through the software: (a) material culture, (b) socio-political realia, and (c) behaviour/practices, whereas thought patterns/values and language culture are not dealt with at all.

(a) *Material culture. Tell Me More. Special Edition* contains a collection of *Cultural texts*, a number of which are arranged into categories such as: *Geography*, *Cuisine*, *Literature*, *Art and Architecture*, and *Entertainment*. At difficulty levels 1-3 each of the texts is reduced to a single sentence accompanied with a relevant drawing or photograph. At the more advanced levels (4-10), each cultural text is an informative paragraph, appended with an image.

The texts titles reveal which areas of material culture are tackled within the program: *Indian Cuisine*, *The Sandwich*, *Sunday Roast*, *The British Pub*, *British Cheese*, *William Shakespeare*, *Oscar Wilde*, *Roald Dahl*, *Winnie the Pooh* (the character), *The Angel of the North*, *The National Trust*, *The Turner Prize*, *John Constable*, *Hadrian's Wall*; *the Beatles*, *Monty Python*, *Cricket*, *Pantomimes*, *Edward Elgar*, *The Edinburgh Festival*, *British cinema*. The geographical texts cover places of interest in the UK, including: London, the Giant's Causeway, Stonehenge, Canterbury and the Lake District.

The *Vocabulary workshop* contains picture/word association activities which involve the names of objects, occasions, and rooms in the home, through which material culture might also be acquired.

More artefacts can be seen in the video dialogues which are featured, for instance, in Lessons 3, 6, and 9: kitchen utensils, tableware, tent accessories (pegs, tent poles, the ground sheet, and mattresses), and car parts (brake pads, the dashboard, indicators, a jack, and a wheel brace).

(b) *Socio-political realia*. The program gives learners an opportunity to learn the socio-cultural realia of different countries through an online service which features a weekly *Tell Me More* lesson, provided in association with the *Euronews* television news channel. Every week's lesson is based on authentic video footage from *Euronews*, whereby learners can find out, e.g. how a Danish farmer has been using the European Union's subsidies in order to modernise his farm. Learners can also watch an authentic video interview with an expert talking about the European Common Agricultural Policy (*Tell me More*, the weekly online lesson of 23.07.2011).

Another source of socio-political knowledge in the program are the *Cultural texts,* which are themed as: *History*, and *Society and Economy* (73 texts). Learners can find out here about major historical events in British history, e.g. the Great Fire of London, Henry VIII, The Civil War, or The Battle of Hastings.

They also learn what social changes British society underwent between the 1970s and the 1990s in texts entitled: *The 1970s*, *The 1980s*, and *The 1990s.* They can additionally expand their knowledge of the basic socio-political processes and institutions in Britain through texts such as: *Devolution*, *Privatisation*, *The Trade Unions*, *The NHS*, *Britain in Europe*, and *English Around the World*.

In addition, the program offers map-based activities, where learners increase their familiarity with elements of UK topography: *Rivers* and *Lakes*, *Relief*, *Seas and Oceans*, *Islands*; or the position of UK countries, cities and towns. The same features of topography can also be learnt with regard to the remainder of the European continent, including: external and internal waters, land relief, country borders, cities and towns. The topography of the world, outside Europe, is also covered along with country borders.

(c) *Behaviour/practices*. From the *Cultural texts,* themed as: *Traditions*, *Cuisine*, and *Entertainment,* learners can find out about cultural behaviour and practices followed in Britain, including: the *Guy Fawkes Night*, *The Loch Ness Monster*, *The Legend of St George*, *The Proms*, *Driving in Britain*, *The British Measurement System*; *The Picnic*, *the British Pub*, *Tea*, *Sunday Roast*; *Rugby*, *Monty Python*, *Cricket*, and *Pantomimes*.

Other forms of behaviour and practices are depicted in the video dialogues which the program contains. Learners can observe the characters featured there, who are: preparing and holding a birthday party; planning and preparing a meal for the guests who are coming soon (using kitchen tools and work sharing); setting the table (laying the table, asking a child for help); camping (enquiring about a space for a tent at a campsite reception, erecting a tent); or having a car serviced.

The action-oriented component (skills of interpreting and relating, and skills of discovery and interaction). None of the intercultural skills is practised within the program. Learners do not interpret cultural phenomena; they do not compare their mother tongue and native culture with other languages or cultures. Learners are not encouraged to consult varied sources or engage in cooperation with partners through project work. Neither do they practice intercultural communication, for which no provisions are made through tools or instructions.

The program does not contain activities where learners would be able to self-assess their own intercultural skills, while the computer-assessed cultural quizzes which it features are not intercultural in character and focus on declarative, fact-based knowledge – not skills.

The 3 testing tools within the CALL package are all language-based. *The Progress Test* tracks learners' progress in language learning; the *Language Achievement Test* assesses learners' language level at the end of the course; and the tool named *Level equivalences* is a tabular document which helps users relate their language achievement test scores to a specific language level of the Common European Framework of Reference. Both the language tests which learners can take within the program, *The Progress Test* and the *Language Achievement Test,* measure only language skills and knowledge.

The educational component (critical cultural awareness). *Tell Me More. Special Edition* does not foster the development of the educational component of intercultural competence, because the software lacks activities which would involve learners in a comparative analysis or judgement of cultural materials.

The technology-related features. The program is equipped with 3 technological features which may facilitate intercultural learning: (a) alternative navigation routes, (b) advanced search options and (c) supplementary cultural materials. The remainder of the features contained within the evaluation checklist, i.e. task authoring tools, cultural explanation, annotation tools, and online communication tools, are absent from the program.

As far as the quality of the audio-visuals is concerned, it must be underlined that the images which *Tell Me More* offers are not very clear. For instance, in the *Geography* section of *Cultural texts* Stonehenge is illustrated by a distant dark photograph of the place. In effect, it is hardly possible to recognise that the structure pictured is a stone circle.

In particular cases photographs are replaced with drawings, which are of rather low quality, and very unclear, e.g. in the *Geography* section of *Cultural texts*, the Giant's Causeway or St Michael's Mount are barely recognisable in the drawings. The picture of St Michael's Mount resembles an impressionistic painting, and may be hard to interpret.

In other situations, the drawings are not even illustrations of the content that they accompany. For example, Winnie the Pooh is presented through an image of a honey spoon with the quotation "Silly Old Bear" – the lack of a proper image of the character may have been caused by copyright issues.

(a) *Alternative navigation routes*. 3 navigation routes are permitted in the software, each determined by one of the three working modes in which learners can use the program: the *Free-to-Roam mode*, the *Guided mode* and *Dynamic mode*.

In the *Free-to-Roam mode* learners can construct their own lessons out of the activities available in the program, depending on their learning objectives. In the *Guided mode* the learner selects learning objectives as well as the time limits of the course and the software prepares a personalised learning path for him/her, accordingly. In the *Dynamic mode* the program systematically evaluates the learner's progress and tailors activities to his/her needs.

(b) *Advanced search options*. *Tell Me More. Special Edition* provides a simple word search tool whereby learners can consult the pronunciation of a word of their choice. The vocabulary items which are part of the program content are arranged in four major lexical groups: *Daily Life*,

Intellect and Reason, *Society and Institutions*, and *Professional Life*, which, in turn, fall into multiple sub-groups.

Yet, what distinguishes the program from other CALL packages is a search utility which allows learners to access specific types of learning resources, including maps and cultural texts.

(c) *Supplementary cultural materials*. The weekly *Tell Me More* online lessons, provided in association with the *Euronews* television channel, feature authentic video footage. As it has already been presented, one of the video lessons focuses on: European agriculture, issues affecting European farmers and the agricultural policies of the European Union (Tell me More, the weekly lesson of 23.07.2011). Such materials facilitate cultural learning, which complements the course content.

In sum, the software helps learners develop only the cognitive component of intercultural competence (knowledge) while completely neglecting the remainder of its elements: attitudes, intercultural skills and critical cultural awareness.

Technology-wise, it offers 3 interculturally useful features: (i) alternative navigation routes, (ii) advanced search options, and (iii) supplementary cultural materials.

The results of the evaluation of the *Tell Me More. Special Edition 1000h* program with regard to the checklist criteria are summarised in tabular form in Appendix F.

4.4 Tell Me More Junior (13-15)

Program overview. This program is a multimedia language course, manufactured by Auralog, and released in Poland in 2007 by Techland. The software comes on 2 CD-ROMs: CD-ROM 1, for 11-13-year-old learners, and CD-ROM 2, for 13-15-year-olds.

As CD-ROM 1 (age 11-13) targets primary school learners, only CD-ROM 2 (age 13-15) was selected for the purpose of the research study, because the sample was supposed to include software targeting learners at the level of lower/upper secondary school.

The program is designed to serve two language proficiency levels: Beginner and Intermediate, and the age group which CD-ROM 2 addresses is that of older primary (lower secondary) and upper secondary learners.

The target language skills to be developed within the program include: listening, speaking, reading, writing, and the language areas the software concentrates on are: grammar, vocabulary and culture.

The course content comprises 57 types of activities, and the program permits language practice within 3 streams: communication, culture and games as well as topics.

User's manual. Tell Me More Junior (13-15) is accompanied by a printed user's manual, which suggests that the focus of the software is on the four fundamental language skills. Although no reference to culture as a teaching/learning goal is made, the manual refers users to *Cultural texts*, which are part of the program content.

Content overview. The software offers users 4 learning paths: *Communicative Activities 1*, *Communicative Activities 2*, *Culture and Games*, and *Themes*. Although the program purports to teach learners how to communicate, in *Communicative Activities 1* and *Communicative Activities 2,* it has a clear language focus, with activities such as: gap filling exercises; dictations; and activities involving the manipulation of language forms, e.g. conjugations, transformations and scrambled words. This path also offers dialogues accompanied by multiple-choice comprehension questions.

The *Culture and Games* learning path embraces the *Culture* component, which focuses on the culture of the United Kingdom along with elements of international culture. However, culture is reduced to geography, entertainment and traditions.

The *Games* component is devoted to language practice, and contains: mystery phrases activities, crossword puzzles and word search puzzles.

The *Themes* learning path is categorised thematically into units such as: *Body and health*, *Describing an object*, *Accommodation*, *Family and acquaintances*, *Time*, and *Animals*. This section purports to aim at developing vocabulary, speaking skills and pronunciation, and its focus is on language. The activities offered here include: sentence pronunciation, word pronunciation, word associations, word order activities, picture/word associations, word order activities with speech recognition and multiple-choice dialogues. It is worth observing that what is labelled as speaking practice within this learning path constitutes pronunciation practice.

The affective component (attitudes). *Tell Me More Junior* carries very little cultural input, and it apparently prioritises language practice. Even the culture that is contained within the program content is not brought forward sufficiently for learners to be able to analyse, or interpret it. That is why learners cannot develop their attitudes towards otherness at large, or other cultures. All in all, the evaluation conducted revealed that the affective component of intercultural competence is completely omitted in the program.

The cognitive component (knowledge). The cognitive component of intercultural competence within the program is developed with reference to its 3 aspects: (a) material culture, (b) socio-political realia and (c) behaviour and practices.

(a) *Material culture*. In the *Culture and Games* section of the program there are a number of cultural texts which in a single sentence present iconic figures, cultural events and beauty spots of Britain, including: The Beatles, the Edinburgh Festival, The Proms, the Loch Less Monster, British newspapers, Canterbury, and the Lake District. Each of the sentences is accompanied by a photograph or drawing, although particularly the latter is of poor quality.

The program also contains a number of activities with a cultural focus, e.g. in the *Culture and Games* section, where learners are expected to match quotations with: appropriate historic figures, e.g. Mary Stuart; pop stars, e.g. the Beatles and Elvis Presley; literary characters, e.g. Romeo and Juliet; and poets, e.g. William Blake.

Language-focused matching activities include photographs of artefacts, e.g.: the French horn, cars stuck in London's traffic, suit and tie, a weighing scales, a clap board and a university graduate's beret, which may implicitly develop the knowledge of material culture.

All in all, the material culture depicted in the program concerns mostly elements of art (literature and music), cultural event, history, national symbols and artefacts.

(b) *Socio-political realia* are presented in the program mostly in the *Culture and Games* path, where learners are given an opportunity to learn: the position of the countries, counties, cities and towns of the United Kingdom.

Apart from British maps, in the *English Around the World* section learners also work with maps of the world in order to learn the position of: English-speaking countries, other countries of the world, and the world's major cities. In addition, one of the maps featured within the program indicates where selected nationalities live in the world.

Learners consolidate their knowledge of geography by: matching points on a blank UK map to the names of large cities; matching photos of world cities to appropriate landmarks, matching pictures to the names of international beauty spots, or identifying British cities, rivers and lakes as well as the capital cities of Europe on a map.

In the cultural texts in the *Culture and Games* section, learners additionally find out that "English is the native language of over 350 million people all over the world" (*Tell Me More Junior 13-15*, the *Cultures and Games* path: *English Around the World*), and in the photo/text matching activities included in the program they can see photographs of the representatives of different social groups, e.g. Ivy League graduates, NHS doctors, or a coal miner at work.

(c) *Behaviour/practices*. Selected forms of behaviour and cultural practices are depicted in photographs which are part of the photo/text matching activities that learners perform. The practices include: listening to the BBC, playing rugby, playing cricket, reading a newspaper, taking a steam boat cruise, or holidaying at a seaside resort.

Cultural texts also inform learners about social/cultural occasions that the British people participate in, such as: the Guy Fawkes Night, the Edinburgh Festival and The Proms.

The action-oriented component (skills of interpreting and relating, and skills of discovery and interaction). Learners do not interpret cultural phenomena in the program as culture is scarcely presented. Cultural presentation most frequently takes the form of a factual sentence with basic information, but it is not followed by proper explanation or culture-focused activities. Too little is presented for learners to interpret.

The program does not make learners compare their own mother tongue and native culture with the target language and other cultures. They might study language differences on their own because a translation functionality is available, but it is restricted to particular tasks: dialogues, grammar explanation, glossary and cultural texts; and the option has a clearly utilitarian purpose.

Learners' attention is not directed towards language or cultural similarities and differences, and the tasks offered focus exclusively on the target language form; only occasionally on culture. It is particularly visible in the *Culture* and *Games* path, where despite opportunities for it, no references are made to learners' mother tongue or native culture.

No opportunity is created for students to consult other cultural resources, e.g. online encyclopaedias, interviews with native speakers, or media publications. An exception might be the online services about the United Kingdom and the USA available from the program, but the cultural resources are limited to articles written by the program authors, as well as official and unofficial websites. Learners are not referred to offline resources, such as: interviews, encyclopaedias, or collectable artefacts.

Despite the fact that the program offers a large number of cultural resources online, on closer inspection, it is hard to claim that the online resources are diverse as only the materials relating to one theme, *Work* and *Travel*, are based on a range of resources: tourist guides, online atlases, and a radio website, where learners can listen to live programmes.

The other resources are limited in range, and at times consist of a single internet link only. What is more, the themes which the resources tackle are limited to: *Work*, *Travel*, and *Moving Abroad*, which are not directly related to the teaching content of the software.

Learners are not inspired to participate in project work, where they would need to cooperate with others in order to enhance their cultural exploration and intercultural development.

Intercultural communication cannot be practised within the program, either. Learners could theoretically do it through the online forum utility featured within the software by contacting learners from abroad, but the forum is not functional; an error message informs users that the forum is under maintenance. Moreover, it must be realised that communication per se, even if it is intercultural, does not automatically foster intercultural development as it must be properly planned, guided by set aims, and followed by reflection. Learners using *Tell Me More Junior* are guided towards none of these.

Self-assessment of intercultural skills is also absent from the software due to the lack of appropriate instructions and tools which might serve the purpose. Thus, learners do not reflect on their own intercultural skills here.

The educational component (critical cultural awareness). Learners do not work on the development of critical awareness as they are not instructed to compare or judge cultural resources. Within the very program cultural materials are limited in scope, and cultural learning is likely to occur only accidentally, whereas the online cultural resources, which are supposed to be accessed by learners on a self-study basis, lack guidance towards work focused on critical cultural awareness.

The technology-related features. *Tell Me More Junior (13-15)* contains 3 technological functionalities which are likely to foster intercultural learning: (a) alternative navigation routes, (b) supplementary cultural materials, and (c) online communication tools.

No advanced search options are provided within the software as learners can perform only a simple word search. Task authoring tools are not provided, and program users have to rely only on the preset tasks already supplied within the program.

Cultural explanation utilities are absent from the program, and the little culture presented in the program is not appended with any commentary.

The audio-visual materials that the program offers are simple photographs/drawings which contain artefacts or famous landmarks, but the graphics are very unclear in places, e.g. it is impossible to recognise the French horn from the photograph that is supposed to present it as only a small fragment of it is visible. Other images, e.g. the drawings which contain the Lake District or the Loch Ness monster, are very unclear.

(a) *Alternative navigation routes*. Learners can access content within the software by navigating through the learning paths: *Communicative Acts*, *Culture and Games*, and *Themes*. In this manner they can select between the specific communicative skills, elements of cultural knowledge, or topics, that they wish to work on, respectively.

Alternatively, users can navigate through the program content by using the *Reference tools*, which are available in the top right corner of the users' graphic interface. The tool displays a pop-up window with a set of clickable links which lead to content categorised as language-focused features: *Grammar Explanations*, *Conjugation Tool*, and *Glossary*; as well as culture-focused elements: *Cultural Texts* and *Maps*.

(b) *Supplementary cultural materials*. *Tell Me More Junior* provides learners with multiple supplementary cultural materials through its online services. One of the features available online is the *Quote of the week*, a quotation by a representative of the target language culture, e.g. a quote from American writer Mark Twain.

The remainder of the resources are grouped within a collection of cultural articles entitled *the Horizons*, whose content falls into 3 sections: *Work*, *Travel*, and *Moving Abroad*.

The *Work* section comprises articles on how to write a C.V. and a covering letter in English when applying for a job. Interestingly enough, the material is accompanied by cultural advice and comments, e.g. an explanation of the British/American system of academic qualifications.

The *Travel* section features an article which presents UK countries as tourist destinations along with photographs and a comprehensive list of hyperlinks to 55 authentic websites, run by institutions and private individuals, which offer information and guidance for tourists travelling to the UK, Ireland, and the USA, e.g. the *English Tourist Board*, *Go Ireland*, *About Britain*, the *Castles of Wales*, or *New York*.

The USA is presented in this section through websites which contain: US maps and guides (the *US National Atlas* website); city tours, sites and views (*The Grand Canyon* website); food and music (the *Creole and Cajun Recipe Page*, or the *KDHX* website of a St Louis local radio station).

The *Moving abroad* section offers articles on life in Britain and the USA as well as information for potential immigrants. The collection of texts for those planning to move to Britain covers the following: Entering Britain (*Visas*, *Work Permits*, *Registering with the Police and Residence Permits*, *Studying in the UK*, *Elections*, *Employment in the UK*, *Social*

Security, including useful hyperlinks to e.g. the Home Office website), Health Care and Social Security as well as Daily Life (*A New Place to Live*, *Electricity*, *Gas and Water*, *Telephone*, *Driving in Britain*, *Highway Code*, *Opening a Bank Account*, *Tax*, *Working Hours*, *Holidays and Public Holidays*, *Education*, *Service Opening Times*, *Importation of Animals*).

The collection of texts on the USA comprises themes such as: Entering the United States (*Do I need a visa*?, *Work*, *Study*, *Residency*) along with hyperlinks to relevant websites, e.g. Immigration and Naturalization Service; Staying in the United States (*Social Security*, *Identification*, *Driving*, *Consular registration*, *Healthcare*, *Income tax*, and *Finding a job*); and Daily Life (*Banking procedures*, *Telephone*, *Renting an apartment*, *Shopping Malls*, *How to pay*, *Sales tax*, *Tips*, *Currency*, *The post office*, *Units of measure*, *Public holidays*, *Education*, *Alcohol and cigarettes*, and *Climate*).

(c) *Online communication tools*. The software offers learners two tools for online communication. One of them is the *Tell Me More* users' forum for asynchronous, text-based communication. This utility permits communication with other users of the program from all over the world, and might help learners to establish and maintain intercultural contacts. However, at the time of the evaluation the forum website was under maintenance, and it was not operational.

The other communication tool available to *Tell Me More Junior* users is an online chat service called *Pen Pals*, which allows synchronous, text-based communication with other program users from all over the world. Yet, at the time of the evaluation the Pen Pals website was also under maintenance. As the researcher was informed by a consultant at the Polish publisher's customer service line, the international manufacturer of the *Tell Me More* software has apparently discontinued the web services, and they are unlikely to be resumed.

In sum, the software helps learners develop only the cognitive component of intercultural competence (knowledge) while neglecting the other elements of it: attitudes, intercultural skills and critical cultural awareness.

Technology-wise, it offers three features: (i) alternative navigation routes, (ii) supplementary cultural materials online, and (iii) two online communication tools, both under maintenance.

The results of the evaluation of the *Tell Me More Junior (13-15)* program with regard to the checklist criteria are summarised in tabular format in Appendix F.

4.5 Profesor Henry

Program overview. This program is also a multimedia language course, originally produced by Edgard, Poland. The software comes on 8 CD-ROMs and an additional Audio CD with PM3 clips.

Profesor Henry does not target a specific age group; thus, it may be stated that it was designed for a general audience, including adolescent learners. The package is aimed to develop mostly two language skills: listening and speaking; and the language areas that it targets are grammar and vocabulary. The course content includes 25,000 words, sentences and expressions along with 18 types of activities.

User's manual. The program is accompanied by a printed user's manual, in which the language levels featured within the software are reported to range from A1 to C2, according to the Common European Framework of Language Reference (CEFR).

The *Grammar* component of the program tackles grammar structures; the *Vocabulary* component is supposed to increase learners' vocabulary store; and the *Listening and Conversation* component aims to facilitate language development through audio-video materials.

In the manual for the *Vocabulary* component, the program authors state that the program has been enriched by pop-up materials, displayed optionally at the end, or during, activities, which contain e.g.: quotations from famous people, photographs, and proverbs along with Polish translation and recorded native-speaker pronunciation.

As the authors maintain, the purpose of these materials is to increase learners' interest in learning the culture of a given foreign country. This feature, however, is available only within the *Vocabulary* component of the package.

Content overview. The *Vocabulary* component gives learners an opportunity to learn lexis along with the pronunciation of particular words and sentences. It also offers exemplary sentences and Polish translation. The vocabulary practice consists in learners: choosing or typing the word that they can hear as well as selecting the right Polish translation.

Additional activities, whose aim is to consolidate the vocabulary taught involve: listening to words accompanied by their written forms and photos which illustrate meaning; matching photos with word labels; selecting the words that learners hear, or typing the names of objects that learners hear pronounced under corresponding photos.

The *Grammar* component permits learners to use 4 learning modes: the *Learn* mode, the *Repetitions* mode, the *Handbook* mode and the *Pronunciation trainer* mode. In the *Learn* mode users perform language-focused activities based on isolated sentences, with little or no context provided. The activities involve: filling tables with appropriate language forms, multiple-choice/open gap filling, jumbled words, jumbled sentences and sentence transformation.

In the *Repetitions* mode, learners can revise the material taught and verify their success through systematic assessment, set by the program on the basis of their performance.

The *Handbook* mode offers content categorised grammatically as e.g.: *Articles*, *Modal verbs*, or *Conditionals*. Within each category pronunciation, exemplary sentences and illustrative photos are available.

The *Pronunciation trainer* mode comprises grammatically categorised language items and allows learners to practise pronunciation by listening to a model answer and recording themselves. Learners can compare their own recordings with the model by referring to voice amplitude graphs and spectrograms.

In addition, a dictionary is available to them, which contains target language words with Polish translations, and letter symbols indicating grammatical categories.

In the *Listening and Conversations* component content is divided into thematic sets: *Free Time and Hobby*, *Culture and Entertainment*, *Society*, and *Houses and Accommodation*. Learners mostly work on language related to the texts which they initially listen to. Afterwards, they are supposed to select out of a number of multiple choice images the one which corresponds to the word that they have heard. Learners are also given a choice of words, and they select one on the basis of a definition that they can hear.

Another type of activity requires learners to listen to a longer conversation, illustrated by a photograph, where they are required to choose a sentence which best summarises the content. They also perform: multiple-choice comprehension questions, matching, true/false and gap-filling activities.

This component allows learners to use a dictionary as well as a mini dictionary of phrases.

The affective component (attitudes). *Profesor Henry* does not cater for the development of the affective component of intercultural competence as learners using the software are not instructed to work on their attitudes towards otherness.

Learners' cultural perspectives, from which they approach other cultures, are not brought to the fore in the activities that the program contains. Therefore, if a shift in learners' stance on difference occurs as they are using the program, it happens due to chance rather than as part of the learning process which the software is supposed to promote.

The cognitive component (knowledge). The development of 4 aspects of the cognitive component of intercultural competence is fostered by the program: (a) material culture, (b) socio-political realia, (c) behaviour and practices, and (d) thought patterns/values. Languaculture is not represented in any manner.

(a) *Material culture*. The program features vocabulary-focused activities which are enriched by randomly displayed pop-up windows, including cultural data such as: quotations from famous people, proverbs, and photographs of famous British/American landmarks.

As the program authors explicitly maintain in the user's manual, the purpose of these materials is to increase learners' interest in exploring the culture of the foreign country in question. The photographs depict, amongst others: the London Eye; the centre of Edinburgh; the Waterloo Station, London; The National Gallery, London; the Big Ben Tower and the Houses of Parliament; HMS Belfast, London; The Natural History Museum, London; Edinburgh Castle; Bodium Castle, England; Canary Wharf, London; Chestow Castle, Wales; Conwy Castle; North Wales; the Dingle Peninsula, Ireland; The Brazen Head pub, Dublin, Ireland; the Double-decker sightseeing bus; the Hoover Dam, Nevada/Arizona, USA; the Ancient Anasazi Ruins Cliff Palace, Colorado, USA; Capitol, Washington D.C., USA; San the Xavier Del Bac Mission church, Tuscon, USA; Niagara Falls, New York, USA; or Sunset Beach, Oahu, Hawaii.

Amongst the quotations from famous people which learners become acquainted with through the pop-up feature, there are also the words of renowned writers, e.g. Mark Twain.

In activities whose aim is to consolidate the vocabulary learnt through the program learners see and hear words accompanied by photographs. Subsequently, they match the photographs with appropriate labels; indicate what they hear while listening to an audio clip; or type under the photographs the names of objects which they can hear. These activities familiarise learners with a selection of artefacts, e.g. within the *Art* theme, they see objects relating to painting, photography or sculpture.

More material culture, celebrities, show business products (films), and famous cities, can be learnt from the video clips which the program offers in the *Speaking and Listening* component.

For instance, in the *Best Film* video a number of speakers talk about their favourite films, they describe selected film scenes, directors, discuss the cast, and say what they find special about the films. The titles discussed are iconic American productions, e.g.: *The Wizard of Oz*, *Breakfast at Tiffany's* or *The Birds*.

In another video learners watch a dialogue between football fans who are watching a live game. The speakers discuss differences between British and Italian football, or the qualities of particular players.

The *Speaking and Listening* section also contains listening texts conveying cultural information, e.g. *Wonders of America* is a listening text which cites general information about the topography and vital statistics of the USA as well as its beauty spots and scenery, e.g. Yellowstone or The Grand Canyon.

The *Media and Information* theme includes a video where a number of native speakers are interviewed about their favourite British newspapers. Amongst other things, learners find out what titles the speakers read and what stories their favourite newspapers cover.

Within the *Travel And Holiday* theme, the videos present the best places to visit in the UK, e.g. the Cheddar Gorge, the Scottish Highlands, Bath, Cornwall, or London's attractions: Tate Modern, the National Gallery and the British Museum.

(b) *Socio-political realia*. The *Vocabulary* section of the program offers sentence learning activities which carry information about selected facts from the history of the world, e.g. a sentence within the *History* theme reads: "The first European settlement in America was established by Vikings" (*Profesor Henry*, the Vocabulary section). Other sentences convey the following historical knowledge, pertaining also to non-English-speaking countries: "The crown jewels are kept in the Tower of London"; "The Inquisition tortured heretics"; "Karl Habsburg was the last emperor of Austria"; or "The coronation of Queen Elizabeth took place in 1953" (*Profesor Henry*, ibid.).

The video clips featured in the *Listening and Speaking* section of the program are also a rich source of information about socio-political institutions and social life, e.g. in the *Society* theme Hyde Park is presented with the Speaker's Corner, its principles and history.

The *Media and Information* theme includes a video documentary about *The History of London*. The *Life Styles* theme contains a video about *Intercultural London*, the city's minorities and minority districts. The *Houses and Accommodation* features a video about types of housing in Britain and the British people's attitude towards them.

(c) *Behaviour/practices*. People's behavioural patterns and cultural practices are presented in the video and images contained within the *Vocabulary* component of the program, including e.g. ways of spending free time, leisure activities or societal practices. For instance, a video about London in the *Culture and Entertainment* theme depicts what people can do at the city's attractions; another video presents the London

Underground and the practices of Tube travellers, while images present other settings, e.g. a game of cricket at Central Park, Wallasey.

The *Listening and Speaking* component of *Profesor Henry* features listening texts where different speakers talk about the leisure activities of the British people, e.g. cricket, football, fishing, pub going, gardening, playing tennis, football and rugby.

Other listening texts reveal practices relating to institutions which shape people's lives in Britain, e.g. learners listen to: 6th form college students talking about their first day at school and the courses that they are taking; or a fragment of a court hearing where the prosecutor is questioning the defendant.

The videos included in the same component of the program illustrate other forms of behaviour: football fans singing chants, a customer talking to a music shop assistant, the culture-determined traditional practices of London's ethnic minorities, commuting practices, Londoners' past time activities (visiting parks and pub going), or a medical check-up.

(d) *Thought patterns/values*. The *Listening and Speaking* audio-video recordings contain interviews with a number of British people who talk about their views, beliefs and feelings relating to various areas of life and culture, e.g. a video in the *Society* theme shows an interview with people from Ireland, Scotland, England and Wales about the manner in which they tend to stereotype other national groups.

Within the *Houses and Accommodation* theme a video demonstrates types of housing in Britain and the British people's attitudes towards them, while the *Media and Information* theme contains video interviews with people who discuss the newspapers which they read, their believes about the papers and the stories published there.

In the *Life Styles* theme a video entitled *Intercultural London* reveals what attitudes London's ethnic minorities have towards the English language as well as their mother tongues.

In the *Man and the Environment* theme a listening text features interviews in which various people talk about their attitude to animals, e.g.: a phobia of cockroaches, a fondness of cats, a hobby of collection zebra figurines.

Finally, the *Life Styles* theme includes a listening text which is a record of interviews with 3 British immigrants to Poland, who talk about their reasons why, and the circumstances in which, they arrived in the country. Learners additionally find out examples of the particular Britons' stereotypical views of Poland, which they held before they started visiting the country regularly.

Another resource through which learners can explore the thought patterns and values of different national groups and people from different areas of the world are the pop-up quotations which accompany language practice activities in the *Vocabulary* section. Exemplary quotations are: “To know is nothing at all, to imagine is everything” by Anatole; or “Soldiers win battles and generals get the credits” by Napoleon Bonaparte.

The action-oriented component (skills of interpreting and relating, and skills of discovery and interaction). *Profesor Henry* does not develop learners’ intercultural skills. Users are not invited to interpret the cultural phenomena which they are exposed to, but are rather expected to acquire the factual knowledge as it comes.

The program does not feature tasks which would involve intercultural or interlanguage comparison. Learners might analyse differences between their own culture and that of other countries on their own, but the software does not stimulate them to do so.

Characteristically, even the activities that carry cultural information focus exclusively on language practice, and culture is treated by the program authors as an addition to mainstream learning. A confirmation of that is the fact that the cultural pop-ups in the program can be deactivated by program users from the *Settings* menu.

Learners using the program are not requested to refer to other cultural resources; they do not perform any project work, either. It is impossible for learners to practice intercultural communication within the program as it is devoid of internet connectivity, and thus, it offers no communication tools.

Self-assessment of intercultural skills is not practised within the software due to the lack of adequate guidance and tools which would permit learners to reflect on how well they can handle the challenges of intercultural communication, or what intercultural skills they have managed to develop.

The educational component (critical cultural awareness). The program does not foster the development of the educational component of intercultural competence. Learners neither compare nor judge the cultural materials which they make use of. Although culture is presented through a number of resources: photographs, textual materials, video documentaries and interviews, learners do not relate them to one another; they do not analyse the materials in terms of the perspectives that they represent, or the purposes for which they were created; the value of the materials for intercultural learning is not assessed.

The technology-related features. *Profesor Henry* contains four technological functionalities which are likely to facilitate intercultural learning: (a) alternative navigation routes, (b) advanced search options, (c) annotation tools, and (d) supplementary cultural materials. Task authoring tools, cultural explanation and online communication tools are not available within the program.

As far the audio-visual materials which are used in the software are concerned, it must be underlined that the photographs are relatively large, and good in quality, but the captions by which they are accompanied are too general, and do not inform learners what the images depict.

What is more, in places, cultural inaccuracies appear, e.g. an outline map of the British Isles, including the Republic of Ireland (Eire), is presented against the Union Jack as the background, which is likely to mislead learners into thinking that the map shows the United Kingdom of Great Britain and Northern Ireland.

In the light of the above, it cannot be stated that the audio-visuals within the software are particularly insightful.

(a) *Alternative navigation routes*. The program content may be accessed in a number of ways. Learners may set the program so that it randomly selects the language content, e.g. vocabulary, which they wish to learn from a particular thematic category. In this case content is automatically graded.

If learners use *Custom Settings*, they can filter out the content according to: themes, level of difficulty, parts of speech (e.g. nouns/verbs), or language units (e.g. words/sentences).

The *Search database* utility allows learners to compile their own lessons based on the components of their choice: a particular thematic set, level of difficulty, parts of speech (e.g. nouns or verbs) and language units (e.g. words/sentences) as well as collections of words which they can add to the program, including self-recorded pronunciation. In this way learners can precisely specify the words to be learnt.

(b) *Advanced search options*. The program enables learners to search its database according to: thematic sets, difficulty level, parts of speech (nouns/verbs) and language units (words/sentences). They can also search their own collection of words added to the program.

The words to be searched can be precisely specified, and the search is user-customised. The words which the program finds are accompanied by information about: the part of speech, the level of difficulty, language unit, theme as well as pronunciation. What is particularly useful for the learner from the perspective of intercultural learning is the fact that the words searched can be located by theme. However, the search functionality lacks a feature which would permit learners to access particular audio-visual materials.

(c) *Annotation tools*. An annotation tool is available to users in the program through which they can annotate the content with their own remarks on the language learnt, or examples of usage. However, the notes entered by learners might easily be used for cultural commentary. The program displays the notes on the screen during activities in order to facilitate learning. Yet, the tool is limited in functionality as it permits commentaries of up to 80 characters only, including spacing.

(d) *Supplementary cultural materials*. Supplementary cultural materials are limited in the software and they take two forms. The more explicit form is that of the afore-mentioned cultural pop-ups, displayed optionally during vocabulary-focused activities. The pop-up windows contain quotations from famous people, annotated photographs, and proverbs along with Polish translation and recorded pronunciation by a native speaker.

More implicit cultural supplements appear in particular vocabulary-focused activities, where the language content is displayed against a background featuring the outline maps of selected world countries along with relevant national flags.

In sum, the software helps learners develop only the cognitive component of intercultural competence (knowledge), while it omits the remainder of its elements: attitudes, intercultural skills and critical cultural awareness.

Technology-wise, it offers four features: (i) alternative navigation routes, (ii) advanced search options, (iii) an annotation tool and (iv) supplementary cultural materials online.

The results of the evaluation of *Profesor Henry* with regard to the checklist criteria are summarised in a tabular form in Appendix F.

4.6 New Reflex English

Program overview. This software is a multimedia language course, released by Young Digital Poland S.A., Poland, currently known as Young Digital Planet, and it is based on two other language courses: *Euro Plus+ Angielski Rozmówki* and the *Reflex* series.

The program is offered on 4 CD-ROMs, and it targets the following language levels: Beginner, Pre-Intermediate, Intermediate and Advanced. The age groups which the software addresses include adolescents and adults, and the language skills which it focuses on are: listening and speaking; the language areas to be developed are grammar and vocabulary.

The course content comprises 2,700 words, phrases and expressions organised within 10 units, and it permits the user to perform language practice within thematic sections, e.g. *Shopping* or *Entertainment,* whose content falls into skill areas, including: conversational and pronunciation practice as well as grammar and vocabulary.

User's manual. The *New Reflex English* program lacks a user's manual. The software offers users only brief installation instructions on the face of each of the CD-ROM discs on which it is delivered.

The program menu features a table summarising the course content, which bears four elements: *Grammar*, *Vocabulary*, *Comprehension* (without specifying whether it is reading or listening comprehension) and *Pronunciation/Conversations*. The menu includes no explicit reference to culture.

Content overview. The program contains 10 units: 8 units featuring new target language material to be learnt, which come under themed titles, e.g. *A Cosmopolitan City* or *A Good Meal*, and two review units.

The graphic interface is apparently modelled after the interface of the *EuroPlus+* package, and so is the organization of the content. Each unit contains sections, referred to as lessons, which fall into the following categories, denoting their focus: *Presentation-grammar*, *Presentation-vocabulary*, *Situations*, *Communication*, and *Summary*. Each lesson contains a number of screens which are labelled as pages.

The affective component (attitudes). Within this program learners do not engage in activities where they could reflect on their attitudes towards other cultures, or their own culture. They are not encouraged to develop their attitudes towards otherness, neither are they challenged to delay judgment of the familiar as well as the unfamiliar. Therefore, it may be concluded that the program does not foster learners' affective development.

The cognitive component (knowledge). As far the knowledge component of intercultural competence is concerned, in *New Reflex English* learners can work on its 3 aspects: (a) material culture, (b) socio-political realia, and (c) behaviour and practices, i.e. the most salient cultural elements. At the same time, the implicit aspects, thought patterns/values and languaculture, are not dealt with at all.

(a) Material culture. In Unit 1 *A Cosmopolitan City* learners perform an exercise in which they at first watch a video clip introducing them to the national symbols and artefacts of selected world countries, and afterwards, match capital cities with appropriate countries. The national symbols and artefacts featured in the video are objects, or people, traditionally, or stereotypically, associated with particular countries and nationalities.

For instance, France is presented through: the Versailles, the king, and perfume; Spain is introduced through: the Corrida ring, the bull, and the matador's articles: clothes, and a red rag.

In the lesson *A Good Meal* an American meal called *fish chowder* is introduced through a simple explanation incorporated into the Polish translation and a video clip which lists its main ingredients. In the *Changing Money* unit, the pound sterling is mentioned as the British currency.

The *Secret of Canterville* lesson focuses more on art, including a mention of a modern art exhibition and ballet dancing at the Edinburgh Festival.

(b) *Socio-political realia*. There are very few examples of socio-political realia which learners can acquire from the program. One of them appears in Unit 1 *A Cosmopolitan City*, in which learners perform an exercise where they match capital cities to appropriate countries, e.g. Paris/ France or Tokyo/Japan.

In another exercise within the same unit learners find out and memorise the capital cities of selected world countries by matching both. Additionally, the program teaches learners geography through a video which demonstrates where the countries and cities in question are located on a map.

(c) *Behaviour and practices*. A few instances of culture-determined behaviour and practices are introduced in Unit 1 *A Cosmopolitan City* through a video clip which features: wearing a perfume (France); playing the guitar (Spain); bowing (Japan), playing classical music (Austria); or reading newspapers and drinking tea (England).

The *Good Meal* lesson contains a video which demonstrates the procedure of laying the table. In the *Changing Money* lesson, users watch a video which tackles practices relating to changing money, e.g. it is explained where money can be changed, and a relevant scene is presented. The *Room No. 34* lesson demonstrates to learners how to book a hotel room, and how a guest is received at a hotel's reception desk.

The entitled *That's Too Expensive* features video scenes which present the daily actions of: shopping at a local open-air market; arranging a meeting for lunch with friends; planning a trip; and booking accommodation.

The action-oriented component (skills of interpreting and relating, and skills of discovery and interaction). The development of intercultural skills is not fostered by the software as learners do not interpret culture. Examples of culture are presented on an as-is basis, without analysis or reflection on the learner's part.

Wherever language is being dealt with, the focus is exclusively on the target language form, thus, learners do not compare their mother tongue or native culture with the target equivalents.

For instance, in the *Presentation – Grammar* and *Presentation – Vocabulary* sections the Polish translation of grammar forms is provided, but it is there for comprehension purposes, exclusively. What follows is language work focused on the target language form, and the grammar explanation does not make any references to learners' native language. Translation tasks featured within the program do not bring forward commonalities, or contrasts, between learner's mother tongue and the target language, either.

The software does not refer learners to other sources of cultural know-how, and learners are not required to participate in any form of project work. Intercultural communication is not practised as no tools are available for that purpose.

Finally, learners do not self-assess their own intercultural skills, because there is no guidance towards it, or tools that could serve the goal. None of the activities within the software require learners to reflect on, or assess, their own intercultural skills.

The educational component (critical cultural awareness). Learners cannot develop their critical awareness when working with the program because *New Reflex English* does not feature activities in the course of which they would be able to compare cultural materials, or judge the content provided. It appears that the elements of culture which are part of the program content are supposed to be uncritically acquired by the learner as they come.

The technology-related features. Only one technology-related feature which could foster the development of learners' intercultural competence is part of the *New Reflex English* program. It is a note-taking tool which enables learners to add their own commentary to particular pages of the course. The content of such commentary is exclusively at the learner's discretion, thus, it may serve the purpose of intercultural learning.

For instance, learners could note down cultural explanation there, or make a record of their emotional reaction to a newly-observed cultural difference. The other possible technological features which could potentially foster intercultural learning are absent from the program.

Alternative navigation routes do not exist in the software as learners can access content only from the *Contents menu*, which contains links to all the units. Each link takes the learner to a screen where the unit components are displayed, including sections such as: *Presentation-grammar*, *Presentation-vocabulary*, *Situations* or *Communication*. Each of these sections features several short lessons, which cannot be accessed alternatively.

Search options in the program are reduced to a simple word search within the *AZ Vocabulary* tool, which is a mini glossary containing words with Polish translations. Learners are not able to search the content of the course thoroughly; neither can they search any of the media included, e.g. photographs or audio/video clips.

Task authoring tools and cultural explanation are absent from the program, while the audio-visuals do not assist learners in intercultural learning. For instance, the videos featured may facilitate the mechanical memorisation of national symbols, or artefacts along with the countries which they represent, but they do not carry any cultural explanation or commentary.

What is more, as pantomime is systematically used to present situations in the video clips, all the learner can see in the footage is dark silhouettes acting against a bright background. In effect, no detail is presented and the scenes depicted lack context.

Supplementary cultural materials or online communication tools are not offered within the software due to the fact that it is devoid of internet connectivity.

Overall, the software helps learners develop only the cognitive component of intercultural competence (knowledge), while it completely neglects the remainder of its elements: attitudes, intercultural skills and critical cultural awareness. Technology-wise, it offers only a single feature, an annotation tool, which could support intercultural learning.

The results of the evaluation of the *New Reflex English* program with regard to the checklist criteria are summarised in a tabular form in Appendix F.

5. Summary of the findings

- Only one of the programs evaluated, EuroPlus+ *Reward,* at least in part, allowed the development of the affective component of intercultural competence, i.e. learners' attitudes.
- All the six programs under examination permitted the development of the cognitive component of intercultural competence, but they all mostly focused on its most salient aspects: material culture, socio-political realia and cultural/behavioural practices.
- Three programs additionally fostered the learning of cultural thought patterns and values: *English+ one pack*, *EuroPlus+ Reward* and *Profesor Henry*.

- The only two CALL packages which contained elements of languacultural instruction were *EuroPlus+ Reward* and *English+ one pack*. However, to do justice, it must be underlined that, while *English+ one pack* contains only a single activity focused on languaculture, *EuroPlus+ Reward* tackles the component far more systematically.
- Training in the pragmatic component of intercultural competence was permitted only within one program: *EuroPlus+ Reward*. It enabled learners to: interpret cultural phenomena and compare native language and culture with other languages and cultures (the development of the skills of interpreting and relating) as well as practice intercultural communication (the skills of discovery and interaction). However, the only type of activity which allowed the practice of the latter group of skills was intercultural communication.
- Only one CALL program, *EuroPlus+ Reward*, enabled learners to increase their critical cultural awareness through activities based on comparing and judging intercultural materials.
- Five programs offered users alternative navigation routes through the content: *English+ one p@ck*, *EuroPlus+ Reward*, *Tell Me More. Special Edition 1000h*, *Tell Me More Junior (13-15)* and *Profesor Henry*.
- Three programs featured advanced search options: *EuroPlus+ Reward*, *Tell Me More. Special Edition 1000h*, and *Profesor Henry*.
- None of the programs contained task authoring tools, with the use of which teachers would be able to develop more interculturally-oriented tasks, or expand the (inter)cultural resources already provided within the software.
- Cultural explanation was available only in *EuroPlus+ Reward*. The remainder of the software evaluated lacked this functionality and left content without a cultural commentary.
- Only in the case of one program, *EuroPlus+ Reward*, did the audio-visual aids provide learners with a deeper insight into the culture presented. The culturally informative aids comprised: images, audio and video clips, including authentic documentaries.
- Three programs, *EuroPlus+ Reward*, *Profesor Henry* and *New Reflex English*, equipped learners with annotation tools, which could be used to append content with a record of cultural data, emotions or cultural commentaries.
- Supplementary cultural materials were provided by five of the programs: *English+ one p@ck*, *EuroPlus+ Reward*, *Tell Me More.*

Special Edition 1000h, *Tell Me More Junior (13-15)* and *Profesor Henry*. Within the programs the supplementary materials were accessible through online services, available from the program menu. The supplements were provided in the form of cultural texts and news articles, accompanied by graphics, or hyperlinks to authentic websites, which might lend themselves to intercultural learning.
- Three programs, *English+ one p@ck*, *EuroPlus+ Reward*, and *Tell Me More Junior (13-15)*, featured online communication tools, which, at least in theory, enabled learners to contact representatives of other cultures. *English+ one p@ck* and *Tell Me More Junior (13-15)* offered tools for synchronous/asynchronous text-based communication; but only *EuroPlus+ Reward* permitted a voice connection in addition to text-based utilities.

A graphic summary of the overall findings of the predictive CALL software evaluation conducted in the course of the research in Module II is demonstrated in Appendix F.

Conclusions. The research was motivated by the main three research questions cited below:

- To what degree and in what manner do Polish EFL teachers implement information and communication technology in order to teach the target language?
- To what degree and in what manner do Polish EFL teachers implement information and communication technology in order to teach culture and develop their learners' intercultural skills?
- Does CALL software targeting lower/upper secondary school level audience available in Poland permit the development of learners' (inter)cultural competence, and which components of intercultural competence does it address?

What follows is an account of the general findings of the research, based on the data obtained in the course of the studies administered within Module I and Module II. The findings are presented with regard to the specific research questions (cf. Chapter Six & Chapter Seven).

Question 1: *In what technological conditions and organisational circumstances do Polish teachers of English work at school?*

The information on the technological conditions and organisational circumstances in which Polish teachers work at school was elicited directly from EFL teachers. Therefore, it is based on the teachers' personal knowledge and experience.

86.5% of the EFL teachers were able to use computers at school, either on a regular basis or moderately frequently, and only less than 2% of the teachers did not have access to information and communication technology at school.

In the case of 48.5% of the teachers, the school computers were available in the regular classroom, and **91.3% of the teachers had computers available at the computer suite. Self-access computers were located mostly at the school library** (86.4%), and in considerably fewer cases, the computers were installed in other locations: the school hall (9.7%) or the common room (3.9%). All in all, the teachers were far more likely to be able to use computers in the school library rather than in the regular classroom.

Only 30.7% of the teachers were permitted to use the computer suite for EFL lessons very regularly, and 33.7% could do so fairly regularly. Over a third of the teachers (35.6%) were not able to run EFL lessons in the computer suite, or did it infrequently. Access to the computer suite was apparently limited due to school regulations, as **most of the teachers** (69.2%) **regularly needed to book the computer suite** for an EFL lesson in advance.

Less than 50% of the teachers (36.19%) **claimed that they had CALL software available at school.** An almost equal proportion of the teachers (40%) knew that there was no CALL software at the teachers' disposal where they worked. A considerably large proportion of the teachers (20%) could not adamantly confirm, or disconfirm, the availability of CALL software at their school, which might suggest that they lacked interest in that matter.

Almost all the teachers (98.1%) **had access to the internet at school.** All of the subjects whose schools were equipped with an internet connection had **connectivity available in the computer suite** (as stated by 98.1% of the teachers). Simultaneously, only **50.5% of the teachers could use the internet in the regular classroom**.

It occurred that the internet could be accessed in the school library to a far greater extent (as stated by 76.7% of the teachers) than in the classroom (50.5%), which implies that in case the teachers could not use the computer suite, it was easier for them to request learners to access the internet outside the classroom rather than attempt to use the internet during the lesson.

Only roughly a quarter of the teachers (26.2%) declared that their school was equipped with a wireless web connection (Wi-Fi). One must be aware of the fact that although a Wi-Fi connection may increase the availability of the web on the school premises, the efficacy of this solution is determined by the technology implemented.

Given that 20% of the teachers could not estimate the age of the computers they had available at school, a large **majority of the teachers** (54.7%) **qualified the school computers as *aging/relatively old* (3-5 years)**, i.e. the hardware was capable of serving most CALL purposes and operating up-to-date software. 20% stated that they had to work on computers which were old, i.e. over 5 years of age. If one bears in mind that a further **5.3% of the subjects estimated the age of their school computers as *brand-new/relatively new,*** it may be concluded that **60% of the subjects examined were able to utilise computers which were technologically fit for most CALL purposes**.

Other ICT resources, apart from desktop computers, available to over 50% of the teachers, included: printers (85.6%) and multimedia projectors (82.7%), laptops (66%), interactive boards (55.8%) and scanners (52.9%).

All in all, it may be concluded that although schools appear to be equipped with both computers and internet connectivity, what poses problems to EFL teachers who would like to utilise ICT for the purpose of computer-assisted language teaching is **limited access, either due to the regulations of use, or the localisation of hardware at school**.

Question 2: *What attitudes towards information and communication technology do Polish teachers of English display?*

The teachers displayed a very positive attitude towards the computer as a tool in EFL teaching. A majority of the teachers (73.4%) believed that **computer-assisted language learning is more intensive than non-CALL instruction**. An even larger majority 85.6% of the teachers agreed that **computer-assisted language learning is more effective** than conventional, non-CALL learning, and that **multimedia facilitate learning** by contextualising the teaching content.

A very large proportion of the teachers (96.2%) expressed the view that the **computer permits the use of authentic materials**, and a sizeable majority (76.9%) agreed that the **computer activates learners** by granting them more autonomy than in a non-CALL lesson.

Roughly the same proportion of the teachers (79.8%) believed that the **computer has a motivational power for learners**, and 94.3% of the teachers agreed that the **computer diversifies learning** by incorporating various learning styles and strategies.

Finally, 92.3% of the teachers expressed the belief that the computer develops professionally and personally useful skills.

As far the role of ICT in the EFL classroom is concerned, a majority of the teachers (83.5%) disagreed with the statement that ICT unnecessarily ruins the teaching/learning routine in the classroom. **Large proportions of the teachers disconfirmed that: ICT permits only the kind of work that can be equally well performed without it, and** that it **distracts attention from what is being taught** (76.9% and 75.7%, respectively). Additionally, a substantial majority (77.9%) believed that **ICT facilitates the teacher's and learner's job.**

In sum, it may be stated that the teachers had a very positive attitude towards both the computer as a tool in EFL teaching as well as the role of ICT in the EFL classroom.

Question 3: *What kinds of computer skills/qualifications do Polish teachers of English possess?*

Most of the teachers (87.6%) **did not have formal ICT qualifications**. Those who did, gained the qualifications primarily through computer courses.

All the teachers (100%) **could operate the computer and handle the most basic tasks** which they are likely to face **in a CALL lesson**, e.g. power on, reset, shut down the computer and operate the basic peripherals: the mouse and keyboard. A vast majority (88.6%) **could also connect peripheral devices,** such as: a printer, scanner or video camera, **to the computer**, but only slightly over 50% of the teachers (56.2%) could perform basic troubleshooting. **A definitive minority of the teachers could handle more complex repairs** (17.1%) **or assemble a new computer** (3.8%).

Most of the teachers declared to possess computer skills useful for EFL teachers, e.g. they could: create multimedia presentations (66.7%); install and use CALL software (71.4% and 70.5%, respectively), use basic applications (87.1%), search the contents of optical discs (88.6%), and use word processors (98.1%).

A substantial majority of the teachers also possessed the essential internet skills: using online communicators (82.9%), searching information online (97.1%); and all the teachers were able to browse internet pages and send/receive e-mails (100%).

A clear-cut minority of the teachers could cope with more sophisticated software-relating operations, e.g.: installing VLEs (5.7%); designing (12.4%) and uploading (10.5%) web pages; or authoring electronic tests (32.4%).

It may be concluded that, **despite the lack of formal qualifications, the teachers had acquired the most necessary ICT skills.**

Question 4: *Do they use information and communication technology in their teaching; what kind of information and communication technology do they utilise; and in what manner do they utilise it?*

A vast majority of the teachers (93.3%) **implemented ICT in EFL teaching,** and the most common purposes for which they used ICT involved: **preparing materials** (75.2%), **using peripheral devices** (89.4%), and **accessing online content** (77.2%).

At the same time, a clear minority of **the teachers created web pages** (1%), **uploaded materials online** (13.7%), **contacted learners via chat** (3.8%) or **engaged learners in work based on online blogs** (3%).

The most commonly used **computer-enhanced channel of teacher-learner communication was e-mail** (36.2%), and the most frequently used types of software which the teachers utilised were: **electronic dictionaries** (43.7%) and **computerised coursebook supplements** (47.1%).

The least frequently utilised software included: CALL programs (72.3% of the teachers used it rarely, or not at all), virtual learning environments (**VLEs**) (82.7%), **concordancers** (93%), **games** (83.2%), **parsers** (98%), **interactive computerised stories** (76%), and **spreadsheets** (86.3%).

The computer media most frequently implemented in EFL teaching were: **text, audio-pictorial media** (audio clips, photos and images) and **video clips.**

On average **the teachers devoted roughly a fifth of their teaching time** (19.7%) **to computer-assisted language teaching.** When teaching English through ICT, **most of the teachers rarely, or never, engaged learners in laptop-based work** (96%) and **work in the computer suite** (62.8%).

The teachers were more likely to use **a single computer in the classroom** (55.4% did so), or **ask learners to work with computers outside the classroom** (66.3% did it), e.g. in the school library or at home.

Most of the teachers **used computers for material presentation** (72.4%) and fostering **learner autonomy** (62.8%), while the smallest proportions of them resorted sto computerised learner-learner communication (35.3%) and electronic testing (42%). Roughly half of the teachers used computers in order to document learners' knowledge (49.5%).

Question 5: *Do they use information and communication technology in order to develop their learners' intercultural competence?*

Only a slight majority of the teachers (55.2%) declared that **they used computers for teaching culture** in the EFL classroom. Those who did so maintained that the computer media which they most frequently used in teaching culture were: **photos, video clips, images, audio clips, text,** and **maps**. The media for which the teachers displayed the least preference were hypertext and animations.

The aspects of culture most commonly taught by the teachers through ICT were: **cultural events** (39%)**, people** (36.2%) **and places** (35.2%). At the same time, the most neglected aspects were: material culture (16.2%) as well as thought patterns, views and values (16.2%).

The largest proportions of the teachers implemented ICT so that their learners could: **analyse images and photos** (34.3%); **practise virtual ethnography** (26.7%); **make notes** and **create texts about their own culture** (23.8%).

The cultural activities involving online communication which the teachers arranged were based on **asynchronous, text-based communication,** i.e. e-mail (27.6%). Smaller proportions of the teachers used online forums (18.1%), or online communicators (15.2%), which permit synchronous/asynchronous communication. The least frequently used mode of communication in teaching culture was videoconferencing (1%).

The teachers mostly organised **online communication activities in which their learners shared thoughts** (26.2%). To a lesser extent, their learners exchanged information (15.2%), or presented their own culture (10.5%).

An overwhelming majority of the teachers very infrequently, or never, used typically intercultural internet techniques, such as: telecollaboration, e-mail tandems (95.7%), webquests (87.9%), culture assimilators (97.9%), literature online (81.6%) and e-journals (92.7%). At the same time, the most frequently used technique out of these was literature online, but it was utilised by only 18.4% of the teachers.

Question 6: *What are the potential deterrents which discourage teachers from implementing information and communication technology in the Polish EFL classroom?*

The most serious deterrent that discouraged the teachers from implementing ICT in the EFL classroom were **technical problems** (61.2%). The other deterrents, cited relatively frequently, were: **lack of ICT skills** (38.8%) and **lack of proper orientation in software** (31.1%). Given that only a minority of the teachers could perform complex computer repairs (17.1%), technical glitches appear to pose a genuine problem to teachers in the EFL classroom. Out of all the other deterrents, added by 26.2% of the teachers in total, two were singled out as the most serious: **lack of time** (9.2%) and **lack of access to computer hardware** (9.2%).

The research results implied that the teachers were in need of more CALL training, which would involve both the technical aspects of the use of ICT as well as a focus on computer-assisted language teaching.

Question 7: *Does CALL software targeting lower/upper secondary school level audiences available in Poland permit learners to work on the major components of intercultural competence such as: attitudes, knowledge, skills of interpreting and relating, skills of discovery and interaction, critical cultural awareness?*

It is very unlikely that CALL software targeting lower/upper secondary school level audiences, available in Poland, permits learners to work on **the affective component** of intercultural competence as only 2 programs within the sample, *EuroPlus+ Reward* and – to a much lesser extent – *English+ one p@ck*, featured activities which tackled on learners' attitudes.

The element of intercultural competence whose development is most likely to be facilitated by CALL software is **the cognitive component**, i.e. **cultural knowledge** – all the 6 programs within the sample permitted this type of work. However, it must be added that CALL programs primarily focus on three aspects of cultural knowledge: material culture, socio-political realia and cultural behavioural and practices – all the programs (N=6) within the sample contained relevant activities. **Thought patterns and values are less likely to be developed** (3 programs featured this aspect of cultural knowledge at all: *English+ one p@ck*, *EuroPlus+ Reward* and *Profesor Henry*), and **the least practised element of cultural knowledge in CALL software is languaculture** as only 2 programs,

EuroPlus+ Reward and *English+ one p@ck*, highlighted the relations between language and culture.

CALL software addressed to lower/upper secondary school level audiences very **infrequently allows learners to practice the intercultural skills** of interpreting and relating, **or the skills of discovery and interaction** – only one program, *EuroPlus+ Reward*, permitted it.

In general, activities focused on the skills of discovery and interpretation are absent from CALL software as in the single program that tackled them, *EuroPlus+ Reward*, only one such skill was developed: intercultural communication. The skills of interpreting and relating are practised through the interpretation of cultural phenomena and interlanguage/intercultural comparisons.

CALL programs are highly unlikely to assist learners in increasing their critical cultural awareness, i.e. developing the educational component of intercultural competence through activities involving the comparison and judgement of intercultural materials – only one program within the sample, *EuroPlus+ Reward*, enabled learners to do it at all.

All in all, it may be stated that within the six programs evaluated, only *EuroPlus+ Reward* truly supported intercultural/crosscultural learning in EFL instruction as the content and activity types that it offered reached beyond cultural knowledge, and allowed the development of attitudes, intercultural skills as well as critical cultural awareness.

The remainder of the programs emphasised only declarative, fact-based knowledge, promoted by the more traditional *British Studies/Landeskunde* approach to teaching culture. Therefore, it may be concluded that **most CALL software for lower/upper secondary school learners does not genuinely allow intercultural learning**. What is more, even when the knowledge component is present within software, **most frequently knowledge is presented with a single culture in mind** – without an intercultural comparison.

In addition, **CALL software predominantly reduces culture to its most salient aspects**, which are the easiest to teach, **while neglecting the less visible aspects:** thought patterns and values, or languaculture, which all require in-depth exploration.

Question 8: *Does CALL software targeting lower/upper secondary school level audience available in Poland feature technological functionalities which facilitate intercultural learning?*

The results obtained indicate **that CALL software** targeting the lower/upper secondary school audience available in Poland **is rather**

unlikely to include technological functionalities which would facilitate intercultural learning in the EFL classroom, and if such functionalities are available, they are most frequently limited to a small number.

It is most likely that CALL software will offer users **alternative navigation routes** through the content and **supplementary cultural materials** (both functionalities were featured in 5 programs within the sample: *English+ one p@ck*, *EuroPlus+ Reward*, *Tell Me More. Special Edition 1000h*, *Tell Me More Junior (13-15)* and *Profesor Henry*.

Learners can navigate the programs either by using a selection of **working modes** (e.g. *Tell Me More. Special Edition*), **learning paths** (e.g. in *Profesor Henry*), **content themes** (e.g. in *Tell Me More Junior*), or **language categories** (e.g. in *Profesor Henry* or *English+ one p@ck*).

The **supplementary materials** available in the programs are mostly **online services**. They are accessible to learners in the form of **cultural texts** (e.g. in *English+ one p@ck*); **news articles accompanied by graphics** (e.g. in *EuroPlus+ Reward* and *Tell Me More. Special Edition*); **hyperlinks to authentic websites**, which lend themselves to intercultural learning (e.g. in *English+ one p@ck*); **cultural pop-ups**, containing quotations from famous people, annotated photographs, and proverbs; or cultural information conveyed through **background graphics** (e.g. in *New Reflex English*).

Advanced search options are less frequently featured within CALL programs – 3 programs offered this functionality: *EuroPlus+ Reward*, *Tell Me More. Special Edition 1000h*, and *Profesor Henry*.

With the use of advanced search utilities learners can browse through the program content via: **purpose-designed navigation tools** (e.g. in *Tell Me More. Special Edition*), through which illustrative aids, e.g. maps, or grammar explanation, can be reached; **more advanced search engines**, which allow queries based on: lexical themes, level of difficulty, language functions or even user-defined categories (e.g. in *Profesor Henry*); or **utilities which search content by unit or lesson** (e.g. *EuroPlus+ Reward*).

Cultural explanation is very infrequently available in CALL software, and only one program in the sample, the *EuroPlus+ Reward*, featured this functionality.

In general, CALL programs offer language and cultural content without an adequate cultural commentary. As the only exception demonstrates, if cultural guidance is provided, it may take the form of **video commentaries** which accompany particular activities. The commentaries may help learners **collect knowledge** about a specific culture, or **relate different cultures** to one another, which transforms learning into an intercultural experience. Explanation may **elucidate cultural phenomena**, such as behavioural/social patterns (verbal and non-verbal) and factual information, as well as **provide coaching in crosscultural communication.**

Most CALL programs do not include insightful audio-visual materials – only one program in the sample, *EuroPlus+ Reward*, contained them. It happens that the graphics used are: **unclear, sketchy drawings of poor quality** (e.g. in *Tell Me More. Special Edition* or *English+ one p@ck*); they are only **loosely related to the content** that they accompany (e.g. in *Profesor Henry*); or **they lack annotation** (e.g. in *New Reflex English*). Video materials may also be **deprived of cultural background** (e.g. in *New Reflex English*), and audio recordings may **lack a proper cultural commentary** (e.g. in *English+ one p@ck*).

As the only program in which the audio-visual aids provided learners with a deeper cultural insight (*EuroPlus+ Reward*) illustrates, images, audio and video clips may be culturally informative, but they must be designed with that purpose in mind. Images accompanying language-focused activities may assist learners in acquiring additional cultural insight. Videos may be provided as documentary films in which selected aspects of culture can be explicitly presented in greater detail along with the socio-cultural context. Audio and video clips may expose learners to real language, as it is actually spoken in a given area, and they may additionally bring to the fore aspects of culture which, otherwise, remain implicit, e.g. interviews may reveal people's thought patterns and values.

Annotation tools are less likely to be offered within CALL software. 3 programs, *EuroPlus+ Reward*, *Profesor Henry* and *New Reflex English*, equipped learners with annotation utilities, which could be used for appending content with a record of cultural knowledge, emotions, or cultural commentaries.

When such tools are provided, they may enable learners to **add their own commentary** to particular course lessons (e.g. as in *Profesor Henry* or *EuroPlus+ Reward*). As the content of the commentary is exclusively at the learner's discretion, and it may serve the purpose of intercultural learning.

In addition, the annotation tool may occasionally feature more elaborate functionalities and display the learner's commentary on the screen during activities which feature relevant language or cultural elements, as exemplified by *Profesor Henry*.

Only selected CALL programs, *English+ one p@ck*, *EuroPlus+ Reward*, and *Tell Me More Junior,* provide learners with **online**

communication tools, which, at least in theory, create opportunities for learners to contact representatives of other cultures.

The communication that the tools permit is **most likely to be text-based** (as in *English+ one p@ck* and *Tell Me More Junior)*, and it is **less likely to involve a voice connection** – the only program in the sample which allowed it was *EuroPlus+ Reward*. However, even in text mode, learners can contact others both **synchronously**, i.e. in real time, and **asynchronously**. While the former may constitute an opportunity for intercultural communicative practice which resembles face-to-face communication, Corbett (2005) and Rollin and Harrap (2005) highlight the usefulness of the latter for emotionally safe intercultural training, as asynchronous communication gives learners time to reflect on the potential difference, culture clashes, or intercultural conflicts which they are likely to experience.

Question 9: *What are the potential implications of the findings for the broader EFL profession and EFL classroom?*

The findings and conclusions of the research study have a number of vital implications:

- It appears that, although a large majority of Polish schools are equipped with computers and internet connectivity, what remains a problem for EFL teachers is lack of access to the hardware. In order to amend the situation, it is necessary for school authorities to: (i) increase the number of regular classrooms with at least a single computer installed; (ii) as well as review the regulations which govern EFL teachers' access to the computer suite.
- Internet access at school, and the degree to which ICT is implemented in EFL/culture teaching, may be relatively easily increased by installing a Wi-Fi connection, which renders the internet available on all the school premises, provided that the quality of the hardware used meets the appropriate standard.
- As most teachers need to book the computer suite for an EFL lesson in advance, which is likely to deter them from implementing ICT in their lessons, selected EFL lessons ought to be scheduled to take place in the computer suite. On the one hand this solution would spare schools organisational problems, on the other hand it would help EFL teachers plan ICT-enhanced lessons in advance.
- Teachers who cannot run EFL lessons in a computer-enhanced classroom may alternatively organise tasks involving self-access work modes, which require learners to use ICT outside the

classroom, e.g. in the school library, the students' club, the common room, the school hall, or at home.

- There is a need for more computer-assisted language learning software at schools. Simultaneously, teachers ought to be systematically updated on the range of CALL programs which are available to them.
- At a majority of schools teachers can work with computers which lend themselves to most CALL tasks. However, due to the fact that computer hardware ages rapidly, it is mandatory for school authorities to systematically upgrade it.
- In order to increase the diversity of ICT-based work modes which teachers are capable of implementing, the range of peripheral devices available at school ought to be expanded; as the research indicates, the devices that Polish schools are still underequipped with are: scanners, interactive whiteboards, laptops, digital still cameras and video cameras.
- Polish EFL teachers' attitudes towards ICT are positive, thus, it appears that their awareness in that area has been sufficiently developed; what ought to be done, however, is creating opportunities for the implementation of ICT in EFL teaching.
- A vast majority of Polish EFL teachers lack formal ICT qualifications. Yet, they have managed to develop basic ICT skills to an extent which permits them to handle most CALL tasks in the classroom. Nevertheless, teachers are in need of training which would focus on two areas: (i) the technical aspects of ICT, with particular emphasis on troubleshooting procedures; and (ii) CALL materials, including materials evaluation procedures, which would help teachers understand the pedagogical value of CALL software as well as select appropriate resources for specific pedagogical purposes. Such training should also embrace instruction in the methodology and use of the less commonly implemented computer applications, such as: concordancers, computer games, parsers, and spreadsheets.
- Since a very small proportion of teachers creates online materials and uploads them to the internet, it is necessary to provide EFL teachers with training in Web 2.0 technologies, whereby they would become content purveyors, not only content recipients. Such training could be enriched by techniques in test authoring in order to empower teachers to design electronic tests.
- EFL teachers require training in (inter)cultural teaching as in their practices they predominantly focus on the most salient aspects of

culture (events, people and places) while neglecting culture-determined thought patterns, views and values.

- EFL teachers lack training in ICT-enhanced intercultural teaching, which would increase their awareness of the potential benefits of computer-assisted intercultural education and familiarise them with computerised techniques in intercultural teaching, e.g.: telecollaboration, including synchronous intercultural communication via chatrooms or online communicators; e-mail tandems; webquests; culture assimilators; literature online; and e-journals.
- If CALL software available to EFL teachers is supposed to enhance intercultural teaching, it is necessary to incorporate into it activities which would target the affective (attitudes), pragmatic (skills) and educational (critical cultural awareness) components of intercultural competence; these aspects are neglected in the software available at the moment. In addition, the cognitive component should be enriched in its scope so that, apart from material culture, socio-political realia and cultural behaviour and practices, it also covers the more implicit aspects of culture: thought patterns and values, and languaculture.
- In order to allow genuine intercultural learning, CALL software for lower/upper secondary school learners ought to assist them in exploring intercultural differences through tasks featuring bi- or multi-cultural content, which would permit crosscultural exploration.
- The user's interface of CALL programs ought to be extended to implement features which would facilitate intercultural learning, in particular: advanced search options, cultural explanation, insightful audio-visuals, annotation tools and online communication utilities.
- Advanced search options should be extended so that they permit learners to access not only the content per se, but also the audio-visual aids available within the program.
- The authors of CALL software ought to take greater care in appending even language-focused activities with additional cultural commentary, which would increase the pedagogical value of the software by turning it into a valuable tool for both language and intercultural education.
- CALL software should be designed with far more attention to the quality of the audio-visual aids that it features, e.g. so that they correspond with the content which they accompany and facilitate learners' understanding of the cultural phenomena which they illustrate. This can be done by improving the clarity of the aids as well as by adequate cultural annotation.

- CALL software ought to allow learners to insert their own notes into the program content so that they could record cultural data, collect cultural explanations or keep a cultural diary. Ideally, such tools ought to display the content of learners' annotation during relevant activities.
- In an age of ICT, all contemporary CALL software ought to include online synchronous/asynchronous communication tools, which would permit learners to practice genuine intercultural communication, or asses their own intercultural skills in action. At the same time, CALL software manufacturers must systematically maintain the communication tools that they offer so that they remain fully functional in the long run. Otherwise, the applicability of CALL programs to intercultural EFL teaching is seriously diminished.
- Finally, it must be underlined that the afore-mentioned functionalities to be added to CALL programs do not constitute a technological challenge; one of the oldest two programs evaluated was already equipped with most of them. Therefore, the problem at issue here is the degree to which the broader ELT profession has so far managed to raise CALL software manufacturers' awareness of the importance of intercultural language education. Improvement in this area could be achieved by prioritising intercultural training within the education system, e.g. through an increase in the presence of intercultural elements in the curriculum as well as in school examinations.

The following conclusions might be generalised from the outcomes of the research study:

- Although Polish schools are in general equipped with computer hardware and internet connectivity, EFL teachers' access to ICT is frequently limited due to school regulations and the technological solutions used.
- Teachers who are not able to run ICT-enhanced EFL lessons in the classroom could alternatively involve learners in computer-based work on a self-access/self-study basis.
- Polish schools are underequipped with ICT peripheral devices and CALL software.
- The quality of ICT hardware available at schools is adequate for most CALL tasks in the EFL classroom, subject to systematic maintenance and upgrading.
- Polish EFL teachers' attitudes towards ICT as well as CALL are positive.

- A vast majority of Polish EFL teachers lack formal ICT qualifications; nevertheless, they possess basic computer skills.
- Polish EFL teachers require ICT training in ICT troubleshooting procedures and CALL materials, including materials evaluation.
- Polish EFL teachers are primarily Web 1.0 users, and they display few Web 2.0 skills; that is, they are mostly content recipients.
- While teaching culture, Polish EFL teachers, first and foremost, concentrate on the most salient aspects of culture while neglecting its implicit elements.
- CALL software for lower/upper secondary school learners primarily features activities which target the cognitive aspects of culture while neglecting the affective, pragmatic and educational components of intercultural competence.
- Polish EFL teachers lack training in ICT-enhanced intercultural teaching, particularly with reference to: awareness of the potential benefits of ICT-enhanced intercultural teaching to language learners, and the use of computerised techniques in synchronous intercultural communication.
- Most CALL software does not offer genuinely intercultural activities as the ones that it contains are predominantly monocultural.
- CALL programs targeting lower/upper secondary school learners contain very few functionalities which would facilitate intercultural teaching/learning in the EFL classroom. However, the absence of the desirable tools is not caused by technological challenges; it rather stems from the lack of the CALL software manufacturers' awareness of the importance of the intercultural language education.
- Despite the presence of intercultural training in European and Polish educational documents as well the Polish examination system (the *Matura* exam), as illustrated by the *Common European Framework of Reference* (2001) or *Informator o egzaminie maturalnym od roku 2008. Język angielski* (CKE 2008), CALL programs have not responded to the need for intercultural teaching.

Validation of the research findings. The researcher took care in order to ensure both internal and external validity (Seliger & Shohamy 1989) of the research.

Internal validity of research studies refers to the degree to which the data interpretation conducted is not likely to have been affected by factors beyond the scope of the study (Seliger & Shohamy 1989). Measures were taken to increase the validity of the research with regard to subject variability, subject population size and the time of administration.

Subject variability. As the subject sample within Module I was selected through convenience/snowballing sampling, an attempt was made to collect data from a wide range of locations across Poland. As a result, the sample was recruited from venues with larger as well as smaller populations across Poland, including: Białystok, Bydgoszcz, Gdynia, Lublin, Łowicz, Łódź, Radom, Sieradz, Skierniewice, Warszawa, Zgierz and Zduńska Wola. Thanks to the procedure, the data were collected in locations in the north, east, centre, and west-of-centre of Poland. It must also be born in mind that the population of teachers examined is likely to have been recruited from a wider range of locations, given that the questionnaire used in the study was administered at teacher training colleges, teacher development centres and higher education institutions, which offered postgraduate, or diploma, courses for in-service teachers from various locations across the country.

Moreover, it must be underlined that the sampling procedure yielded a subject sample which was diverse in composition with regard to: age, gender, professional experience, professional position and professional status.

Subject population size. In Seliger and Shohamy's (1989) view, the larger the subject population, the less likely it is to be subject to personal variability. Therefore, the researcher made an endeavour to increase the return rate of the questionnaire by collecting the questionnaire forms from the subjects in person.

The return rate was also increased by the distribution of questionnaires in relatively compact settings, where they could be relatively easily collected, e.g. in the teacher's room at school, or during teacher training courses.

Timing. It was intended not to allow the time of administration to exert an influence on the quality of the data obtained. Therefore, no time limit was imposed on the respondents who filled in the questionnaire paper, and the subjects were not under the pressure of time while responding to the questionnaire. For the same reason, filter questions were applied, and the questionnaire was designed to contain mostly close-ended questions, where the subjects were required to only circle, tick or number relevant response categories.

External validity denotes the degree to which the findings of a particular study can be extended to contexts beyond the setting in which the study was administered (Seliger & Shohamy 1989). Attempts were made in order to increase the external validity of the research in terms of: population characteristics, the descriptive explicitness of the independent variable, researcher effects and research methods.

Population characteristics. The subject population reflected the target population examined within the study in that it was composed of representatives of: both genders, varying degrees of teaching experience (novice/experienced teachers), EFL teachers/EFL teacher trainers and a comprehensive range of professional positions, as determined by professional development.

Descriptive explicitness of the independent variables. The researcher explicitly defined the variables under examination (cf. sections 1 & 2 of Chapter Four and sections 1 & 2 of Chapter Seven). This was done with a view to explicating the phenomena under investigation to researchers who might potentially wish to replicate the study in other settings.

Researcher effects. The researcher avoided exerting an influence on the respondents while they were filling the questionnaire form by limiting his interaction with them to the absolute minimum. The respondents did not receive any commentary from the researcher pertaining to the goals of the questionnaire beyond the written instructions with which they were provided in the introductory note.

The respondents were left on their own when filling the questionnaire in order to reduce the approval motive effect (Larsen-Freeman & Long 1991), i.e. the respondents' intention to please the researcher; in this manner they could concentrate on the questionnaire paper and respond to the questions without the researcher in mind.

Research methods/techniques. As the researcher intended to collect data which would be truthful, he assured the respondents of the complete anonymity of the data analysis procedures. With that in mind, the questionnaire was designed so as not to contain questions which would allow identification of the subjects, e.g. names or exact age.

In order to reduce the self-flattering effect (Larsen-Freeman & Long 1991), i.e. the respondents' tendency to project a positive image of themselves through the responses that they provide, the researcher did not inform the subjects about the exact purpose of the study. The research aim was introduced to them in a very general manner in the introductory note at the top of the questionnaire paper.

The searcher also endeavoured to avoid *the response set effect* (Baker 1994), i.e. the respondents' tendency to proceed through a series of *matrix questions* (Cohen et al. 2007) rapidly, by mechanically marking the same response option each time. This was avoided by placing blocks of matrix questions in separate parts of the questionnaire paper, or by breaking them into sections preceded by sub-questions. It was done so in the case of Section E of the questionnaire, where a sub-question separating the two series of matrix questions was placed at the very bottom of the page. In this manner the respondents needed to pause, read the sub-question and turn the page overleaf before they proceeded through the questionnaire.

In addition, prior to implementation, the questionnaire utilised within Module I and the software evaluation checklist utilised within Module II were both consulted with 10 independent judges, and amended in accordance with the feedback gathered. The questionnaire had also been piloted on a group of EFL teachers representative of the target population, and modified on the basis of the data obtained.

Recommendations for further research. One of the drawbacks of the research was the limited sample size, which considerably limits the reliability of broader generalisations made on the basis of the results obtained. In the light of the above, it would desirable to replicate the study on a larger population of Polish EFL teachers, or alternatively, on an equal-sized subject sample selected on a random basis.

The research data were collected through a questionnaire, which is an instrument of a high degree of explicitness, whose very nature might have exerted an influence on the results obtained. In addition, the part of the questionnaire which investigated Polish EFL teachers' implementation of ICT in their daily school practices relied on the teachers' reports, and not actual classroom data. Thus, in the future, action research ought to be administered, whereby teachers' classroom practices could be observed directly. This kind of study would yield factual evidence, which would not be subject to teachers' projections of what they genuinely do.

The predictive evaluation of the CALL software, conducted within Module II was administered by a single researcher. As Tomlinson (2003) recommends, even materials evaluations carried out with the use of a set of explicit criteria – as was the case within the research study – ought to be ideally conducted by "more than one evaluator" (Tomlinson 2003: 32).

Consequently, the CALL software evaluation might be additionally performed by yet another, independent evaluator, who would utilise the same evaluation checklist and produce his/her own evaluation report. In this manner the validity of the results obtained could increase.

Finally, it must be remembered that the intercultural potential of the CALL software under study was examined through predictive evaluation. A potentially interesting aim of a future study would be to examine how particular intercultural elements of CALL software translate into classroom practices, i.e. whether they authentically allow EFL teachers to work on the specific components of the intercultural competence of their learners. In other words, the predictive evaluation might be verified through empirical, or retrospective, evaluation (Ellis 1997).

APPENDIX A

OVERVIEW OF RESEARCH MODULE I

Module I	
Research aims	To investigate technological conditions/circumstances in which Polish teachers of English work at school; To investigate Polish EFL teachers' attitudes towards information and communication technology; To establish Polish EFL teachers' computer skills/qualifications; To investigate whether Polish EFL teachers use information and communication technology in their teaching, what kind of information and communication technology they utilise, and in what manner they utilise it; To investigate whether Polish EFL teachers use information and communication technology in order to develop learners' intercultural competence; To establish the potential deterrents which discourage Polish EFL teachers from implementing information and communication technology in the Polish EFL classroom; To examine whether there are any differences in perception of the role of ICT in language teaching and utilisation of ICT in the teaching practice between selected groups of Polish EFL teachers distinguished by: age, gender, qualifications, teaching experience, type of school, stage of professional development, and professional status

Research method	Descriptive (Focused description)
Research technique	Structured questionnaire
Number and general characteristics of subjects (N)	(N=105) professionally active teachers of English from Poland, employed at primary, lower secondary school, upper secondary school, language school as well as teacher training college
Timing	VIII-X.2010 Designing the research questions
	II.2011-III.2011 Preparing the first draft of the questionnaire III-IV.2011 Piloting and consulting the questionnaire IV.2011 Revising the questionnaire IV-VI.2011 Administering the questionnaire VI-VII.2011 Analysing the data obtained
Data analysis	Quantitative analysis

APPENDIX B

RESEARCHER'S COPY OF THE QUESTIONNAIRE

INFORMACJA: Niniejszy kwestionariusz jest anonimowy i stanowi część badania, którego celem jest ustalenie zakresu w jakim nauczyciele języka angielskiego w Polsce wykorzystują technologie informacyjne i komunikacyjne w swojej pracy.
Uprzejmie proszę o wpisanie w luki, zakreślenie lub zaznaczenie ☑ właściwych odpowiedzi.

A. Dane osobowe i profil zawodowy nauczyciela
A1. Płeć: ❑ **K** ❑ **M** **A2.** Wiek: ❑ poniżej 30 lat
❑ 30-40 lat ❑ powyżej 40 lat
A3. Posiadane kwalifikacje:
❑ dyplom ukończenia (N)KJO ❑ licencjat
❑dyplom ukończenia studiów wyższych ❑ dyplom ukończenia studiów wyższych zawodowych
❑ doktorat ❑ inny tytuł:______________________________

A4. Wykształcenie uzupełniające: (studia podyplomowe/ kursy/ egzaminy/ certyfikaty)

____

A5. Stopień awansu zawodowego:
❑ nie dotyczy ❑ stażysta ❑ nauczyciel kontraktowy
❑ mianowany ❑ dyplomowany

A6. Staż w zawodzie nauczyciela języka angielskiego: _______ lat.
A7. Typ placówki, w której jesteś zatrudnion(y/a):
❑ przedszkole ❑ szkoła podstawowa ❑ gimnazjum
❑ szkoła ponadgimnazjalna ❑ szkoła językowa
❑ kolegium nauczycielskie

A8. Sektor edukacji: ❑ państwowy ❑ prywatny
A9. Tygodniowy wymiar godzin dydaktycznych: _______

B. Szkolna infrastruktura komputerowa

B1. Gdzie w Twojej szkole znajdują się komputery?

❑ biura administracji ❑ biblioteka ❑ pracownia komputerowe
❑ sale lekcyjne ❑ świetlica ❑ klub uczniowski
❑ hall ❑ szkoła nie posiada komputerów

Na poniższe pytania odpowiedz: 1. Zawsze, 2. Często, 3. Czasami, 4. Rzadko, 5. Nigdy

B2. Jak często w Twojej szkole nauczyciel może korzystać z komputerów szkolnych? 1 2 3 4 5

B3. Jak często można prowadzić zajęcia z języka obcego w pracowni komputerowej? 1 2 3 4 5

B4. Czy wymagana jest wcześniejsza rezerwacja pracowni komputerowej? 1 2 3 4 5

B5. Czy Twoja szkoła posiada oprogramowanie do nauki języka angielskiego? ❑ Tak ❑ Nie ❑ Nie wiem

B6. Czy Twoja szkoła ma dostęp do internetu?
❑ Tak ❑ Nie ❑ Nie wiem

B7. Gdzie w szkole jest dostęp do Internetu?

❑ wszędzie (łącze bezprzewodowe) ❑ biura administracji ❑ biblioteka ❑ pracownia komputerowa
❑ sale lekcyjne ❑ świetlica ❑ klub uczniowski ❑ hall ❑ inne miejsca: ____________________

B8. Określ szacunkowy wiek komputerów, które są do dyspozycji nauczycieli:

❑ poniżej1 roku ❑ 1-2 lata ❑ 3-4 lata ❑ 5 lat ❑ powyżej 5 lat ❑ Nie wiem

B9. Jaki sprzęt komputerowy i urządzenia współpracujące z komputerem są dostępne w szkole:

❑ komputery stacjonarne ❑ laptopy ❑ projektor multimedialny
❑ tablica interaktywna ❑ skaner ❑ drukarka
❑ drukarka/skaner/xero w jednym ❑ kamera cyfrowa
❑ aparat cyfrowy ❑ inne,______________________________
❑ nie wiem

C. Stosunek do idei wykorzystywania komputerów w nauczaniu języka angielskiego
Na poniższe pytania odpowiedz: 1. Zdecydowanie tak, 2. Raczej tak, 3. Nie wiem 4. Raczej nie, 5. Zdecydowanie nie
C. Na ile zgadzasz się z poniższymi stwierdzeniami?
C1. Nauka wspomagana komputerowo jest bardziej intensywna 1 2 3 4 5
C2. Nauka wspomagana komputerowo jest bardziej efektywna 1 2 3 4 5
C3. Multimedia wspomagają naukę ponieważ prezentują treści w kontekście 1 2 3 4 5
C4. Komputer pomaga wykorzystywać materiały autentyczne 1 2 3 4 5
C5. Komputer uaktywnia uczniów, którzy stają się bardziej samodzielni 1 2 3 4 5
C6. Komputer motywuje uczniów 1 2 3 4 5
C7. Komputer urozmaica naukę (pozwala na wykorzystanie różnorodnych stylów/strategii uczenia się) 1 2 3 4 5
C8. Komputer rozwija umiejętności niezbędne uczniom w życiu zawodowym/prywatnym 1 2 3 4 5

Technologia komputerowa:
C9. niepotrzebnie burzy dotychczas obowiązujący schemat nauczania i uczenia się 1 2 3 4 5
C10. powoduje chaos i kłopoty z dyscypliną na lekcji 1 2 3 4 5
C11. pozwala robić tylko to, co i tak można zrealizować bez jej wykorzystania 1 2 3 4 5
C12. odwraca uwagę od nauczanych zagadnień 1 2 3 4 5
C13. ułatwia pracę ucznia i nauczyciela 1 2 3 4 5

D. Znajomość obsługi komputera
D1. Zaznacz umiejętności z zakresu obsługi sprzętu komputerowego, które posiadasz. Potrafię:
❑ używać myszki i klawiatury
❑ uruchamiać, resetować i wyłączać komputer
❑ podłączyć do komputera drukarkę, skaner, kamerę video, itp.
❑ rozwiązywać problemy z wadliwie działającym sprzętem (np. brak dźwięku)
❑ wymienić np. kartę graficzną lub pamięć RAM w komputerze
❑ złożyć nowy komputer

D2. Zaznacz umiejętności z zakresu obsługi oprogramowania komputerowego. Potrafię:

❑ korzystać z programów typu: *Notatnik*, *WordPad*, *Paint*
❑ wysyłać i odbierać wiadomości e-mail
❑ przeglądać strony internetowe (np. w programach *Interbet Explorer*, *Firefox*, *Google Chrome*)
❑ edytować teksty (np. w programach: *Microsoft Word*, *Open Office Writer*, *Star Office Writer*)
❑ tworzyć prezentacje multimedialne (np. w programach: *PowerPoint*, *Open Office Impress*)
❑ korzystać z programów obliczeniowych, np. arkuszy kalkulacyjnych: *Excel*, *Calc*
❑ przeszukiwać zawartość dysków CD, DVD, bluRay
❑ wyszukiwać informacje w Internecie (np. w wyszukiwarce *Google*)
❑ korzystać z komunikatorów internetowych (*Skype*, *GG*, *MS Messenger*)
❑ instalować programy komputerowe
❑ korzystać z programów do nauki języka ang. (np.: *Euro Plus+*, *Tell Me More*, *Professor Henry*)
❑ tworzyć testy komputerowe (np. w programach: *Hot Potatoes*, *QuizMaster*)
❑ korzystać z platform e-learningowych (np.: *Moodle, Librus, Vulcan*)
❑ samodzielnie instalować platformy e-learningowe (np.: *Moodle*)
❑ tworzyć strony internetowe
❑ umieścić strony www w internecie
❑ programować (np. w językach: *Basic* , *C++*, *Java*)

D3. Czy posiadasz certyfikaty, dyplomy ukończenia studiów podyplomowych lub inne dokumenty, które potwierdzają Twoją wiedzę i umiejętności z zakresu obsługi komputera?

❑ tak, posiadam:______________________________________
❑ nie

E. Wykorzystanie komputera w nauczaniu języka angielskiego

E1. Czy w jakikolwiek sposób wykorzystujesz komputer w nauczaniu języka angielskiego?

❑ Tak ❑ Nie (Jeśli wybrałeś opcję *Nie*, przejdź do pytań w sekcji G.)

Na poniższe pytania odpowiedz: 1. Zawsze, 2. Często, 3. Czasami, 4. Rzadko, 5. Nigdy

E2. Czy przygotowujesz materiały dydaktyczne za pomocą komputera? 1 2 3 4 5

E3. Czy przygotowujesz testy/ćwiczenia komputerowe? 1 2 3 4 5

E4. Czy korzystasz z urządzeń peryferyjnych (np. drukarka, skaner) 1 2 3 4 5

E5. Czy wykorzystujesz materiały internetowe? 1 2 3 4 5

E6. Czy tworzysz strony internetowe dla uczniów? 1 2 3 4 5

E7. Czy udostępniasz materiały dla uczniów w internecie? 1 2 3 4 5

Jakie?______________________________ _______________________

E8. Czy kontaktujesz się z uczniami poprzez e-mail? 1 2 3 4 5

E9. Czy korzystasz z czatów internetowych w kontaktach z uczniami? 1 2 3 4 5

E10. Czy Twoi uczniowie pracują w oparciu o blogi? 1 2 3 4 5

Jak często na lekcjach wykorzystujesz programy komputerowe wymienione poniżej?

E11. multimedialne programy do nauki języka angielskiego 1 2 3 4 5

E12. platformy e-learningowe (np.: *Moodle, Librus)* 1 2 3 4 5

E13. elektroniczne słowniki/encyklopedie 1 2 3 4 5

E14. dołączone do podręcznika materiały komputerowe 1 2 3 4 5

E15. programy typu „concordancers” 1 2 3 4 5

E16. gry komputerowe 1 2 3 4 5

E17. programy typu „parser” 1 2 3 4 5

E18. interaktywne historyjki/opowiadania 1 2 3 4 5

E19. programy do tworzenia prezentacji multimedialnych (np. *PowerPoint*) 1 2 3 4 5

E20. programy kalkulacyjne (np. *Excel*)? 1 2 3 4 5

E21. Ponumeruj poniższe media od 1 do 7 wg częstotliwości z jaką je wykorzystujesz. Media, z których nie korzystasz wcale oznacz cyfrą 0.

__tekst __ obrazki __ zdjęcia __ mapy

__ animacje __ nagrania audio __ nagrania video

E22. Ile procent czasu średnio poświęcasz na nauczanie języka wspomagane komputerem (CALL)? ________ %

Jak często korzystasz z komputerów w następujący sposób? **Odpowiedz: 1. Zawsze, 2. Często, 3. Czasami, 4. Rzadko, 5. Nigdy**
E23. wykorzystuję jeden komputer w klasie 1 2 3 4 5
E24. uczniowie pracują w klasie na laptopach 1 2 3 4 5
E25. zajęcia odbywają się w pracowni komputerowej 1 2 3 4 5
E26. uczniowie wykonują zadania na komputerze po lekcji, np. w domu lub bibliotece 1 2 3 4 5

Jak często wykorzystujesz komputery w poniższych celach? **Odpowiedz: 1. Zawsze, 2. Często, 3. Czasami, 4. Rzadko, 5. Nigdy**
E27. prezentacja materiału 1 2 3 4 5
E28. testowanie 1 2 3 4 5
E29. wspieranie samodzielnej pracy ucznia 1 2 3 4 5
E30. utrwalanie wiadomości 1 2 3 4 5
E31. dokumentowanie wiedzy ucznia 1 2 3 4 5
E32. komunikacja między uczniami 1 2 3 4 5

F. Wykorzystanie komputera w nauczaniu kultury
F1. Czy wykorzystujesz komputery w nauczaniu kultury? Jeśli nie, przejdź do sekcji G. Jeśli tak, odpowiedz na pytania poniżej.

F2. Ponumeruj poniższe media od 1 do 7 wg częstotliwości z jaką je wykorzystujesz w **nauczaniu kultury**. Media, z których nie korzystasz wcale oznacz cyfrą 0.
__tekst online __hypertext (tekst z linkami) __ obrazki __ zdjęcia __ mapy __ animacje __ nagrania audio __ nagrania video

F3. Jakich aspektów kultury uczysz z wykorzystaniem technologii komputerowej?
❑ geografia ❑ instytucje ❑ ludzie ❑ wydarzenia kulturowe ❑ miejsca ❑ zachowania ❑ poglądy/wartości
❑ kultura materialna (artefakty) ❑ powiązania między językiem i kulturą
❑ stereotypy ❑ inne____

F4. Jakiego rodzaju ćwiczenia kulturowe wykonują na komputerach uczniowie?
❑ sporządzają notatki ❑ tworzą teksty o kulturze własnej/obcej ❑ analizują obrazki, zdjęcia ❑ obserwują wirtualnie obcą kulturę
❑ komunikują się z przedstawicielami innych kultur
❑ analizują własną komunikację z przedstawicielami innych kultur
❑ inne____

F5. Które narzędzia komunikacji Twoi uczniowie wykorzystują w celu pogłębiania wiedzy kulturowej?
❑ e-mail ❑ fora internetowe ❑ czat ❑ grupy dyskusyjne ❑ blogi ❑ komunikatory internetowe ❑ video konferencje
❑ inne ______________________ ❑ żadne

F6. Zaznacz cele, w jakich Twoi uczniowie wykorzystują internetowe narzędzia komunikacyjne:
❑ wymiana poglądów z innymi
❑ wymiana informacji kulturowych z innymi
❑ prezentacja kultury rodzimej

F7. Jak często wykorzystujesz na zajęciach następujące techniki internetowe?
Na pytanie odpowiedz: 1. Zawsze, 2. Często, 3. Czasami, 4. Rzadko, 5. Nigdy
tele-kolaboracja 1 2 3 4 5 email tandems 1 2 3 4 5
webquest 1 2 3 4 5 asymilatory kulturowe 1 2 3 4 5
literatura online 1 2 3 4 5 e-journals 1 2 3 4 5

G. Czynniki zniechęcające do wykorzystywania TiK
G1. Co zniechęca Cię do wykorzystywania techniki komputerowej?
❑ koszty ❑ problemy techniczne ❑ brak wystarczających umiejętności ❑ brak orientacji w dostępnym oprogramowaniu
❑ niechęć uczniów do pracy z komputerem
❑ inne ______________________ ❑ nic

Serdecznie dziękuję, za udział w niniejszym badaniu. Państwa odpowiedzi pozwolą na głębsze poznanie poruszanych zagadnień. Wyniki badania omówione zostaną z zachowaniem Państwa anonimowości. Z wyrazami szacunku, Mariusz Marczak.

APPENDIX C

RESPONDENT'S COPY OF THE QUESTIONNAIRE

INFORMACJA: Niniejszy kwestionariusz jest anonimowy i stanowi część badania, którego celem jest ustalenie zakresu w jakim nauczyciele języka angielskiego w Polsce wykorzystują technologie informacyjne i komunikacyjne w swojej pracy.
Uprzejmie proszę o wpisanie w luki, zakreślenie lub zaznaczenie ☑ właściwych odpowiedzi.

A1. Płeć: ❑ **K** ❑ **M** **A2.** Wiek: ❑ poniżej 30 lat
❑ 30-40 lat ❑ powyżej 40 lat

A3. Posiadane kwalifikacje:
❑ dyplom ukończenia (N)KJO ❑ licencjat
❑dyplom ukończenia studiów wyższych ❑ dyplom ukończenia studiów wyższych zawodowych
❑ doktorat ❑ inny tytuł:____

A4. Wykształcenie uzupełniające: (studia podyplomowe/ kursy/ egzaminy/ certyfikaty)

____

A5. Stopień awansu zawodowego:
❑ nie dotyczy ❑ stażysta ❑ nauczyciel kontraktowy
❑ mianowany ❑ dyplomowany

A6. Staż w zawodzie nauczyciela języka angielskiego: _______ lat.

A7. Typ placówki, w której jesteś zatrudnion(y/a):
❑ przedszkole ❑ szkoła podstawowa ❑ gimnazjum
❑ szkoła ponadgimnazjalna ❑ szkoła językowa
❑ kolegium nauczycielskie

A8. Sektor edukacji: ❑ państwowy ❑ prywatny

A9. Tygodniowy wymiar godzin dydaktycznych: _______

B1. Gdzie w Twojej szkole znajdują się komputery?
❑ biura administracji ❑ biblioteka ❑ pracownia komputerowe
❑ sale lekcyjne ❑ świetlica ❑ klub uczniowski
❑ hall ❑ szkoła nie posiada komputerów

Na poniższe pytania odpowiedz: 1. Zawsze, 2. Często, 3. Czasami, 4. Rzadko, 5. Nigdy
B2. Jak często w Twojej szkole nauczyciel może korzystać z komputerów szkolnych? 1 2 3 4 5
B3. Jak często można prowadzić zajęcia z języka obcego w pracowni komputerowej? 1 2 3 4 5
B4. Czy wymagana jest wcześniejsza rezerwacja pracowni komputerowej? 1 2 3 4 5
B5. Czy Twoja szkoła posiada oprogramowanie do nauki języka angielskiego? ❑ Tak ❑ Nie ❑ Nie wiem
B6. Czy Twoja szkoła ma dostęp do internetu? ❑ Tak ❑ Nie ❑ Nie wiem
B7. Gdzie w szkole jest dostęp do Internetu?
❑ wszędzie (łącze bezprzewodowe) ❑ biura administracji ❑ biblioteka ❑ pracownia komputerowa
❑ sale lekcyjne ❑ świetlica ❑ klub uczniowski ❑ hall ❑ inne miejsca: ____________________

B8. Określ szacunkowy wiek komputerów, które są do dyspozycji nauczycieli:
❑ poniżej1 roku ❑ 1-2 lata ❑ 3-4 lata ❑ 5 lat ❑ powyżej 5 lat ❑ Nie wiem

B9. Jaki sprzęt komputerowy i urządzenia współpracujące z komputerem są dostępne w szkole:
❑ komputery stacjonarne ❑ laptopy ❑ projektor multimedialny
❑ tablica interaktywna ❑ skaner ❑ drukarka
❑ drukarka/skaner/xero w jednym ❑ kamera cyfrowa
❑ aparat cyfrowy ❑ inne, np.:__________________________________
❑ nie wiem

Na poniższe pytania odpowiedz: 1. Zdecydowanie tak, 2. Raczej tak, 3. Nie wiem 4. Raczej nie, 5. Zdecydowanie nie

C. Na ile zgadzasz się z poniższymi stwierdzeniami?

C1. Nauka wspomagana komputerowo jest bardziej intensywna 1 2 3 4 5

C2. Nauka wspomagana komputerowo jest bardziej efektywna 1 2 3 4 5

C3. Multimedia wspomagają naukę ponieważ prezentują treści w kontekście 1 2 3 4 5

C4. Komputer pomaga wykorzystywać materiały autentyczne 1 2 3 4 5

C5. Komputer uaktywnia uczniów, którzy stają się bardziej samodzielni 1 2 3 4 5

C6. Komputer motywuje uczniów 1 2 3 4 5

C7. Komputer urozmaica naukę (pozwala na wykorzystanie różnorodnych stylów/strategii uczenia się) 1 2 3 4 5

C8. Komputer rozwija umiejętności niezbędne uczniom w życiu zawodowym/prywatnym 1 2 3 4 5

Technologia komputerowa:

C9. niepotrzebnie burzy dotychczas obowiązujący schemat nauczania i uczenia się 1 2 3 4 5

C10. powoduje chaos i kłopoty z dyscypliną na lekcji 1 2 3 4 5

C11. pozwala robić tylko to, co i tak można zrealizować bez jej wykorzystania 1 2 3 4 5

C12. odwraca uwagę od nauczanych zagadnień 1 2 3 4 5

C13. ułatwia pracę ucznia i nauczyciela 1 2 3 4 5

D1. Zaznacz umiejętności z zakresu obsługi sprzętu komputerowego, które posiadasz. Potrafię:

❑ używać myszki i klawiatury
❑ uruchamiać, resetować i wyłączać komputer
❑ podłączyć do komputera drukarkę, skaner, kamerę video, itp.
❑ rozwiązywać problemy z wadliwie działającym sprzętem (np. brak dźwięku)
❑ wymienić np. kartę graficzną lub pamięć RAM w komputerze
❑ złożyć nowy komputer

D2. Zaznacz umiejętności z zakresu obsługi oprogramowania komputerowego. Potrafię:

❑ korzystać z programów typu: *Notatnik*, *WordPad*, *Paint*
❑ wysyłać i odbierać wiadomości e-mail
❑ przeglądać strony internetowe (np. w programach *Interbet Explorer*, *Firefox*, *Google Chrome*)
❑ edytować teksty (np. w programach: *Microsoft Word*, *Open Office Writer*, *Star Office Writer*)
❑ tworzyć prezentacje multimedialne (np. w programach: *PowerPoint*, *Open Office Impress*)
❑ korzystać z programów obliczeniowych, np. arkuszy kalkulacyjnych: *Excel*, *Calc*
❑ przeszukiwać zawartość dysków CD, DVD, bluRay
❑ wyszukiwać informacje w Internecie (np. w wyszukiwarce *Google*)
❑ korzystać z komunikatorów internetowych (*Skype*, *GG*, *MS Messenger*)
❑ instalować programy komputerowe
❑ korzystać z programów do nauki języka ang. (np.: *Euro Plus+*, *Tell Me More*, *Professor Henry*)
❑ tworzyć testy komputerowe (np. w programach: *Hot Potatoes*, *QuizMaster*)
❑ korzystać z platform e-learningowych (np.: *Moodle, Librus, Vulcan*)
❑ samodzielnie instalować platformy e-learningowe (np.: *Moodle*)
❑ tworzyć strony internetowe
❑ umieścić strony www w internecie
❑ programować (np. w językach: *Basic* , *C++*, *Java*)

D3. Czy posiadasz certyfikaty, dyplomy ukończenia studiów podyplomowych lub inne dokumenty, które potwierdzają Twoją wiedzę i umiejętności z zakresu obsługi komputera?

❑ tak, posiadam:______________________________________
❑ nie

E1. Czy w jakikolwiek sposób wykorzystujesz komputer w nauczaniu języka angielskiego?

❑ Tak ❑ Nie (Jeśli wybrałeś opcję *Nie*, przejdź do pytań w sekcji G.)

Na poniższe pytania odpowiedz: 1. Zawsze, 2. Często, 3. Czasami, 4. Rzadko, 5. Nigdy

E2. Czy przygotowujesz materiały dydaktyczne za pomocą komputera? 1 2 3 4 5

E3. Czy przygotowujesz testy/ćwiczenia komputerowe? 1 2 3 4 5

E4. Czy korzystasz z urządzeń peryferyjnych (np. drukarka, skaner) 1 2 3 4 5

E5. Czy wykorzystujesz materiały internetowe? 1 2 3 4 5

E6. Czy tworzysz strony internetowe dla uczniów? 1 2 3 4 5

E7. Czy udostępniasz materiały dla uczniów w internecie? 1 2 3 4 5

Jakie?______________________________ ______________________

E8. Czy kontaktujesz się z uczniami poprzez e-mail? 1 2 3 4 5

E9. Czy korzystasz z czatów internetowych w kontaktach z uczniami? 1 2 3 4 5

E10. Czy Twoi uczniowie pracują w oparciu o blogi? 1 2 3 4 5

Jak często na lekcjach wykorzystujesz programy komputerowe wymienione poniżej?

E11. multimedialne programy do nauki języka angielskiego 1 2 3 4 5

E12. platformy e-learningowe (np.: *Moodle, Librus)* 1 2 3 4 5

E13. elektroniczne słowniki/encyklopedie 1 2 3 4 5

E14. dołączone do podręcznika materiały komputerowe 1 2 3 4 5

E15. programy typu „concordancers" 1 2 3 4 5

E16. gry komputerowe 1 2 3 4 5

E17. programy typu „parser" 1 2 3 4 5

E18. interaktywne historyjki/opowiadania 1 2 3 4 5

E19. programy do tworzenia prezentacji multimedialnych (np. *PowerPoint*) 1 2 3 4 5

E20. programy kalkulacyjne (np. *Excel*)? 1 2 3 4 5

E21. Ponumeruj poniższe media od 1 do 7 wg częstotliwości z jaką je wykorzystujesz. Media, z których nie korzystasz wcale oznacz cyfrą 0.

__tekst __ obrazki __ zdjęcia __ mapy

__ animacje __ nagrania audio __ nagrania video

E22. Ile procent czasu średnio poświęcasz na nauczanie języka wspomagane komputerem (CALL)? _______ %

Jak często korzystasz z komputerów w następujący sposób? **Odpowiedz: 1. Zawsze, 2. Często, 3. Czasami, 4. Rzadko, 5. Nigdy**

E23. wykorzystuję jeden komputer w klasie 1 2 3 4 5
E24. uczniowie pracują w klasie na laptopach 1 2 3 4 5
E25. zajęcia odbywają się w pracowni komputerowej 1 2 3 4 5
E26. uczniowie wykonują zadania na komputerze po lekcji, np. w domu lub bibliotece 1 2 3 4 5

Jak często wykorzystujesz komputery w poniższych celach? **Odpowiedz: 1. Zawsze, 2. Często, 3. Czasami, 4. Rzadko, 5. Nigdy**

E27. prezentacja materiału 1 2 3 4 5
E28. testowanie 1 2 3 4 5
E29. wspieranie samodzielnej pracy ucznia 1 2 3 4 5
E30. utrwalanie wiadomości 1 2 3 4 5
E31. dokumentowanie wiedzy ucznia 1 2 3 4 5
E32. komunikacja między uczniami 1 2 3 4 5

F1. Czy wykorzystujesz komputery w nauczaniu kultury? Jeśli nie, przejdź do sekcji G. Jeśli tak, odpowiedz na pytania poniżej.

F2. Ponumeruj poniższe media od 1 do 7 wg częstotliwości z jaką je wykorzystujesz w **nauczaniu kultury**. Media, z których nie korzystasz wcale oznacz cyfrą 0.
__tekst online __hypertext (tekst z linkami) __ obrazki __ zdjęcia __ mapy __ animacje __ nagrania audio __ nagrania video

F3. Jakich aspektów kultury uczysz z wykorzystaniem technologii komputerowej?
❑ geografia ❑ instytucje ❑ ludzie ❑ wydarzenia kulturowe ❑ miejsca ❑ zachowania ❑ poglądy/wartości
❑ kultura materialna (artefakty) ❑ powiązania między językiem i kulturą
❑ stereotypy ❑ inne______________________________________

F4. Jakiego rodzaju ćwiczenia kulturowe wykonują na komputerach uczniowie?
❑ sporządzają notatki ❑ tworzą teksty o kulturze własnej/obcej ❑ analizują obrazki, zdjęcia ❑ obserwują wirtualnie obcą kulturę
❑ komunikują się z przedstawicielami innych kultur
❑ analizują własną komunikację z przedstawicielami innych kultur
❑ inne____

F5. Które narzędzia komunikacji Twoi uczniowie wykorzystują w celu pogłębiania wiedzy kulturowej?
❑ e-mail ❑ fora internetowe ❑ czat ❑ grupy dyskusyjne ❑ blogi ❑ komunikatory internetowe ❑ video konferencje
❑ inne ____________________________________ ❑ żadne

F6. Zaznacz cele, w jakich Twoi uczniowie wykorzystują internetowe narzędzia komunikacyjne:
❑ wymiana poglądów z innymi
❑ wymiana informacji kulturowych z innymi
❑ prezentacja kultury rodzimej

F7. Jak często wykorzystujesz na zajęciach następujące techniki internetowe?
Na pytanie odpowiedz: 1. Zawsze, 2. Często, 3. Czasami, 4. Rzadko, 5. Nigdy
tele-kolaboracja 1 2 3 4 5 email tandems 1 2 3 4 5
webquest 1 2 3 4 5 asymilatory kulturowe 1 2 3 4 5
literatura online 1 2 3 4 5 e-journals 1 2 3 4 5

G1. Co zniechęca Cię do wykorzystywania techniki komputerowej?
❑ koszty ❑ problemy techniczne ❑ brak wystarczających umiejętności ❑ brak orientacji w dostępnym oprogramowaniu
❑ niechęć uczniów do pracy z komputerem
❑ inne ____ ❑ nic

Serdecznie dziękuję, za udział w niniejszym badaniu. Państwa odpowiedzi pozwolą na głębsze poznanie poruszanych zagadnień. Wyniki badania omówione zostaną z zachowaniem Państwa anonimowości. Z wyrazami szacunku, Mariusz Marczak.

APPENDIX D

OVERVIEW OF RESEARCH MODULE II

Research aims	To investigate whether CALL software available in Poland targeting lower/upper secondary school level audiences permits learners to work on the major components of intercultural competence: attitudes, knowledge, skills of interpreting and relating, skills of discovery and interaction, critical cultural awareness; To investigate whether CALL software available in Poland targeting lower/upper secondary school level audience features technological functionalities which facilitate intercultural learning;
Research methods	Descriptive (Focused description)
Research instruments	Software evaluation checklist, researcher's notes
Number and general characteristics of subjects (N)	(N=6) multimedia Computer-Assisted Language Learning (CALL) programs available to Polish teachers of English and learners at the level of lower and upper secondary school
Timing	VIII-X.2010 Designing the research questions
	VIII.2010-III.2011 Preparing the first draft of the evaluation checklist III-IV.2011 Consulting the checklist VII-VIII.2011 Conducting the software evaluation VIII-IX.2011 Analysing the data
Data analysis	Quantitative and qualitative analysis

APPENDIX E

CALL SOFTWARE EVALUATION CHECKLIST

Software / Evaluation criteria	English+ one pack	EuroPlus+ Reward	Tell Me More SE	Tell Me More Junior	Profesor Henry	New Reflex English
CONTENT-BASED FEATURES						
Attitudes (Do learners…)						
1. work on their attitudes?						
Knowledge (Does the culture taught comprise…)						
2. material culture?						
3. socio-political realia?						
4. behaviour/practices?						
5. thought patterns/values?						
6. languaculture?						
Skills of interpreting and relating (Do learners…)						
7. interpret cultural phenomena?						
8. compare L1/C1 with L2/C2?						
Skills of discovery and interaction (Do learners…)						
9. consult varied sources?						
10. do project work?						
11. practice IC communication?						
12. self-assess their own IC skills?						
Critical cultural awareness (Do learners…)						
13. compare/judge materials?						

Software / Evaluation criteria	English+ one pack	EuroPlus+ Reward	Tell Me More SE	Tell Me More Junior	Profesor Henry	New Reflex English
TECHNOLOGY-RELATED FEATURES (Does the software feature…)						
14. alternative navigation routes?						
15. advanced search options?						
16. task authoring tools?						
17. cultural explanation?						
18. insightful audio-visuals?						
19. annotation tools?						
20. supplementary cultural materials?						
21. online communication tools?						

APPENDIX F

CALL SOFTWARE EVALUATION RESULTS

Software / Evaluation criteria	English+ one pack	EuroPlus+ Reward	Tell Me More SE	Tell Me More Junior	Profesor Henry	New Reflex English
CONTENT-BASED FEATURES						
Attitudes (Do learners…)						
1. work on their attitudes?	○	●	○	○	○	○
Knowledge (Does the culture taught comprise…)						
2. material culture?	●	●	●	●	●	●
3. socio-political realia?	●	●	●	●	●	●
4. behaviour/practices?	●	●	●	●	●	●
5. thought patterns/values?	●	●	○	○	●	○
6. languaculture?	●	●	○	○	○	○
Skills of interpreting and relating (Do learners…)						
7. interpret cultural phenomena?	○	●	○	○	○	○
8. compare L1/C1 with L2/C2?	○	●	○	○	○	○
Skills of discovery and interaction (Do learners…)						
9. consult varied sources?	○	○	○	○	○	○
10. do project work?	○	○	○	○	○	○
11. practice IC communication?	○	●*	○	○	○	○
12. self-assess their own IC skills?	○	○	○	○	○	○
Critical cultural awareness (Do learners…)						
13. compare/judge materials?	○	●	○	○	○	○

Software / Evaluation criteria	English+ one pack	EuroPlus+ Reward	Tell Me More SE	Tell Me More Junior	Profesor Henry	New Reflex English
TECHNOLOGY-RELATED FEATURES (Does the software feature…)						
14. alternative navigation routes?	●	●	●	●	●	○
15. advanced search options?	○	●	●	○	●	○
16. task authoring tools?	○	○	○	○	○	○
17. cultural explanation?	○	●	○	○	○	○
18. insightful audio-visuals?	○	●	○	○	○	○
19. annotation tools?	○	●	○	○	●	●
20. supplementary cultural materials?	●	●	●	●	●	○
21. online communication tools?	●	●*	○	●*	○	○

*not functional at the time of the evaluation

BIBLIOGRAPHY

ACTFL (1999) *Standards for Foreign Language Learning: Preparing for the 21st Century*. [online] [cited 31 July 2010] Access: http://www.actfl.org/i4a/pages/index.cfm?pageid=3392.

Agar, M. (1994) *Language shock: Understanding e culture of conversation*. New York: William Morrow and Company.

—. (1996) *The Professional Stranger: An Informal Introduction to Ethnography*, 2nd edition. San Diego: Academic Press.

Ahmad, K., Corbett, G., Rogers & Sussex, R. 1985. *Computers, Language Learning and Language Teaching*. Cambridge: Cambridge University Press.

Alderson, J.C. and Bachman, L.F. (2007) Series Editors' Preface. In Chapelle, C.A. & Douglas, D. *Assessing Language through Computer Technology*. Cambridge: Cambridge University Press, pp. ix–xi.

Alderson, J. Charles. (1986) Computers in Language Testing. In Leech, G. & Candlin, C. (eds.) *Computers in English Language and Research*. London: Longman.

Aleksandrowicz-Pędich, L., Draghicescu, J. Issaiass, D. & Śabec, N. (2003) The views of teachers of English and French on intercultural competence in language teaching. In Lázár, I. (ed.) *Incorporating intercultural communicative competence in language teacher education*. Strasbourg: Council of Europe.

Aleksandrowicz-Pędich, L. (2005) *Międzykulturowość na lekcjach języków obcych.* Białystok: Wydawnictwo Uniwersytetu w Białymstoku.

—. (2006) *Rozwijanie kompetencji interkulturowej na studiach biznesowych. Propozycje programowe*. Białystok: Wydawnictwo Uniwersytetu w Białymstoku.

—. (2007) Interkulturowość w kształceniu językowym w Polsce i innych krajach europejskich. In Komorowska, H. (ed.) *Nauczanie języków obcych. Polska a Europa*. Warszawa: Wydawnictwo SWPS Academica.

Alexander, R. J. (1999) Caught in a global English trap, or liberated by a *lingua franca*? Unravelling some aims, claims and dilemmas of the English language teaching profession. In Gnutzmann, C (ed.) *Teaching and Learning English as a Global Language: Native and Non-Native Perspectives.* Tuebingen: Stauffenburg Verlag.

Alptekin, C. (1993) Target-language culture in EFL materials. *ELT Journal* 47 (2), pp. 136-143.

Andrews, M. (1998) Introducing British Studies into Hungarian Secondary Schools. In Byram, M. & Fleming, M. (eds.) *Language Learning in Intercultural Perspective.* Cambridge: Cambridge University Press.

Archer, C.M. (1986) Culture bump and beyond. In Valdes, J.M. (ed.) *Culture Bound.* Cambridge: Cambridge University Press.

Ash, S. (2007) The United States of America – The Land of Opportunity. In Ronowicz, E. & Yallop, C. (eds.) *English. One Language, Different Cultures*. Continuum.

Asher, J. (1982) *Learning Another Language Through Actions: The complete teacher's guidebook.* Los Gatos, Calif.: Sky Oaks Productions.

Atkinson, T. & Davies, G. (2008) Computer Aided Assessment (CAA) and Language Learning. In Davies, G. (ed.) *Information and Communications Technology for Language Teachers (ICT4LT), Slough, Thames Valley University* [online] [cited 17 April 2009] Access: http://www.ict4lt.org/en/en_mod4-1.htm.

Baker, T.L. (1994) *Doing Social Research*. New York: McGraw-Hill.

Bakhtin, M. (1992) *The Dialogic Imagination: Four Essays*. AustIn University of Texas Press.

Bandura, E. (2000) Rozwijanie kompetencji interkulturowej w nauczaniu języka angielskiego. In Komorowska (ed.) *Nauczanie języków obcych w zreformowanej szkole.* Warszawa: IBE.

—. (2007) *Nauczyciel jako mediator interkulturowy*. Kraków: Tertium.

—. (2009) Lekcje wspierające rozwój kompetencji interkulturowej. In Komorowska (ed.) *Skuteczna nauka języka obcego.* Warszawa: CODN.

Banks, A. (1975) 'French Without Language'. *Harvard Today* 18(1), pp.4.

Bañados, E. (2005) 'A Blended-learning Pedagogical Model for Teaching and Learning EFL Successfully Through an Online Interactive Multimedia Environment'. *CALICO Journal* 23 (3), pp. 533-550.

Barro, A., Byram, M., Grimms, H., Morgan, C. & Roberts, C. (1993) Cultural Studies for Advanced Language Learners. In Graddol, D., Thomson, L. & Byram, M. (eds.) *Language and Culture*. Clevedon: BAAL and Multilingual Matters.

Barro, A., Jordan, S. & Roberts, C. (1998) Cultural practice in everyday life: the language learner as ethnographer. In Byram, M. & Fleming, M. (eds.) Language Learning in Intercultural Perspective. Cambridge: Cambridge University Press.

Bax, S. (2003) 'CALL – past, present and future.' *System* 31/1, pp. 13-28.

Beaujour, M. & Ehrmann, J. (1967) A Semiotic Approach to Culture. Foreign Language Annals 1(2), pp. 152-163.

Belz, J.A. (2003) 'Linguistic Perspectives in the Development of Intercultural Competence in Telecollaboration.' *Language Learning & Technology* 7, no. 2 [online] [cited 8 June 2009] Access: http://llt.msu.edu/vol7num3/belz/.

Bennett, M. J. (1993) Towards ethnorelativism: A developmental model of intercultural sensitivity (revised). In Paige, R.M. (ed.) *Education for the Intercultural Experience*. Yarmouth, ME: Intercultural Press.

—. (1997) How not to be a fluent fool: Understanding the cultural dimension of language. In Fantini, A.E. (Vol. ed.) & Richards, J.C. (Series ed.) *New ways in teaching culture, New ways in TESOL series II: Innovative classroom techniques*. Alexandria, VA: TESOL.

—. (1998) Intercultural communication: A current perspective. In Bennett, M.J. (ed.) *Basic concepts of intercultural communication: Selected readings*. Yarmouth, ME: Intercultural Press.

Bélisle, C. (2007) *eLearning and Intercultural dimensions of learning theories and teaching models*. Paper submitted to the FeConE (Framework for eContent Evaluation) project. May 2007 [online] [cited: 29 August 2009] Access: http://www.elearningeuropa.info/files/media/media13022.pdf.

Belz, J. (2005) 'Intercultural questioning, discovery and tension in Internet-mediated language learning Partnerships'. *Language and Intercultural Communication* 5(1), pp. 3-39.

Bernaus, M., A., Andrade, A.I., Kervran, M., Murkowska, A. & Sáez, F.T. (2007) (eds.) *Plurilingual and pluricultural awareness in language teacher education*. Council of Europe Publishing.

Birdwhistell, R.L. (1960) Kinesics and Communication. In Carpenter, E.S. & McLuhan, M. (eds.) *Exploration s in Communication*. Boston: Beacon Press.

Blum-Kulka, S. House, J. & Kasper, G. (eds.) (1989) Cross-Cultural Pragmatics: Requests and Apologies. Vol. XXXI. In *Advances in Discourse Processes* Freedle, R.O. (ed.) Norwood, N.J.: Ablex.

Boas, F. (1986) Language and thought. In Valdes, J.M. (ed.) *Culture Bound*. USA: Cambridge University Press.

Bock, R.D. & Mislevy, R.J. (1982) Adaptive EAP estimation of ability in a microcomputer environment. *Applied Psychological Measurement* 6, pp. 431-444.

Bogusławski, A. (2006) Pedagogiczne paradoksy językoznawstwa, *Kwartalnik Pedagogiczny* 4 (202), pp. 13-25.

Bolt, R. (2001) The Foreign Language Classroom, Culture and British Studies – Reflections and Suggestions. In Houten, M. & Pulverness. A. (eds.) *New Directions New Opportunities. British Studies Conference*

Proceedings. Puławy Poland 9-12 March, 2000. Kraków: The British Council.

Bonvillain, N. (1997) *Language, Culture, And Communication: The Meaning Of Messages*. Upper Saddle River, NJ: Prentice Hall.

Bourdieu, P. (1991) *Language and Symbolic Power*. Cambridge: Polity Press.

Brandl, K. (2005) 'Are you Ready to Moodle?' *Language Learning and Technology* 9, no. 2 [online] [cited 8 June 2009] Access: http://llt.msu.edu/vol9num2/review1/.

Bredella, L. (1998) Is Intercultural Understanding Possible? In Bredella, L. & Haack, D. (eds.) *Perceptions and Misperceptions: the United States and Germany*. Tübingen Narr.

Bredella, L. (1992) 'Towards a pedagogy of intercultural understanding'. *Amerikastudien [American Studies] 37*(4), pp. 559-594.

Breen, M.P. & Candlin, C.N. (1980) 'The essentials of a communicative curriculum in language teaching'. *Applied Linguistics* 1/2, pp. 89-112.

Brett, P. (2001) 'The rationale for the usefulness of multimedia for language learning'. *Network* 1, pp. 11-16.

Brislin, R.W. (1990) *Applied Cross-Cultural Psychology*. London: Sage.

Brislin, R., Cushner, K., Cherrie, C. & Young, M. (1986) *Intercultural interactions: A practical guide.* Beverly Hills: Sage Publications.

Brooks, N. (1968) *Language and Language Learning*. Foreign Language Annals 1, pp. 204-217.

Brown, J.D. (1986) *Learning A Second Culture.* In Valdes, J.M. (ed.) *Culture Bound.* USA: Cambridge University Press.

Buchowska, A. (2004) Promoting Learner Autonomy through Webquest Activities In Miatluk, H. et al (ed.) *Linguistic Research and Language Teaching.* Białystok: Wydawnictwo Uniwersytetu w Białymstoku.

Budzko, A. (2005) Defining culture for foreign language teaching and its correlation with the level of languae proficiency. In Miatluk, H. & Bogacki, K. (eds.) *Language, Society and Problems of Intercultural Communication*. Białystok: Uniwersytet w Białymstoku.

Buttjes, D. & Byram, M. (1991) (eds.) *Mediating Languages and Cultures*. Clevedon: Multilingual Matters.

Byram, M. (1984) 'Cultural Studies in Language Teaching'. *Modern Languages* 65/4, pp. 204-212.

—. (1989) *Cultural Studies in Foreign Language Education*. Clevedon, Philadelphia: Multilingual Matters.

—. (1991) 'Teaching Culture and Language: Towards an Integrated Model'. In Buttjes, D. & Byram, M. (eds.) *Mediating Languages and Cultures.* Clevedon: Multilingual Matters.

—. (1997) *Teaching and Assessing Intercultural Communicative Competence*. Clevedon: Multilingual Matters.

—. (2000a) Intercultural Communicative Competence: the Challenge for Language Teacher Training. In Mountford, A. & Wadham-Smith, N. (eds.) *British Studies: Intercultural Perspectives*. Longman and the British Council.

—. (2000b) 'Assessing Intercultural Competence in Language Teaching'. *Sprogforum* 18, vol. 6, pp. 8-13.

—. (2003) Introduction. In Byram, M. (ed.) *Intercultural Competence*. Strasbourg: Council of Europe.

—. (2006) How to... develop intercultural competence. An interview with Professor Michael Byram conducted by Ewa Bandura. In Pulverness, A. (ed.) *The Best of the British Studies Web Pages*. British Council Poland.

—. (2008) *From Foreign Language Education to Education for Intercultural Citizenship*. Clevedon, Buffalo, Toronto: Multilingual Matters.

Byram, M. & Fleming, M. (1998) Introduction. In Byram, M. & Fleming, M. (eds.) *Language Learning in Intercultural Perspective: Approaches through Drama and Ethnography.* Cambridge: Cambridge University Press.

Byram, M., Gribkova, B. & Starkey, H. (2002) *Developing the Intercultural Dimension in Language Teaching.* Strasbourg: Council of Europe Publishing.

Byram, M., Morgan, C. & Colleagues (1994). *Teaching-and-Learning Language-and-Culture.* Clevedon: Multilingual Matters.

Byram, M. & Tost Planet, M. (2000) Introduction. *Social Identity and European Dimension. Intercultural Competence through Foreign Language Learning.* Strasbourg: Council of Europe Publishing.

Byram, M. & Zarate, G. (1996) *Młodzież wobec różnic. Propozycje dla nauczycieli.* Warszawa: Fundacja Edukacja dla Demokracji.

Byram, M. & Zarate, G. (eds.) (1997) *The Sociocultural and Intercultural Dimension of Language Learning and Teaching.* Council of Europe Publishing.

Camilleri Grima, A. (2002) *How Strange! The Use of anecdotes in the development of intercultural competence.* Strasbourg: Council of Europe Publishing.

Camilleri Grima, A. & Fitzpatrick, A. (2003) Teachers and Learners: new roles and competences. In Heyworth, F. (ed.) et al. *Challenges and Opportunities in Language Education . Contributions of the European*

Centre of Modern Languages 2000-2003. Strasbourg: Council of Europe Publishing.

Canale, M. & Swain, M (1980) 'Theoretical bases of communicative approaches to second language teaching and testing competence: An experiment in foreign language testing'. *Applied Linguistics* 1(1), pp. 1-47.

Canagarajah, A. S. (1999) *Resisting Linguistic Imperialism in English Teaching*. Oxford: Oxford University Press.

Carel, S. (2001) Students as virtual ethnographers: Exploring the language-culture connection. In M. Byram, Nichols, A. & Stevens, D. (eds.) *Developing intercultural competence in practice*. Clevedon: Multilingual Matters.

Carrier, M. (2006) 'Technology in the Future Language Classroom'. *Modern English Teacher* 15, no.3, pp.5-15.

Cevasco, M.E. 2000. British Studies at the University of Sao Paulo. In Mountford, A. & Wadham-Smith, N. (eds). *British Studies: Intercultural Perspectives*. Harlow: Longman in association with The British Council.

Chapelle, C.A. (2001) *Computer Applications in Second Language Acquisition.* Cambridge: Cambridge University Press.

Chapelle, C.A. & Douglas, D. (2006) *Assessing Language through Computer Technology*. Cambridge: Cambridge University Press.

Chomsky, N. (1965). *Aspects of the Theory of Syntax*. Cambridge, Mass.: MIT Press.

Claypole M (2003) Blended Learning: new resources for teaching Business English. In Pulverness, A. (ed.) *IATEFL Brighton Conference Selections*. Canterbury: IATEFL, UK.

COALA (2007) *Kompetencja międzykulturowa w kształceniu nauczycieli języków obcych na potrzeby edukacji wczesnoszkolnej*. Warszawa: Atut.

CODN (2000) *Europejskie Portfolio Językowe dla dorosłych.* Warszawa: CODN.

—. (2004) *Europejski system opisu kształcenia językowego: uczenie się, nauczanie, ocenianie*. Warszawa: CODN.

—. (2004) *Europejskie Portfolio Językowe dla uczniów od 10-15 lat.* Warszawa: CODN.

—. (2006) *Europejskie Portfolio Językowe dla uczniów od 6-10 lat.* Warszawa: CODN.

—. (2007) *Europejskie Portfolio Językowe dla uczniów od 3-6 lat.* Warszawa: CODN.

Cohen, L., Manion, L. & Morrison, K. (2007) *Research Methods in Education*. USA and Canada: Routledge.

Cole, J. & Foster, H. (2007) *Using Moodle* (2nd Edition). Sebastopol: CA.: O'Reilly Media, Inc.

Collie, J. (1998) Teaching British Cultural Studies: Reflections on some Methodological Issues. In Byram, M. & Fleming, M. (eds.) *Language Learning in Intercultural Perspective.* Cambridge University Press.

Cooper, A. (1998) Mind the gap! An ethnographic approach to cross-cultural workplace communication research. In Byram, M. & Fleming, M. (eds.) *Language Learning in Intercultural Perspective.* Cambridge University Press.

Corbett, J. (2003) *An Intercultural Approach to English Language Teaching*. Clevedon: Multilingual Matters.

—. (2005) *Minding the gap: intercultural approaches to ELT*. CD-ROM. Durham: The British Council.

—. (2010) *Intercultural Language Activities*. Cambridge: Cambridge University Press.

Corder, S. P. (1968) Film and Television in Modern Language Teaching. In Jalling, H. (ed.) *Modern Language Teaching*. London: Oxford University Press.

Council of Europe (1982) *Recommendation No. R (82) 18E concerning Modern Languages.*

—. (1984) *Recommendation No. R (84) 18 of the Committee of Ministers to Member States on the Training of Teachers in Education for Intercultural Understanding, Notably in a Context of Migration*. Adopted by the Committee of Ministers on 25 September 1984 at the 375th meeting of the Ministers' Deputies.

—. (2001) *Common European Framework of Reference for Languages*. Cambridge: Cambridge University Press.

—. (2001) *Recommendation 1539 (2001) on the European Year of Languages*.

—. (2004) *European Language Portfolio. Principles and Guidelines.* DGIV/EDU/LANG (2000) 33 rev. 1. Revised in June 2004[online] [cited: 21 July 2010] Access: http://www.coe.int/t/dg4/portfolio.

—. (2008) *White Paper on Intercultural Dialogue*. [online] [cited: 29 July 2010] Access: http://www.coe.int/dialogue.

—. (2009) *Autobiography of Intercultural Encounters.* [online] [cited: 29 July 2010] Access: http://www.coe.int/t/DG4/AUTOBIOGRAPHY/.

Crozet, C. & Liddicoat, A.J. (eds.) (1997) *Teaching culture as an integrated part of language teaching: an introduction. ARAL* Series S, no. 14, pp.1-22.

Crystal, D. (2001) 'To surf or not to surf: that *is* the question'. *Network* 1, pp. 3-10.

Cunningsworth, A. (1995) *Choosing Your Coursebook*. Oxford: Heinemann.

Cushner, K. & Brislin, R.W. (1996) *Intercultural Interactions. A Practical Guide.* Thousands Oaks, CA: Sage Publications.

Czaplikowska, R. (2007) *Zastosowanie technologii informacyjnej w kształceniu nauczycieli na przykładzie III NKJO w Sosnowcu*. Paper presented at the conference 'IV Międzynarodowa Konferencja Edukacyjna – Ustroń 2007' [online] [cited 1 September 2008] Access: http://spnjo.polsl.pl/konferencja/materialy/referaty/calus.pdf.

Damen, L. (1987) *Culture Learning: The Fifth Dimension in the Language Classroom*. Reading, MA: Addison Wesley.

Danova, R. (1998) Foreground Sources of English Language and Culture. In Cherrington, R. & Davcheva, L. (eds.) *Teaching Towards Intercultural Competence. Conference Proceedings*. Sofia: Tilia/The British Council.

Davies, A. (1991) *The Native Speaker in Applied Linguistics*. Edinburgh: Edinburgh University Press.

Davies G. (2009) 'CALL Software and Website Evaluation Forms'. In Davies G. (ed.) *Information and Communications Technology for Language Teachers (ICT4LT)*, Slough, Thames Valley University [online][cited: 02 August 2010] Access: http://www.ict4lt.org/en/index.htm.

Dawson, K. (2002) *Practical Research Methods. A User-Friendly Guide To Mastering Research*. Oxford: How to Books Ltd.

Delanoy, W. (1995) 'Cultural Learning in the FL-Classroom: from "Landeskunde" to "New Cultural Studies"'. *British Studies Now. Anthology.* Issues 1-5, pp. 37-42.

Dodd, C. (2001) Working in tandem: An Anglo-French project. In Byram, M., Nichols, A, & Stevens, D. (eds.) Developing Intercultural Competence in Practice. Clevedon: Multilingual Matters.

Dodge, B. (1995) *Some Thoughts about Webquests* [online][cited 12 August 2006] Access: http://webquest.sdse.edu/about-webquests.html.

—. (2000) *The Webquest Page* [online][cited 12 August 2006] Access: http://webquest.sdse.edu/webquest/webquest.html.

Douglas Brown, H. (1986) Learning a second culture. In Valdes, J.M. (ed.) *Culture Bound*. USA: Cambridge University Press.

—. (1998) Learning a second culture. In Byram, M. & Fleming, M. (eds.) *Language Learning in Intercultural Perspective.* Cambridge University Press.

Dudeney, G. (2000) *The Internet and the Language Classroom*. Cambridge: Cambridge University Press.

—. (2006) How… to work with a webquest. In Pulverness, A. (ed.) *The Best of the British Studies Web Pages*. British Council Poland.

Dunnett, S.C., Dubin, F. & Lezberg, A. (1986) English language teaching from an intercultural perspective. In Valdes (ed.) *Culture Bound*. Cambridge: Cambridge University Press.

Duranti, A. (1997) *Linguistic Anthropology*. New York: Cambridge University Press.

ECML (2007) Languages for social cohesion: language education in a multilingual and multicultural Europe [online] [cited: 21 July 2010] Access: www.ecml.at/documents/mtp2E.pdf.

Edelhoff, C. (1997) Lehrerfortbildung and interkulturelles lehren and lernen im fremdsprachenunterricht. In Baumgratz & Stephan (eds.) *Fremdsprachenlernen als beitrag zur internationalen verstdndigung. Inhaltliche and organisatorische perspektiven der lehrerfortbildung in europa*. München: Ludicium.

Edgington, B. (2000) A Comparative Approach to Teaching British Studies and Perspectives. In Mountford, A. & Wadham-Smith, N. (eds.) *Intercultural Perspectives*. Harlow, England: Longman in association with The British Council.

Ellis, R. (1997) 'The empirical evaluation of language teaching materials'. *ELT Journal* 51, pp. 36-42.

Eurydice (2008) *Key Data on Information and Communication Technology in Schools in Europe. 2008 Edition*. Brussels: Education, Audiovisual and Culture Executive Agency.

Fantini, A.E. (2000) 'A Central Concern: Developing Intercultural Competence'. *SIT Occasional Paper Series*, no. 1, pp. 25-33.

—. (2002) 'Academic Mobility Programs and Intercultural Competence'. *SIT Occasional Paper Series*, no. 3, pp. 15-19.

Fenner, A. (2000) Cultural awareness. In Fenner, A. & Newby, D. (ed.) *Approaches to Materials Design in European Textbooks: Implementing Principles of Authenticity, Learner Autonomy, Cultural Awareness*. Graz: ECML/Council of Europe Publishing.

Fenner, A. & Newby, D. (ed.) (2000) *Approaches to Materials Design in European Textbooks: Implementing Principles of Authenticity, Learner Autonomy, Cultural Awareness*. Graz: ECML/Council of Europe Publishing.

Fiske, J. (1989) *Reading the Popular*. Boston: Unwin Hyman.

Fitzpatrick, A. (2003) Resources, tools, aids and other devices. In Heyworth, F. (ed.) et al. *Challenges and Opportunities in Language*

Education. Contributions of the European Centre of Modern Languages 2000-2003. Strasbourg: Council of Europe Publishing.

Fleming, M. (1998) Cultural awareness and dramatic art forms. In Byram, M. & Fleming, M. (eds.) *Language Learning in Intercultural Perspective*. Cambridge University Press.

Fowler, S.M. & Blohm, J. (2004) An Analysis of \methods for Intercultural Training. In Landis, D., Bennett, J.M. & Bennett, M.J. (eds.) *Handbook of Intercultural Training*. Thousand Oaks: Sage Publications, pp. 37-84.

Frydrychova Klimova, B. (2008) 'Blended Learning'. *English Teaching Professional* 58, September, pp. ?-?.

Furnham, A. & Bochner, S. (1986) *Culture shock: Psychological reactions to unfamiliar environments*. London: Methuen.

Furstenberg, G., Levet, S., English, K., & Maillet, K. (2001) 'Giving a virtual voice to the silent language of culture: The Cultura project'. *Language Learning and Technology* 5 (1), pp. 55-102.

Gajek, E. (2002a) *Komputery w nauczaniu języków obcych*. Warszawa: Wydawnictwo Naukowe PWN.

—. (2002b) Kryteria ewaluacji programów komputerowych i stron internetowych wspomagających naukę języków obcych. In Komorowska, H. (ed.) *Ewaluacja w nauce języków obcych*. Białystok: Wydawnictwo Uniwersytetu w Białymstoku.

—. (2007) Technologia informacyjna i komunikacyjna (TIK) w edukacji językowej w Polsce i innych krajach europejskich. In Komorowska, H. (ed.) *Nauczanie języków obcych - Polska a Europa*. Warszawa: Wydawnictwo SWPS Academica.

—. (2009) Lekcje z wykorzystaniem technologii informacyjnej. In Komorowska, H. (ed.) Skuteczna n*auka języka obcego. Struktura i przebieg zajęć językowych*. Warszawa: CODN.

Gałkowski, B. (2006) 'Kompetencja formuliczna a problem kultury i tożsamości w nauczaniu języków obcych', *Kwartalnik Pedagogiczny* 4 (202), pp. 163-180.

Gardner, R.C. & Lambert, W. (1972) Attitudes and Motivation in Second Language Learning. Rowley, Mass.: Newbury House.

Garton, A. F. (1992) *Social Interaction and the Development of Language and Cognition*. Hove/Hillsday: Lawrence Earlbaum Associates.

Gautheron-Boutschatsky, C., Escalle, K., Androulakis, G. & Rieder, K. (2004) In Zarate, G., Gohard-Radenkovic, A., Lussier, D. & Penz, H. (eds.) *Cultural mediation in language learning and teaching*. Council of Europe Publishing.

Geertz, E. (1973) *The Interpretation of Cultures: Selected Essays*. New York: Basic.

Gigon, M.O. (1998) To be or not to be: motivating students through theatre. In Cherrington, R. & Davcheva, L. (eds.) *Teaching Towards Intercultural Competence. Conference Proceedings*. Sofia: Tilia/The British Council.

Global Gateway (2010) The official project website. [online][cited: 09 August 2010] Access: www.globalgateway.org.uk.

Głowacka, B. (2005) *Przewodnik metodyczny dla nauczycieli do Europejskiego Portfolio Językowego dla uczniów od 10-15 lat*. Warszawa: CODN.

Gnutzmann, C. (2000) *Lingua Franca (especially English): Functions, Role, Evolution – Teaching and Learning Issues – Striving for Plurilingualism.* Strasbourg: Council of Europe Publishing.

Godwin-Jones, B. (2001) 'Language Testing Tools and Technologies'. *Language Learning and Technology* 5, no. 2 [online] [cited 17 April 2009] Access: http://llt.msu.edu/vol5num2/emerging/default.html.

Gohart-Radenkovic, A., Lussier, D., Penz, H. & Zarate, G. (2004) Reference fields and methodologies. In Zarate, G., Gohard-Radenkovic, A., Lussier, D. & Penz, H. (eds.) *Cultural mediation in language learning and teaching.* Council of Europe Publishing.

Goodenough, W.H. (1964) Cultural anthropology and linguistics. In Hymes, D. *Language in Culture and Society*. New York: Harper and Row.

Goodson, I.F. & McGivney, V. (1985) *European Dimensions and the Secondary School Curriculum*. Brighton: Falmer.

Gozdawa-Gołębiowski, R. (2006) 'Interkulturowość czy antykulturowość? Rozważania nad nauczaniem angielszczyzny międzynarodowej', *Kwartalnik Pedagogiczny* 4 (202), pp. 93-112.

Graddol, D. (2006) *English Next*. The British Council.

Graham, R. (2007) *Blended Learning Systems: Definition, Current Trends and Future Directions*. Brigham Young University, USA. [online][cited: 02 August 2010] Access: http://www.uab.edu/it/instructional/technology/docs/blended_learning_systems.pdf.

Greenall, S. (1994) *Reward.* Oxford: Heinemann.

Grosjean, F. (1982) *Life With Two Languages. An Introduction to Bilingualism.* Cambridge: Mass.: Harvard University Press.

Guenova, V. et al. (2000) Training module in English: The Role of Social Identity in Intercultural Competence Acquired through Language Learning. In Byram, M. & Tost Planet, M. *Social Identity and*

European Dimension. Intercultural Competence through Foreign Language Learning. Strasbourg: Council of Europe Publishing.

Hall, E. (1959) *The Silent Language.* New York: Doubleday.

—. (1966) *The Hidden Dimension.* London, Sydney, Toronto: Bodley Head.

Halliday, M.A.K. (1990). New Ways of Meaning: A Challenge to Applied Linguistics. A paper presented at the 10th World Congress of Applied Linguistics, Thessaloniki, Greece, April.

Halverson, R.J. (1985) 'Culture and vocabulary acquisition: A proposal'. *Language Annals* 18(4): 327-332.

Hammersley, M. & Atkinson, P. (1995) *Ethnography: Principles in Practice*, 2nd edition. London: Routledge.

Hampden-Turner, C.M. & Trompenaars, F. (2000) *Building Cross-Cultural Competence: How to Create Wealth from Conflicting Values.* New Haven, Conn.: Yale University Press.

Hanna, B. E. & de Nooy, J. (2003). 'A funny thing happened on the way to the forum: Electronic discussion and foreign language learning'. *Language Learning & Technology* 7 (1), pp. 71-85.

Hanušova, S. (2006) *Coursebook evaluation*. Katedra angliského jazyka a literatury. Brno: Pedagogická fakulta Masarykovy Univerzity [online][cited: 02 August 2010] Access: http://svp.muni.cz/ukazat.php?docId=355.

Heider, F. (1957) *The Psychology of Interpersonal Relationships.* New York: Wiley.

Heinze, A. & Procter, C. (2004) 'Reflections On The Use Of Blended Learning'. Conference Proceedings *Education in a Changing Environment 13th-14th September 2004,* pp. .

Heyworth, F. (2003) 'Language education in a multilingual and multicultural Europe – the context'. In Heyworth, F. (ed.) et al. *Challenges and Opportunities in Language Education . Contributions of the European Centre of Modern Languages 2000-2003*. Strasbourg: Council of Europe Publishing.

Hinkelman, D. (2005) 'Blended Learning: Issue Driving an End to Laboratory-Based CALL'. *JALT Hokkaido Journal* 9, pp. 17-31.

Hockett, Ch. (1960) 'The Origin of Speech'. *Scientific American* 203, pp. 89-96.

Holly, D. (1990). The unspoken curriculum - or how language teaching carries cultural and ideological messages. In Harrison, B. (ed.) *Culture and the Language Classroom. ELT Documents 132.* London: Macmillan. Modern English Publications and the British Council.

Huber-Kriegler, M., Lázár, I. & Strange, J. (2003) *Mirrors and Windows. An Intercultural Communication Textbook.* Strasbourg: Council of Europe Publishing.

Hughes, G.H. (1986) An argument for culture analysus in the second language classroom. In Valdes, J.M. (ed.) *Culture Bound*. USA: Cambridge University Press.

Humphrey, D. (2007) *Intercultural Communication Competence: The State of Knowledge*. Report prepared for CILT. The National Centre for Languages. Development of NOS in intercultural Skills Project 26th May 2007. [online][cited: 02 August 2010] Access: http://data.cilt.org.uk/standards/donnareport.pdf.

Hutchinson, T. & Waters, A. (1987) *English for Specific Purposes. A learning-centered approach*. Cambridge: Cambridge University Press.

Hymes, D. (1967) Models of the interaction of language and social setting. Journal of Social Issues XXIII/2, pp. 8-28.

—. (1972) *On communicative competence*. Philadelphia: University of Pennsylvania Press.

Inal, B. (2006) 'Coursebook Selection Process and Some of the Most Important Criteria to be Taken into Consideration in Foreign Language Teaching'. *Journal of Arts and Sciences*, 5 May, pp. 19-29.

Informator o egzaminie maturalnym od roku 2008. Język angielski. (2008) Centralna Komisja Egzaminacyjna.

Irishkanova, K., Röcklinsberg,, Ozolina, O. & Zaharia, J.A. (2004) Empathy as part of intercultural mediation. In Zarate, G., Gohard-Radenkovic, A., Lussier, D. & Penz, H. (eds.) *Cultural mediation in language learning and teaching.* Council of Europe Publishing.

Jandt, F.E. (2001) *Intercultural Communication*. Thousand Oaks, London, Delhi: Sage Publications.

Jones, N. (1990) Reader, Writer, Text. In Carter, R. (ed.) *Knowledge about Language and the Curriculum: a LINC reader*. London: Hodder and Stoughton.

Johnson, J. (1979) Living Language: USA Culture Capsules for ESL Students. Rowley, Mass.: Newbury House.

Kachru, B.B. (1985). Standards, codification and sociolinguistic realism: The English language in the outer circle. In Quirk, R. & Widdowson. H. (eds.) *English in the world: Teaching and learning the language and literatures*. Cambridge: Cambridge University Press.

—. (2004) *Asian Englishes: beyond the canon*. Hong Kong: Hong Kong University Press.

Kachru, B.B. & Smith, L.E. (2008) *Cultures, Contexts and World Englishes*. New York and London: Routledge.

Kalnberzina, V. (2000) Latvian module: Understanding 'Social Identity'. In Byram, M. & Tost Planet, M. *Social Identity and European Dimension. Intercultural Competence through Foreign Language Learning.* Strasbourg: Council of Europe Publishing.

Kaplan, D. & Manners, R.A. (1972) *Culture Theory.* Englewood Cliffs, N.J.: Prentice Hall.

Kastendiek, H. (2000) Proposals for a Comparative Landeskunde Approach. In Mountford, A. & Wadham-Smith, N. (eds.) *Intercultural Perspectives.* Harlow, England: Longman in association with The British Council.

Kern, R. & Warschauer, M. (2000) Theory and practice of network-based language teaching. In Warschauer, M. & Kern, R. (eds.) *Network-based language teaching: Concepts and practice.* New York: Cambridge University Press.

Khanevitch, Z. (2005) Culture and communication: the mass media and their influence on popular culture. In Bogacki, K., Miatliuk, H. & Skrada, L. (eds.) *Language, Society, and Problems of Intercultural Communication.* Białystok: Wydawnictwo Uniwersytetu w Białymstoku.

Kilickaya, F. (2004) 'Guidelines to Evaluate Cultural Content in Textbooks'. *The Internet TESL Journal* X, No. 12 [online][cited: 02 August 2010] Access: http://iteslj.org/Techniques/Kilickaya-CulturalContent/.

Kluckhohn, C. & Kelly, W.H. (1945) The concept of culture. In Linton, R. (ed.) *The Science of Man in the World Culture.* New York: Columbia University Press.

Kluckhohn, C. & Kroeber, A.L. (1952) *Culture: A Critical Review of Concepts and Definitions.* Cambridge, Massachusetts: The Museum.

Kohonen, V., Jaantinen, R., Kaikkonen, P. & Lehtovaara, J. (2001) *Experiential Learning in Foreign Language Education.* Harlow, England: Longman.

Kolb, D. (1984) *Experiential learning.* Englewood Cliffs, N.J.: Prentice Hall.

Kołodziejczyk, D., Lynn, J. & Żylińska, J. (2000) Culture and Nationhood: First Stages in the Development of Comparative Cultural Studies. In Mountford, A. & Wadham-Smith, N. (eds.) *Intercultural Perspectives.* Harlow, England: Longman in association with The British Council.

Komorowska, H. (1999) *Metodyka nauczania języków obcych.* Warszawa: Wydawnictwo Szkolne i Pedagogiczne.

—. (2006a) Intercultural competence in ELT syllabus and materials design. *Scripta Neophilologica Posnaniensia* VIII, pp. 59-83.

—. (2006b) 'Język i kultura w dydaktyce języków obcych'. *Kwartalnik Pedagogiczny* 4 (202), pp. 27-45.

—. (2006c) Teaching English as a lingua franca. In Zybert, J. (ed.) *Issues in Foreign Language Learning and Teaching.* Warszawa: Wydawnictwo Uniwersytetu Warszawskiego.

—. (2009) *Metodyka nauczania języków obcych.* Warszawa: Fraszka Edukacyjna.

Korhonen, K. (1999) 'Intercultural Communication through Hypermedia'. *Intercultural Communication*, August, issue 1.

Krajka, J. (2007) *English Language Teaching in the Internet-Assisted Environment.* Lublin Maria Curie-Skłodowska University.

Krajka, J. & Grudzińska, Z. (2002) Using the Internet in the Language Classroom to Foster Learner Independence – Ideal and Reality. *IATEFL Poland Teacher Development and Autonomous Learning SIG Newsletter,* 7 May, pp. 9-16.

Kramsch, C. (1989) New Directions in the Teaching of Language and Culture. In *NFLC Occasional Papers. National Foreign Language Center at the John Hopkins University*, pp. 1-13.

—. (1993) *Context and Culture in Language Teaching.* Oxford: Oxford University Press.

—. (1998a) The privilege of the intercultural speaker. In Byram, M. & Fleming, M. (eds.) *Language Learning in Intercultural Perspective.* Cambridge: Cambridge University Press.

—. (1998b) *Language and culture.* Oxford: Oxford University Press.

—. (1999) 'The cultural component of language teaching'. *British Studies Now. Anthology.* Issues 6-10, pp. 85-95.

Krashen, S. (1982) *Principles and Practice in Second Language Acquisition.* New York: McGraw-Hill.

Krauss, R.M. & Chiu, C.-Y. (1998) Language and social behaviour. In Gilbert, D.T., Fiske, S.T., and Lindzey, G. (eds.) *The handbook of social psychology*, No. 2. New York: McGraw-Hill.

Kroeber, A.L., & Kluckhohn, C. (1952) 'Culture: A critical review of concepts and definitions.' *Harvard University Peabody Museum of American Archeology and Ethnology Papers, 47.*

Kuper, A. (1999) *Culture: The Anthropologist's Account.* Cambridge: MA: Harvard University Press.

Kurek, M. (2004) 'Webquests – projekty internetowe na lekcjach języka angielskiego'. *Języki obce w szkole* 2, 72-76.

Kurtchenia, E. (2005) Role-play a s a guide in "Tiptoeing through the mine fields" of the cross-cultural understanding. In Bogacki, K., Miatliuk, H. & Skrada, L. (eds.) *Language, Society, and Problems of Intercultural Communication*. Białystok: Wydawnictwo Uniwersytetu w Białymstoku.

Kühlmann, T.M. & Stahl, G.K. (1998) 'Anforderungen an Mitarbeiter in internationalen Tätigkeitsfeldern'. *Zeitschrift Personalführung* 11, pp. 44-55.

Lakoff, G. & Johnson, M. (1980) Metaphors We Live By. Chicago: University of Chicago Press.

Lanham, E. & Zhou, W. (2003) 'Cultural Issues in Online Learning – Is Blended Learning a Possible Solution?'. *International Journal of Computer Processing of Oriental Languages* 16, no. 4, pp. 275–292.

Larsen-Freeman, D. (1986) *Techniques and Principles in Language Teaching*. Oxford: Oxford University Press.

Larsen-Freeman, D. & Long, M. (1991) *An Introduction to Second Language Acquisition Research*. New York: Longman.

Larson, D.A. & Smalley, W.A. (1972) *Becoming Bilingual: a Guide to Language Learning*. New Canaan, CN: Practical Anthropology.

Lázár, I. (2007) Guidelines for the teaching of intercultural communicative competence (ICC). In Lázár, I., Huber Kriegler, M., Lussier, D., Matei, G.S. & Peck, C. (eds.) *Developing and assessing intercultural communicative competence. A guide for language teachers and teacher educators*. Strasbourg: Council of Europe Publishing.

Leach, E. (1982) *Social Anthropology*. Glasgow: Fontana.

Le Page, R. & Tabouret-Keller, A. (1985) *Acts of Identity. Creole-Based Approaches to Language and Ethnicity*. Cambridge: Cambridge University Press.

Lessard-Clouston, M. (1997) Towards an Understanding of Culture in L2/FL Education. In Ronko, K.G. *Studies in English*, 25, 131-150 Japan: Kwansei Gakuin University Press.

Levine, D.R. & Adelman, M.B. (1993) *Beyond Language*. Englewood Cliffs, NJ: Prentice-Hall Regents.

Levy, D. (2007) 'Culture, Culture Learning and New Technologies: Towards a Pedagogical Framework Language'. *Learning & Technology 11, no. 2, pp. 104-127.*

Lewandowska-Tomaszczyk, B. (2000) Computers, language corpora and their applications. In Lewandowska-Tomaszczyk, B., Osborne, J. & Schulte, F. *Computers in Language Studies*. Piotrków Trybunalski: Wyższa Szkoła Pedagogiczna w Kielcach.

Liaw, M. (2006) 'E-Learning and the Development of Intercultural Competence.' *Language Learning & Technology* 10, no. 3, pp. 49-64 [online][cited: 07 August 2010] Access: htp://llt.msu.edu/vol10num3/liaw/.

Loveday, L. (1981) *The Sociolinguistics of Learning and Using a Non-Native Language*. London: Pergamon.

Lubecka, A. (1994) 'Nauczyciel języka obcego - ekspertem w dziedzinie kultury?' *Języki Obce* w *Szkole* 5, pp. 387-392.

Lustig, M.W. & Koester, J. (1999) *Intercultural Competence: Interpersonal Communication Across Cultures*. New York and Harlow: Addison Wesley Longman.

Lussier, D., Auger, R., Urbanicová, V., Armengol, M., De la Serna, P. & De Miguel, M.C. (2007) Representations of other cultures in the context of the initial and ongoing training of teachers. In Lázár, I., Huber Kriegler, M., Lussier, D., Matei, G.S. & Peck, C. (eds.) *Developing and assessing intercultural communicative competence. A guide for language teachers and teacher educators. Strasbourg: Council of Europe Publishing.*

Łuczak-Łomża & Metera-Debaene (2002) *Zanim wybierzesz podręcznik. Metody oceniania materiałów do nauki języków.* Warszawa: Fraszka Edukacyjna.

Łyp-Bielecka, A. (2008) Czy wykorzystanie technologii informacyjnej na lekcji języka obcego może zwiększyć motywację uczniów? In Michońska-Stadnik, A. & Wąsik, Z. *Nowe spojrzenia na motywację w dydaktyce języków obcych.* Tom 2. Wrocław: Wydawnictwo Wyższej Szkoły Filologicznej we Wrocławiu.

Malinowski, B. (1922) *Argonauts of the Western Pacific*. London: George Routledge.

Malysheva, O. (2005) Cultural diversity in education in the USA. In Miatluk, H. & Bogacki, K. (eds.) *Language, Society and Problems of Intercultural Communication*. Białystok: Uniwersytet w Białymstoku.

Marczak, M. (2004) 'Inventive Webquest'. In Pulverness, A. (ed.) (2006) *The Best of the British Studies Webpages*. British Council Poland [CD-ROM] Access: ./data/www/wq/n_wq.htm.

Masie, E. (2006) The Blended Learning Imperative. In Bonk, C. J. & Graham, C.R. (eds.) *The Handbook of Blended Learning: Global Perspectives, Local Designs*. San Francisco, CA: Pfeiffer.

Mason, R. & Rennie, F. (2006) *E-Learning: The key concepts.* Abington, Oxon: Routledge.

Mason, R. & Rennie, F. (2008) *E-Learning and Social Networking Handbook*. New York, NY; Abingdon, Oxon: Routledge.

McCarthy, M. & Carter, R. A. (1994) *Language as Discourse: perspectives for language teaching*. London: Longman.

McDonnell, M. & Connolly, F. (2007) *The Blended Approach: Computer Assisted and Traditional Language Learning in Aviation English Training*. A paper delivered at the Second Icao Aviation Language Symposium (Ials/2). Icao Headquarters, Montréal, Canada 7 – 9 MAY 2007 [online][cited: 07 August 2010] Access: http://www.icao.int/icao/en/anb/meetings/ials2/Docs/19.Connelly.pdf.

McDonough, J. & Shaw, C. (1993) *Materials and Methods in ELT*. Oxford, UK; Cambridge, USA: Blackwell.

Medgyes, P. (1992). 'Native or non-native: who's worth more?' *ELT Journal* 46 (4), pp. 340-349.

—. (2001). When the teacher is a non-native speaker. In M. Celce-Murcia (Ed.),Teaching English as a second or foreign language. Boston: Heinle & Heinle.

Meinardi, M. (2007) 'Shared and Mutual Knowledge in Language Learning. Where our worlds overlap'. *Modern English Teacher* 16, no. 1, pp. 65-70.

MEN (2008) *Rozporządzenie Ministra Edukacji Narodowej z dnia 23 grudnia 2008 r. w sprawie podstawy programowej wychowania przedszkolnego oraz kształcenia ogólnego w poszczególnych typach szkół,* Dziennik Ustaw z 2009 Nr 4, poz. 17.

Midgeley, M. (1980) *Beast and Man. The Roots of Human Nature*. London: Methuen.

Mikes, G. (1946) *A Handbook for Beginners and More Advanced Pupils*. London/New York: Wingate.

Miles, M. & Huberman, M. (1994) *Qualitative Data Analysis* (second edition). Beverly Hills, CA: Sage.

Montgomery, M., & Reid-Thomas, H. (1994) *Language and Social Life*. England: The British Council.

Montgomery, M. (1995) 'Institutions and Discourse' *British Studies Now. Anthology Issues 1-5*. The British Council, pp. 25-28.

—. (2003) Foreword. In Corbett, J. *The Intercultural Approach to English Language Teaching*. Clevedon, Buffalo, Toronto: Multilingual Matters.

Moran, P.R. (2001) *Teaching Culture. Perspectives in Practice*. Boston: Heinle & Heinle.

Morain, G.G. (1986) Kinesics and cross-cultural understanding. In Valdes, J.M. (ed.) *Culture Bound*. USA: Cambridge University Press.

Morgan, C. (1998) Cross-cultural encounters. In Byram, M. & Fleming, M. (eds.) *Language Learning in Intercultural Perspective. Approaches through drama and ethnography*. Cambridge University Press.

Motteram, G. & Sharma, P. (2009) 'Blending Learning in a Web 2.0 World'. *International Journal of Emerging Technologies & Society* 7, no. 2, pp: 83-96.

Müller-Hartmann, A. (2000) 'The Role of Tasks in Promoting Intercultural Learning in Electronic Learning Networks'. *Language Learning & Technology* 4, No. 2, pp. 129-147.

Müller-Jacquier, B. (2000). Linguistic Awareness of Cultures. Grundlagen eines Trainingsmoduls. In Bolten, J. (ed.) *Studien zur internationalen Unternehmenskommunikation*. Leipzig: Popp.

National Center for ESL Literacy Education (2003) *Software Evaluation Guidelines* [online][cited: 02 August 2010] Access: http://www.cal.org/caela/esl_resources/SoftwareEvalGuidelines.pdf.

National Language Security Initiative. The U.S. Department of Education. [online] [cited: 31 July 2010] Access: http://www.languagepolicy.org/documents/legislation/NSLI.pdf.

Nedkova, M. & Davcheva, L. (1998) Intercultural Training for Student Teachers of English and Geography. In Cherrington, R. & Davcheva, L. *Towards Intercultural Competence. Conference Proceedings.* Sofia: Tilia/The British Council.

Neumeier, P. (2005) 'A closer look at blended learning – parameters for designing a blended learning environment for language for language teaching and learning'. *CALICO Journal* 23 (3), pp. 163-178.

Neuner, G. (2003) Socio-cultural interim worlds in foreign language learning and teaching. In Byram, M. (ed.) *Intercultural Competence*. Strasbourg: Council of Europe.

Noblitt, J. (1989) 'Technology and language learning'. *Academic Computing*, October, pp. 56.

Nostrand, H.L. (1967a) A Second Culture: New Imperative for American Education. In Michel, J. *Foreign Language Teaching. An Anthology*. London: Collier-MacMillan.

—. (1967b) *Background Data for the Teaching of French*. Seattle: University of Washington.

Nostrand, H. (1989) 'Authentic texts and cultural authenticity: an editorial'. Modern Language Journal, 73(1), pp. 49-52.

Ochs, E. & Schieffelin, B. (1984) Language Acquisition and Socialization: Three Developmental Stories and Their Implications. In Shweder, R. & LeVine, R.A. (eds.) *Culture Theory: Essays on Mind, Self, and Emotion*. New York: Cambridge University Press.

O'Dowd, R. (2003) 'Understanding the "Other Side": Intercultural Learning in a Spanish-English E-Mail Exchange'. *Language Learning & Technology* 7, no. 2 [online][cited: 07 August 2007] Access: http://llt.msu.edu/vol7num2/odowd/, pp. 118-144.

Osborne, J. (2000) Computers and the foreign language teacher and learner. In Lewandowska-Tomaszczyk, B., Osborne, J. & Schulte, F. (eds.) *Computers In Language Studies*. Piotrków Trybunalski: Kielce Pedagogical University Affiliated College Press.

Paikeday, T. (1985) The Native Speaker is Dead! Toronto: Paikeday Publishing Inc.

Paradowski, M. (2008) 'Winds of Change in the English Language - Air of Peril for Native Speakers?' *Novitas-ROYAL* 2(1), pp. 92-119.

—. (2010) Anti-native-speaker-hegemony rationale. Version 3. *Knol*. 2010 Feb 18 [online] [cited 17 April 2010] Access: http://knol.google.com/k/michał-b-paradowski/anti-native-speaker-hegemony-rationale/2qpvzotrrhys1/30.

Parmenter, L. (2003) Describing and defining intercultural communicative competence – international perspectives. In Byram, M. (ed.) *Intercultural Competence*. Strasbourg: Council of Europe.

Partington, A. (2001) Corpora-based description in teaching and learning. In Aston, G. (ed.) *Learning with corpora*. Houston, TX: Athelstan.

Pawelec, A. (2006) 'Relatywizm językowy. Czy można „przyswoić sobie" inny język?', *Kwartalnik Pedagogiczny* 4 (202), pp. 155-162.

Peck, C., Rot Gabrovec, V., Čankovă, M., Lazar, I. & Vief-Schmidt, G. (2007) Materials and activities to develop intercultural competence. In Lázár, I., Huber Kriegler, M., Lussier, D., Matei, G.S. & Peck, C. (eds). *Developing and assessing intercultural communicative competence. A guide for language teachers and teacher educators*. Strasbourg: Council of Europe Publishing.

Penz, H. (2001) Cultural awareness and language awareness through dialogic social interaction using the Internet and other media. In Brit-Fenner, A. (ed.) *Cultural awareness and language awareness based on dialogic interaction with texts in foreign language learning*. Council of Europe Publishing.

Pfeiffer, W. (2001) *Nauka języków obcych. Od praktyki do praktyki*. Poznań: Wagros.

Pinker, S. (2002) *The Blank Slate*. London: Penguin Books.

Poelzl, U. (2003) Signalling cultural identity: the use of L1/Ln in ELF. *Vienna English Working Papers*. Vol. 12 no 2, pp. 3-23.

Podstawa programowa kształcenia ogólnego dla szkół podstawowych (2008) [online] [cited: 21 December 2008] Access:

http://www1.reformaprogramowa.men.gov.pl/project_rozporządzenia.

Porto, M. (2000) Integrating the Teaching of Language and Culture. In Mountford, A. & Wadham-Smith, N. (eds.) *Intercultural Perspectives*. Harlow, England: Longman in association with The British Council.

Preston, D. (1981) 'The ethnography of TESOL'. *TESOL Quarterly* 15(2), pp. 105-116.

Pulverness, A. (1999) ‘English as a foreign culture: ELT and British Cultural Studies’. *British Studies Now. Anthology Issues 6-10*. The British Council: 100-104.

Raw, L. (1998) Intercultural competence: does it exist? In Cherrington, R. & Davcheva, L. (eds). *Teaching Towards Intercultural Competence. Conference Proceedings*. Sofia: Tilia/The British Council.

Reid-Young, A. (2003) 'The key to successful e-learning is b-learning.' *HCI, Journal of Information Development*. Retrieved February 7 [online] [cited: 21 January 2009] Access: http://www.hci.com.au/hcisite2/journal/Key%20to%20elearning%20is %20blearning.htm

Richards, J.C. & Rodgers, T.S. (1986) *Approaches and methods in language teaching: A description and analysis*. Cambridge: Cambridge University Press.

Riley, P. (2007) *Language , Culture and Identity.* London, New York: Continuum.

Risager, K. (2007) *Language and Culture Pedagogy*. Clevedon, Buffalo, Toronto: Multilingual Matters.

Roberts, C. (1995) ‘Ethnographic Approaches to Cultural Learning’. *British Studies Now. Anthology Issues 1-5*. The British Council, pp. 49-52.

Robinson, G. (1988) *Crosscultural Understanding*. London: Prentice Hall.

Rollin, H. & Harrap, A. (2005) ‘Can E-Learning Foster Intercultural Competence’. *Brookes eJournal of Learning and Teaching* 1, issue 3, pp. k-8.

Ronowicz, E. (2007) Introduction. In Ronowicz, E. & Yallop, C. (eds.) *English: One Language, Different Cultures*. Continuum.

Ronowicz, E. & Yallop, C. (2007) *English:* One *Language, Different Cultures.* London, New York: Continuum.

Ruben, B. D. (1976). 'Assessing communication competency for intercultural adaptation'. *Group and Organization Studies* 1, pp. 334-354.

Ruciński, S. (1988) *Wychowanie jako wprowadzenie w życie wartościowe*. Warszawa: Wydawnictwa Uniwersytetu Warszawskiego.

Salaberry, R. (2001) 'The use of technology for second language learning and teaching: a retrospective'. *The Modern Language Journal* 85, no. 3, pp. 39-56.

Samovar, L. & Porter, R. (1972) *Intercultural communication: A reader*. Belmont, CA: Wadsworth, Inc.

Samovar, L., Porter, R. & Jain, N. (1981) *Understanding Intercultural Communication*. Belmont, CA.: Wadsworth.

Savignon, S. (1972) *Communicative competence: An experiment in foreign language testing*. Philadelphia: Centre for Curriculum Development.

Schulte, F. (2000) Information and Communication Technology (ICT) and Major Trends and Western/European Societies. In Lewandowska-Tomaszczyk, B., Osborne, J. & Schulte, F. *Computers in Language Studies*. Piotrków Trybunalski: Wyższa Szkoła Pedagogiczna w Kielcach.

Schumann, J. (1986) 'Research on the acculturation model for second language acquisition'. *Journal of Multilingual and Multicultural Development* 7: 379-392.

Seelye, H. (1974) *Teaching culture: Strategies for foreign language educators*. Skokie, IL: National Textbook Company.

Seelye, H.N. (1988) *Teaching Culture*. Lincolnwood. Il.: National Textbook Company.

Seliger, H.W. & Shohamy, E. (1989) *Second Language Acquisition Research Methods*. Hong Kong: Oxford University Press.

Selinker, L. (1972) 'Interlanguage'. *International Review of Applied Linguistics* 10, pp. 201-239.

Sell, R.D. (1995) 'Culture, Foreign Language Education and Literature'. *British Studies Now. Anthology*. Issues 1-5, pp. 29-31.

Sercu, L. (1998) In-service teacher training and the acquisition of the intercultural competence. In Byram, M. & Fleming, M. (eds). *Language Learning In Intercultural Perspective. Approaches through drama and ethnography*. Cambridge University Press.

Shandar, E. (2005) Intercultural class projects. In Miatluk, H. & Bogacki, K. (eds.) *Language, Society and Problems of Intercultural Communication*. Białystok: Uniwersytet w Białymstoku.

Sharma, P. & Barrett, B. (2007) *Blended Learning. Using technology in and beyond the language classroom*. Oxford, England: Macmillan Publishers Limited.

Sharwood-Smith, M. (2007) British shibboleths. In Ronowicz, E. & Yallop, C. (eds.) *English. One Language, Different Cultures*. Continuum.

Shaughnessy, M. (2003) 'CALL, commercialism and culture: inherent software design conflicts and their results'. *ReCALL* 15 (2), pp. 251-268.

Shaw, N. (2004) *Global Gateway. Bringing an International Dimension to Education.* A multimedia presentation. London: The British Council.

Shawback, M.J. & Terhune, N.M. (2002) 'Online interactive courseware: using movies to promote cultural understanding in a CALL environment.' *ReCALL* 14, issue 01, pp. 85-95.

Sheldon, L. (1988) 'Evaluating ELT textbooks and materials'. *ELT Journal* 42, pp. 237-246.

Sik, P. (1998) The internet for intercultural competence. In Cherrington, R. & Davcheva, L. (eds). *Teaching Towards Intercultural Competence. Conference Proceedings*. Sofia: Tilia/The British Council.

Silverwood, T. (2007) 'Blended Learning Made Easy'. *Studies in Humanities and Social Sciences* 74, pp. 115-121.

Skopinskaja, L. (2003) The role of culture In foreign language teaching materials: an evaluation from an intercultural perspective. In Lázár, I. (ed.) *Incorporating intercultural communicative competence in language teacher education.* Kapfenberg: Council of Europe Publishing.

Slowman, M. (2007) 'Making Sense of Blended Learning'. *Industrial and Commercial Training* 39, no. 6, pp. 315-318.

Sobkowiak, P. (2008) 'Lektorat języka angielskiego w dobie globalizacji', *Języki Obce w Szkole* 4, pp. 76

Stubbs, M. (1995) 'Collocations and cultural connotations of common words.' *Linguistics and Education* 7, no. 4, pp. 379-390.

Suchodolski, B. (1987) *Dzieje kultury polskiej*. Warszawa: Polska Agencja Wydawnicza Interpress.

Suler, J. (2004) 'The Online Disinhibition Effect'. *Cyber Psychology & Behavior* 7, pp. 321-326.

Sztompka, P. (2002) *Socjologia. Analiza społeczeństwa.* Kraków: Wydawnictwo Znak.

Tajfel, H. (1981) *Human Groups and Social Categories*. Cambridge: Cambridge University Press.

Tarleton State University (2004) *About Distributed Education, What is Distributed Education?*[online] [cited: 21 January 2009] Access: http://www.qualityresearchinternational.com/glossary/distributededucation.htm.

Tavangarian D., Leypold, M., Nölting, K., Röser, M. & Voigt, D. (2004) 'Is e-Learning the Solution for Individual Learning? *Electronic Journal of e-Learning* 2, issue 2, pp. 273-280.

Teeler, D. & Gray, P. (2000) *How to Use the Internet in ELT*. Harlow: Pearson Education Limited.

Thanasoulas, D. (2001) 'The Importance of Teaching Culture in the Foreign Language Classroom'. *Radical Pedagogy* 3, issue 3 [online] [cited: 22 July 2010] Access: http://radicalpedagogy.icaap.org/content/issue3_3/7-thanasoulas.html.

Tomalin, B. & Stempleski, S. (1993) *Cultural Awareness*. Oxford: Oxford University Press.

Tomczak, A.M. (2005) Studying non-verbal communication for intercultural awareness. In Bogacki, K., Miatliuk, H. & Skrada, L. (eds.) *Language, Society, and Problems of Intercultural Communication*. Białystok: Wydawnictwo Uniwersytetu w Białymstoku.

Tomlinson, G. (2003) Materials Evaluation. In Tomlison, G. (ed.) *Developing materials for language teaching*. London, New York: Continuum.

Toyoda, E. & Harrison, R. (2002) 'Categorization of Text Chat Communication between Learners and Native Speakers of Japanese'. *Language Learning & Technology* 6, no. 1, pp. 82-99.

Tsiplakides, I. (2011) Selecting an English Coursebook: Theory and Practice. *Theory and Practice in Language Studies* 1, no. 7, pp. 758-764.

Tsvirko, E. (2005) Cultural Awareness and communicative competence in the EFL classroom. In Miatluk, H. & Bogacki, K. (eds.) *Language, Society and Problems of Intercultural Communication*. Białystok: Uniwersytet w Białymstoku.

United Nations General Assembly (2001) *Global Agenda for Dialogue among Civilizations*. Resolution adopted by the General Assembly. A/RES/56/6.

Underwood, J. (1984) *Linguistics, Computer and the Language Teacher*. Rowley, MA.: Newbury House.

Valette, R.M. (1986) The culture test. In Valdes, J.M. (ed.) *Culture Bound*. Cambridge: Cambridge University Press.

Valdes, J.M. (1986) *Culture bound: bridging the cultural gap in language teaching*. Cambridge: Cambridge University Press.

Vygotsky, L.S. (1962) *Thought and language*. Edited and translated by Hanfmann, E. & Vakar, G. Cambridge, MA, NY: MIT Press; John Wiley.

—. (1978). *Mind in society: The development of higher mental processes*. Cambridge, MA: Harvard University Press.

Wardhaugh, R. (1976) *The Context of Language*. Rowley, Mass.: Newbury House.

Ware, P.D. & Kramsch, C. (2005) 'Toward an intercultural stance: Teaching German and English through telecollaboration.' *The Modern Language Journal* 89(2), pp. 190–205.

Warschauer, M. (1996) 'Computer Assisted Language Learning: an Introduction'. In Fotos, S. (ed.) *Multimedia Language* Teaching. Tokyo: Logos International, pp. 3–20.

—. (1997) 'Computer-mediated collaborative learning: Theory and practice'. *Modern Language Journal* 81/4. pp. 470-481.

—. (2000) 'The Death of Cyberspace and the Rebirth of CALL'. *English Teachers' Journal Computer* 53, pp. 61–67.

—. (2002) 'Reconceptualizing the Digital Divide'. *First Monday* 7, no. 7 [online][cited: 12 December 2010] Access: http://firstmonday.org/htbin/cgiwrap/bin/ojs/index.php/fm/article/view Article/967/888.

Warschauer, M. & Healey, D. (1996) 'Computer and language learning: an overview'. *Language Teaching* 31, pp. 57-71.

Weaver, G.R. (1986). Understanding and coping with cross-cultural adjustment stress. In Paige, R.M. (ed.) *Cross-Cultural Orientation, New Conceptualizations and Applications.* Lanham, MD: University Press of America.

Whorf, B.L. (1956) *Language, Thought, and Reality*. Cambridge, Mass.: MIT Press.

Williams, R. (1965) *The Long Revolution*. Harmondsworth: Penguin.

Winter, G. (1986) German-American student exchange: adaptation problems and opportunities for personal growth. In Page, R.M. (ed.) *Cross-Cultural Orientations: New Conceptualizations and Applications*. London: University Press of America.

Wood, D. (1998) *How Children Think and Learn.* Oxford: Blackwell Publishers.

Wylie, L. & Stafford, R. (1977) *Beaux Gestes: A Guide to French Body Talk*. Cambridge, Mass.: The Undergraduate Press.

Zarate, G. (2003) Identities and plurilingualism: preconditions for the recognition of intercultural competences. In Byram, M. (ed.) *Intercultural Competence*. Strasbourg: Council of Europe.

Zarate, G., Gohard-Radenkovic, A., Lussier, D. & Penz, H. (2004) Recommendations. In Zarate, G., Gohard-Radenkovic, A., Lussier, D. & Penz, H. (eds.) *Cultural mediation in language learning and teaching.* Council of Europe Publishing.

Zawadzka, E. (2004) *Nauczyciele języków obcych w dobie przemian.* Kraków: Oficyna Wydawnicza Impuls.

Żylińska, M. (2003) 'Podejście interkulturowe, czyli o konieczności zmian w nauczaniu języków obcych'. *Języki obce w szkole* 6, pp. 49-61.

—. (2007) *Postkomunikatywna dydaktyka języków obcych w dobie technologii informacyjnych. Teoria i praktyka.* Warszawa: Fraszka Edukacyjna.

Index